EXHIBITING AMERICA

The Smithsonian's National History Museum, 1881–2018

DAVID K. ALLISON AND HANNAH PETERSON

A Smithsonian Contribution to Knowledge

Smithsonian
Scholarly Press
WASHINGTON, D.C.
2021

Published by SMITHSONIAN INSTITUTION SCHOLARLY PRESS
P.O. Box 37012, MRC 957, Washington, D.C. 20013-7012
https://scholarlypress.si.edu

Library of Congress Cataloging-in-Publication Data
Names: Allison, David K., 1950- author. | Peterson, Hannah (Hannah L. C.), author. |
    Smithsonian Institution Scholarly Press, issuing body.
Title: Exhibiting America : the Smithsonian's national history museum, 1881-2018 /
    David K. Allison and Hannah Peterson.
Other titles: Smithsonian's national history museum, 1881-2018 | Smithsonian contribution
    to knowledge.
Description: Washington, D.C. : Smithsonian Scholarly Press, 2021. | Series: A Smithsonian
    contribution to knowledge | Includes bibliographical references. |
Identifiers: LCCN 2020042794 (print) | LCCN 2020042795 (ebook) | ISBN 9781944466404
    (paperback) | ISBN 9781944466398 (Adobe pdf)
Subjects: LCSH: National Museum of American History (U.S.)—Exhibitions. | National
    Museum of American History (U.S.)—History. | National museums—Washington (D.C.)
    | National characteristics, American. | United States—Civilization—Exhibitions. |
    United States—History—Exhibitions.
Classification: LCC E169.1 .A4435 2021 (print) | LCC E169.1 (ebook) | DDC 973.074753—
    dc23 | SUDOC SI 1.60:AM 3
LC record available at https://lccn.loc.gov/2020042794
LC ebook record available at https://lccn.loc.gov/2020042795

ISBN: 978-1-944466-39-8 (online); 978-1-944466-40-4 (print)

Publication date (online): 18 February 2021

*A finished museum is a dead museum,
and a dead museum is a useless museum.*

—George Brown Goode,
assistant secretary for the National Museum, 1889[1]

Contents

Preface

On a Tuesday evening in late November 2018, we—David and Hannah—were holed up as usual in our windowless basement office. Surrounded by stacks of paper, reference materials, and old Smithsonian guidebooks, our office chairs pulled to the space between our desks, we were having one of our typical impassioned conversations about our research. What were we so excited about that day? Who knows—all that is certain is that it caught us both by surprise when the words slipped out: "Maybe we should write a book?" In less than half an hour, we had a rudimentary outline sketched out on notebook paper. By the next day, we had completed a full outline, finalized the periodization of the book, and divided the necessary research and writing between us.

Although we had spent six months researching at this point, the idea of writing an extensive monograph had been far from our minds. Our first purpose was documentation: to learn about the history of the museum and to compile the sources we had used so others could use them for reference. David was set to retire and did not want to commit to another multiyear project. Hannah was a recent graduate of St. John's College and had never worked on so large a project before. But somehow, once it had been spoken, the idea of a book was infectious. We never looked back.

The project had begun with David, who worked at the National Museum of American History for 32 years, from 1987 to 2019, as a curator, department chair, and ultimately associate director for curatorial affairs. Throughout this period, he devoted his efforts primarily to studying the museum's collections and using them to create exhibitions, publications, and programs to help the museum's audiences understand the history of the United States and its relevance today. He spent little time thinking about the importance of the museum's own story. But over time, he gradually recognized the many ways that history shaped the museum's role as one of the nation's principal storytellers.

Thus, as David approached retirement, he determined that he should research the history of the museum and find ways to share it with others. John Gray, then director of the museum, and Sue Fruchter, deputy director, strongly supported these efforts. John and David had numerous conversations on why the study would be valuable and what its focus should be. Ultimately, David was granted three years of half-time employment in "phased retirement" to conduct the investigation that led to this book.

David determined to focus on the history of the exhibitions the museum had created, because they were its principal product and the way it primarily communicated with its millions of visitors. Moreover, he had spent the majority of his career planning, creating, and managing exhibitions, including three large, long-term displays, and several dozen smaller ones. He believed this extensive experience would help him better understand and tell the story of the changing character of exhibition development at the museum. He began with some trepidation, however. He was well aware of the uneven quality of the museum's records on exhibitions, having been involved in preserving some of them himself. Initially, he was also uncertain what it would be possible to accomplish through this effort. Perhaps he could do no more than compile a body of select historical reference materials.

When John Gray and David first began discussing a history project for the museum, they decided to consider a suggestion from David's wife, and recruit an intern from St. John's College in Annapolis, Maryland. At St. John's, unlike most American colleges and universities, study is not based on selective courses directed toward a major in a single field of knowledge. Instead, students there follow a fixed curriculum of study for a general degree in liberal arts based on reading and analyzing original texts created by fundamentally important writers and thinkers in the Western tradition, from Plato to Einstein.

John and David both had strong connections at St. John's, as did David's wife, whom he met there. David had taken his Bachelor of Arts degree there in 1973, and John had been a graduate student and later a member of the college's Board of Visitors and Governors. St. John's students do not study the historical texts in their curriculum in traditional ways. Rather, they focus on the significance of the fundamental ideas inherent in them and how these ideas shaped human development. By including a St. John's student in the team working on the history of the museum, John and David thought that the study might be more insightful. With the help of a faculty member at St. John's, they recruited Hannah. She stood out because she already had experience with the Smithsonian, having worked as an intern with the Smithsonian Folklife Festival in the summer of 2017. Hannah joined the project in June of 2018 as a summer intern and continued working with David through August 2019.She was then appointed as a research associate and became a chief collaborator and ultimately coauthor of this book.

We spent our first summer in collaboration exploring the historical sources we found, and deep in conversation about the larger story of the museum. We had found richer materials than we had expected—sometimes in unusual places. Official records in the Smithsonian Archives were highly valuable, but incomplete. One important supplement was several file cabinets of documents and images compiled by the museum's Public Affairs Office that were stored in a dusty basement office. They had barely survived shredding several times. The materials dated from the 1960s through the 1990s and included a variety of sources that we found nowhere else. Beyond this material, we conducted discussions with long-time staff members, some of whom had squirreled away their own personal copies of notes, draft scripts, drawings, and brochures. We found relevant records at the Library of Congress and in archives of universities where museum staff members had gone after they left the Smithsonian. From eBay, we purchased a few critical Smithsonian publications that were not preserved by the Smithsonian libraries. These additional sources, plus David's personal experience, helped us flesh out our story beyond what we found in official files.

Our search was exhilarating. We believed that, using all the materials we had located, we could write a compelling narrative that would give readers a good general overview of how the museum had originated and developed over time. Although we located numerous published sources on aspects of the museum's history, no other authors had tried to tell the story we had found. Thus, in November 2018, we developed an outline for our book. It stated that our goal was to:

> Provide a thoughtful and engaging overview and analysis of the changing ways the Nation's largest, broadest, and most visited national history museum has presented America's story in its exhibitions, from its beginning through the present; suggest some challenges that will face the museum in future years;... [and] give readers the experience of being in the museum in different eras and seeing how it presented history in different ways.

One of the most significant parts of this plan was the idea of giving our readers the *experience* of the museum at different periods of its history. Early in the project, we had become captivated by the hundreds of old exhibit photographs that we discovered in the records. Although the images from decades past were sometimes faded and dated (and occasionally included amusing examples of the fashions of past eras), they began to bring to life for us the exhibits that we were learning about. In some ways, this was a revelation.

On our first meeting, David had taken Hannah on a tour of the museum that began in an unexpected location: the *Power Machinery* exhibition on the first floor. Tucked out of the way, accessible only by walking through the *Electricity* exhibition, *Power Machinery* rarely attracts much attention, but it has an important claim to fame as the oldest exhibition still standing on the museum floor. Although diminished over the years, *Power Machinery* had opened with the new museum building—in 1964.

Presented with only the *Power Machinery* exhibition as it currently stands, you would be forgiven for thinking that the museum of 1964 was a less-than-exciting place. There are no large images on the case walls, just simple, silk-screened black text on white backgrounds. There are no buttons to press, no videos to watch, and no human-interest stories. There is only hulking machinery, labeled with technical explanations. As we began to explore the museum of the 1960s through photographs, however, it became clear that this out-of-date exhibition was not, after all, an accurate representation of the "modern" Museum of History and Technology—the initial name of the institution. Historic photographs showed exhibits that were bright and colorful, decorated with elegant silk-screen design work, with machinery in motion to demonstrate its operation, elaborate settings to display the everyday life of the past, and sometimes, oddly enough, even live animals. This was the image of the museum of an earlier era that we wanted to recreate for our readers: a museum that drew its thousands of visitors because it was full of life and wonder.

Over the next 10 months, we drafted our manuscript. Hannah was the principal author for sections of chapter 3 and all of chapter 4, while David wrote the other chapters. However, the whole book was a joint effort, as we actively discussed all our research and conclusions.

Our shared experience at St. John's influenced our work in several important ways. In our study there, we focused on understanding central ideas in major philosophical and historical books. Thus, we were both deeply interested in the ideas that museum leaders and curators intended to communicate in the museum's exhibitions. Likewise, we were interested in how these intentions were shaped by the realities of exhibition planning and development, including what artifacts were available, what space could be used, sources of funding, and the staff members involved—including curators, designers, museum specialists, educators, media planners, and others.

Our educational background also influenced how we divided the history of the museum into eras that were characterized by shifts in goals and approaches to exhibitions. In our studies at St. John's, we had traced developments in the ideas underlying Western philosophy, science, and literature from ancient Greece to modernity, and this seemed to us a similar, albeit far more limited task. We recognized that such determinations are always somewhat arbitrary and subject to debate. We saw that there were many continuities as well as differences between eras. On the other hand, distinguishing distinct eras in the museum's past provided a basis for comparison of the changing ways the museum presented American history—how it chose to "exhibit America."

Finally, we were determined that our account should include not just plans and how they changed, but also sample images of what visitors saw. Given the restrictions of a printed book, and using the limited images that have been preserved, we wanted our readers to get a sense of what it was like to visit exhibitions at the museum in different eras. In fact, we realized that for many readers, these images would be more compelling than our text, just as museum visitors remember more what they see than the exhibition text they read. In a manner analogous to Socrates's admonition that reading about ideas is never an adequate substitute for discussing them, we knew that reading our descriptions of exhibits was but a shadow of what it meant to walk through and experience them.

In conducting our research and writing, we were aided by many people who had worked in or with the museum. Some discussed our findings and tentative conclusions with us. Others helped us locate sources we would never have found on our own. We are especially grateful for the invaluable assistance of Ellen Alers, Amy Bartow-Melia, Joan Boudreau, Nigel Briggs, Clare Brown, Trina Brown, Pedro Colón, Nancy Davis, Barney Finn, Sue Fruchter, Lisa Kathleen Graddy, John Gray, Pam Henson, Valeska Hilbig, Robert Johnstone, Jennifer Jones, Katharine Klein, Peter Liebhold, Bonnie Campbell Lilienfeld, Andrea Lowther, Melinda Machado, Peter Manseau, Art Molella, Howard Morrison, Shelley Nickles, Shannon Perich,

Harry Rubenstein, Fath Davis Ruffins, Lauren Safranek, Ivan Selin, Mitch Toda, Hal Wallace, Tim Winkle, Helena Wright, and Bill Yeingst.

To assist us in the research portion of our project, we recruited two interns, whose outstanding efforts can be seen in this final work. Caroline Young, a history and business student at the University of North Carolina at Chapel Hill, came in the early phase of the project in the summer of 2018. She conducted research on a variety of topics, including how the history of the museum was reflected in Smithsonian annual reports. She digitized dozens of valuable sources and hundreds of images of museum exhibitions. Grace Trumbo joined us as part of a degree program in art history at Whitworth University in Spokane, Washington. She worked with the project during the fall of 2018. Grace compiled the chart in the appendix of this book that shows the relationship of museum directors and Smithsonian secretaries. She also researched and scanned numerous documents and images from the Library of Congress as well as Smithsonian archives and office files. These included multiple editions of guidebooks to the museum's exhibitions. She did an independent study of the series of exhibit posters the museum produced from the 1960s to the 1990s, analyzing them from both artistic and historical perspectives. Finally, she completed the task of reorganizing the large collection of documents and images that the team had digitized during its initial year of research.

Several of our colleagues were kind enough to read our entire manuscript and give us helpful comments and corrections. Their assistance helped us avoid many errors in fact and interpretation. Our special thanks to John Gray, Melinda Machado, Art Molella, Howard Morrison, Harry Rubenstein, and Ivan Selin. Bob Selim, who for many years was the museum's lead editor, stepped out of retirement to make a detailed edit of the manuscript that markedly improved its syntax and readability. We are especially grateful to him for this dedicated effort. Finally, we thank Ginger Minkiewicz, Myka Bangert, and other staff members at Smithsonian Scholarly Press for their assistance in preparing our book for publication.

The Smithsonian is among America's most unique and characteristic institutions. Its democratic mission to "increase and diffuse knowledge" is closely linked to the nation's highest ideals. We were honored to have the opportunity to uncover and share some of its remarkable history.

David K. Allison and Hannah Peterson
July 2020

Figure 1-1. The Star-Spangled Banner, the flag that inspired the national anthem, on display in 2018, shown with the first verse of the song.

CHAPTER 1

Introduction

The Star-Spangled Banner: An American Icon

Visitors to the National Museum of American History in the twenty-first century were encouraged to begin their tour by viewing the Star-Spangled Banner, the flag that inspired the national anthem. More than anything else they would see, this display symbolized the museum's responsibility to preserve the nation's most important artifacts and exhibit the American story to millions from across the nation and around the world. Like almost everything else in the museum's vast collection, the flag had a compelling history.

Most visitors were surprised to learn that "The Star-Spangled Banner," set to the words of Francis Scott Key's poem "The Defence of Fort M'Henry," did not officially become the national anthem of the United States until 1931.[2] Furthermore, Americans tend to think that their anthem is a song about the flag as a patriotic symbol. However, it is actually a song about this particular flag, which was raised at Fort McHenry in Baltimore, Maryland, on the morning of 14 September 1814, during the War of 1812. That action showed all who witnessed it that the fort had not surrendered after a fierce bombardment by British warships. Its heroic stand became a turning point in the conflict, which is often called the second war of American independence: it demonstrated that the United States would endure. When Key's poem became the national anthem, the flag he saw became a unique national treasure. Coincidentally, it was already in the Smithsonian.

The museum had acquired it through serendipity, as it has so many of its important artifacts. In the decades following the War of 1812, the family of Lieutenant Colonel George Armistead, who commanded Fort McHenry during the bombardment, had kept the flag as a prized possession. It was little known outside Baltimore. Occasionally, the family brought it out for patriotic ceremonies, but Americans did not yet consider it an irreplaceable national treasure. As was a common practice with memorabilia during this era, the Armistead family would occasionally even snip off pieces of the flag and give them to veterans or other honored citizens as souvenirs.[3]

After George Armistead's death in 1818, the flag passed to his widow, Louisa Hughes Armistead. Upon her death in 1861, it passed to her daughter, Georgiana Armistead Appleton. During the years she owned the flag, it gradually became

Figure 1-2. The Star-Spangled Banner hanging outside the Smithsonian Institution Building ("the Castle"), 1907.

recognized as an important national artifact. When Georgiana died in 1878, she bequeathed the flag to her son, Eben Appleton. He too recognized the flag's growing significance, but still turned down most requests to loan it for display, partly because it was so fragile.

Early in the twentieth century, Appleton decided he should donate the flag to a public institution for permanent preservation. He first considered giving it to Baltimore or the state of Maryland. However, by chance, one of his cousins, John B. Baylor, was a colleague of Smithsonian Secretary Charles Walcott. Baylor recommended that Appleton consider donating it to the Smithsonian's National Museum, which was increasingly becoming recognized as an appropriate repository for prized artifacts of American history. Appleton became convinced that this was the best plan.

In 1907, he loaned the flag to the Smithsonian. When it arrived, it was unfurled and temporarily hung outside the museum for a documentary photograph.

In 1912, Appleton converted the loan to a gift. Later he stipulated that the Smithsonian could neither loan the flag nor display it in other locations. As is clear in the photograph, the flag was already in poor condition when Appleton transferred it to the Smithsonian, and it was not even in suitable condition for long-term display there.

In 1914, curators arranged for its conservation following the best practices of the era. Under the leadership of Amelia Fowler, a team of seamstresses worked for eight weeks to detach it from a canvas to which it had been tacked in 1873, and carefully sewed it onto a new linen backing. This required approximately 1,700,000 stitches. Fowler later acquired a patent for her process of "new and useful improvements in preserved fabric display."[4] Museum curators could now safely put the flag on view. They displayed it in one of the largest cases in the museum, but even there, it had to be folded.

Over the following decades, the Smithsonian would display the flag in four increasingly dramatic ways, as the chapters that follow will discuss. Each time, curators, designers, and educators had to address a set of important issues. Although these were particularly challenging when presenting the museum's most iconic object, similar concerns must be addressed in every exhibition. The essence of the museum's mission has always been to illuminate the history of the United States through exhibitions of "material culture," objects of historical significance.

Figure 1-3. The Star-Spangled Banner on display in the U.S. National Museum, 1928.

Each time the flag was displayed, the first issue was designing a physical setting. This was particularly difficult because the flag was not only large and fragile, but also had great symbolic importance. In several instances, the museum literally designed or redesigned portions of its building to provide an impressive setting for the flag, which heightened the experience of encountering it. Next came the challenge of interpreting the flag as both a specific artifact with a particular history and a timeless symbol of the nation as a whole. This became even more important after Key's poem became the national anthem in 1931. Third was planning the detailed design of the presentation. Would the flag be enclosed in a case or displayed in the open? How would it be lit? How much interpretive labeling would be provided? Should it be supplemented with media, including performances of the anthem, video, or an interactive display? The final issue was preserving the flag for future generations. Balancing conservation needs with continuous display is particularly challenging with dyed fabrics. Yet, as with every national treasure in the Smithsonian's collection, there is no substitute for seeing the real thing. As Smithsonian curators have often remarked, "Our goal is to tell the real story with the real stuff."

Five Eras in Museum History

The Smithsonian has displayed exhibits of American history since it opened its first museum. Initially, however, they were only a subordinate section of the U.S. National Museum, which focused on natural history. Years later, American history became the focus of a specialized Smithsonian museum that would have a series of names: the Museum of History and Technology, the National Museum of History and Technology, the National Museum of American History, and, most recently, the National Museum of American History, Kenneth E. Behring Center.

This book traces five distinct eras in Smithsonian exhibitions of American history. Three of these were determined by major alterations in the physical setting for the museum: the opening of the U.S. National Museum during the first era, the opening of the Museum of History and Technology in the second era, and the renewal of public space in the National Museum of American History in the fifth era. The third and fourth eras centered on programmatic changes for the exhibitions of the museum: development of new exhibitions related to the bicentennial of the American Revolution in the third era, and a focus on American social history in the fourth era. No previous study of the museum has sought to identify and then analyze distinctions between different eras in its development. This is fundamental to gaining a comprehensive perspective of how the museum has changed over time.

The discussion of every era includes a floor plan for a specific year at the end of that period that epitomizes the era as a whole. Each plan provides a snapshot of all the major exhibitions visitors could see at the time. Written descriptions and images of the exhibitions explain not only what they were intended to convey but also show how they looked and felt.

Discussing the full range of displays on each floor plan is critical to documenting in a thorough manner the multiple ways that the museum "exhibited America" over 130 years. The broad scope of the floor plans is a reminder that the exhibitions were always a blend of old and new. No "renovation" has ever brought a complete transformation. Moreover, the exhibits that ended up on the museum floor were determined by a wide variety of factors. Some were large and involved hundreds of artifacts, images, and audiovisual components. Others included only a handful of objects and images. Some were major institutional priorities and were shaped by staff at multiple levels, including the museum's senior staff and occasionally even the secretary of the Smithsonian. Many of these also had external consultants and advisors who contributed to the planning. Others resulted from the thinking and planning of only a few or even just one curator and designer. Some were intended to last decades. Others were on display for only a few months or years. Many fell between these two extremes. The costs of some were borne by the museum itself, while others, especially in more recent eras, required raising millions of dollars from outside funders to supplement the museum's own resources. Comparing the range of different exhibition projects illuminates the varied factors and how they conditioned the resulting displays.

This approach also helps balance a limitation in previous historical works on the museum.[5] Previous scholarly analysis of the museum's exhibitions examined only one or a limited set of exhibitions in limited time periods. In addition, earlier studies frequently focused more on planning and intent than on discussing what finally resulted on the museum floor and was seen by visitors. Perhaps this was because archival records on planning are more plentiful and coherent than discussions of final results. Indeed, the best records of the latter are often images of final displays—a principal reason so many are included here.

Tracing the history of the museum's exhibits through five different eras reveals long-term trends and challenges that shaped the institution throughout its existence. After developing them in the book, we summarize and discuss them in the final chapter:

- Should the museum focus on the role of the United States as part of a wider world or its internal, nationalistic history? This relates particularly to the varied ways the Star-Spangled Banner was displayed in different eras.
- Would the full set of exhibitions on display at any one time present a complete or coherent presentation about United States history, or would they present a miscellany of disjointed perspectives?
- Would exhibitions be devoted to presenting objects in collections or exploring historical themes? Would they be devoted to demonstrating technological and social progress of the United States or to exploring citizens' evolving sense of the nation's identity? And how effectively would exhibitions move from initial plans to the reality of what ultimately went on display?
- As the museum changed, how would legacies of past exhibitions and collections shape those that followed?
- Finally, was the role of the museum to focus fundamentally on the history of American diversity or the struggle for national unity?

As we conducted our study, we were inspired by the epigraph we chose for this book: "A finished museum is a dead museum, and a dead museum is a useless museum." It was a statement from George Brown Goode, the greatest visionary among the founders of the Smithsonian's National Museum. We believe that Goode's thought captures a spirit that has animated the Smithsonian throughout its history. It comes from an address he delivered to the Brooklyn Institute in 1889 entitled "The Museums of the Future." He said, in part:

> When a museum building has been provided, and the nucleus of a collection and an administrative staff are at hand, the work of the museum begins, and this work, it is to be hoped, will not soon reach an end. **A finished museum is a dead museum, and a dead museum is a useless museum.** One thing should be kept prominently in mind by any organization which intends to found and maintain a museum, that the work will never be finished....My prayer for the museums of the United States and for all other similar agencies of enlightenment is this—that they may never cease to increase.[6]

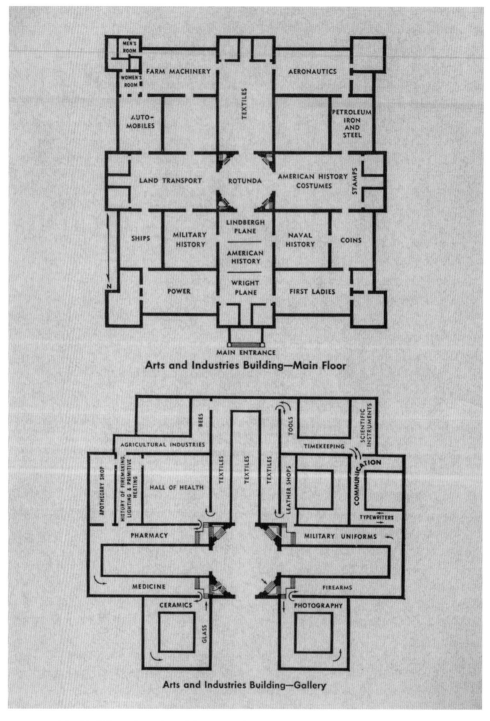

Figure 2-1. The 1962 floor plan. The exhibitions in the Arts and Industries Building were mostly on the main floor. The gallery map shows exhibits on the second-floor balconies in the same building, which were accessed by stairs. The unlabeled areas were openings to the ground floor. In 1962, the graphic arts collection was still on display in the original Smithsonian Institution Building ("the Castle").[7]

CHAPTER 2
The Nation's Attic (1876–1964)

The Era

In 1881, the Smithsonian established the U.S. National Museum as a comprehensive institution that would collect artifacts for research and reference in all areas of learning, then present exhibitions to diffuse knowledge based on them to the public. Even before the museum opened, it was clear that one building would not be enough to cover such a vast compass. In 1903, Congress authorized a second building, which became the home of the Smithsonian's natural history collections and exhibitions. Remaining in the National Museum Building was the Department of Arts and Industries, which contained collections of science, engineering, history, medicine, and crafts. The museum was then designated the Arts and Industries Building, and its staff filled the museum floors with new exhibitions related to these subject areas.

For the next 40 years, as the Arts and Industries Building aged, the collections and exhibitions multiplied, and the museum became increasingly crowded with haphazardly arranged displays. It gradually degenerated into what the public came to call "the nation's attic." Throughout those years, museum leaders advocated abandoning the building and creating one or more new museums, but their appeals went unanswered.

This era extended from 1876 to 1964, from the opening of the U.S. National Museum in 1881 to the museum's exhibits modernization program in the 1950s–1960s. The floor plan we chose to epitomize it dates from 1962, near the end of the era. The chapter focuses primarily on the later years of this lengthy period, exploring how the legacy of exhibitions at the U.S. National Museum would affect the future Museum of History and Technology. The exhibitions on display in 1962 dated from the 1910s through the 1940s. They showed collections in standardized cases with little interpretation or context. However, they were being replaced by new displays created under the exhibits modernization program. Within it, curators and designers employed interpretive settings, advanced graphic design, more extensive labeling, and improved lighting. Their experiments foreshadowed the style of exhibitions that would characterize the Museum of History and Technology.

Prelude: A Spectacular Debut

The Smithsonian's National Museum Building debuted in the limelight.[8] On 4 March 1881, it was the venue for President James Garfield's inaugural ball. Because it had the largest open space of any building in Washington at the time and was brand new, it was well suited for the gala. Exhibitions had not been installed, so there was ample room for mingling, dancing, and partying. Not incidentally, Garfield had been a regent of the Smithsonian from 1865 to 1873, and again from 1877 to 1880. He said he considered this "the most pleasant duty of my official life."[9] Smithsonian leaders had recognized soon after the election that his inaugural would be a great opportunity to impress leading Washingtonians of the grandeur and significance of their new facility—at a time when they were looking to the federal government for increasing recognition and support.

The building was decorated with patriotic banners and bunting. A temporary wooden floor was laid because the permanent tile floor was not yet ready. Both gas lights and a new kind of illumination, electric lights, were temporarily installed. Seemingly small details were addressed at the highest level. At a meeting in early February, for example, the Hall and Promenade Committee ratified the selection of 100 pieces of dancing music and 50 pieces of promenade music. They also wrangled over whether the hundreds of boxes for storing the plush hats of guests could be made of unplaned instead of finished wood. Smithsonian Secretary Baird reportedly

Figure 2-2. Exterior of the National Museum, ca. 1889.

said he thought that unplaned boxes would be "disgraceful to the place and…that they were only fit for a pigsty."[11] The committee approved the planed lumber.

Inauguration Day began with a heavy storm of wind, snow, and rain, but by 11:00 am the skies had cleared and President Garfield was able to deliver his lengthy inaugural address at the Capitol. Everyone was then ready to party. That evening, some 3,000 to 5,000 lucky guests poured into the National Museum Building to celebrate. They marveled at the lighting and were overwhelmed by the huge *Statue of America* installed in the center of the building, holding an electric bulb in her hand.

According to the *Washington Post*,

> The ball last night proved a fitting close to the [inauguration]. The large hall of the new museum building was lit up by gas and electric lights, beautifully decorated and thronged with a brilliant assemblage. The President held a reception from 9 until 11 o'clock, at which hour dancing began. The affair was in every respect a success.[12]

Now the work of installing the exhibitions began. The U.S. National Museum would not open to the public until months later, in October 1881. Its initial displays established patterns and precedents that would shape the Smithsonian's history museum far into the future.

Figure 2-4. The inaugural decorations were reportedly "artistic, munificent, and attractive, embellished by the coats-of-arms of the different states, handsomely festooned with State flags and seals."[13] On the left and right of the center arch are the insignia of President James A. Garfield and Vice President Chester A. Arthur.

Joseph Henry, George Brown Goode, and Creating the National Museum

What led to the creation of the National Museum? In 1826, James Smithson, an English scientist, bequeathed his estate to the United States of America "to found at Washington, under the name of the Smithsonian Institution, an establishment for the increase and diffusion of knowledge among men." His fortune came to the United States as 104,960 British gold sovereigns—worth $508,318.46 at the time (approximately $13 million in 2018), a princely sum to the new nation. Equally significant were his two collections—books and minerals. These became the seeds of the Smithsonian library and Smithsonian museums.[14]

Determining how to manage the Smithson bequest took Congress many years. Some questioned whether this money, from a British aristocrat who had never even visited the United States, should be accepted at all. Others disputed whether it should be used to create a national university, an astronomical observatory, or a host of other things.[15] Not until 1846 did President James K. Polk sign into law the bill establishing the Smithsonian Institution. It created a board of regents, led by the vice president and chief justice, to oversee the new body. Among other things, the bill stated that the regents

> shall cause to be erected a suitable building, of plain and durable materials and structure, without unnecessary ornament, and of sufficient size, and with suitable rooms or halls, for the reception and arrangement, upon a liberal scale, of objects of natural history, including a geological and mineralogical cabinet; also a chemical laboratory, a library, a gallery of art, and the necessary lecture rooms.[16]

The regents and the secretary of the Smithsonian, whom they would appoint, were left to determine the details of how this authorization should be interpreted. Clearly, the bequest should be used for scientific research. Should it also be used to establish a museum?

Secretary of War Joel Poinsett, a physician and avid naturalist, thought so. He was concerned about what should be done with scientific collections already being gathered by explorers studying Western lands and the world's oceans. These included the U.S. Navy's ongoing United States Exploring Expedition (called the Wilkes Expedition because it was directed by Lieutenant Charles Wilkes). It had been dispatched in 1838 to explore and survey the Pacific Ocean and surrounding lands, and it was accumulating large quantities of scientific specimens.

In May 1840, Poinsett had joined with around 90 other national leaders interested in science and learning—members of Congress, scientists, clergymen, and prominent citizens—to establish a National Institution for the Promotion of Science.[17] Its objectives were to promote science and the useful arts and to establish a national museum of natural history that would preserve scientific collections such as those being gathered by the Wilkes Expedition.[18]

This group believed that the new Smithsonian Institution, once in operation, might be the ideal organization to manage a national museum that could preserve and catalog these valuable objects. Unfortunately, that could not happen immediately, because the initial Smithsonian Institution Building, which came to be called "the Castle" due to its design, was not completed until 1855. For the present, the commissioner of patents in the Department of the Interior agreed to hold the collections coming in from the Wilkes Expedition, those of other exploring expeditions, and even the collections from the James Smithson bequest.

The Smithsonian regents chose Princeton Professor of Natural History Joseph Henry to serve as the institution's first secretary. He believed firmly that the mission of the Smithsonian should be fostering scientific research and publication, not managing a museum. Moreover, he was concerned that the cost of caring for scientific collections would require a substantial portion of the limited interest being paid from Smithson's bequest, which was the only funding the institution initially had. As far as he was concerned, the collections being gathered in the Patent Office should find a home somewhere else.

A decade later however, Secretary Henry had changed his mind, for several reasons. First, in 1850 he had hired Spencer F. Baird, a naturalist, ornithologist, and dedicated collector, as assistant secretary. When Baird came to the Smithsonian, he brought his own substantial collections with him. Unlike Henry, Baird favored the idea of establishing a museum within the Smithsonian. Second, the institution had become a major collector of artifacts itself—from the Pacific Railroad Survey, the Mexican Boundary Survey, other government expeditions, and individual explorers. In fact, these were already four times greater in bulk than that which the Patent Office was holding and wanted to transfer.[19] Finally, the new building, which opened in 1855, had enough space to store the collections the Patent Office wanted to give to the Smithsonian. Thus, Henry wrote,

> Since experience has shown that the building will ultimately be filled with objects of natural history belonging to the general government, which, for the good of science it will be necessary to preserve, it may be a question whether, in consideration of this fact, it would not be well to offer the use of the large room immediately for a national museum, of which the Smithsonian Institution would be the mere curator, and the expense of maintaining which should be paid by the general government.[20]

Critical to Henry's change of heart was that Congress cover the cost of the transfer and care of these "national collections." It decided to do so, and the collections were transferred in 1858.[21] When the National Institution itself folded in 1861, its holdings were also transferred to the Smithsonian. Henry now summarized the combined collections of the Smithsonian as consisting of:

> First, those of the naval expeditions; second, those of the United States geological surveys; third, those of the boundary surveys; fourth, those of surveys for railroad routes to the Pacific; fifth, of miscellaneous expeditions under the War and Navy Departments; sixth, those of miscellaneous collections presented or deposited by societies and individuals; and, lastly, of an extensive series of the results of explorations prosecuted by the Institution itself.[22]

One of the reasons the Smithsonian agreed to take all government scientific collections was to centralize them for efficiency. Henry planned to weed out duplicate objects and transfer them to colleges and universities who could use them for their own research and educational purposes.[23] This seemed like a very concrete and useful way to "diffuse knowledge," as Smithson had mandated. In contrast to later periods of its history, the Smithsonian indeed spent many years giving away thousands of objects to other institutions.

Taking official responsibility for national collections marked a fundamental turning point in the history of the Smithsonian. Henceforth, expanding, researching, caring for, and exhibiting them to the public would become a core component of its mission—indeed, it became the only work that most Americans ever associated with the institution. It also marked the point when the Smithsonian became a permanent public–private partnership, funded not only by a private bequest and additional donations, but also by substantial public funding, which soon became its principal source of support.

With this change, the Smithsonian now had become the de facto home not only of the national collections, but also of a national museum. This new role was now regularly noted in Smithsonian reports and scientific publications. Congress, however, did not officially recognize it until it had decided to fund a building to house it.[24] This development took years—and happened in a surprising way.

In 1866, John L. Campbell, a professor of mathematics, natural philosophy, and astronomy at Wabash College in Indiana, proposed to Philadelphia Mayor Morton McMichael that the United States celebrate the upcoming centennial of the American Revolution with a major international exhibition in Philadelphia. What better way could there be to dramatically highlight the nation's growth and achievements in its first century? Soon other supporters of the idea jumped on the bandwagon. They included Philadelphia's venerable Franklin Institute, which suggested that the display be hosted in the spacious Fairmount Park, along the Schuylkill River.

The Philadelphia City Council approved the idea in January 1870. In 1874, President Ulysses S. Grant finally agreed that the federal government should participate in the exhibition and appointed a government board to manage its involvement. Representing the Smithsonian on it was Spencer F. Baird, assistant Smithsonian secretary and curator of the National Museum. He suggested that the Smithsonian take a leading role in planning government exhibitions for the centennial. He asked his young associate, George Brown Goode, to handle most of the details.

The board's initial plans included a Smithsonian exhibition to be housed with other government exhibitions in a building devoted solely to them. They also proposed that this building should be designed so that it would be "capable of removal to Washington after the close of the Exhibition, to be used as a National Museum at the capital of the nation."[25] The board's solution presented a clever way for the Smithsonian to leverage the government's participation in the centennial celebration to meet the institution's own needs.

Congress, however, refused to approve this scheme. Instead, it chose to house all the government displays in a building paid for from the appropriations of the various departments and bureaus, including the U.S. Army and Navy, which would have exhibits there. The Smithsonian received a limited appropriation of $67,000 for its displays. When the exhibition ended, the government building, instead of coming to Washington, was to be sold to help the government recoup some of its outlay.[26]

Still sensing opportunity in the centennial, the Smithsonian took responsibility for coordinating a combined exhibition of its display with the Fish Commission and the Indian Bureau of the Department of the Interior. The exhibition was divided into five sections: Smithsonian Activities, Animal Resources, Fisheries, Mineral Resources, and Anthropology.

The Centennial Exhibition was a resounding success. It ran from 10 May to 10 November 1876. Thirty-seven countries participated, and nearly 10 million people

Figure 2-5. Smithsonian exhibits at the Centennial Exhibition in Philadelphia, 1876.

visited. If there was ever any doubt, this extravaganza made clear that there was a huge audience for public displays about American industry, science, and history. When the Centennial Exhibition was over, the Smithsonian offered to review and add to its collections significant objects that other exhibitors did not want to take back. Many countries agreed. Though the institution had brought 21 freight-car loads of exhibit materials to the exhibition, double that number came back to Washington.[27]

The Smithsonian estimated that the value of gifts from foreign governments was around $1 million. The regents later said of them, "The intrinsic value of the donations is moreover enhanced by the circumstances under which they were made. They came to us in the one hundredth year of our life as a nation, in token of the desire of the governments of the world to manifest their interest in our destiny."[28] Few of the objects in the main hall at the Centennial Exhibition initially came to the Smithsonian. Philadelphia entrepreneurs believed that they could maintain the building and many of the exhibited objects as an ongoing display in Philadelphia. When this venture failed in 1881, however, some of those objects also trickled into the Smithsonian.[29]

Everyone understood that the Smithsonian Castle was insufficient to hold this wealth of new treasures. Since the institution had not been allowed to keep the building used in Philadelphia, it had no choice but to build a new one. In the Smithsonian's 1876 annual report to Congress, Baird wrote,

It will, however be readily understood that the Smithsonian Building will be entirely inadequate to accommodate this collection in its return from Philadelphia, especially as even now it is overcrowded and packed from top to bottom with thousands of boxes, for the proper exhibition of the contents of which there is no space or opportunity at the present time. It is to be hoped that action at an early day will be taken by Congress looking toward a proper provision for this emergency, especially when it is realized that the materials are thus available for a National Museum that shall be equal, in its extent and completeness and it its educational advantages, to that of any nation in the world."[30]

Congress did not fund a new building in 1876, when the request was first made, but after further lobbying by the regents and other Smithsonian supporters, it appropriated $250,000 for a national museum in 1879. In the meantime, the collections were stashed in the Armory Building, which stood east of the Castle, on the same site where the Smithsonian would erect its National Air and Space Museum a century later.

Even before the Centennial Exhibition ended, Secretary Henry and his assistant Spencer Baird had begun working with Montgomery C. Meigs, quartermaster general of the U.S. Army, to develop preliminary plans for a museum building. They felt that having concrete ideas to show Congress and others would help encourage the appropriation. Moreover, Meigs, who had previously worked on the extension of the U.S. Capitol and other public building projects in Washington, could use his connections to build enthusiasm for the plan.[31] Smithsonian leaders also consulted architect Adolph Cluss, of the firm Cluss & Schultz, who had worked on the reconstruction of the Smithsonian Castle after a disastrous fire in 1865. Cluss was ultimately hired to design the new museum.

Joseph Henry died on 13 May 1878, before funding for the museum was guaranteed. The regents quickly named Spencer Baird as his successor, and he assumed the position only four days later. With his own responsibilities broadened, Baird now looked to his assistant George Brown Goode to take principal responsibility for the museum project.

Cluss's final design for the National Museum followed the general style of buildings at the Centennial Exhibition. It was also like buildings at earlier exhibitions, such as the New York Crystal Palace Exhibition and the 1867 Paris Exhibition. Taking the form of a Latin cross, it included a dome, numerous galleries, a central rotunda, and large windows. Most of the exhibition area was on the ground floor to facilitate access. The plan provided maximum exhibit space for exceedingly low cost—only six cents per square foot (approximately $1.60 in 2018).

The resulting structure had 80,300 square feet of display space. It was divided into 17 halls that freely communicated with each other by wide and lofty archways. Extending from the central dome were four naves, each 65 feet wide and 117 feet long. The side walls were 42 feet high. The floor beams, girders, and roofs were all of iron, and the floors were of marble and tile. To reduce cost, the building was made of high-quality red bricks—over five million of them. It also required 3,000 barrels of cement, 1,200 cubic yards of concrete, 470 tons of wrought iron, 31,000 square feet of glass, and other materials.[32]

Assuring good illumination in the building was critical. Initially, there would be no artificial lighting in the exhibit areas. In addition to eliminating interior walls, Cluss used high exterior walls pierced with windows throughout, to let light from above filter into every public space. Skylights were included that avoided direct sun and allowed light to come in from every angle.[33]

Scholars of Cluss's designs consider the National Museum Building his "master-work." Historian Cynthia R. Field explained that the edifice

> incorporated all his training and thinking about architectural and design ideas. The building was as unique in appearance as it was in function, be-cause it was the first National Museum building ever designed in the United States.... For this museum he practiced a modern approach to design, wherein the expression of structure and adaptability to function were embodied in the measure of aesthetic success.[34]

Decades later, in 1971, the building would be added to the National Historical Register. The application claimed it was the "best preserved example in the United States of 19th century 'world's fair' or 'exposition' type architecture.... It reflects the three principal requirements of this type of architecture: to enclose and cover a very large area; to present a tasteful, dramatic, and pleasing exterior; and to be inexpensive to construct."[35]

If the structure was Cluss's masterpiece, the planned organization of the museum's exhibits revealed the brilliance of George Brown Goode. Baird named him assistant director of the National Museum in 1880, and in 1887, assistant secretary in charge of the museum. He remained in that position until his death in 1896, at the age of only 45.

Goode's definition of the goals, organizing principles, and structure of the National Museum, as well as his management of its exhibitions during its initial years, profoundly shaped the future of the Smithsonian. His influence persisted even after the National Museum broke up in the twentieth century into separate museums, including the Museum of History and Technology. Indeed, the breadth of his vision still resonated in the Smithsonian's strategic plans of the twenty-first century, as leaders sought to find coherence in the manifold activities in which the Smithsonian had become involved.

Goode, an ichthyologist who had received his master's degree at Harvard under Professor Louis Agassiz, came to the Smithsonian in 1872 to work under Assistant Secretary Spencer Baird. When Goode took the lead in coordinating government participation in the 1876 Centennial Exhibition, he labored tirelessly on this project, spending 14-hour days selecting objects, planning displays, organizing transportation, and assembling an encyclopedic catalog. It eventually drove him to a nervous breakdown and extended leave of absence.[36] However, he loved the work and would devote himself to museum collections and exhibitions for the rest of his life.

In a remembrance of Goode written soon after his death, Samuel P. Langley, who followed Baird as secretary of the Smithsonian, and under whom Goode also worked for many years, noted this about the traveling displays that Goode regularly organized:

Figure 2-6. George Brown Goode, ca. 1880.

> Nowhere were Mr. Goode's administrative talents more strongly shown than in an exhibition. The plans of the floor space, the cases, the specimens were all carefully arranged in advance. Boxes were especially made of lumber which could be utilized for cases or platforms. Cases were marked, and not very long before the opening of the exposition the entire mass would be deposited on the bare space assigned to the Smithsonian exhibition. Usually other exhibitors had their material half arranged by this time, and the fear was expressed by sympathetic bystanders that the Smithsonian would not be ready. The cases would be unpacked, and the specimens put in them in whatever position they happened to stand, and up to the last day all would seem to be in confusion; but Doctor Goode knew his resources and his men as a general knows his army. Suddenly all detailed work would come to an end, and in the course of a few hours, as if by magic, the entire exhibit would be put in place.[37]

Goode's most lasting influence was in his systematic thinking about the National Museum's goals, organization, and structure. The museum, he believed, had three basic goals. It should be a *museum of record*, which preserves the material foundation of scientific knowledge; a *museum of research*, which supports scholars in identifying and grouping objects in their "most philosophical and instructive relations"; and a *museum of education*, which illustrates with specimens "every kind of natural object and every manifestation of human thought and activity by displaying descriptive labels adapted to the popular mind." This brief summary of the museum's mission was repeated year after year in published guides.[38]

Goode's view of what the museum should contain and how it should be arranged was all-encompassing. In a section of the Smithsonian's 1881 report to Congress, he posited that "the chief requisite to success in the development of a great museum is a perfect plan of organization and a philosophical system of classification." The structure he proposed was based on anthropology, but, as he explained, the word "anthropology" being applied in its most comprehensive sense. It should exhibit the physical characteristics, the history, the manners, past and present, of all peoples, civilized and savage, and should illustrate human culture and industry in all their phases; the earth, its physical structure and its products, is to be exhibited with special reference to its adaptation for use by man and its resources for his future needs. The so-called natural history collections—that is to say, the collections in pure zoology, geology, and botany—should be grouped in separate series, which, though arranged on another plan, shall illustrate and supplement the collections in industrial and economic natural history. The classification proposed should provide a place for every object in existence which it is possible to describe, or which may be designated by a name. When the object itself cannot be obtained, its place should be supplied by a model, picture, or diagram. The following plan of classification is proposed for provisional use; the experience of future years will doubtless make it wise to introduce into it numerous changes.... Only the principal divisions of the classification are now presented, a more detailed exposition being reserved for the next report.

OUTLINE OF A SCHEME OF MUSEUM CLASSIFICATION

Divisions.

I. Mankind
II. The Earth as Man's Abode
III. Natural Resources
IV. The Exploitative Industries
V. The Elaborative Industries [i.e. human arts, industries, and technology]
VI. Ultimate Products and their Utilization
VII. Social Relations of Mankind
VIII. Intellectual Occupations of Mankind[39]

Although clearly characterized by the racial prejudices of the era, this broad structure provided Goode with a framework to display everything the National Museum already had, or might collect in the future, not only from the United States but from anywhere in the world. For the next 15 years, Goode strove to make the National Museum an institution that organized all human knowledge and shared it with the public, free of charge. In his mind, this was an ideal way to carry out James Smithson's mandate to "diffuse knowledge."

The First Exhibitions

The museum opened to the public in 1882. Door guards recorded 152,744 visitors from February to the end of the year—15,000 more than viewed displays that remained in the Smithsonian Castle.[40] Hundreds of thousands of tourists and residents were eager to see more Smithsonian exhibitions. Installation of additional cases

Figure 2-7. Visitors to the National Museum Building, 1898.

continued through that year and for several years to come. Yet even during the museum's first year of operation, Secretary Baird knew the building would not be large enough to display the rapidly expanding collections of the Smithsonian as new agencies of the government, including the Geological Survey, transferred more specimens. He soon began petitioning Congress for a second building.[41]

While Goode's concept was comprehensive, it did not translate easily into a plan for laying out displays of objects the Smithsonian collections actually included. Moreover, many of his colleagues objected to the structure. By the time he reported

Name of department.	1882.	1883.	1884.	1885–'86. (a)	1886–'87.	1887–'88.	1888–'89.	1889–'90 (b)
Arts and industries:								
Materia medica..........	....	4,000	4,442	4,850	5,516	5,762	5,942	(c) 5,915
Foods................ ..	....	1,244	1,580	822	877	877	911	1,111
Textiles................	....	....	2,000	3,063	3,144	3,144	3,222	3,288
Fisheries ....:.....	....	....	5,000	9,870	10,078	10,078	10,078	10,080
Animal products......... ..	....	....	1,000	2,792	2,822	2,822	2,918	2,949
Graphic arts............	....	....	....	....	....	....	....	(d) 600
Transportation and engineering	....	....	....	....	....	....	....	1,250
Naval architecture	....	....	600	....	....	....	600	(e) 600
Historical relics............	....	....	....	1,002				
Coins, medals, paper-money, etc	....	....	....	1,005	}13,634	14,640	14,990	20,890
Musical instruments.......	....	....	....	430	417	427	427	447
Paints and dyes............	....	....	....	2,278	2,238	3,011	3,011	3,132
The Catlin Gallery	....	....	....	77	100	100	109	197
Physical apparatus	....	....	....	500	500	500	500	(f)
Oils and gums	....	....	....	250	251	251	251	263
Chemical products.........	....	....	....	{197 / 659	198 / 661	198 / 661	213 / 688	} 1,112
Domestic animals...........	....	....	....	....	....	....	....	66
Ethnology...............	....	....	200,000	500,000	503,764	505,464	506,324	508,830
American aboriginal pottery.	....	....	12,000	25,000	26,022	27,122	28,222	29,269
Oriental antiquities.........	....	....	....	....	....	....	850	3,485
Prehistoric anthropology ...	35,512	40,491	45,252	65,314	101,659	108,631	116,472	123,677
Mammals (skins and alcoholics)	4,660	4,920	5,694	7,451	7,811	8,052	8,275	8,836
Birds......................:	44,354	47,246	50,350	53,945	54,987	56,484	57,974	60,219
Birds' eggs and nests........	....	....	40,072	44,163	48,173	50,055	50,173	51,241
Reptiles and batrachians	....	....	23,495	25,344	27,542	27,664	28,405	29,050
Fishes	50,000	65,000	68,000	75,000	100,000	101,350	107,350	122,575
Vertebrate fossils............	....	....	....	....	....	....	....	(g) 512
Mollusks	33,375	......	400,000	460,000	425,000	455,000	468,000	471,500
Insects	1,000	....	151,000	500,000	585,000	595,000	603,000	618,000
Marine invertebrates	11,781	14,825	200,000	350,000	450,000	515,000	515,300	520,000
Comparative anatomy:								
Osteology..................	3,535	3,640	4,214	{10,210	11,022	11,558	11,753	12,326
Anatomy	70	103	3,000	}				
Paleozoic fossils	......	20,000	73,000	80,482	84,491	84,649	91,126	92,355

Figure 2-8. Growth of the collections, 1882–1890.

on progress in installing the museum in 1884, he admitted that its varied departments would in fact use different ways of presenting their objects.[42] Ultimately, the installed exhibitions were organized around the subject areas of the divisions, not the grand anthropological structure Goode had originally outlined. As the chapters ahead will relate, this early example of how the realities of exhibition development altered initial grand plans would be repeated many times.

One important aspect of Goode's approach remained in place, however. The Anthropology Division continued to include all the major collections that later would become the responsibility of a separate Museum of History and Technology, where they would be interpreted in different ways than Goode had imagined. Figure 2-8 shows the relative size of the collections in 1890 and how they had expanded since 1882.

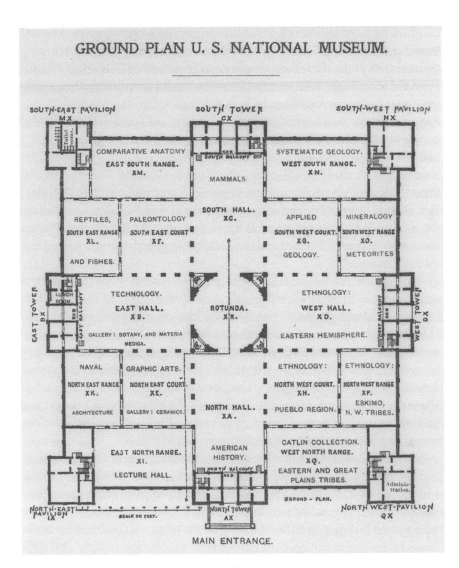

Figure 2-9. Floor plan of the museum in 1890.[43]

The plan in Figure 2-9 shows how the museum looked to the public in 1890. Clearly, it was primarily a museum of natural history, with a wide variety of objects from the paleontology, botany, mineralogy, and ethnology collections. Much space in the North Hall at the main entrance was devoted to displaying George Catlin's remarkable paintings of American Indians. Also on view near the entrance were George Washington's uniform and camp kit, Martha Washington's bed curtains, china presented to the Washingtons by the Marquis de Lafayette, and portraits of the first couple. Visitors found a wealth of objects related to President Ulysses S. Grant given to the Smithsonian jointly by his widow and financier William H. Vanderbilt. Vanderbilt had purchased the collection from General Grant in 1885 to help him cover debts for bad investments but had never wanted to keep the objects. Where should they go? Why not the Smithsonian?

By this time, the Smithsonian already had on display many of the curiosities that would later earn it the nickname of "the nation's attic." Visitors could see a printing press reportedly used by Benjamin Franklin, spectacles worn by Thomas Paine when he wrote *Common Sense*, muskets given to President Thomas Jefferson by the emperor of Morocco; a pocket knife of Daniel Boone's, the hair of 14 presidents, from George Washington to Franklin Pierce, a coat worn by General Santa Anna in the Mexican War, a section of a tree cut down by musket balls at the Battle of Spotsylvania, and even rejected models of the Washington Monument. The technology collections included a model of James Eads's St. Louis bridge, the John Bull locomotive, pharmacopeias of many nations, and a large collection of boat models.[44]

To keep down costs and enhance flexibility in displaying objects, Goode standardized the design of cases as much as possible. They were all of mahogany, and most of them eight feet, eight inches long and of uniform height. They could easily be used to create walls or sections on the museum floor without additional exhibit furniture. These were supplemented by other case designs when vertical displays were unnecessary. This closely packed forest of mahogany cases gave the National Museum its distinctive look. It was something designers of the Museum of History and Technology would be anxious to abandon when they planned their new museum in the 1950s.

Figure 2-10. North Hall of the National Museum with history relics.

Figure 2-11. Relics of George Washington.

Figure 2-12. East wing transportation exhibits.

Figure 2-13. Cases in the Boat Hall of the National Museum.

Splitting the Museum

In 1903, Congress finally decided to heed the constant pleas of the Smithsonian for a new building. Initially, they approved an expenditure of $1.5 million. Unlike their predecessors in the 1880s, Smithsonian leaders this time did not thank Congress and gratefully do the best they could with this appropriation. Experience had shown that if the institution did not seek to get more of its needs met at this critical juncture, it would have to wait long years to obtain additional support.

Experience had also taught the Smithsonian that the design of the new building should not be based on what had been appropriate for large, temporary exhibitions. The new building had to be suitable for a permanent institution devoted to perpetual preservation and care of objects and scientific research as well as public education and display. To make their case, the regents formed a special committee that documented "the pressing needs of additional room for the proper exhibition of specimens belonging to the National Museum."[45] Instead of agreeing with an initial plan for using the $1.5 million, they presented a "plan B" that was more than twice as expensive: $3.5 million. Their case was persuasive. In 1903, Congress approved this much larger appropriation for expenditure beginning in 1904.[46]

The new building opened in 1911. In later years, it would be called the Natural History Museum and still later the National Museum of Natural History. But at this point, it was simply called the second building of the National Museum. Its facilities were far better suited for the full range of museum work than those of the original building. The collections moved there were primarily those related to natural history. As Charles Wolcott, who became secretary of the Smithsonian in 1907, reported in the 1911 Annual Report:

> The most important item of interest in connection with the National Museum during the year was the completion on June 20, 1911, of all structural work on the new building, just six years after the excavations for the foundation were commenced.... [The new building] is massive and imposing in appearance. It is well lighted. There is little room that cannot be utilized. More than one-half of the 10 acres of floor space is placed at the service of the public in the interest of popular education, while the remaining space is used for reserve collections and laboratories of the scientific departments and divisions and for the maintenance of the building and the operation of the heating, lighting, and ventilating plant. The greater part of the natural-history collections, including ethnology, have been removed to the new structure; while in the old building space is now afforded for the proper display of objects pertaining to the arts and industries, including the collection illustrating the graphic arts and the art textiles, and also for the large and interesting series illustrative of American history. Although there has yet been no formal dedication of the new building, the exhibition halls are being opened to the public one after another as the reinstallation of the exhibits progresses.[47]

Visitation continued to grow. In 1911, 207,010 came to the older National Museum Building, 151,112 to the new museum building, and 107,085 to the galleries in the Smithsonian Institution "Castle" Building.[48]

By 1919, the two buildings of the museum were being officially being called the Natural History Building and the Arts and Industries Building. The separation of the collections into the two locations led to administrative changes. The secretary decided to reorganize the Anthropology Department. The divisions of ethnology, prehistoric archeology, historic archeology, and physical anthropology moved to the Natural History Building. The divisions of history, mechanical technology, and the sections of ceramics, music, medicine, photography, art textiles, and period costumes now became the Arts and Industries Division and stayed in the Arts and Industries Building. This new combined division and its collections would form the nucleus of the Museum of History and Technology in the 1950s.[49]

Meanwhile, curators kept collecting. Among the largest and most significant additions were objects related to World War I, which had just ended on 11 November 1918. In collaboration with the War and Navy Departments, the Smithsonian acquired a large quantity of materials related to the war, which it reported in 1919, "will probably form one of the most important collections ever undertaken by it."[50] It included uniforms, weapons, shop models, medals, mementos, photographs, and combat art. In the new era of military aviation, the Smithsonian's dreams were even greater:

> Through arrangement with the Army and Navy the museum is planning to exhibit examples of every plane, engine, radio apparatus, and other accessory in production in the United States at the time of the armistice, and has secured for this exhibit the temporary metal structure erected on the Smithsonian grounds in 1917 by the War Department for the use of the Air Service.[51]

Although this grand aspiration went unfulfilled, the collections that the Smithsonian did acquire later became central to the National Air and Space Museum.

To display this material properly, the Smithsonian argued once again that it needed still another museum building. Even in the aftermath of victory in World War I, the request failed at this point. Displays of World War I objects were mounted in the Natural History Building, the Arts and Industries Building, and the temporary aviation museum mentioned in the quotation above.

Arts and Industries on Display

With the natural history collections gone, the curators of the arts and industries collections had an entire museum building to themselves. Over time, they gradually filled it with a wide variety of displays. The floor plan in Figure 2-14 shows how it appeared in 1933. That year, 581,802 visitors came to the museum, fewer than the previous year due to the Great Depression.[52]

The displays now ranged from health to ceramics to military uniforms to agriculture—including a living beehive. These were still primarily collections arrayed in exhibit cases, or what would later be called "open storage," but they were organized in new ways. Most displays were designed to show technical progress or illuminate key technical principles in their respective fields. Even the graphic arts and photography exhibits were more about improved technology than visual art. In contrast to this were displays focused specifically on politics or biography, such as the Hall of History, with its "personal belongings and medals of honor of statesmen, warriors, scientists, and authors."[53]

Two exhibitions related specifically to women's history. The first, opened in 1914, was a collection of women's "period costumes" that focused primarily on the first ladies of the United States. This will be discussed in a subsequent section. In sharp contrast to this was a display of objects related to women's suffrage donated by

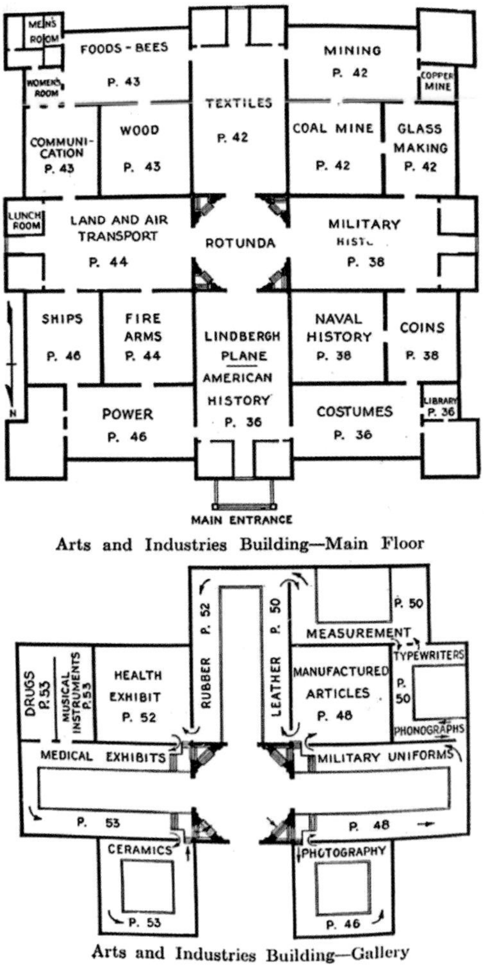

Figure 2-14. Floor plan of the Arts and Industries Building in 1933.

Arts and Industries Building—Main Floor

Arts and Industries Building—Gallery

the National American Woman Suffrage Association. The exhibition resulted from the advocacy of suffragette Helen Hamilton Gardener. Soon after the nineteenth amendment was approved by Congress in June 1919, Gardener, who ran the organization's Washington office, petitioned the Smithsonian to accession a selection of objects she would donate to commemorate the landmark event and then create an exhibition based on them. The objects included the red shawl that Susan B. Anthony wore at suffrage conventions, a copy of the 1848 Declaration of Sentiments and Resolutions, the table on which Elizabeth Cady Stanton drafted the declaration, photos of the congressional signing ceremonies, and the gold pen Gardener had purchased for the momentous occasion. Gardener's persistence led to a small exhibition entitled *An Important Epoch in American History* opening in 1920, months before the amendment was ratified by all the states required and became law.[54] Subsequently, a selection of the items were displayed in a standard case as Collection of the National Woman Suffrage Association. Despite this early activity, the museum devoted little further attention to women's political history in its exhibitions until the 1980s.

Figure 2-15. Women's suffrage collection, including Susan B. Anthony's portrait and shawl and other materials related to the passage of the nineteenth amendment.

Now displayed in the center of the building was the plaster cast model for the *Statue of Freedom* that had stood atop the U.S. Capitol building since 1863. In 1890, the model replaced the *Statue of America*, which had been on view when the National Museum opened. The female figure depicted in this new sculpture was an allegorical symbol of the nation. She wore a Native American–style blanket over her left shoulder. In her right hand was a sheathed sword, and her left held a laurel wreath of victory and the shield of the United States. She wore a military helmet adorned with stars and an eagle's head crowned by an arching crest of feathers. This statue became the central icon of the Arts and Industries Building, a role that the Star-Spangled Banner would assume decades later in the Museum of History and Technology. Surprisingly, the *Statue of Freedom* would never be displayed in the museum. However, in 2008, it was loaned to the new Capitol Visitor Center and displayed there, prominent once again.

Due in part to the collecting that followed World War I, military history was now given significant exhibition space. Particularly noteworthy were objects related to General John "Black Jack" Pershing, commander of the American Expeditionary

Figure 2-16. *Statue of Freedom*, icon for the Arts and Industries Building.

Forces in that war, including his headquarters map showing the location of forces on Armistice Day, 11 November 1918.

Visitors could also see many weapons, ship models, and uniforms. The uniform cases in Figure 2-17 displayed examples dating from the American Revolution through World War I.

Two of the most popular exhibitions were those on mining and photography. The mining display included a large model of the copper mine at Bingham Canyon, Utah. Models were increasingly being used in the museum to help visitors imagine historical artifacts in context. The photography exhibition included scores of images, from daguerreotypes to contemporary prints. It also displayed hundreds of photographic appliances, including cameras, shutters, and lenses.

After the relocation of the natural history artifacts, arts and industries curators were delighted to have a whole building to exhibit their collections, but they were increasingly dissatisfied with the limitations of the structure. As their collections increased, there was no space to display new accessions unless they were crammed into existing cases. Storage spaces overflowed. Offices were inadequate and poorly equipped. Climate control was abysmal. As visitation to the museum grew, the lack

Figure 2-17. Military uniforms exhibition.

Figure 2-18. Mining exhibition.

Figure 2-19. One case in the photography exhibition.

of adequate restrooms, food service, and seating left patrons tired, hungry, and uncomfortable. The building had been designed to have only natural lighting, and thus had windows everywhere. Artificial lighting was later added, but natural light still streamed in. Too much of it damaged many objects, such as textiles and paper artifacts. A strong consensus developed that the building was no longer acceptable for a national museum devoted to permanently preserving national treasures.

Frank Taylor, Leonard Carmichael, and Modernizing Exhibitions

By the time World War II ended, the Arts and Industries Building was more confusing and disorganized than ever. While Smithsonian collections had continued to expand, space to exhibit them had not. In 1946 a Smithsonian National Air Museum was formally authorized by Congress, but without a new museum building to display its collections. Some of the new air museum's objects were being exhibited in the aviation building. However, it had a low ceiling that did not allow display of aircraft suspended overhead. Consequently, some of those were hung in Arts and Industries Building—where no one else was using the overhead space.

A walking tour outlined in a Smithsonian guide of the era gave a sense of the random grouping of the museum's displays. Visitors entering the building would see the Wright Brothers' pathbreaking Kitty Hawk *Flyer* and Charles Lindberg's *Spirit of*

St. Louis hovering above them. Displayed on the floor were random historical relics of American leaders, including Abraham Lincoln's life mask, Admiral Peary's polar trophies, and a desk on which Thomas Jefferson drafted the Declaration of Independence. Adjacent to this area were gowns of the first ladies, a numismatics display, and an exhibition about the U.S. Navy and Marine Corps. Next came stamps, mementos of American political leaders, and a dollhouse depicting American family life from 1900 to 1914. Overhead, there were two Curtiss airplanes of 1909 and 1912. And that was just one corner of the museum.

There were no clear hallways between exhibitions and no directional signs. The sole bathroom in the building was all the way to the rear and hard to find. In some ways the serendipity of exhibit arrangement was charming and surprising, and many visitors enjoyed the eclectic mix. But the building's reputation as "the nation's attic" was more deserved than ever.

Smithsonian leaders were aware of the problems, and of the potential of gaining greater congressional support now that World War II had ended in American victory. In 1946 and 1947, they persuaded Congress to introduce bills to create not only a new history museum, but also a new museum for engineering and industry and a new air museum. However, none of these initiatives received funding.[55]

Much could still be done. In 1948, Assistant Secretary of the Smithsonian John W. Graf created a subcommittee of the Smithsonian Planning Committee to develop a program for modernizing the Smithsonian exhibitions in all its existing museum buildings. These now comprised the Smithsonian Institution Building ("the Castle"), the Arts and Industries Building, the Freer Gallery, the Natural History Building, and the temporary aviation building. Graf appointed Frank Taylor, the new curator of the Engineering Department, to head the subcommittee.

Taylor and his colleagues took this assignment very seriously and issued a scathing critique of the current situation. In their report, they wrote:

> The exhibition element of the institution's work has reached a low level of accomplishment. This is due to the lack of money and staff to carry on exhibition work and, possibly the more important reason, to the preoccupation of the staff and administration with other elements of the work, such as research, preservation, and exploration.... Exhibits of many sections were 'finished' by [curators'] predecessors many years before their time and...they have had neither the need nor the incentive to undertake exhibition work.[56]

To illustrate the seriousness of the issue, committee members described the worst exhibits in each building. Taylor chose the photography exhibition in Arts and Industries. He wrote:

> [The cases] are literally jampacked with old and new photographic and motion picture equipment. Most of it is of great technical interest. It looks as though it was installed by someone who was looking away and possibly carrying on a conversation while putting the objects on the shelves. The labels

Figure 2-20. Secretary Carmichael welcomes Lady Bird Johnson to the First Ladies Hall in the National Museum, 1962.

are generally only single line names and numbers typed on drab paper.... Ninety per cent of the material now displayed would be more usefully housed in reference storage cases. Until this is done, no real improvement in exhibition is possible.[57]

The cost to fix this exhibition alone: $16,000.

The Smithsonian Planning Committee had proposed a budget of $100,000 to be spent on modernization across the institution. The subcommittee boldly estimated that the cost to make a significant difference was much higher: $4 million. Secretary Alexander Wetmore was not willing to lobby for this level of funding in addition to asking for new buildings, so little was done. Significant progress would require a new leader.

In 1953, Leonard Carmichael replaced Wetmore as secretary of the Smithsonian. He was the first secretary who was neither a physical nor biological scientist, and the first since Joseph Henry who was not promoted to the position from inside the institution. In his 11 years at the Smithsonian, Carmichael would make many major changes—focused especially on the institution's museums and exhibitions.

Born in 1898, Carmichael received his bachelor of science degree from Tufts University and PhD in experimental psychology from Harvard. He taught at Princeton, Brown, and the University of Rochester before becoming president of Tufts University in 1938. During World War II, he served as director of the National Roster of Scientific and Specialized Personnel, helping recruit talented staff for work on radar, the atomic bomb, and other technical areas. In 1953, he left Tufts to become secretary of the Smithsonian. Even in this post, he continued to work in his field, publishing, for example, *Basic Psychology*, a popular text for general readers, in 1957.[58]

Carmichael came to the Smithsonian determined to modernize it and make it a much stronger educational institution that reached the general public, especially those who visited its museums. He was anxious to take on the challenges that the modernization subcommittee had detailed. In his first annual report to Congress, Carmichael wrote:

[Many of our visitors] are impressionable high-school seniors on what may well be their one trip to Washington. It is thus borne in upon everyone connected with the Smithsonian Institution that our exhibits must be prepared in such a way that they will most effectively tell these eager and earnest visitors the story of America's natural history and of the rise of the industrial and scientific greatness of America. These future leaders of our Nation cannot help being wiser in all that they do concerning our country if they see in our halls [sic] examples of the ingenious productions of great inventors and leaders of the past.[59]

This heartfelt sentiment energized Carmichael's commitment to a modernization program for the institution's museums and exhibitions that began in his first year and continued throughout his tenure. Over that 11-year period, Carmichael made huge strides forward. He secured $36 million of congressional funds to build the new Museum of History and Technology. He also chose and installed its founding director, Frank Taylor, who would guide this challenging project to successful completion. Elsewhere in the Smithsonian, he directed the creation of the National Portrait Gallery and acquisition of the historic Patent Office Building to house both it and the Smithsonian's American Art Museum. He added two new wings to the National Museum of Natural History. He revitalized the Smithsonian Astrophysical Observatory and moved it to Cambridge, Massachusetts.

Year after year, he also obtained hundreds of thousands of dollars to modernize exhibitions in all the Smithsonian museums. These included many remaining in the original U.S. National Museum building, some of which will be discussed further below, and all those installed at the new Museum of History and Technology. There were many more at the National Air Museum and the Museum of Natural History, including displays on dinosaurs, gems and minerals, anthropology, and botany. These improvements brought spectacular results. Between 1953 and 1963, annual visitation to the Smithsonian increased from 3,429,000 to 10,309,000.

During Carmichael's tenure, Smithsonian collections increased from 34 million cataloged objects to 57 million. Among the most noteworthy for the Natural History Museum were the Hope Diamond and the 11-ton, 13-foot-tall Fénykövi elephant known as Henry. For the Museum of History and Technology, they included the gunboat *Philadelphia,* a stellar collection of Russian gold coins, the Syz collection of European porcelains, the IBM collection of early astrolabes, gowns of first ladies and White House china, 66 examples of early telephone technology from Bell Telephone Laboratories, and the 1401 locomotive, the heaviest object to be installed in the new museum. In addition to being a master in attracting government funding, Carmichael also doubled the value of the Smithsonian endowment, from $11 million to $22.5 million.

Hall of First Ladies (1955)

The first and most successful exhibition modernized in the Arts and Industries Building was the *First Ladies* display. The collection on which it was based had an interesting background. Two private citizens, Cassie Mason Myers Julian-James and Rose Gouverneur Hoes, conceived the idea of creating the collection in the early twentieth century. Washington society figures, they came to believe that the first ladies' dresses represented American fashion at the highest level in ways that exemplified broader social change in the nation.

Over the next several years, they helped the Smithsonian acquire gowns of 15 first ladies. Most significant was a donation in 1912 by Helen Taft, first lady at that time, of the gown she had worn to her husband's inaugural ball three years earlier. This gift set a precedent that would be followed by all subsequent first ladies.[60]

The first version of the first ladies exhibition, entitled *Collection of Period Costumes*, opened in February 1914. It was an immediate success. The *Washington Star* reported,

> In a secluded corner of the National museum, somewhat out of the beaten path followed by sightseeing throngs, there is an exhibition that will bring joy to the heart of every feminine visitor to the National Capital. Here, in a dimly lighted room, made smoky by warlike relics of former glory which repose in glass cases under lock and key, on all sides, famous White House ladies of bygone generations may be viewed: and if the visitor is of the proper temperament, an acquaintanceship may be cultivated that will prove an unending enjoyment.[61]

Figure 2-21. *First Ladies* exhibition, ca. 1912.

Figure 2-22. *First Ladies* exhibition in the 1930s.

Women, who were fascinated by the beautiful dresses, saw the first ladies as trend-setters and exalted role models. The oldest dress on display had been worn by Martha Washington, while the newest came from Helen Herron Taft. The dresses were shown in lines of standard mahogany cases with minimal labeling and no context.

In 1931, the exhibition was moved to a more spacious gallery, but the presentation remained a simple collections exhibition that included only dresses, accessories, and minimal explanation.

Then, in the early 1950s when the Smithsonian was deciding which exhibits to modernize, Margaret Klapthor and other curators made a persuasive argument that the first ladies exhibition should be included:

> The collection of Dresses of the First Ladies . . . is one of the most popular and most well-known exhibits in this country. . . . At the present time the collection is poorly exhibited and inadequately lighted. The dresses are crowded in the cases in which they are displayed. . . . The Collection has become for the people of the United States a symbol of our system of government. It is a visual expression of American democracy. The Collection contains dresses worn by the wives of planters, farmers, lawyers, tradesmen, statesmen, soldiers, teachers,—men from every walk of life who have been elected to the highest office in our government. It is a panorama of history with emotional appeal which can be understood by all.[62]

Figure 2-23. The modernized First Ladies Hall in the 1950s.

Moreover, the collection now included original furniture, paneling, and decorations from the White House at various periods, as well as fashion accessories. A new form of display was in order.

> It has become important to preserve for the people of the United States an idea of the transitional periods of decoration through which the [White House] has passed. The Smithsonian Institution has already in its possession the materials to create such a picture, and the coordination of these specimens into graceful and dignified settings for the dresses seems appropriate and logical.[63]

The Smithsonian authorized $75,000 to renovate the exhibition.[64] Instrumental to creating it was a dynamic young designer, Benjamin W. Lawless, who worked closely with Klapthor. After military service in World War II, Lawless earned bachelor's and master's degrees in fine art at the University of Illinois at Urbana-Champaign. After a one-year stint as an art museum director in Saginaw, Michigan, he joined the Smithsonian in 1953.[65] Lawless later told a reporter that when he arrived at the Smithsonian,

> My first thought was; "Does this place need help!" I said I'd just work here six months, redoing the First Ladies' Hall. We spent our time cutting away lace that had been sewn over the plunging fronts on those gowns. Then they learned I could build models, so I kind of got involved.[66]

Lawless shaped all the projects of the exhibits modernization program and later became chief designer at the Museum of History and Technology. He would have a huge impact on determining the look and feel of the new museum. He stayed with the Smithsonian for 28 years, until 1981.

Presiding at the opening of the new First Ladies Hall on 24 May 1955 was Mamie Eisenhower, whose dress it included. The elegant display showed dresses representing every presidential administration in eight period settings based on architectural details and furniture from the White House. It also included a sizable collection of White House china of various presidential administrations.

Remembering the National Museum's debut, while also referencing the crowded condition of the current museum, the *Washington Post* reported:

> Last evening's ceremonies awakened memories of the Garfield ball, when the Smithsonian had just been finished—a band played in the rotunda and guests danced in the space now filled with exhibits.... [They] sat in chairs beneath the Spirit of St. Louis and the Wright Brother's airplane while the scarlet-coated Marine band played in front of a display of American wartime uniforms.[67]

The museum could not have chosen a better way to launch its modernization program. This use of period settings that allowed visitors to compare the dresses from different eras to each other was a smashing success that illustrated the value of contextual presentation.

Hall of Health (1957)

Like other modernized exhibitions, the new Hall of Health replaced a series of crammed, standardized cases displayed along a hallway. In it, according to the *Washington Post*, "the miracle of life becomes a three-dimensional reality."[68] Besides historical artifacts, it used a wealth of graphic illustrations and models. Dramatically featured in the center of the gallery was the "transparent woman," which "by means of electronics, light, and sound, shows the location and explains the function of the major organs of the body."[69] Every 15 minutes, a recorded voice from above explained functions of the body. At an interactive station, visitors could use an oversized stethoscope attached to an oscilloscope screen that let them "see" their hearts beating.[70]

The general goal of the room was to exhibit "man's knowledge of his body then and now." It touched on embryology, growth, bones and muscles, dental health, the heart and circulation, digestion and respiration, the endocrine system, the nervous system, and health in old age.[71] There was also a "health theater" where visitors could rest and view media presentations.

Hall of Telephony (1957)

The modernized *Telephony* exhibition opened in March 1957. It first summarized the work of earlier inventors who contributed to knowledge of sound and its communication, ending with the inventions of Alexander Graham Bell. Then it traced the story from the first practical telephones to the present, moving from wired to electronic

Figure 2-24. Public health exhibition, 1925.

Figure 2-25. The modernized Hall of Health, 1957.

Figure 2-26. The modernized *Telephony* exhibition.

devices to solid-state technology. Besides historical artifacts, the exhibition included models, graphic illustrations, recorded narration, and contemporary telephones.

This display differed from the other exhibitions in the building. It was produced and presented not by Smithsonian staff but by the Bell Telephone Laboratories Exhibit Department. It was donated to the Smithsonian on behalf of the Bell Telephone System and the Independent Telephone Companies.[72] The benefit of the outside support was demonstrated in the quality of the presentation and the wide range of important objects it included, which the Smithsonian would not have been able to obtain on its own. Besides donating the exhibition, the sponsors committed to help the Smithsonian keep the exhibition up to date.

Although the museum maintained close connections with many corporations, there are few examples when it allowed one of them to produce an entire exhibition on its own, even if, as in this case, the museum had helped shape the content. The extent to which industrial sponsors should be involved in Smithsonian exhibition development would become much more controversial in subsequent years.

Hall of Power Machinery (1957)[73]

The modernized Hall of Power Machinery boasted a dramatic new form of presentation. Instead of just static artifacts, it included moving engines, modes, murals, diagrams, and schematic mechanisms. They showed the progress of technology from primitive wind-powered and water-powered machines to steam and gas turbines.[74] Frank Taylor, at this time assistant director of the National Museum, summed up the educational message,

> The exhibit shows the evolution of machines men have made to convert natural supplies of energy—coal, water, oil—into mechanical work. It also

Figure 2-27. Hall of Power Machinery.

shows the need to make these machines portable and more efficient. Finally, it shows the development of electrical transmission to make mechanical energy available at every point it is needed in industry.[75]

Within a few years, Taylor and his associates would seek to populate a brand-new and much larger museum with many exhibitions that had similar goals. The successful modernization program was proof that it would be a major improvement over its predecessor.

A Legacy in Museum Collections

The exhibits modernization program established a compelling new direction for future exhibitions in the Smithsonian's national history museum. An even more important legacy from the years in the Arts and Industries Building was provided by the artifacts the curators had collected during this era. As the charts in this chapter document, most areas in which the museum collects in the twenty-first century were established during this period. Moreover, this was when museum staff acquired many of the museum's most famous "national treasures." These include the Star-Spangled Banner, the George Washington and Ulysses Grant relics, the Jefferson desk, the early first ladies' gowns, the John Bull locomotive and other early transportation objects, and hundreds of artifacts related to printing, graphic arts, and photography. Staff in subsequent eras were continually challenged to create innovative displays of these legacy artifacts that were relevant to new generations of Americans.

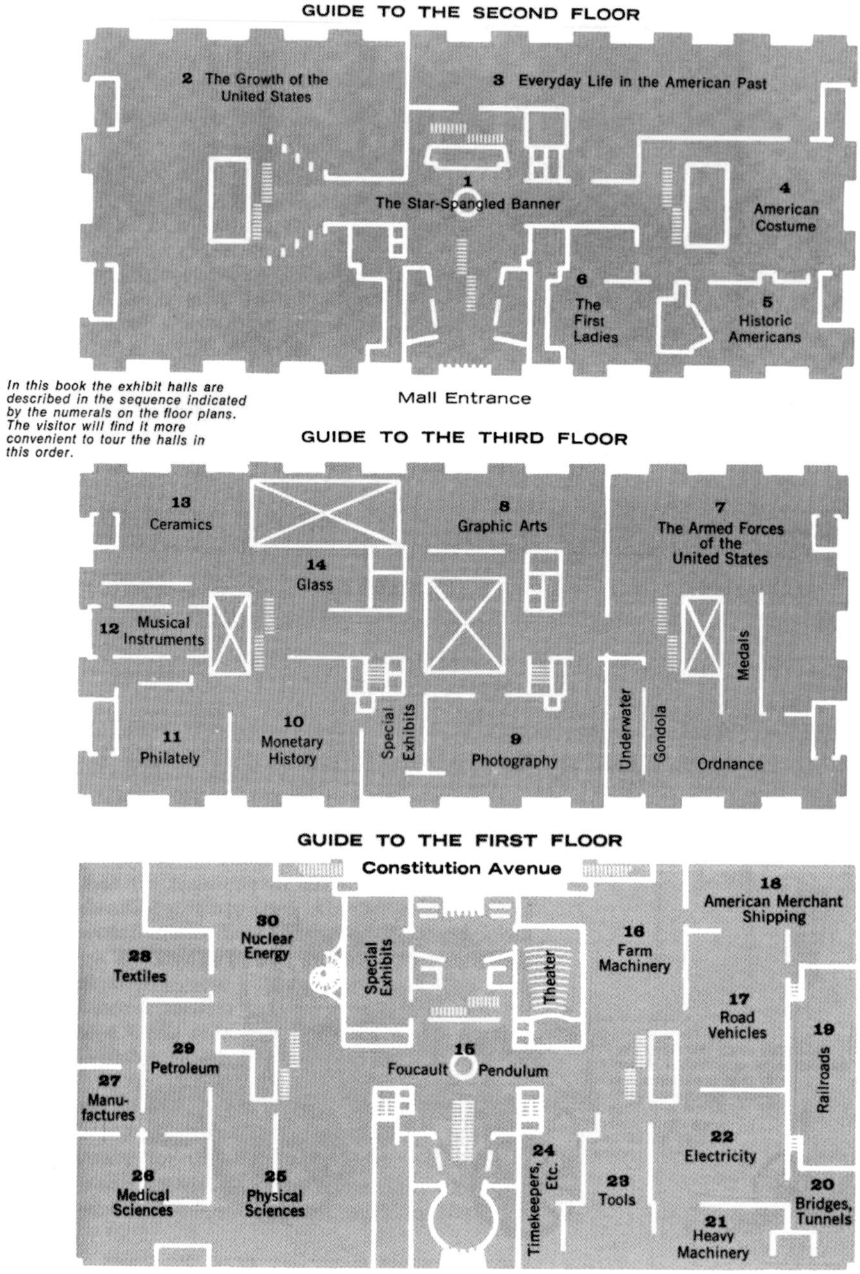

GUIDE TO THE SECOND FLOOR

2 The Growth of the United States

3 Everyday Life in the American Past

1 The Star-Spangled Banner

4 American Costume

6 The First Ladies

5 Historic Americans

In this book the exhibit halls are described in the sequence indicated by the numerals on the floor plans. The visitor will find it more convenient to tour the halls in this order.

Mall Entrance

GUIDE TO THE THIRD FLOOR

13 Ceramics

14 Glass

8 Graphic Arts

7 The Armed Forces of the United States

12 Musical Instruments

Medals

11 Philately

10 Monetary History

Special Exhibits

9 Photography

Underwater Gondola

Ordnance

GUIDE TO THE FIRST FLOOR

Constitution Avenue

28 Textiles

30 Nuclear Energy

Special Exhibits

Theater

16 Farm Machinery

18 American Merchant Shipping

17 Road Vehicles

19 Railroads

29 Petroleum

15 Foucault Pendulum

27 Manufactures

26 Medical Sciences

25 Physical Sciences

Timekeepers, Etc.

24

23 Tools

22 Electricity

21 Heavy Machinery

20 Bridges, Tunnels

Figure 3-1. The 1968 floor plan is taken from an in-depth 1968 guidebook to the museum that was prepared by its curators.[76] The numbers on the floor plan recommended an order for touring all the exhibitions, moving from the second to the third and finally the first floor. The descriptions of the exhibitions in this chapter follow that order. Although the museum opened in 1964, the exhibitions shown here were not finished until 1968.

CHAPTER 3

A Museum of History and Technology (1964–1969)

The Era

The Smithsonian's Museum of History and Technology opened in 1964 with the goal of presenting "the inspiring story of the United States—its origins, struggles, development, traditions, [and] strength."[77] *It was to be a thoroughly modern museum that was proudly patriotic. The building included not only modular and flexible exhibition spaces, but also easy navigation, visitor amenities, staff offices, artifact storage, and conservation facilities. The Smithsonian wanted the new museum to be well organized, aesthetically pleasing, and visitor friendly. It was to have a comprehensive introductory exhibition that would provide the context for all the other displays. They were to be a mix of thematic presentations for general visitors and collection halls that provided in-depth explorations of specific subjects.*

This era extended from 1964 to 1969, beginning with the installation of the initial exhibitions and extending through the completion of the first full version of the museum. It ended with the appointment of Daniel Boorstin as director, who would bring a fundamentally new approach to its goals and exhibitions.

The floor plan we chose to epitomize the era dates from 1968, when all its exhibitions were finally in place. Although the museum did not achieve all its goals, it was enormously popular, attracting millions of visitors every year. It was a vast improvement over what had been displayed in the Arts and Industries Building.

The order in which the exhibits are discussed in this chapter follows the numerical sequence listed on the floor plan, except for Historic Americans, which is included with the group of second-floor thematic exhibitions. Note that many of the names on the floor plan are abbreviations of the full names of the exhibit halls.

The initial exhibitions in the museum had impressive endurance. While some were replaced in less than a decade, others lasted for 40 years or more. As of 2019, sections of one original exhibition, Power Machinery, *were still on display, and several of the largest, most iconic objects—George Washington's statue, the gunboat* Philadelphia, *and the 1401 locomotive—had never been relocated.*

Prelude: A Presidential Dedication

On the evening of 22 January 1964, Washington government and society leaders, along with foreign dignitaries, gathered for a gala opening of the Museum of History and Technology. Smithsonian Secretary Leonard Carmichael served as master of ceremonies. His tireless and effective advocacy with Congress was largely responsible for securing the $36 million appropriation for the institution. It was his ultimate achievement at the Smithsonian—he would retire at the end of the month.

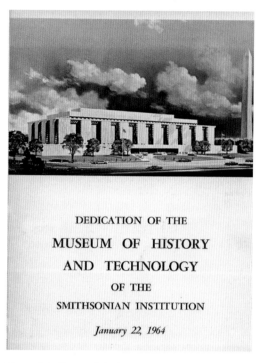

Figure 3-2. Cover of dedication program brochure for the new museum, 1964.

Museum Director Frank Taylor sat with other leaders on the stage. The internal design of the building and the organization of its exhibitions had resulted primarily from his strategic planning, which had matured over several decades. This new institution, a striking contrast to both the U.S. National Museum and subsequent Natural History Museum, realized Taylor's bold vision of what a truly "modern museum" should be.

The Smithsonian had long expected that President John F. Kennedy would give the keynote address at the dedication, but his assassination two months earlier had dashed those plans. In the wake of the tragedy, President Lyndon B. Johnson spoke instead. In his remarks, he posited ways that the museum's iconic artifacts should be used to foster patriotism. He said, in part:

> It pleases me a great deal tonight to come here to perform the role of dedicator in this building of knowledge which is the inheritor of all that has gone before....
>
> I would hope that there will come to this building the children of the nation. For here is recorded, as William Faulkner expressed it, the agony and the sweat of the human spirit, the victory of the freedom and genius of our country. Here, young children see, with their own eyes, yes, even to touch with their own hands, the ripe fruit of America's historical harvest. Whitney's cotton gin, Singer's sewing machine, McCormick's reaper, Edison's phonograph, Bell's telephone—they are all here, a part of this treasure-house of our inheritance. The more we understand the meaning of the past, the more we appreciate the winning of the future.

Figure 3-3. President Lyndon B. Johnson dedicating the Museum of History and Technology.

If this Museum did nothing more than illuminate our heritage so that others could see a little better our legacy, however so small the glimpse, it would fulfill a noble purpose. I am glad to be here. I am always glad to be where America is.[78]

The next day, a Thursday, the museum welcomed its first 8,000 visitors. On the following Saturday, the number swelled to 23,000, and on Sunday, to 54,943—outnumbering even those who flocked to see the *Mona Lisa* at the Louvre that day.

Despite these record-breaking crowds, however, many reviewers of the new museum were unimpressed. The external design, which was intended to be an innovative modern twist on the classical architectural styles of the buildings around it, was widely disparaged by architectural critics. One sniffed that it had "all the dignity of a recently remodeled department store."[79] Many commentators also noted that despite years of work, only 10 of the 40 planned exhibitions in the new museum were open,[80] and even this small percentage could be perplexing. In a comprehensive review, "Inside the New Museum" published in the *Washington Star* in March 1964, reporter Hugh Wells wrote:

George Washington may be half nude. The original "Star-Spangled Banner" has a white stripe patched with red. The Maryland State flag has no gold cross at the top of the pole. Nobody can explain why the Foucault pendulum proves that the world goes around. And the building may not be a landmark in the history of architecture.

Yet he still understood why the museum was a huge hit with the American public.

The kids who are crawling over [the] 1401 [locomotive] are in seventh heaven.[81] When the doors of the new $36 million Museum of History and Technology opened two months ago, the crowds surged forward like a Roman phalanx—and the people have kept coming despite the unkind cracks.[82]

Even if the museum had a bland exterior and an eccentric mix of displays—or perhaps because of them—it had succeeded. Between 1964 and the completion of the first full generation of exhibitions, as shown on the 1968 floor plan (Figure 3-1), Taylor and his staff produced 286,000 square feet of exhibitry. These more than doubled what had been on view in the Arts and Industries Building in the 1950s. Although the exhibitions did not ultimately deliver everything Taylor imagined, they realized his grand vision to a far greater degree than any subsequent director would ever achieve. More important, the basic structure of the museum that Taylor developed has endured.

A False Start

Ever since the 1910s, leaders of the Arts and Industries Division of the United States National Museum had struggled with making effective use of the cheaply constructed Arts and Industries Building they had inherited. They thought it was largely a waste of effort. Thus, in the years following World War I, they began conceiving ideas for a new museum building—or perhaps as many as four more—to complement the already completed Natural History Building. The leaders petitioned Congress to fund new homes for museums of engineering and technology, civil history, aviation, and fine arts.

The Museum of History and Technology grew in part out of the vision for one of these: a proposed National Museum of Engineering and Industry.[83] It was developed and promoted by Carl Mitman, curator of mineral and mechanical technology at the U.S. National Museum, and supported by his young assistant, Frank Taylor. A former mining engineer himself, Mitman was dedicated to celebrating the contributions of significant engineers to American history. His notion was a museum that would explain and highlight the history of industry and engineering in America. It would start with exhibits outlining the "Sciences Fundamental to Industry," such as mathematics, physics, and chemistry. Next it would exhibit "basic industries," such as agriculture and transportation, and "derived industries," such as textiles and graphic arts. Mitman dreamed of displays filled with original machines, replicas, scale models, photographs, and even moving pictures. These, he thought, would help visitors understand the workings of mechanical artifacts and their place in industry and America as a whole. In the U.S. National Museum's Annual Report to Congress in 1920, Mitman argued his case,

> The commanding place in the world which the United States has reached in the short space of seventy-five years is due largely to the full development and utilization of mechanical power in the exploitation of her natural resources. It is this that has made it possible for the people of the United States to enjoy a standard of living far and above that under which the peoples of the rest of the world exist and still no public sign of appreciation is to be found anywhere. What more suitable monument could there be, therefore, than a Museum of Engineering, and where could there be found a more logical place for it than as a part of the great National Museum?[84]

Congress gave Smithsonian leaders the opportunity to seek partners in American industry to help support the museum. For several years, Mitman worked closely with Holbrook Fitz-John Porter, a self-employed consulting engineer in New York, to help develop a coalition. They were successful in gaining endorsement from professional societies of mechanical, mining, civil, and electrical engineers. However, these tentative commitments never led to financial support. Mitman and Taylor at the Smithsonian continued to develop ideas for the museum, but as years passed and the United States entered the Great Depression, it was clear that the plan was going nowhere. Nonetheless, Taylor would return to some of his earlier thinking in later years when he directed development of the new Museum of History and Technology.

Frank Taylor and Creating the Museum of History and Technology

Born on Capitol Hill in Washington, D.C. on 25 March 1903, Frank Taylor joined the Smithsonian staff as an untrained laboratory apprentice in the model shop at the age of 19. He gradually advanced to museum aide, then assistant curator. He worked closely with his mentor, Carl Mitman. Acting on his advice, Taylor took a leave of absence from the museum to earn his bachelor's degree in engineering from the Massachusetts Institute of Technology in 1928. This led to his becoming curator in the Division of Engineering. From that time on, except for military service in World War II from 1943 to 1945, he would spend his entire career at the Smithsonian.

Upon his return from the war, Taylor was deeply disappointed in the run-down, dated exhibitions he found. He would soon become an agent of change. In 1948, as discussed in the previous chapter, he was asked to lead the planning for exhibition modernization across the Smithsonian.

During this period, it was becoming clear that for both fiscal and logistic reasons, Congress was unlikely to authorize more than one new Smithsonian museum in the next several years. Therefore, Taylor and his allies worked to fashion a conceptual

Figure 3-4. Frank Taylor in his Smithsonian workshop, 1925.

plan not for a museum focused solely on engineering, but for a new institution that would pull together disparate collections from across the Smithsonian. The plan was deliberately flexible rather than doctrinaire in determining which these would be.

Originally, they grouped together collections and staff in history, science, technology, and aeronautics. They also wanted to add the anthropology and ethnology departments located in the Natural History Building, which was suffering from its own space shortages. Then, in 1946, Congress decided to authorize (but not fund) a National Air Museum. Thus, aeronautics was dropped from the plan and would remain separate. The National Air and Space Museum would finally open decades later, in 1976.

The remaining pieces were united under a grand concept somewhat reminiscent of George Brown Goode's vision in the 1880s: a Museum of Man. This broad new institution was to cover the whole of human history, not just American history, and interweave collections and exhibitions that would display a wide range of activities and interests of mankind.

Just like Goode's earlier plan, however, this one soon failed for practical, not theoretical reasons. The curators in the Department of Anthropology decided to pull out of the group because they felt they were more closely aligned with the curators and scientists in natural history than with those working in history and technology. Moreover, they believed that their space needs would eventually be met with the addition of new wings on their current building.

The Cultural History section of the Division of Ethnology decided it should be included in the new museum because it focused on American colonial history while the remainder of the division concentrated on Native Americans. In addition, Graphic Arts, which, for administrative reasons, had been managed within the Division of Engineering for many years, wanted to remain in the mix. Finally, the Smithsonian's National Collection of Fine Arts decided to transfer its collections of ceramics and glass to the new museum. These were the groups that became the foundation of the Museum of History and Technology. Notably, they included both international and American collections.

Figure 3-5. Cover of the 32-page promotional brochure for the proposed new museum.

Years later, when talking about how the museum had been organized, Frank Taylor admitted that the planning was based on happenstance, opportunity, and administrative convenience rather than a grand conceptual scheme. He urged his readers to dismiss "the thought that the MHT was designed 'in a vacuum' or with 'a clean slate' and sprang into being as a theoretically conceived or ideal scheme."[85] With a wink, he added that he and his colleagues only "*acted* as though we conceived the combination by sheer logic and rational thinking."[86]

The name of the museum itself had also emerged serendipitously. Taylor later recalled, "we made a decision to have only science and technology and history in the building, and we wondered what we would call it. I believe it was Grace Rogers, who is now Grace Rogers Cooper, curator of the Division of Textiles, who offered the name of 'History and Technology,' which is very simple and very descriptive of what would be in the building."[87]

Even given the heterogeneous assembly of collections and staff, Taylor was convinced that he could create a coherent, successful, and meaningful museum—an institution that would be a huge improvement over "the nation's attic." Over the next several years, he and Leonard Carmichael, the new Smithsonian secretary, devoted themselves feverously to creating that institution. Taylor recollects an early conversation with Carmichael, who promised him: "You bring me something that I can sell, and I'll sell it!"[88] And sell it he did.

To help make the case for the new institution, Taylor and his colleagues created an illustrated promotional brochure in 1953. It posited three main reasons that the United States should create a Museum of History and Technology:

- To house the collections that now overflow the antiquated and uneconomical Arts and Industries building of the United States National Museum
- To illustrate by means of these historical collections the cultural and technological development of our Nation from colonial times
- To place before the millions who visit the Nation's Capital each year a stimulating permanent exposition that commemorates our heritage of freedom and highlights the basic elements of our way of life.[89]

The turning point came two years later. In 1955, Carmichael took the lead in securing the authorization for the new museum building by testifying in a congressional hearing before the Subcommittee on Buildings and Grounds of the Committee on Public Works. In a passionate and patriotic speech, he made his case. He argued that the Arts and Industries Building was totally unsuited to remain the nation's museum—calling it "a building that even in its earliest days was considered a cheaply built shell." Its poor conditions had already resulted in the loss of valuable, unique national treasures.[90]

He explained that the new museum, with its organized series of exhibition halls, would be the "Nation's unique history book of objects," and that it would tell the story of American national progress.[91] Attempting to appeal to the national pride and patriotism that had enveloped the country following its World War II victory, he compared the United States to its other Western counterparts, suggesting that their museums of history, science, and technology put the United States to shame. He even suggested that a patriotic national history museum might act as an effective defense against Russian Cold War–era propaganda, by offering proof that America was the birthplace of many inventions that Russia was attempting to claim. A new museum in the nation's capital, granted the funds and attention that had been lacking during the Depression and the war era, would cement America's progress for citizen and foreign visitors alike. As Carmichael said:

Here, then, is an area in which the Smithsonian can uniquely serve an outstanding national need. The museum we envision—from its foyer, where we propose to enshrine the original Star-Spangled Banner, through the whole sweep of its exhibit halls—is planned to instill in each citizen a deepened faith in our country's destiny as champion of individual dignity and enterprise. Equally, it is conceived to instill in each foreign visitor admiration and respect for our ever-expanding social and technological horizons.[92]

Just two months later, the government authorized the construction of "a Museum of History and Technology for the Smithsonian Institution," and allocated $36 million to cover the costs of its design and construction.[93]

While Carmichael and the regents lobbied Congress and explained the purpose for the new museum, Taylor focused on practical concerns. In 1955, he became chairman of an ad hoc "Committee to Continue Planning for the Museum of History and Technology" and began developing a comprehensive master plan for the new museum. He devoted personal attention to all the specifics. His plans ranged from concepts of exhibition groups—10 "Growth of America" exhibitions and 10 "Science and Technology in Industry" exhibitions—to calculations of appropriate ceiling heights and types of flooring. By 1956, he had a complete "Checklist and Outline of Requirements for the Museum of History and Technology,"[94] which was handed to the architects to be incorporated into the design of the building.

After the initial authorization in 1955, the museum's planners made steady progress. In 1956, they hired the prominent architectural firm McKim, Mead & White, famous for their renovation of the White House at the turn of the century, to design the building. In 1957, an administrative change formally established the Museum of Natural History and the Museum of History and Technology as independent entities within the Smithsonian. They were no longer merely divisions of the U.S. National Museum. In August 1958, ground was broken for the new museum.

Structure of the Modern Museum

The Museum of History and Technology offered the Smithsonian the first opportunity in more than 50 years to design and construct a new building. The Arts and Industries Building, which had been completed in 1881, had been deemed too small, too old, and, most significant, too old-fashioned to be the site of the new and thoroughly modern museum. But how should a truly "modern museum" be structured?

The Smithsonian's promotional brochure had criticized the Arts and Industries Building on six basic points: it was too small, it lacked necessary facilities such as storerooms and laboratories, it was arranged haphazardly, its systems were old and

Figure 3-6. Architectural model of the planned Museum of History and Technology, ca. 1958.

Figure 3-7. Frank Taylor surveys the museum under construction.

outmoded, it was inconveniently located, and finally, it had "neither artistic merit nor historical significance."[95] However, a modern museum had to do more than just rectify these deficiencies. It had to be a multifaceted institution. Ever the engineer, Taylor said it had to be an "efficient museum machine."[96] What did he intend?

The modern museum would be flexible. Although the new building was deliberately designed with its initial series of exhibits in mind, museum leaders understood the building should be easily adaptable for future developments. To this end, the exhibition halls were structured so that only the walls surrounding elevators, stairs, and mechanical shafts were permanent. Electrical ducts were placed under the floors, and ceilings were constructed of removable panels so that lighting patterns in new exhibitions could be reworked.

The modern museum would be spacious. A common criticism of the Arts and Industries Building was its lack of space. It failed to provide room for the ever-expanding historical and technological collections. Frank Taylor observed that the building "remained so crowded that the exhibits were difficult to organize or even to confine to allotted spaces. Textiles flowed into locomotives, military collections pressed hard upon exhibits of early gowns, and airplanes hung over everything."[97] The new museum, by contrast, would offer more than twice the exhibition space that the Arts and Industries Building did, as well as upper floors for staff and storage. The exhibition floors would have wide, spacious corridors that would easily allow for both the expected large crowds and the thoughtful placement of interesting historical artifacts. The exhibitions too would be designed with a new, "modern" approach:

fewer, more isolated objects, with wide paths between them so visitors could look at them from multiple perspectives.

The modern museum would be accommodating. The museum building was to be easily accessible to as wide a range of visitors as possible. Originally, the two main entryways were designed with no steps leading up to either entrance. When small stairways were later added to the Madison Drive side, ramps were also included to keep the entrance accessible.

Museum leaders anticipated the crowds of schoolchildren that would visit the museum, although they imagined local students coming for afternoon trips more than the tour groups from all over the country that were characteristic of later years. To accommodate them, the building included a covered driveway and entrance on the south side of the first floor. Buses could come directly up to the building so students could enter safely into an area designed to receive and orient them.

The modern museum would be effective. The U.S. National Museum, despite its reputation as the "nation's attic," had always been immensely popular with visitors. It attracted collectors and other laypeople interested in specific subjects, professionals from various industries, and many, many visitors with general interests. The exhibitions in the new building were carefully designed to appeal to both generalists and specialists. Over 50 percent of the exhibitions were to be heavily collections-based. These were the foundation of the museum—displays such as the first ladies' gowns, numismatics, stamps, and transportation vehicles. Other exhibitions would be broader and more thematic. These halls were intended to appeal to general visitors or those with only a limited time to spend in the museum. As the 1953 promotional brochure stated:

> Experience has shown it [to be] good museum practice to present the best known and most popular items in the Museum so that the average visitor can see them comfortably in two hours or less. For this arrangement to be most effective, the items should be placed in a compact series of related halls developing a sustained theme.[98]

This primary series of halls Taylor envisioned was initially entitled *Growth of America*. They were intended to present a chronological history of the technological and social growth of America, illustrated by the museum's most beloved objects. A second series was to be *Science and Technology in Industry*. Its exhibitions would contextualize scientific and technological artifacts in the industries that made use of them, such as petroleum or textiles.

The modern museum would be innovative. Besides the new techniques of design and display that had been explored during the exhibits modernization program in the Arts and Industries Building, Taylor wanted to pioneer the use of new technology. He mandated that the new building must be equipped with built-in television cameras. These would allow staff to create educational programs directly in relevant exhibitions, and then connect with audiences across the nation and even around the world.

The modern museum would be intuitive. The Arts and Industries Building had been poorly organized. The main entrance led not into a lobby or orientation space but directly into one of the most crowded areas in the building. The layout was a maze of halls, courts, ranges, and balconies, where exhibitions spilled into each other and many were accessible only from other exhibitions.

In the new museum, public entrances would be obvious and inviting and the grounds would feature outdoor exhibits such as sculptures and fountains, to welcome and encourage visitors to approach the building. On entering, visitors would find wide-open lobby spaces, with signs, landmark objects, and clear lines of sight to direct them to the exhibitions in which they were most interested.

The modern museum would be comfortable. The Arts and Industries Building was infamously crowded, cluttered, and uncomfortable—it had no air-conditioning to fight the sweltering D.C. summers and had only a single pair of bathrooms to serve all museum visitors. The new building, by contrast, would have visitor comfort everywhere. Increasing exhibition space was part of the answer, but Taylor also believed the design should never let visitors feel "shut in." A press release written about the new layout explained his intentions:

> Tired visitors are not receptive ones, so many features of the building have been designed to lessen museum fatigue. Moving stairways, benches and chairs in inviting arrangements throughout the halls, windows providing frequent glimpses of the outdoors, a variety of flowing materials, and adequate ventilation and temperature control will be provided. Variations in the levels of lighting and in the predominating colors used from hall to hall will promote comfort and relief in viewing the exhibits and stimulate the visitor's interest. The visitor who may expect to visit Washington only once and who wishes to make his museum stay a long one will have the choice of a cafeteria or snack bar for refreshment.[99]

The modern museum would be patriotic. Its goal was more than simply the increase and diffusion of general knowledge: the modern museum attempted, in a way that the U.S. National Museum never did, to instill a certain understanding of the world and the United States' place in it. Remington Kellogg, the overall director of the U.S. National Museum at the time of the Museum of History and Technology's opening, explained that the new museum was needed

> for the opportunity it gives to awaken in citizen and foreigner alike a clear understanding of the inspiring story of the United States—its origins, struggles, development, traditions, strength. Its exhibits are planned to instill in each citizen a deepened faith in his country's destiny as a champion of individual dignity and enterprise, in each foreigner a renewed respect for our ever-expanding social and technological horizons.[100]

Figure 3-8. *Infinity* sculpture being installed, 1967.

Entering the Modern Museum

Visitors to the museum in 1968, four years after it opened, now found its three floors full of exhibitions. By design, their experience began even before they entered the building. In 1967, José de Rivera's abstract sculpture *Infinity* had been installed outside the entrance from the National Mall. Its gleaming stainless-steel surfaces shimmered in the sun as the artwork rotated slowly around its axis every six minutes. Walter O. Cain, chief architect of the building, had it installed there to highlight the fact that although this was a museum of history, it was also distinctly modern. He said that the sculpture "gives off halations and brilliant refractions of light which create compositions of their own, infinite in number, never repeating, yet interdependent with, and deriving from, the form of the sculpture." A *Washington Star* reporter saw it less poetically as an "atomic age version of how the ancients used to dramatize bodies revolving in the universe."[101]

Figure 3-9. The Star-Spangled Banner hanging in Flag Hall on the second floor, 1973. In front of it was a circular opening to the first floor of the museum, through which passed the wire for the Foucault pendulum. (The wire is not visible in this image.)

Figure 3-10. Visitors watch the Foucault pendulum.

Surrounding the building were flags of the 50 states of the nation, symbolizing that the United States was a federal republic. Carved into the large marble walls around the entrance were inspiring quotations from three of the individuals responsible for creating and shaping the Smithsonian: James Smithson, John Quincy Adams, and the first secretary, Joseph Henry. The carvings had been handcrafted by James Saris, a Greek immigrant, who spent months on the job—each single letter taking two and a half hours of work.[102] His favorite statement was Joseph Henry's, which concluded,

> Narrow minds think nothing of importance but their own favorite pursuit, but liberal views exclude no branch of science or literature, for they all contribute to sweeten, to adorn, and to embellish life…science is the pursuit above all which impresses us with the capacity of man for intellectual and moral progress and awakens the human intellect to aspiration for a higher condition of humanity.[103]

Upon entering the building on the second floor, visitors walked into the spacious and grandiose Flag Hall and saw the Star-Spangled Banner, exhibited fully unfurled for the first time in a Smithsonian exhibition. It stood as an enduring symbol of both the unity of the nation and the significance of the museum. Filtered air was constantly blown across the flag's surface, to protect it from dust and lint. Behind it was an image that allowed visitors to compare what remained of the flag with it original size.

The Star-Spangled Banner represented the museum's commitment to history. To symbolize its commitment to technology, the institution installed another large and impressive object in the center of the first floor: a Foucault pendulum. The pendulum's wire was attached to the ceiling of Flag Hall and descended through an oculus in front of the flag to the first floor below. The pendulum bob oscillated slowly back and forth every nine and a half seconds. As the earth rotated around it, the bob gradually knocked over a series of pins, demonstrating the rotation of the earth.[104] This dynamically embodied the triumph of scientific knowledge over the primitive human belief that the sun rotated around the earth.

The Second-Floor Thematic Exhibitions

Growth of the United States (1968)

Growth of the United States was intended to be the new museum's star attraction. It was to focus on broad historical themes, rather than a single collection. Museum leaders told the press, "what makes the exhibit unique is that it contains not the relics and objects of a single subject, but many different items from each period to show how Americans lived in that time."[105] The display was to fill the entire west wing of the museum's second floor and cover all of American history, from Native Americans in the year 1000 to the present day.

Frank Taylor's initial plan projected 10 exhibition halls, each based on a significant period of the country's history. This was later reduced to five larger halls occupying the same space. Machines, weapons, costumes, period settings, vehicles, and more would be intermixed, and "exhibited for their value in graphically communicating the meaning of the period."[106] Using objects to communicate thematic ideas was rare among American museums of the era. At the Smithsonian, an interdisciplinary exhibition that drew from many departments and collections was unheard of. The 1968 guidebook to the museum stated:

> The introductory hall is to be followed by a chronological sequence of three main sections, each representing a century in American life, and a concluding hall. In the exhibits, objects from each century of American experience—from the arts, technology, and science—are interrelated and interpreted in the context of the individual periods.[107]

In *Growth of the United States*, a train would represent not only a technological achievement but also a cultural milestone in American economic growth. Taylor explained: "A typical exhibit will be a pioneer [sic] locomotive purchased in England in 1831 by the proprietors of an early American railroad. It will illustrate the beginning in America of corporate ventures into enterprises too large for the resources of one or two associated individuals."[108]

The complexity of this new approach and the diversity of the collections it would require meant, Taylor believed, that none of the museum's current staff had the necessary training and expertise to curate it. In 1957, he hired Anthony Garvan, professor of American civilization at the University of Pennsylvania, whom he considered a national expert in material culture studies.

Garvan became head curator of the Civil History Division, but he worked at the museum only on a part-time basis. He continued to live in Philadelphia and maintained his professorship at the University of Pennsylvania. Taylor later described this unusual situation:

> Tony Garvan never came on our staff. He worked about half time.... He had a Corvette which he drove at high speed from Philadelphia to Washington twice a week both ways. He was quite an attractive and sometimes dramatic sort of person but really an excellent man. [With his help] we had invented an answer to the question we knew we would be asked, "What is the Smithsonian going to do in this building, just more of the same old thing?" Our answer was a concept called the "Growth of the United States," which was a kind of a summation of all that would be seen in the building. It was an exhibit in itself which showed the very finest things we had from the period of exploration and discovery through the whole history of the United States with outstanding things. Dr. Garvan helped perfect that.[109]

Garvan had been educated at Yale and had a particular interest in historic preservation. Although he had never worked in a museum, this interest led him to make connections with the burgeoning public history community. He developed a pioneering master's degree program in museum studies at the University of Pennsylvania. In 1951, he had published a book, *Architecture and Town Planning in Colonial Connecticut*, which explored the colonial era through architecture and material culture. When planning *Growth of the United States*, he wrote,

> [O]bjects taken by themselves while often illustrative of particular events, can give direct evidence of human achievements apart from their immediate design and manufacture. As an illustration any writing upon paper or other surface is evidence of the state of writing, of writing materials, pen, inks, etc, in fact of the technology of writing. But no historian would dream of stopping there; obviously he must probe the meaning and the value of the written text. In the same way each machine and each object included in this museum has two levels of meaning – the one technological, the other cultural.[110]

Although Garvan conceived brilliant theories on the relationship between physical objects and history, he struggled to implement them in practical and affordable displays. Because the huge new exhibition was not tied to any particular collection, objects Garvan wanted to include had to be taken from other curators' collections. Since the curators, in turn, often expected to exhibit them in their own displays, this could lead to strong disagreements. This situation was further exacerbated by Garvan's eccentric personality and part-time, elite status.

In his negotiations, Garvan could become ethereal in articulating his plans to use the objects thematically rather than literally. At times, he might embarrass his colleagues by pointing out provocative connections that they themselves had not recognized. On other occasions, they would argue with him about the accuracy of his views. As Frank Taylor remembered, the tugging and pulling became a continuing challenge. Frequently he had to step in personally to arbitrate.[111]

Garvan began by writing the script for Hall III (1750–1851), which was one of his personal areas of interest and expertise. Work moved quickly, with Garvan producing page after page of conceptual ideas for cases showing compelling artifacts. However brilliant the thinking, this led to problems. Museum leaders had a limited budget and primarily wished to use objects already in the museum's extensive collections. But Garvan wanted to borrow or acquire hundreds of new objects because they would better illustrate the points he wanted to make. John Ewers, who was then responsible for exhibits planning for the new building, noted dryly: "The fact that a considerable number of objects are specified which are not in the museum's collections will present problems in the layout of the hall as well as in procurement by the curator."[112]

Garvan conceived of the exhibition as a broad anthropological look at American civilization. His inspiration came from his academic background. He organized the exhibition into cases or "units" bearing names from the Human Relations Area Files (HRAF) categorical system that he had used at Yale. The HRAF databases were designed to compare and contrast ethnographic resources of different civilizations. The original labels in Garvan's planned hall employed HRAF categories such as "The Preservation of Food" or "The Processing of Basic Materials." Although most exhibit labels later abandoned this academic language, the basic structure remained.

The many difficulties involved in developing the exhibition delayed its completion. When sections finally began opening in 1967, only Hall II (1640–1750) and

Figure 3-11. Model of *Growth of the United States* exhibition, Halls II and III. Note the Ipswich House (*left*), the eighteenth-century water wheel and Conestoga wagon (*center*), and the John Bull locomotive (*right*). These two halls were the only ones built of five that were planned.

Hall III (1750–1851) were done. The museum promised that the remaining halls would soon follow, but none ever did. The space planned for them would eventually be used for other purposes.

The two sections that were finished were complex, intriguing, and well designed. Hall II explored the period of English colonization in America. It emphasized the transformation of "virtually every class of artifact" from the early years of this period to the later years. The hall covered a wide variety of subjects, some of them broad and abstract, such as Settlement Patterns, Exact Knowledge, Water Transport, or Geography and the Western Border. In the exhibit cases around the edge of the room, these subjects were elegantly illustrated.

In an oral history interview years later, Taylor discussed this newer, more modern style of exhibitry:

> The general technique was to build a modern exhibit, what we call an upright or panel type exhibit with graphics and silkscreened illustrations and maps, with the objects held to the panel, something like illustrations on the page of a book and with the text stenciled on the panels. We would build these, and we would obtain the kinds of fixtures in which they would go in the new building, meaning in many instances cases which we designed and had built. These were quite modern and some were very handsome things.[113]

In the center of the hall was the Ipswich House, the largest single artifact on display in the new museum, and one of the most memorable. It was intended as a

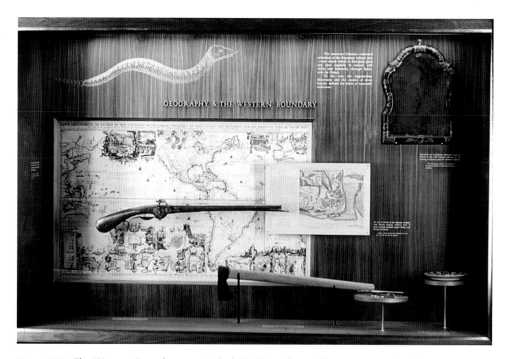

Figure 3-13. The Western Boundary case included objects from different curatorial collections.

dramatic example of how wood construction techniques in America evolved from 1660 to 1750. Wood-framed architecture of this type became an established American tradition. To make the point, most of the exterior of the house was removed, exposing parts of the oak skeleton and supporting beams.

The museum's acquisition of the house had been a fluke. In 1963, curators heard from concerned citizens in Ipswich, Massachusetts, that a vacant eighteenth-century Georgian-style home was to be demolished to make room for a parking lot. They soon concluded that it was a much better example of what they hoped to illustrate than a house they had already collected. So they raced to Massachusetts to save it from the bulldozer.[114]

The house was painstakingly taken apart, transported, and reconstructed in the museum. It was so big that it extended from the second to the third floor of the museum and required a specially redesigned exhibit space. Not surprisingly, it has never moved. When *Growth of the United States* closed in 1976, it was walled off for several decades, as various plans to reopen it faltered. Finally, it went on view again in 2001 in the exhibition *Within These Walls*. We will return to that story in chapter 6.

Another eye-catching feature of Hall II was an eighteenth-century water wheel and mill. The 14-foot wheel turned as though powered by water cascading over it. Actually, the power came from a small electric motor. To add greater authenticity to the scene, the museum initially included a few live ducks. When they didn't work out, chickens were substituted. Soon they too were exiled. Years later, Deputy Director Silvio Bedini commented on the source of this pioneering effort at realism in an amusing article he entitled "Fair is Foul or Foul is Fair":

Figure 3-14. Visitors around the Ipswich House display.

In January 1967...the new exhibit *Growth of the United States* had been opened, featuring a full-size 18th-century house and operating water wheel. The very size of these objects and the nature of the story they attempted to tell required some form of enlivement. [Smithsonian Secretary S. Dillon] Ripley urged that an attempt be made to provide a new dimension. Why not add several Muscovy ducks, he suggested, since this breed existed in 18th-century America? His powers of persuasion resulted in the purchase of five Muscovy ducks. Late one afternoon they were delivered to the exhibit hall, and installed in a pseudo-barnyard area between the house and the mill. The timing left much to be desired. On the evening of the day that the ducks were installed, a formal dinner was scheduled for the regents of the Institution. Because the Growth of the United States Hall was the newest and most exciting exhibit, it had been selected as the setting for the dinner, and tables were set up around the water wheel. By the time that the regents arrived to be seated, the ducks had made their presence amply evident. They had managed to escape the temporary enclosure and had wandered around the area, obviously in great bewilderment, because they left wet and copious evidence of their prowls everywhere, on the floor, on the seats, and around the tables. The labor force responded promptly and heroically to the emergency, and dinner was served as scheduled....

Figure 3-15. The eighteenth-century water wheel. Note the live ducks in the lower left.

The ducks continued to live on in the GOUS for six months, and although it was thought that all was well, some serious problems had developed. First of all, it seemed that no member of the museum staff had either the time or the inclination to feed the ducks and clean their pen. When a little pressure was exerted, the staff was remindful that ducks were not mentioned in their position descriptions...[115]

Visitors moved past the water wheel into Hall III, which covered the period 1750 to 1851. The two halls transitioned seamlessly into one another, with the same structure of exhibit cases around the edges and larger objects in the center.

Hall III featured a blue and red Conestoga wagon, a nineteenth-century bedroom setting, and the John Bull locomotive, reportedly the oldest working locomotive in the world. Other museum treasures were Benjamin Franklin's printing press, George Washington's uniform, Joseph Henry's electromagnet, and the lap desk on which Thomas Jefferson wrote the Declaration of Independence.

Growth of the United States fell far short of providing the promised overview of American history or serving as an introduction and index to all the other exhibitions in the museum. As subsequent chapters will reveal, it became the first of several

Figure 3-16. The Conestoga wagon (*center*) and John Bull locomotive (*right*) were popular objects in *Growth of the United States.*

Figure 3-17. Full view of the John Bull locomotive.

large efforts to create a broad introductory exhibition to the museum, none of which succeeded. Yet the exhibition was far from a failure. It was redeemed by both its innovative, high-quality design and its blend of treasures from the museum's rich collections. Visitors may have seen some of them before in the National Museum, but never presented in such an effective way. Although the exhibition did not give them a full survey of American history, most visitors enjoyed the sections they found.

Everyday Life in the American Past (1964)

Another exhibition, *Everyday Life in the American Past*, became the sort of introductory exhibition that *Growth of the United States* was planned to be. This large display also walked visitors chronologically through history. However, instead of a broad topical sweep, it focused on historically accurate period settings that showed the "belongings and surroundings" of everyday people in different eras. These allowed visitors to step into rooms that ordinary people of past ages had left behind and to experience their daily existence vicariously.

Unlike *Growth of the United States*, *Everyday Life in the American Past* was an expansion and improvement on an earlier Smithsonian exhibition. However, it had been installed not in the Arts and Industries Building but in the Natural History Building. Called the Hall of Everyday Life in Early America, it had opened there in 1957.

The exhibition was the product of a brilliant curator of ethnology, C. Malcolm Watkins. He came to the U.S. National Museum in 1949, after working as a curator

Figure 3-18. California Gold Rush section of the *Everyday Life* exhibition.

and collector for Old Sturbridge Village in Massachusetts. He held his bachelor of science degree from Harvard and wrote freelance articles about antiquities. During World War II, he served in the air force.

Although not trained as a historian, Watkins's interest in material culture was rooted in his parents' passion for historical preservation and his mother's love of ceramics. As a young man, he inherited his grandfather's collection of historical lighting devices, made connections in the Rushlight Club (an organization for lighting historians), and accompanied his mother on digs in abandoned historical kilns. His background led him to a keen interest in preserving and displaying objects and also environments that were as authentic as he could make them. Before Watkins's arrival, the Ethnology Department had focused almost exclusively on Native American studies. He was hired to take charge of what had become a growing collection of non–Native American collections of decorative arts and domestic technology.

At the National Museum, Watkins found a small collection of textiles, ceramics, lighting devices, and musical instruments. He also took charge of the famous Copp family collection, a stellar assortment of colonial American domestic artifacts that had been in the museum since the 1890s. Finally, he became responsible for the museum's first period room on display: a wood-paneled parlor named the Ritter Room, after the woman who donated it.

Unlike period rooms in art museums that were designed to showcase upper-class furniture, ceramics, and other domestic arts in an elegant context, the Ritter Room was intended to give the viewer a connection to everyday life in the past. Although called a parlor, the room was cluttered with kitchenware, bedroom furnishings, and craft tools—shown as it might have looked when actually used, not dressed up for company.

The exhibition quickly became a popular Washington tourist attraction. Both Watkins's personal philosophy and his background at Old Sturbridge had led him to appreciate the material culture of common people.[116] He was interested in how objects had been used, not their aesthetic value. As he expanded the museum's collections, he continued to focus on workaday objects. One of his earliest acquisitions was a large collection of antiques from Edna Greenwood. He had met her through the Rushlight Club, and she later came to Washington to see his Ritter Room. She reportedly turned to him and said, "Malc, we can do better."[117] She subsequently gave the museum over 2,000 artifacts, including preindustrial tools, domestic utensils, textiles, and more.

While the Ritter Room effectively established new ways to display period rooms, Watkins knew that many of its objects were historically inaccurate. They did not faithfully represent the region or era. As he moved on to collect and plan additional period rooms for *Everyday Life in the American Past*, the exhibition that would appear in the Museum of History and Technology, he was determined to make them as authentic in every detail as he could. Only then would they be not only interesting, immersive experiences, but also truly educational.

Figure 3-19. The Ritter Room as it appeared in the Natural History Building, 1956.

A year later, after ground was broken for the Museum of History and Technology, the Division of Cultural History, including Watkins, was transferred to the new museum. His exhibition was scheduled to follow him there. Due to the differences in space available in the new building, it could not simply be "moved," but had to be fully restructured. For example, it was originally intended that the Story House, a seventeenth-century Massachusetts Bay dwelling, would be incorporated into the new exhibition, but the ceiling in the space was too low to accommodate it.

Watkins relished the new opportunity. His goal was to display detailed, accurate period settings of ordinary people's everyday lives: areas in private homes including living rooms, kitchens, and parlors, but also public locations, such as ice-cream parlors or schoolrooms. He wanted visitors not only to see the past, but also to feel as if they were walking through an earlier era. As he later explained to another curator,

> Objects are expressions of their cultures and time frames and that is [why]
> we exhibit them and study them. The mannerisms and shapes and embel-
> lishments of material objects are visual languages and dialects. They emerge
> from the subliminal just as different languages do. They unconsciously
> express meanings, feelings, and intentions on the part of their creators as
> distinctively as words do and different word sounds and vocabularies do....
> If we fail to make the point in [a] label that objects convey cultural meanings
> and why they do, we may fail to come across to the visitor. We need to guide
> the visitor in what may to him be a concept not easy to grasp. We need to
> encourage him to look and observe and think.[118]

He reflected further on his philosophy of exhibitry in an oral history in 1995,

> I don't think we should be snobbish about and be afraid to admit, the ability of a room to create the feeling of a person standing in, if possible, standing actually inside, so that our viewing alcoves can be inserted into the rooms themselves and make it nearly possible for the visitor to say that he had actually been in one of these rooms and had felt the difference in the dimensions, in the appearance, and, of course, with the aid of the objects shown, given some feeling of the life represented by the room.[119]

Watkins was a tireless collector. In his search for accurate settings that came with walls, floors, windows, and doors as well as objects, he scoured the nation for abandoned buildings of a different time—structures the museum could afford to acquire. Sadly, many of them were bereft of furnishings, so Watkins had to piece together objects similar to what they might have once contained. On a few special occasions, however, he was able to acquire rooms that still contained their complete furnishings and therefore ensured the specific accuracy he sought.

In two cases, his quest for historical and affordable accuracy led him to collect rooms inhabited by people connected to his family. One was a Brooklyn dining room from the house where his wife's great-uncle had lived, and the other, his mother's own Massachusetts children's bedroom.

Although a brilliant collector, Watkins was no architect or carpenter. To disassemble the rooms and reconstruct them in the museum, he needed expert assistance. In managing these details, he relied on contract services from George H. Watson, whom he had known as superintendent of construction and maintenance at Old Sturbridge Village. Watson eventually was involved in working closely with Ben Lawless and the museum design staff not only on most of the settings in *Everyday Life*, but also in *Growth of the United States*, the *First Ladies* exhibition, and *Political History*. Much of the character of the new museum relied on his expertise in design and historical reconstruction.[120]

Unlike *Growth of the United States, Everyday Life in the American Past* opened with the new museum in 1964. It encompassed over a dozen period room settings, stretching from a seventeenth-century timber-frame house from Massachusetts to a twentieth-century Washington, D.C., ice-cream parlor. The Ritter Room with which Watkins had started was now remodeled and renamed the Reuben Bliss Parlor. Although the settings were arranged in roughly chronological order, visitors could wander through them freely. Several are particularly illustrative of Watkins's approach.

The nineteenth-century schoolroom represented the one-room schools that played a key role in early American education systems. Besides what appeared in the setting behind glass, it included two replica desks positioned in an alcove. Here visitors could sit and imagine what it was like to be a student in those early days. It also led to an amusing display of exactly the kind of audience engagement and immersion that Watkins was hoping for:

Figure 3-20. The Reuben Bliss Parlor (the revised Ritter Room), 1966.

Figure 3-21. Early nineteenth-century schoolroom.

70

The benches that we put in the visitor's part were not old benches, but were copies of the old benches; they were new. The other benches, of course, as you would suspect, were covered with carved initials and verses and all sorts of inscriptions from bored kids, and we said nothing, we didn't suggest it, but we knew that people who came into that alcove to look at the school from the bench were bound to do the same, and indeed they did. When the school was finally dismantled with the other things in the hall, the 1964 benches were as carved up as the old ones.[121]

Depicted in Figure 3-22 is a private library that Benjamin Comegys added to his Philadelphia home ca. 1880. Watkins collected not only the room with its decorations and furnishings, but also photographs that meticulously documented how it had been arranged in the nineteenth century. These guided how he exhibited it. For the objects that had been lost over the years, he found faithful replacements—some replicas, some exact period duplicates.

Due to Watkins's interests and professional contacts, most of *Everyday Life in the American Past* in the Museum of History and Technology was focused on settings in the Northeast, predominantly related to Anglo-Saxon history. However, shortly after the initial opening of the hall, Watkins worked to add examples of more diverse cultures. The first of these resulted from his deliberate effort to find a western period room.

Figure 3-22. The Comegys library illustrated upper-class life in a major American city.

Figure 3-23. The California kitchen represented western American life in the nineteenth century.

At his wife's suggestion, he chose a Californian ranch kitchen owned by a nineteenth-century miner who remained in California following the gold rush. The beautiful blue-paneled kitchen became one of the most popular settings in the exhibition.

Following the success of the California kitchen, Watkins continued to add displays focused on more diverse groups and locations, including an eighteenth-century adobe dwelling from Santa Fe, New Mexico. The research into California led to an exhibit case on Chinese Americans, and in 1969 Watkins added to the exhibition an African American tenant farmer's house from Southern Maryland.

Political and social history curators, as well as other museum staff, did not believe this provided adequate coverage of African American history. They advocated for additional displays for years. In 1970, Edna Wright, an exhibits editor, summarized her frustrations on the subject in a blunt memorandum to Frank Taylor and Museum Director Daniel Boorstin.

> I understand that the proposed exhibit titled "1619–1865: The Afro-American Experience" is being held under advisement and is not being considered for production this fiscal year. This exhibit, intended as a permanent section of the Hall of Everyday Life in the American Past...was written to overcome the glaring omission of the contribution of this ethnic group in the building and shaping of the United States.
>
> As Exhibits Editor for this hall for the past 10 years, I am aware of its purposes and contents. The other ethnic groups that made major contributions

Figure 3-24. Eighteenth-century adobe house, Santa Fe, New Mexico.

to the settlement and building of this country are represented. The Spanish influence—the largest representation—extends through four large cases and alcoves. The British, French, German, and Dutch have two cases each and the Scandinavian, one. Each exhibition traces the arrival of these peoples from their native lands to North America; relates their struggles for survival; explains how they adapted their customs to the requirements of the new laud and other people; presents items of clothing, household goods, tools, etc.; and illustrates the everyday patterns of their lives.

After the hall was opened a script was written to include African influences but it was never produced. A couple of years later one single case was added to discuss African backgrounds and the concept of slavery. It includes 11 items that were made in Africa but were, in all probability, never used by the slaves that were brought to America. This exhibit does nothing but explain what slavery means....

In keeping with the demands of the times, the Smithsonian has attempted to correct throughout the museum the omission of significant contributions made by Negroes in all phases of history.... The Division of Cultural History continues to receive numerous queries from the public on the subject of black history. This [new] exhibit could serve effectively as an answer to these queries.[122]

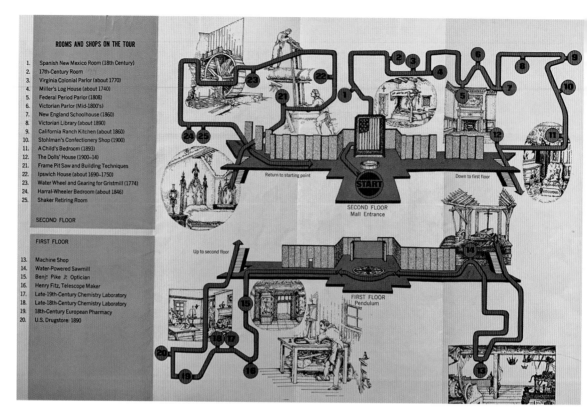

Figure 3-25. Visitors' guide to rooms and shops in the museum, 1970.

Despite this impassioned plea, the proposed display was never produced. Perhaps this was because Boorstin believed it was too controversial, or perhaps it was because the museum was now focused on planning its upcoming bicentennial exhibitions (see the following chapter).

Thus, debate continued about the appropriate scope of *Everyday Life in the American Past*—in large part because it was so significant. Nevertheless, when it opened in 1964, its concrete, historically accurate detail, and the fact that it was all completed on time, made it the most comprehensive chronological overview of American history in the new museum. Although its settings represented only limited segments of the diverse American public, visitors loved how they were transported to earlier times and places, with far different objects than they used in their own homes and schools. The success of the exhibition and subsequent use of settings elsewhere meant that instead of becoming known for object groupings that illustrated abstract historical themes, the museum became renowned for its range of diverse historic settings.

In 1970, after recognizing how much visitors appreciated historic settings, the museum created a special guide that directed them on a tour of 25 rooms and shops. It rated highly when tested with a sample audience. One respondent summarized, "The tour was useful because it made it easier for us to get around the museum and showed us the best parts of the museum."[123]

Figure 3-26. The fanciful parade of "historic Americans," illustrating changing styles of campaigning.

Hall of Historic Americans (1965)

The Hall of Historic Americans was largely built from two collections inherited from the National Museum. The first included historic relics of famous Americans—such as George Washington's uniform and Abraham Lincoln's silk hat. The second encompassed campaign materials and other paraphernalia from presidential elections. Although many of the "historic relics" had belonged to Americans involved in politics, others came from generals, inventors, and other significant individuals. What resulted was a mélange that sought to demonstrate "the growth of American politics and the contributions of various individuals, groups, and institutions to the nation's history."[124]

The scope was very ambitious. The Hall of Historic Americans, which debuted in June 1964, had a goal parallel to that of *Growth of the United States*. It aimed to provide a comprehensive survey of American history based on political history and biography rather than technological and social history. In contrast to *Growth*, *Historic Americans* was organized topically rather than chronologically.

It opened with Robert Frost's poem "The Gift Outright," which the author had recited at the inauguration of President John F. Kennedy. Poignantly displayed beneath the large panel was a handwritten copy from Frost himself, penned for the exhibition. The curators chose the poem for its message that the United States had yet to realize its destiny: it was still becoming. In retrospect, the choice reveals aspects of the attitude of the museum—and much of the nation, about the significance of Native Americans during this era. The land didn't "belong" to the arriving settlers

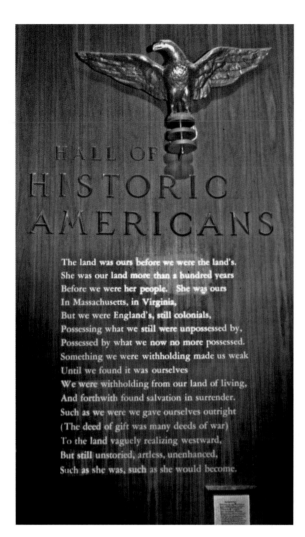

Figure 3-27. Robert Frost's poem, including a handwritten copy penned by the author for the exhibition (*lower right*).

The land was ours before we were the land's.
She was our land more than a hundred years
Before we were her people. She was ours
In Massachusetts, in Virginia,
But we were England's, still colonials,
Possessing what we still were unpossessed by,
Possessed by what we now no more possessed.
Something we were withholding made us weak
Until we found it was ourselves
We were withholding from our land of living,
And forthwith found salvation in surrender.
Such as we were we gave ourselves outright
(The deed of gift was many deeds of war)
To the land vaguely realizing westward,
But still unstoried, artless, unenhanced,
Such as she was, such as she would become.

but would be violently wrested by them from control of native populations who had lived there for centuries.

Following this contemplative opening came an abrupt change: an eclectic, flamboyant campaign parade. Unlike the meticulously accurate settings in *Everyday Life in the American Past*, this display elided historical periods: the papier-mâché figures illustrated changing styles of campaigning. The artifacts dated from 1840 to 1920. A log cabin that evoked "the rough quality of politics in the American West" was followed by a front porch, and then a railroad car illustrating whistle-stop appearances.

Another series of displays showed artifacts related to significant historical figures, including Ulysses S. Grant and his family, George and Martha Washington, and Abraham Lincoln.

The Lincoln display featured a striking figure of the president in a suit he wore the day he was assassinated, and the hat he wore that day on the bureau next to him. His figure was displayed with a hand resting on the back of a carved armchair from the House of Representatives. This was meant to reference a famous photograph of Lincoln taken by Matthew Brady. On the wall was the model for Lincoln's patent

Figure 3-28. A variety of political campaign materials from different eras.

Figure 3-29. President Lincoln's original suit and patent model.

for lifting boats over shoals. Curator Wilcomb Washburn wrote of how he wanted visitors to experience the scene,

> I [thought] it would play Lincoln "straight" and yet convey to the beholder the contradictory impressions he gave to Americans of the period. His grotesqueness would be emphasized, particularly in this day, by his black clothes and by the contrasting white of his face and hands, but these features would at the same time suggest the saintly quality that makes him approach a Christ-figure among American statesmen.[125]

Besides displays on former presidents, the exhibition featured cases depicting the roles of various groups in American history. Several covered other branches of the government. These included objects representing the Senate, the House of Representatives, and the Supreme Court, along with personal mementos of various Congress members. For example, the guidebook called out the "especially interesting" paperweight designed by William Jennings Bryan. Shaped like a miniature plow, it was fashioned from swords that had been condemned by the War Department and etched with the Biblical text, "They shall beat their swords into plowshares."[126]

Besides surveying political groups and institutions, the exhibition featured an eclectic mix of other famous citizens. The American Scholars section presented Robert Goddard's 1928 experimental rocket along with academic regalia and awards. Americans Abroad showed miscellaneous diplomatic gifts to "suggest the roles played by United States citizens in maintaining and extending the nation's international influence."[127] The display included original carbon blocks from Chicago Pile 1, the world's first artificial nuclear reactor.

This focus on *groups* of Americans enabled the museum's earliest movement toward increased inclusivity and diversity. Sections depicting the contributions of women and Native Americans were included when the museum opened. A few years later, another was added on famous African Americans—the first time the museum focused on them as a separate group.

Figure 3-30. Display of "First Americans," designed to highlight their dignity as an independent race.

The Native American display (titled "First Americans") was deliberately designed to offer a nuanced understanding of famous Native Americans. Although his attitude seems racist and insensitive in retrospect, Wilcomb Washburn was progressive for his era. He wrote,

> My purpose would be to break the stereotype of the Indian presently existing in the public mind. The portraits selected would convey an immediate appreciation of the fact that these people were persons with thoughts, feelings, and minds as active as our own. The idea of the Indian as a "savage" is still so strong in the minds of most Americans, that it is nearly impossible to talk intelligently about the subject to them. The portraits, I hope, would do much to move this stumbling block to their understanding. In sum, no attempt would be made to see the Indian either as a tormenting devil or as a tormented angel. He would be represented in this hall, as the white man is, by pictures of him taken in his formal "best," and objects which are the products of his better moments.[128]

The Second-Floor Collection Halls

Hall of American Costume (1964)

Although the first ladies' dresses always received the most attention from visitors, they were not the only display of American costume in the new museum. The American costume collection had been slowly building for several years, having grown partly out of the U.S. National Museum's textiles collection and the Copp family collection mentioned earlier. In the Arts and Industries Building, the costume collection occupied a single wall case, but in the new museum, it was given 7,400 square feet across from the *First Ladies* exhibition. However, even that was enough for only about 30 percent of the total collection.

The Hall of American Costume walked the visitor through the history of dress in the United States from the seventeenth century until the modern fashions of the 1960s. Beyond examples of clothing from various periods, the exhibition also displayed undergarments and accessories, such as shoes, stockings, gloves, jewelry, purses, and parasols.

The exhibition was arranged chronologically into four sections representing the "Four Centuries of Costume in America," and its entrance featured large illustrations to represent each period. The first section, covering the seventeenth century, was the sparsest, as examples of seventeenth-century costume were so rare that the Smithsonian had none. Therefore, this section contained paintings, engravings, and other illustrations that portrayed the styles of that era.

The Smithsonian's eighteenth-century costume collection was a bit more extensive. This section began by displaying the types of fabrics and colors used to make eighteenth century clothing. Then it showed specific examples, including a woman's

Figure 3-31. Trying on a wedding dress in a nineteenth-century dressmaker's salon.

Figure 3-32. This scene of a tea party shows the lacy, elegant dresses of the Edwardian period, 1900–1910.

wedding dress from the years of the American Revolution and a fashionable scarlet hooded cloak known as a "cardinal."

The section devoted to nineteenth-century fashion was by far the most comprehensive. It was further subdivided into five periods of style: 1800 to 1830, 1830 to 1850, 1850 to 1870, 1870 to 1890, and 1890 to 1900. Each highlighted distinct difference in women's dress styles. A period setting in this area, entitled The Dressmaker's Salon, showed a bride-to-be being fitted for a bustle-style wedding gown by a female dressmaker, while her mother (clad in a stylish blue dress) looked on.

The twentieth-century section began with the "Gibson girl" costume popular around the turn of the century; the straight-cut, knee-length flapper dresses of the 1920s; and a display on the classic modern style, the "little black dress."

American Costume was an early example of a loosely thematic hall. Although it attempted nowhere near the breadth of *Growth of the United States*, and although it was more a collections-oriented exhibition than a thematic display, it did follow a strict chronological progression and surveyed a broad range of changes in American style. This modern approach, while potentially more interesting and educational for visitors, had its downsides. The collection, though extensive, was not by any means completely representative of the entire American history of costume. Moreover, it overwhelmingly focused on women's clothing. Although there were some examples of men's and children's attire, they received short shrift compared to women's costumes.

Hall of First Ladies (1964)

Like *Everyday Life in the American Past* the Hall of First Ladies was not a new experiment in presentation. Instead, it was an elaborate upgrade of the already "modernized" *First Ladies* exhibition in the National Museum that had opened in 1955, when the dresses were shown in settings for the first time. The new display was to be even more contextual, more authentic, and better designed. In an oral history interview years later, Frank Taylor discussed the transition:

> [Ben] Lawless, [director of exhibit design,] became identified with the Museum of History and Technology largely because he had started in the [National Museum] and had designed the first renovation of the First Ladies Hall.... He learned a lot from that, and he applied this to the new First Ladies Hall in ways that are quite subtle and not readily observed. For example... when we did it the first time, the viewer looked into a nice setting, nicely done, but he looked through a frame as though he were looking at a picture.... In the new hall, if you've noticed, there are no frames, and the rooms look like pieces cut out of big rooms.... As you walk through you have the impression that what you're looking at is a series of parts of rooms cut out of a much larger one. This is what I meant earlier about our experience with the exhibits renovation program paying off in the exhibits in the Museum of History and Technology.[129]

Figure 3-33. *First Ladies* Blue Room display in the Arts and Industries Building.

Figure 3-34. Improved *First Ladies* display without "picture frames," at the Museum of History and Technology.

Compare the "picture frame" presentation in the National Museum in Figure 3-33 with the "room setting" approach in the Museum of History and Technology in Figure 3-34. These dresses represented first ladies of the 1860s to 1890s.

The content objectives of the new display were clear, straightforward, and limited. They were largely developed by curator Margaret Klapthor, who partnered extremely effectively with Lawless. The display included a dress representing the administration of every president of the United States in the recreation of a White House room. Although all were worn by first ladies, not all of those had been president's wives. In some circumstances, the official duty of hostess of the White House, which formally defined who served as first lady, was performed by a relative or family friend. In developing the exhibition, both curators and designers had learned from previous experience what their audience wanted and enjoyed. A guide to the hall explained,

> The collection is installed in period settings that display the dresses in the type of surroundings in which they were originally worn. In creating these settings, the Museum has, whenever possible, used actual architectural details and furniture and fixtures associated with the White House or the representative First Ladies. Since each setting contains dresses representing a span of

Figure 3-35. First ladies in the recreated East Room of the White House.

several administrations, it has been necessary to select a style of background and furnishing typical of a certain period or of a single administration within a period.[130]

The exhibition also included a collection of White House china that was "the most complete collection...outside the Executive Mansion."[131] The exhibition comprised eight settings in total. Each included plaster mannequins in various poses wearing the gowns. Surprisingly, the faces of the figures were all sculpted from the same model, with only the coiffure varied to give individuality to the figure. The model was a representation of Cordelia, from Shakespeare's *King Lear*. The individual hairstyles, which were based on historical images, were designed to be as authentic as the settings, even if the faces were not.

The simplicity and opulence of the exhibition were its strengths. Unlike many, if not most, of the objects in the museum's collection, these dresses were designed to be seen and admired for their beauty and elegance. They were not shown as evidence of technical progress or American national achievement.

In a broad review of the new museum in the *Washington Evening Star*, reporter Hugh Wells noted that highlights of the museum included "Alexander Graham Bell's original telephone, George Washington's uniform, Eli Whitney's cotton gin, the writing desk on which Thomas Jefferson prepared the Declaration of Independence, plus a veritable flood of farm machinery, automobiles, carriages, clocks, phonographs, typewriters, locks, musical instruments, stamps and guns." He went on, "What draws the feminine ohs is the exhibit of First Lady fashions—their gowns and the rooms they lived in."[132] Which was precisely the point. Perhaps in hindsight, the exhibition could be judged as sexist and stereotyped, but it remained the most popular in the new museum, as had been its predecessor. As will be discussed in later chapters, subsequent versions of the first ladies exhibition had deeper historical objectives, but none would ever again be as large or as elegant as this one.

The Third-Floor Collection Halls

When the collection halls on the third floor opened, the museum made no claim that they were related to each other. The subjects displayed here were those whose objects were generally smaller and lighter than in the collections on the first floor, the other main location for such displays. At the same time, locating collections on the third floor was not intended to diminish their significance, as the museum expected they would still attract visitors interested in their specific subjects. When Secretary Carmichael had promoted such displays in testifying to Congress on establishing the museum, he said,

> Likewise, in the Museum will be shown the Smithsonian's world-famous collections of stamps and coins, guns, watercraft models, and all the others that have made the Institution a mecca for scholars, collectors, and hobbyists, the country over.[133]

Curators for each hall developed their plans independently of the areas around them. Because producing these displays had lower priority than the second-floor exhibitions, none of them opened with the museum in January 1964. They gradually debuted over the subsequent months and years. Among the first were the Monetary History Hall, Philately Hall, and parts of the Graphic Arts Hall. The largest of the third-floor halls, the Armed Forces Hall, still remained incomplete by the end of 1968. In the new museum, this floor was the most reminiscent of the haphazard organization of collections characteristic of the Arts and Industries Building.

Hall of Armed Forces History (1966)

The Hall of Armed Forces History centered on a set of chronological displays that traced the history of the U.S. Army and Navy from their origins in seventeenth-century militia and maritime activities up through the American Revolution, the War of 1812, the Mexican War, and the Civil War. At that point, the United States had become a major world military power. The hall did not have space to take the story further. In the 1970s, as will be explained in the next chapter, the museum developed bold plans to exhibit the comprehensive history of the American military in a military park at an entirely different location.

Besides military conflicts, the displays covered peacetime activities. Among them were the Lewis and Clark Expedition of the Louisiana Purchase, Matthew Perry's diplomacy in Japan, Matthew Fontaine Maury's research into hydrography, and the work of the Army Corps of Engineers in civil engineering. Artifacts featured

Figure 3-36. A general view of the Armed Forces Hall, showing the style of case display.

Figure 3-37. Washington's tent, camp kit (*left*), and portrait.

Figure 3-38. The Continental "gondola" *Philadelphia*, the oldest intact American man-of-war, built in 1776.

Figure 3-39. The gondola *Philadelphia* being installed in the museum while it was under construction.

in these displays included standard weapons, military uniforms, footgear, ship models, flags, scientific instruments, and memorabilia.

Particularly popular were unique objects associated with General George Washington, including sections of the headquarters tent he used during the Revolution, his uniform, and his camp chest.

Also included in this hall were a series of connected galleries that showed special collections. The largest and most significant was the Revolutionary-era gunboat *Philadelphia*, the oldest surviving American fighting vessel. It was one of eight "gondolas" or gunboats designed by General Benedict Arnold to combat the British invasion of upper New York in 1776. Sunk during the Battle of Valcour Island, it remained underwater in Lake Champlain until it was discovered and raised in 1935. It was donated to the museum in 1964 and was so large it had to be installed while the building was under construction (Figure 3-39).

Adjacent to the *Philadelphia* was a display on ordnance. Artifacts shown here traced the development of weapons from the Stone Age to modern times. They

Figure 3-40. The Ordnance section of the Armed Forces Hall.

Figure 3-41. Equipment used in underwater archeology research.

included hand and shoulder firearms, machine guns, edged weapons, and models of heavy ordnance used on both land and sea. Unlike the chronological display on the Armed Forces, this one included weapons and models up to the period of the Cold War.

Another topical section presented military orders, medals, and decorations. Like the ordnance display, this one included non-American objects such as medals of the British Order of the Garter, the Greek Order of the Redeemer, and the Russian Order of Saint Andrew. Outstanding American medals included examples of the Medal of Honor, the Legion of Merit, and the Presidential Medal of Freedom.

Figure 3-42. Diorama of Japanese printmakers creating a complex color illustration.

Finally, the hall included a surprising section on underwater archeology and exploration. Although only indirectly related to armed forces history, it was the research specialty of the head of the division, Mendel L. Peterson, who ranked among the leading researchers in this field in the nation. On display were objects related to the history of this area as well as artifacts recovered in Smithsonian research dives, most of them in the Caribbean. They included ship fittings, trade goods, cannon, small arms, and coins.

Hall of Graphic Arts (1966)

The goal of the Hall of Graphic Arts was to explain the processes and present outstanding examples of graphic works created and produced by hand or photomechanical processes. The most arresting display was a scene of nineteenth-century Japanese printmakers creating and printing a color woodcut in the *ukiyo-e*, or "floating world" style. To create a print from the artist's design, separate wood blocks had to be cut for the multiple colors in the finished print. This required extreme precision.

For the final color print, 25 separate impressions were required to complete the image from 10 printing surfaces on 6 blocks. In Figure 3-42, the artist on the left is rubbing the back of the paper with a bamboo disk to transfer ink from the block to the face of the print, while the man on the right is cutting one of the blocks.

Figure 3-43 shows the seventh progressive proof of 25 separate impressions required to create the colored image in Figure 3-44.

Figure 3-43. "A Rustic Genji," engraved by Kokichiro Mori-kawa, after the seventh step, before color was applied.

Figure 3-44. "A Rustic Genji," engraved by Kokichiro Morikawa, the final impression after 25 steps.

Figure 3-45. Printer display in the Graphic Arts Hall; the Columbian press is the third from the left.

Figure 3-46. Daguerreotype of Louis J. M. Daguerre.

The Japanese printmaking setting included a prized group of wood blocks, color prints, sample pigments, and related tools, all of which had been given to the Smithsonian by the Japanese government in 1889. Its prominence in the hall illustrated the degree to which the graphic arts collection was international in scope, not restricted to American developments in this field. Other woodcuts on display ranged from the fifteenth century to recent years, and included works by Albrecht Dürer, Niccolò Boldrini, Ernst Kirchner, and others.

Further displays gave the history of the varied ways artists create works in print form. The exhibition distinguished clearly between artistic prints and photomechanical reproductions. It contrasted techniques used in wood engraving, mezzotint, line engraving, drypoint engraving, etching, aquatint, lithography, and silk-screening. It also featured four examples of landmark American printing technology, including the Columbian hand press of 1813, the first hand press made in the United States.

Adjoining this hall were galleries used for temporary displays of works selected from the museum's extensive graphic arts collection.

Hall of Photography (1966)

The Hall of Photography hall traced its subject from the earliest written speculations recorded in the eleventh century to the development of modern automated equipment and high-speed films. On display were many historic pieces, ranging from the first daguerreotype camera used in the United States, which had been built

Figure 3-47. Samuel F. B. Morse's daguerreotype camera, 1839, PG.000004.

Figure 3-48. The twin-lens reflex Rolleiflex camera of the 1960s, widely used by professional photographers.

for Samuel F. B. Morse, through the twin-lens reflex Rolleiflex of the 1960s. The exhibition also included a completely equipped photographic darkroom as it existed in the mid-1800s and a model of the laboratory used by William Henry Fox Talbot, inventor of the "negative-to-positive" image capturing and printing process.

Several other displays traced the evolution of photojournalism and demonstrated electrical transmission of photographic images for printing in newspapers on the same day. As with the Hall of Graphic Arts, the Hall of Photography included an area for temporary exhibition of prints from the collection.

Hall of Monetary History and Medallic Art (1964)

The Hall of Monetary History and Medallic Art, which opened in 1964, was largely the same exhibition that had been created as part of the exhibits modernization program in the Arts and Industries Building. The new exhibition included 19 sections tracing the development of money economy from primitive barter to the establishment of modern monetary systems.[134] It also featured a selection of significant medals of the United States and other nations.

The display was notable compared to numismatic displays in other national museums because the objects were arranged in their historical and cultural context, not according to a numismatic classification system. Labeling and imagery explained how the artifacts were related to significant historical events and had been an integral part of the cultural development of human society. The exhibition gave special emphasis to the development of various forms of currencies in North America and their roles in the economic and political growth of the United States.

Here visitors were able to view the world's largest public display of gold coins, as

Figure 3-49. Vladimir and Elvira Clain-Stefanelli (*together on right*) at *History of Money* exhibit case.

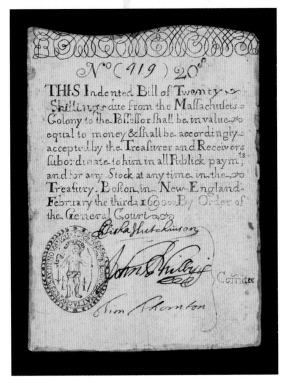

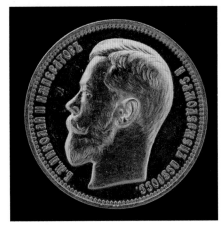

Figure 3-50. Twenty-shilling note, Massachusetts, 1790.

Figure 3-51. Twenty-five ruble pattern coin struck in 1896 during the reign of Nicholas II.

well as selections from the United States Mint collection, which had its inception in the late eighteenth century. Particularly notable were artifacts from the Willis H. Du Pont collection of Russian coins and medals.

Besides coins, currency, and medals, the display included a reconstructed coin stamper designed by Leonardo da Vinci and a nineteenth-century coin screw press.

Figure 3-52. The Curtis Jenny invert stamp, one of the rarest American philately artifacts.

Figure 3-53. Owney, the highly popular and honored mascot of the rail postal service.

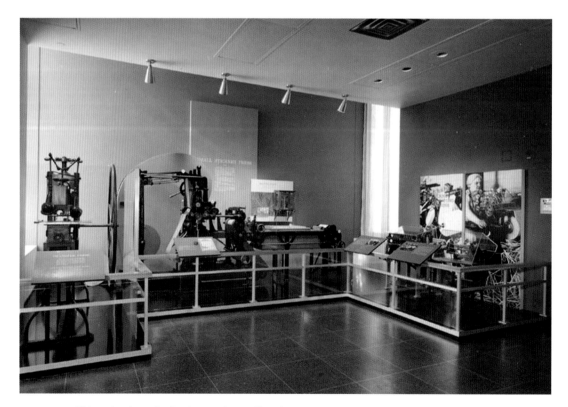

Figure 3-54. This technology display featured a small Stickney press (*center*) as well as a transfer press (*left*) and perforating and coiling machines (*right*).

Hall of Philately and Postal History (1964)

The Hall of Philately and Postal History surveyed the history and technology of written communications, focusing within that story on the production and collecting of postage and revenue stamps. Its numerous display cases traced the subject from ancient to modern times, highlighting the American experience.

A major theme was the continual effort to find better and faster means for processing and delivering mail, as the nation expanded across the continent. The presentation explained such events as the introduction of postage stamps in 1847, fast mail trains between New York and Chicago in 1875, and airmail in 1918.

Visitors flocked to see philatelic rarities, among them the highly valued 24-cent Curtiss Jenny invert single stamp, of which only 100 had been sold. Another crowd-pleaser was the preserved remains of the dog "Owney." He was a stray who had wandered into the Albany, New York, post office in 1888 and soon became a mascot for the Railway Mail Service. Postal clerks took him all over the country, where he received hundreds of tags and medals from his devoted fans.

Serious stamp collectors spent hours with 473 pullout frames that contained more than 3,700 sheets of mounted stamps from all over the world. These were but a small selection of the more than 12 million stamps, postal covers, and other philatelic artifacts in the full collection, which they could also visit by appointment.

Finally, the hall included displays of technology related to every phase of stamp production, from the artist's design through printing, perforating, and coiling.

Hall of Musical Instruments (1965)

The Hall of Musical Instruments contained one of the most important features of the new museum: a room in which curators could regularly give demonstrations and concerts on instruments from the collection. Keeping the artifacts in playing condition was the work of the division's restoration staff. Among the important instruments

Figure 3-55. Musical instrument demonstration.

Figure 3-56. Bowed stringed instruments.

Figure 3-57. Artifacts related to musical stage shows.

shown were a 1718 bass viola da gamba, an eighteenth-century violin from the workshop of Amati in Cremona, a viola by Gennaro Gagliano of 1780, and a 1701 Stradivarius violincello.

In the exhibition, visitors also found displays of American folk instruments, including hammered dulcimers, fiddles, banjos, and mouthbows. These were played at barn dances and other social gatherings. Other cases featured displays on topics such as musical stage shows.

Hall of Ceramics (1966)

The museum's national ceramics collection was developed largely through the donation of valuable private collections. These included the Stanley E. Wires collection of decorated tiles, the Robert McCauley collection of Liverpool jugs, the Ellouise Baker Larsen collection of English earthenware, and the Leon collection of yellow glazed English earthenware. Most important of all was the Hans Syz collection of eighteenth-century porcelains from Europe and Asia, which came to the Smithsonian in 1963. Selections from all of these were featured in the new Hall of Ceramics.

The exhibition traced the history of ceramics from antiquity to the present, and included artifacts from Europe, Asia, and the United States. The opening gallery in the exhibition displayed modern ceramics and recent acquisitions. It featured a ceramic fountain created by Donald Raitz of Alfred University in 1963.

Visitors then walked through four galleries of objects from the Syz collection. They traced the history of porcelain manufacture in eighteenth-century Europe with examples from all the major and most of the minor continental factories of the period. Among the most remarkable were Italian comedy figures modeled in porcelain by Johann Kändler of Meissen, Germany, ca. 1740.

Figure 3-58. Entry to the Hall of Ceramics. The Raitz ceramic fountain is on the right.

Figure 3-59. Meissen figures of Dottore (*left*) and Harlequin (*right*). Hans Syz collection.

Figure 3-60. Display of English earthenware.

Adjoining galleries showed English porcelains of the eighteenth and nineteenth centuries, English earthenware and stoneware of the seventeenth through the nineteenth centuries, and selections from the Stanley Wires collection of ceramic tiles.

The final gallery followed the history of American ceramics from colonial pottery to production ware of the nineteenth century and art pottery of the early twentieth century.

Hall of Glass (1966)

Displays in the Hall of Glass traced the development of glassmaking from antiquity to the present. They explained and illustrated the design and production techniques used in different periods and countries. The artifacts on exhibit ranged from some of the earliest-known glass objects, made in Egypt in the fifteenth century BCE, through examples of European glass of the fourth to the twentieth centuries, to American glassware of recent years. One particularly eye-catching object was a gilt-bronze and glass banquet centerpiece made for Napoleon by his court artisan, Pierre-Phillippe Thomire.

An American cut glass display illustrated techniques such as miter cuts, facets, and flutings. These basic cuts could be combined to create a variety of motifs including the pinwheel, hobnail, vesical, and fan star. Also shown were exceptionally fine pieces of Tiffany glass that had been selected for the Smithsonian and donated by Louis Comfort Tiffany in 1896.

Figure 3-61. Case displays in the Glass Hall.

Figure 3-62. Napoleon's gilt-bronze and glass centerpiece.

Figure 3-63. American cut glass display.

The First-Floor Collection Halls

When envisioning the organization of the new museum in 1956, Frank Taylor thought that new technology exhibitions on the first floor should go beyond simply displaying and describing important artifacts. They should be devoted to explaining "Science and Technology in Industry Today" and illustrate clearly "the technological and scientific developments which are of outstanding importance to the industry." He was thinking particularly of topics such as petroleum, atomic energy, iron and steel, and communications. They might employ models, illustrations, and descriptive labeling that traced key developments up through recent times. These exhibits, he hoped, "will change with appropriate rapidity." Exhibits in other areas, such as watercraft, medical history, and physical science would, in contrast, be modern displays "of the collections for which the Smithsonian Institution is famous." However, these too should "feature the modern with the historical development which produced it."[135]

When the museum opened, the new technology exhibitions on this floor did not clearly fall into one category or the other. Instead, most had elements of both types. All provided more textual context and explanation than their predecessors in the National Museum had done. In many instances, curators and designers included a large number of models made exclusively for the exhibition to illustrate features that were not always clear from historic artifacts. Sometimes these showed the size and scale of industrial equipment or the many steps in a technical process. At other times, they displayed contrasts between different designs or approaches to resolving a technical issue.

To assist them in reaching their goal, curators and designers frequently asked industrial firms to donate models or graphic illustrations that would help explain complex processes to the public. Unlike in later eras, such close ties with industrial firms were not seen as inappropriate or a conflict of interest.

Robert Vogel, who curated the exhibition on civil engineering, reflected deeply on how the new museum should address this field, which had not been the subject of a previous exhibition. He wrote,

> The current philosophy of the National Museum completely rejects the classical "cabinet" technique of museum exhibition by which a collection of relics and artifacts is simply placed before the public, each item bearing a minimum of identification and with no attempt made to relate the objects to one another or to any other parameter of interpretation. If museum exhibits are to be something more than assemblages of curiosities, incapable of arousing anything more in the viewer than patronizing astonishment at the "ignorance" or the "quaintness of things" in the "olden times," it is absolutely essential that the exhibits be attractively displayed, and most vital, arranged with some sort of continuity and interpretation. In plain words, a story must be told, and told effectively.

Figure 3-64. Farm machinery.

In order for an exhibit to tell its story effectively, it must attempt to (1) *stimulate interest*, if possible even in those with none previously...; (2) *stimulate thought*, a function largely of the skill with which its interpretive aspects have been performed; (3) *instruct*, by providing insight into the particularities of the topic; (4) *furnish a sense of historical development and continuity*, meaningful both to the layman and the expert; and (5)...*establish the relationship of the subject area to the rest of the world.*[136]

To varying degrees, Vogel's ambitious goals were shared by his fellow curators as they planned the first-floor displays.

Hall of Farm Machinery (1964)

What's in a name? Sometimes, both the public and museum officials themselves referred to the Hall of Farm Machinery shown on the floor plan at the beginning of this chapter as the "Hall of Agriculture." Even in publications, the names were interchangeable. This confusion was indicative of the evolving nature of the technology exhibitions in the museum. To what extent should they describe collection objects and to what extent should they cover broad themes? As noted in the first chapter, this became an enduring question for the museum over the years.

When the new museum opened, the name *Farm Machinery* was definitely the most accurate for this exhibition. It did not attempt to survey the full history of American agriculture. Rather, it focused on tracing the history of innovation in agricultural technology. Among the most impressive were an array of large machines

Figure 3-65. The new Huber steam tractor.

that dramatically reduced the work of humans and animals in agricultural production. Whereas 90 percent of Americans had been farmers when the nation was founded, by 1960, they amounted to less than 10 percent.

As Figure 3-64 illustrates, this exhibition exemplified the new design approach of displaying objects in the open as much as possible and allowing visitors to see them from all sides. In the center of the hall was a huge 1886 harvester-thresher built by Benjamin Holt. It was the first machine to combine harvesting, threshing, cleaning, and bagging grain. The machine represented a key shift away from gear drives of earlier combines to link belts. Their use meant that if the horses supplying the power bolted, they would only break the belt, not strip the gears. The machine was pulled by teams of 20 or more horses or mules.

Soon, tractors became the technology most identified with American farming, and the exhibition included several important examples. One was the Huber steam tractor, which measured 16 feet long and weighed 20 tons. It was manufactured ca. 1920.[137] This monster could burn either straw or coal. Farmers used it for both plowing and threshing, but generally only on very hard ground, such as found in the Great Plains.

Steam tractors were gradually replaced by lighter and more versatile machines powered by kerosene or gasoline engines. The exhibition included the oldest surviving internal-combustion-engine tractor, the Hart Parr #3. Built by Charles Hart and Charles Parr in Charles City, Iowa, in 1900, it weighed in at 14,000 pounds. Hart and Parr first introduced the word "tractor" when advertising their new device. Soon it was eclipsed by lighter, more versatile vehicles. Also on display was the John

Figure 3-66. Display of innovations in American plows.

Figure 3-67. The living beehive was in the Plexiglas box to the right.

Deere Model D, introduced in 1923, the first tractor built, marketed, and named John Deere. It had a two-cylinder kerosene-burning engine that produced 15 to 22 horsepower.

While the big machines in the Hall of Farm Machinery tended to attract the most visitors, the hall also included important earlier technologies, some illustrated with scale models. On display were hand tools, reapers, mowers, and plows. One panel featured a plow designed by Thomas Jefferson with an attached moldboard that lifted and turned over the sod that the iron blade cut.

Young people at the exhibition loved the section on bees, which reprised a popular display in the Arts and Industries Building. Like its predecessor, it included a live honey-bee hive supplied by the Department of Agriculture. The display described the organization of bee colonies and how they functioned.

Hall of Road Vehicles (1964)

The Hall of Road Vehicles showed representative collections of horse-drawn vehicles, bicycles, fire-fighting equipment, and motorized conveyances. Almost everything on display had been built in America. Each vehicle was shown on the type of road material appropriate for its era. Walking past them all, visitors could follow the progression from horse-drawn to self-powered conveyances. The latter began to outnumber the former around 1905.

Figure 3-68. General view of the Hall of Road Vehicles.

Figure 3-69. Urban omnibus (*left*) and rural passenger wagon (*right*). The display contrasted an 1880 omnibus commonly used in towns and cities with an 1880 hack passenger wagon used in the west on rougher roads.

Figure 3-70. Ford Model T.

The Ford Model T ushered in the automobile age. It gave personal mobility to more than 15 million Americans. Light and powerful, it could negotiate rough roads, and parts for it were generally available at dealers in both urban and rural areas.

Docents in the exhibition gave talks and answered questions to help young visitors learn about the history and technology of transportation. Given Americans' fascination with their cars, it is not surprising that the Road Vehicles Hall was one of the museum's most popular areas.

Figure 3-71. Teaching children about road transportation history.

Hall of American Merchant Shipping (1964)

Since the 1880s, the Smithsonian had assembled one of the premier collections in the United States of merchant ship models. Many them had been on display in the Boat Hall in the National Museum. Now they formed the basis of the Hall of American Merchant Shipping. The models were generally of three types: merchant sailing ships, merchant steam ships, and merchant fishing craft. The display was generally chronological, but the fishing boats were also grouped by the localities in which they

Figure 3-72. Display of merchant sailing ships.

Figure 3-73. Model of Columbus's *Santa Maria.*

Figure 3-74. The paddle steamer *George Law.*

were used. The temporal order of the models allowed visitors to see the technical development of American ship design. While most of the models were selected for technical reasons, others were related to important historical events.

The *Santa Maria,* shown in the model in Figure 3-73, was the largest of the three ships in which Columbus and his comrades sailed to America in 1492, and served as his flagship. The ship ran aground on a reef off the island of Hispaniola and was lost.

This 1852 paddle steamer, *George Law,* was used for the New York to Panama steamship service that took eager prospectors to California during the gold rush.

Besides the full ship models, the exhibition included half-hull models, models of marine engines, and ship plans. Panel displays discussed sail-making, navigation, and knots used by mariners.

Railroad Hall (1964)

The Railroad Hall was organized to show how the evolution of railroad equipment converged toward standard designs. This contrasted sharply with its predecessor exhibition in the National Museum, which had focused on "firsts" and curiosities. Because of the space available, much of the technical explanation was done with scale models, not full-sized artifacts.

The gallery was divided into three main areas. One focused on locomotives, one on rail cars, and the third on street cars. The Locomotives section was the most impressive. At its center, next to a large picture window, was a pair of locomotives. The small one to the left in Figure 3-75 was the wood-burning 1851 *Pioneer*, which served for 40 years on the Cumberland Valley Railroad. Behind it was an 1836 Camden and Amboy passenger car, one of the earliest types of passenger coaches. To the right was the massive coal-fired, 199-ton, 92-foot-long 1401 steam locomotive, built for Southern Railway in 1926. It was used to transport passengers until the early 1950s, when diesel-fueled locomotives replaced those powered by coal. The locomotive was notable for being one of the engines that pulled Franklin Roosevelt's funeral train from Hot Springs, Georgia, to Washington, D.C., in 1946. The comparison of the two engines illustrated clearly how far locomotive design had progressed in 75 years.

The 1401 was the heaviest artifact on display in the museum, and the building was literally structured to accommodate it. The locomotive was trucked to the

Figure 3-75. The *Pioneer* (left) and 1401 (right) locomotives.

Figure 3-76. Installing the 1401 locomotive.

Figure 3-77. Washington, D.C., streetcar, as seen in a later photograph.

museum on the night of 25 November 1961 and positioned on museum property. Track was laid to direct it into in the hall and it entered on 30 November. It has been there ever since.

As in the Locomotives section, the Rail Cars section employed many models to show the transition from simple four-wheel coaches to air-conditioned, stainless-steel streamliners. Other displays in this section explored the history of freight cars, couplers, brake development, and Pullman cars.

Transportation in Washington, D.C., was represented by this streetcar from the Capital Traction Company. Electric cars first appeared in the nation's capital in 1888. By the turn of the century, the city had around 200 miles of line in operation. As in other large American cities, streetcar traffic in Washington began to fall off in the 1920s because of the automobile.

Figure 3-78. Entry to the Hall of Civil Engineering, which focused on bridges and tunnels.

Hall of Civil Engineering (1964)

The Hall of Civil Engineering housed the Smithsonian's first exhibition ever on this topic. Curators thought that focusing on how humans have used technology to go over or under obstacles would be a good way to interest visitors in their somewhat arcane subject. The section on bridges explored developments in both design and the choice of materials as it traced advances in spanning technology.

A series of models, several of which are shown in Figure 3-79, illustrated the evolution of design techniques. They show, from top to bottom, stone arch technology of the Romans, ca. 100 AD, a Chinese cantilever bridge of 1670, a 1779 English cast-iron bridge—the first to use metal, and an 1840 all-metal bridge across the Erie Canal that employed a "bowstring" truss. Also on display were numerous tools used in bridge construction.

Eight more models showed advances in tunneling technology. They highlighted examples of building tunnels in different environments, such as soft ground or hard rock. Included was a model of the Brunel Thames Tunnel, the first to be constructed

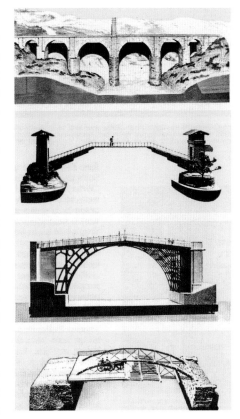

Figure 3-79. Comparative bridge designs.

underwater. To complete it, in 1843, builders used jackscrews to insert a cast-iron shield to provide continuous support in the soft clay of the riverbed. A model of the 1890 St. Clair Tunnel between Port Huron, Michigan, and Sarnia, Ontario, showed the first major underwater tunnel to accommodate full-scale railroad traffic.

Hall of Heavy Machinery (1967)

The Hall of Heavy Machinery, which was also called the Power Machinery Hall, traced the development of power machines from the early steam engine to the internal combustion engine. This was one of the prime factors in the transformation of the United States from an agricultural to an industrial economy.

The exhibition began with the early development of steam engines in Europe and the United States. Among the important artifacts from this early period was Matthew Baldwin's first engine, built in 1829.

Nearby was a large Harlan and Hollingsworth walking-beam steam engine (Figure 3-80), which was kept in operation (using compressed air) for visitors to see. Between 1852 and 1927, this device, which generated 40 horsepower, ran woodworking machines at the Southern Railway's shops in Charleston, South Carolina.

Visitors gaped at a giant piston and connecting rod from one of the steam engines built in 1903 to power New York's first subway. It was one of the largest ever constructed for generating electricity.

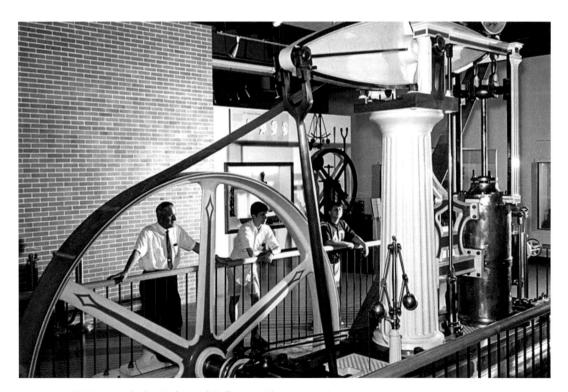

Figure 3-80. Visitors study the Harlan and Hollingsworth steam engine.

Figure 3-81. New York subway piston.

Figure 3-82. The Skinner Universal Uniflow steam engine.

Figure 3-83. Niagara Falls pumping engine.

In the center of the gallery was a Skinner Universal Uniflow reciprocating steam engine of 1926. It allowed steam to flow into cylinders in only one direction to increase the thermal efficiency of the engine.

A contrast to the steam engines was this high-speed pumping engine. It was driven by a water turbine and was used to furnish oil under pressure at the hydroelectric station at Niagara Falls from 1901 to 1929. The exhibition concluded with several examples of diesel engines, which by the 1920s were replacing steam engines for many applications.

Hall of Electricity (1965)

The Hall of Electricity was largely an exploration of the many ways that electrical technology had been developed and used in society. These included power, lighting, measurement, and communications. Many visitors, however, most remembered an amusing display of the "electric kiss," a diorama of a nineteenth-century parlor game that used a static electricity generator to create shocking effects (Figure 3-84).

The exhibition opened in stages that began in 1964 and stretched until the end of the decade. The first section, which debuted in July of that year, focused on a recent technological development: communications satellites. It highlighted the historical

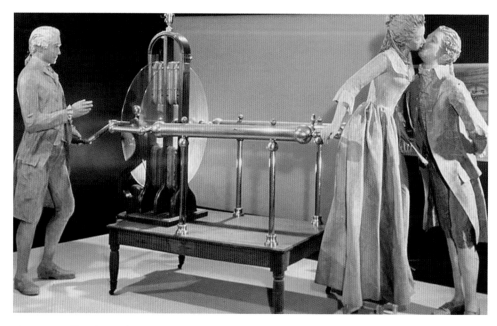

Figure 3-84. The electric kiss.

Figure 3-85. Communications satellites display.

Figure 3-86. Electrical communication display.

development of the rapidly changing field, emphasizing the variety of techniques that had been used to relay information around the world.

A display on electrical science summarized the development of theories of electricity, up through James Clerk Maxwell's theory of electromagnetism. It included many examples of experimental apparatus such as Leyden jars, voltaic cells, and batteries. Of particular note was a battery reportedly used by Joseph Henry, the first secretary of the Smithsonian Institution.

A section on electrical communication focused on the telegraph and telephone and included some of the museum's outstanding artifacts in this area, among them

Figure 3-87. Alexander Graham Bell's telephone, which was demonstrated at the 1876 World's Fair.

Figure 3-88. Thomas Edison's 1879 light bulb.

Samuel Morse's 1844 prototype of the telegraph and early prototypes of telephones made by Alexander Graham Bell and Elisha Gray.

A major section traced the history of power generation from arc-lighting stations to the establishment of the first large isolated power station at Niagara Falls in 1895. It covered early pioneering physicists including George Ohm, Alessandro Volta, and André-Marie Ampère and carried the story forward to the work of Thomas A. Edison. This "Wizard of Menlo Park" was to become one of the most prolific inventors in American history. The exhibition highlighted the range of work he did with electrical technology, with particular emphasis on the creation of a practical incandescent lamp in 1879 and subsequent development of a complete power and lighting system.

Hall of Tools (1964)

The goal of the Hall of Tools was to trace the evolution of toolmaking from hand tools to machine tools. This development transformed the work of American coopers, wheelwrights, blacksmiths, woodworkers, and others. Among the traditional hand tools displayed were the cooper's adz, a hoop tightener, a sun plane, a splitting froe, a spoke pointer, a brace and bit, and a hoof parer. Also shown were Eli Whitney's power-fed milling machine, invented ca. 1818, and Thomas Blanchard's lathe for turning gunstocks, patented in 1819.

Case displays and short films explained the five basic processes of machining: turning, drilling, planing, milling, and grinding, and the tools associated with them.

The highlight of the exhibition was the recreation of a mid-nineteenth-century machine shop, whose machines were restored to operating condition. Among the artifacts were a planing machine, a milling machine, several lathes, and a forge. Also

Figure 3-89. Museum staff installing the milling display.

Figure 3-90. The machine shop setting. Note the distribution belts, shafts, and pulleys that distributed power to the individual machines.

included in the display to give it greater authenticity were a cuspidor (or spittoon) and stovepipe top hat.

Demonstrations of the machines were given on regular schedules. In an early example of interactive exhibits, visitors were able to use telephone handsets to listen to the story of the shop and its equipment. The machine shop was so popular that a version of it was later included in the 1986 *Engines of Change* exhibition. There, the labeling would focus on social rather than technical themes.

Hall of Timekeeping and Light Machinery (1964)

The full name of the exhibition in the Hall of Timekeeping and Light Machinery shown on the floor plan at the beginning of this chapter as "Timekeepers, Etc." was *Timekeepers, Record Players, Typewriters, and Locks.* Later this was changed to the Hall of Timekeeping and Light Machinery or just the Hall of Light Machinery. Insofar as the museum claimed that there was any reason, other than convenience, for grouping this miscellany together, it was that these devices were "all commonly used by man in the modern world."[138]

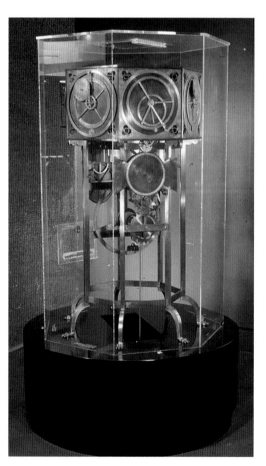

Figure 3-91. Giovanni De Dondi's elaborate astronomical clock.

Timekeeping was the principal subject. Displays traced the history of timekeeping from antiquity to the present and included water clocks, oil clocks, sand glasses, and other devices besides the more common sundials. Examples of mechanical clocks dated from the fourteenth century onward and came from Europe and Asia as well as America. These included a reconstruction of Giovanni De Dondi's renowned astronomical clock of ca. 1381, shown in Figure 3-91. At its top were planetary dials, one on each of the seven sides. Directly below them were dials that indicated hours and minutes of local daylight, month, saint of the day, date, moveable feast days, cycle of the moon, and nodes in the Roman 15-year cycle. The dial showing the time of day was on the front, below the planetary dial of the sun. This was flanked by tables giving times of sunrise and sunset throughout the year.

Featured in the exhibition was a period setting of William Bond's chronometer factory in Boston as it might have looked ca. 1845 (Figure 3-92). This was a reconstruction that used the structure from a contemporary clock factory in Connecticut and original tools from Bond.

Figure 3-92. William Bond's chronometer factory.

It gave visitors a clear sense of the tools and environment common for nineteenth-century workers.

Locks and keys were traced from ancient Egypt through the Renaissance to recent years. Besides examples of the devices, the exhibit showed tools for fabricating locks and keys.

Displayed in the section on record players were Thomas Edison's phonograph of 1877, Alexander Graham Bell's graphophone of 1887, and Emile Berliner's gramophone of 1899. These same three devices would be featured again in the *America's Listening* exhibition of 2018 (see chapter 6).

The section on typewriters explained that they were largely an American innovation, beginning with a patent issued to William A. Burt in 1829. The exhibit included examples from the nineteenth and twentieth centuries showing the evolution of this device.

Hall of Physical Sciences (1966)

Perhaps nothing more clearly symbolized the international character of the science and technology exhibitions in the new museum, as contrasted to the more nationalistic character of the history exhibitions, than the entry to the Hall of Physical Sciences. Here the museum elected to create a setting in Alexandria, Egypt, during the second century AD, where Greek rulers of the province had established a great center of learning. To represent the origins of modern mathematical science, the scene depicted the astronomer Ptolemy conducting observations that led to his monumental work, the *Almagest*, the most noteworthy early treatise on astronomy that has survived. All the instruments in the display were reproductions. On surrounding

Figure 3-93. Locks and keys display.

Figure 3-94. Visitors exploring the typewriter display.

Figure 3-95. Entry to the *Physical Sciences* exhibition.

walls were cases showing collection objects related to ancient and medieval science, including some of the museum's outstanding set of early astrolabes.

In general, the exhibition focused on the evolution of scientific instrumentation and computation from antiquity to the present. Visitors could explore significant discoveries made in a wide variety of fields, including astronomy, chemistry, meteorology, seismology, geodesy, oceanography, hydrography, and physics.

One landmark object shown to illustrate the beginning of modern precision devices was a famous 1775 dividing engine created by English instrument maker Jesse Ramsden (Figure 3-96). It was employed to divide arcs of circles automatically on precision instruments for navigation and science. The instrument had a heavy bronze wheel with 2,160 gear teeth. They engaged a screw that,

Figure 3-96. The Ramsden dividing engine.

when turned six times, rotated the carriage for the stylus exactly one degree. The object to be divided was clamped to the arms of the bronze wheel, with the cutting mechanism above it.

Another treasure was watchmaker Jean L'Epine's 1725 adding machine, which was related to earlier devices made by philosopher Blaise Pascal. L'Epine made the device for King Louis XV of France. It could add numbers by the rotation of discs with a stylus, and even had a mechanism for "carrying" when a digit in a column became greater than 9. It was a significant step toward later mechanical and electrical computing technology.

To illustrate the role of scientific instrumentation in surveying, the museum created a setting depicting surveyors Andrew Ellicott and Benjamin Banneker laying out the boundaries of the District of Columbia, around 1800 (Figure 3-97). Ellicott's instruments included a six-foot zenith-sector telescope, one of the most accurate instruments built in the United States in the late eighteenth century. Banneker was one of the few African Americans recognized in the museum for his technical work.

Several other settings illustrated chemical research. The first, shown in Figure 3-98, represented an eighteenth-century chemistry laboratory and included glassware that had been owned by the famous chemist Joseph Priestley. He made major contributions through his experiments with gases, particularly oxygen. In 1794, Priestley came to America to escape persecution for his religious and political beliefs. A contrasting display showed the 1876 chemical laboratory of Ira Remsen, who co-discovered the artificial sweetener saccharine.

Among the most recent artifacts in the exhibition were a series of pioneering digital computing devices (Figure 3-99). They included sections of the Mark I, ENIAC, SEAC, and UNIVAC digital computers. Together they marked the beginning of the computer industry in the United States.

Figure 3-97. Andrew Ellicott and Benjamin Banneker surveying the District of Columbia boundaries.

Figure 3-98. Recreation of Joseph Priestley's laboratory.

Figure 3-99. Early electrical computing devices.

Figure 3-100. Old World apothecary shop.

Halls of Medical Sciences (1966)

The Halls of Medical Sciences covered four related subjects: pharmacy, dentistry, medicine, and the development of the healing arts. Settings in this exhibition let visitors see how medical practice had changed over time and transformed the relationships involved between practitioners and patients.

The earliest setting reconstructed an eighteenth-century Old World apothecary shop. E. R. Squibb and Sons had imported this unique collection of pharmacy tools, equipment, and fixtures from Germany in 1932. Squibb first displayed it at the Century of Progress Exposition in Chicago (1933–1934), then later gave it to the American Pharmaceutical Association. They, in turn, transferred it to the Smithsonian as a permanent loan. The shop was first displayed at the National Museum, beginning in 1946. It was then enlarged and further developed in the Medical Sciences Hall. While much of the shop was a reconstruction, authentic pieces included the table, lamps, and baroque consoles flanking the table. The drug jars, glassware, and utensils were artifacts dating from the sixteenth to the nineteenth centuries collected by Dr. Jo Meyer of Wiesbaden.

Contrasted to this was a reconstructed 1890 American pharmacy. Inside were complete sets of Limoges milk glass, Queensware drug and ointment jars, glassware, scales, and patent medicines arranged on the shelves. In the rear of the pharmacy was the prescription department with paraphernalia used by druggists of that period laid out on the counter. Many of the fixtures in the shop were from the Roach Drugstore of Washington, D.C.

A dentistry setting featured the office furnishings and dental equipment of Dr. G. V. Black, who practiced in Jacksonville, Illinois. He was dean of the Northwestern University Dental School from 1891 until his death in 1915.

Figure 3-101. Inside an 1890 pharmacy.

Figure 3-102. The medical "influence" machine of the 1890s.

An arresting scene that led into the History of Medicine section showed a patient attached to an "influence" machine in the 1890s. It used static electricity to treat a variety of nervous and muscular disorders. Inside the section, visitors found cases showing more successful innovations including the first heart-bypass pump used on a human, an early iron lung, and the first plastic arterial substitutes for heart surgery.

Writing in the *Washington Evening Star*, reviewer Herman Schaden commented:

Visitors should get a psychological boost from some of the displays. Those early drills, knives, and forceps, ear trumpets and surgical saws, the static machine...that "cured" with electrical shock, the reconstructed early dental office with its torture-room atmosphere—these should make everyone a little happier about today's comparatively pleasant techniques.[139]

The popular medical science exhibits stayed on display for decades, with little change except for reorganization to make room for *Pain and Its Relief* in 1983. All, including the latter, were ultimately replaced by the broader and more thematic exhibition *Science in American Life*, in 1994. It included some medical topics, but they were limited. (Both it and the pain exhibition are discussed in later chapters.) Several attempts were made to reintroduce major medical science exhibitions to the museum in subsequent years, but they failed for lack of funding and strong leadership.

Hall of Manufactures (1968)

In 1968, the Hall of Manufactures displayed a temporary exhibit on Iron and Steel that included a model of a modern blast furnace. Later additions to the hall would trace the technical development of the industry from the process of finding ore through iron making, steel production, and manufacturing of steel products. Additional models donated by industrial partners included one of the Norris Locomotive Works in Philadelphia, which in 1855 was the largest locomotive plant of its era, and one of Ford Motor Company's massive steel plant in River Rouge, Michigan. Although there were plans to move this exhibition to the lower level of the building, it remained on the first floor.

Figure 3-103. Model of a modern blast furnace.

Textiles Hall (1965)

In discussions of what made the Museum of History and Technology unique, Frank Taylor and other museum leaders often cited the example of textiles. The Smithsonian was unusual, they said, because it collected and displayed both textile machinery and textile products. They saw textile manufacture as an excellent subject to illustrate the relationship between technical innovation and societal change.

Figure 3-104. Early American spinning wheel.

Exhibits in the Textiles Hall showed examples of raw materials, implements, and machines that were used to produce and decorate many types of fabrics. Artifacts included spinning wheels, an early drawloom, and devices for tapestry weaving.

The exhibition included Samuel Slater's 1790 carding machine, an important

Figure 3-105. A nineteenth-century Jacquard loom.

Figure 3-106. Public weaving demonstration.

step in the automation of textile manufacture. Slater established the first successful American cotton mill in Rhode Island. His work helped stimulate the Industrial Revolution in the United States. This artifact is one of only two pieces of original Slater machinery still in existence.

Another major highlight was a nineteenth-century Jacquard loom, which used punched cards to program complex designs for damask-weaving machines. Visitors could see how a single craftsperson, using this device, could weave complex, patterned fabrics by themselves. The innovation transformed the silk-weaving industry.

Spinning and weaving demonstrations, given in the hall on a regular schedule, were very popular with visitors of all ages. Other subjects covered in the hall included textile printing, knitting, and embroidery.

Figure 3-107. *Panorama of Petroleum* mural.

Hall of Petroleum (1967)

Gracing the walls of the airport in Tulsa, Oklahoma, in recent years has been a large, 13-foot by 56-foot mural entitled *Panorama of Petroleum*. Painted in 1964 by Delbert Jackson, a Tulsa resident, it depicts the history of famous oilmen of that city, which once called itself the oil capital of the world and today still depends heavily on the petroleum industry. The mural seems a natural way to welcome visitors to Tulsa, but it was not originally intended to hang there. Rather, it was painted to orient visitors to the new Hall of Petroleum at the Museum of History and Technology when the hall opened in 1967, and it was donated to the museum by a group of Tulsa oil men.[140]

In the 1960s, petroleum was the source for more than 80 percent of the energy consumed by the United States, not to mention its being a feedstock for the production of plastics and even pharmaceuticals. The exhibition provided a comprehensive account of all phases of petroleum technology, from exploration to refining and distribution. It included artifacts, working models, and demonstrations that illustrated the origins of modern industrial techniques.

Figure 3-108. Visitors explore the history of gasoline pumps.

Perhaps more than for any other exhibition, the Petroleum Hall depended on support from industry. Philip W. Bishop, curator of the exhibition, told the *Washington Evening Star,*

> Some 50 or 60 companies contributed at least $300,000 and their technical skills toward construction of the exhibits. We are greatly indebted to them, and their engineers, for the funds and knowledge which make our models and replicas accurate and authentic.[141]

Besides studying the models and drilling equipment, visitors were amused to compare early gasoline pumps with those that were familiar to them.

When the exhibition closed in the 1980s, the introductory mural went into storage. In 1998, citizens in Tulsa asked that it be given to them for display at the airport. The Helmerich Foundation, which had helped pay for its creation, together with the Amoco Foundation, contributed $200,000 to have it crated, moved, restored, and displayed.[142] The artifacts shown in the exhibition went into storage. In later years, the museum moved away from exhibitions on petroleum, energy, and natural resources to other topics.

Figure 3-109. Recreation of the Chicago Pile.

Hall of Nuclear Energy (1967)

The Hall of Nuclear Energy depicted what was then envisioned as an inexhaustible source of future power. It was a large, open exhibition that featured memorabilia and equipment associated with major discoveries in understanding the nature of atomic power and its peaceful applications. The exhibition did not cover the development of nuclear weapons. One of the most important displays was a full-scale replica of Enrico Fermi's 1942 atomic pile in Chicago, in which he achieved the first controlled fission reaction.

Another was the original Van de Graaff particle accelerator designed and built by Merle A. Tuve to study the structure of the atom. It was the first machine to attain one million electronic volts.

Yet another was a full-sized demonstration model of the 1951 Princeton stellarator, which was used by physicist Lyman Spitzer to raise the temperature of heavy hydrogen to one million or more degrees centigrade in his research on atomic fusion.

Figure 3-110. The Van de Graaff particle accelerator. The stairway around it goes down to the lower level.

Figure 3-111. The Princeton stellarator.

A Legacy in Museum Structure

The details of the 1968 exhibitions are significant because this initial version of the Museum of History and Technology established an enduring legacy that continued to influence subsequent periods. Moreover, this era was the only time when the museum actually used all the space on its three exhibit floors for public displays. Ever since, significant portions of it have been allocated to other functions, such as office space and artifact storage. No later leaders have had the opportunity to determine as many aspects of the museum experience in the Smithsonian's history museum as did Frank Taylor and his staff. The exterior of the building, with its state flags, *Infinity* sculpture, and inspiring quotations, has remained the same. Although there were later efforts to update building systems, exhibit halls, and visitor amenities, Taylor's initial principles for a "modern museum" remained foundational. The original locations of certain objects and previous exhibits often determined the placement of their successors. The first floor remained the home of technology and transportation; the Greenough statue of George Washington stayed in its central location on the second-floor west wing and introduced political and social history displays; the gunboat *Philadelphia* and military history exhibits never moved from their locations on the third floor. Most notably, the Star-Spangled Banner remained the iconic object that established the core of the museum in the Flag Hall. Finally, the blend of historical and technological exhibitions during this era established benchmarks against which later versions of the museum should be compared. What changed and why? How did the past influence the future? The museum of 1968 echoed through the eras that followed.

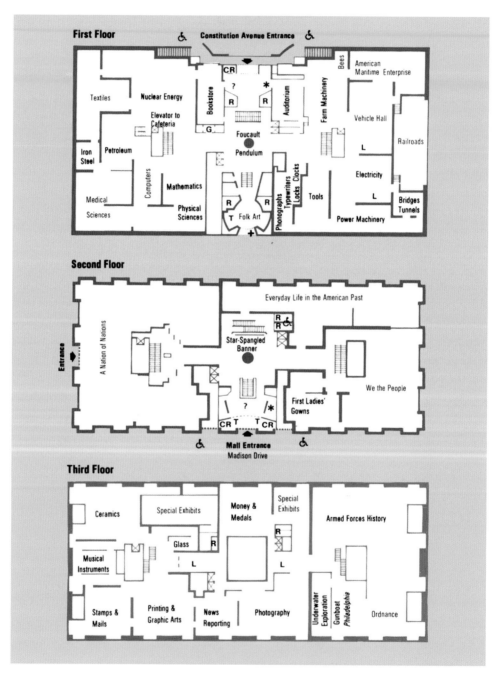

Figure 4-1. The 1976 floor plan shows the major exhibitions visitors would find in the museum in 1976.[143] Although many of the exhibits were holdovers from the opening of the museum, this map shows the first round of exhibition renovations, particularly those opened in celebration of the American bicentennial. Most were located on the second floor.

CHAPTER 4

Celebrating America's Bicentennial (1969–1979)

The Era

Smithsonian leaders used the celebration of the bicentennial of the United States in 1976 as an occasion to make major changes in the National Museum of History and Technology (the Museum of History and Technology had added "National" to its name in 1969). Although a major initiative for an outdoor military park failed, five other large new exhibitions were successfully planned and installed. The most significant was a new introductory exhibition, A Nation of Nations, *that signaled a turning point in the museum's approach to American history. Another,* 1876: A Centennial Exhibition, *used the recently vacated Arts and Industries Building to present a nostalgic look at the nation's Centennial Exhibition in Philadelphia, which had been instrumental in the creation of the Smithsonian's first museum.*

This era extended from 1969 to 1979, beginning with the appointment of Daniel Boorstin as director of the museum and ending with the appointment of Roger Kennedy as director. Under Kennedy's leadership, the museum would change both its name and its focus. The floor plan we chose to epitomize the era dates from 1976, when all the bicentennial exhibitions were open. We discuss these in a thematic order. Then we review the communications exhibitions of the early 1970s following their physical arrangement on the first and third floors.

Prelude: Remembering the Centennial

On 10 May 1876, at 10:30 in the morning, President Ulysses S. Grant, accompanied by 4,000 national guardsmen, sailors, and marines, arrived in front of Memorial Hall in Philadelphia, the site of the Centennial Exhibition. There, he and Mrs. Grant were joined by the Emperor Dom Pedro II of Brazil and the Empress Teresa, the first reigning monarchs to visit the United States. Music that was specifically commissioned for the centennial wafted through the air and speeches followed.[144] President Grant officially opened the celebration with brief remarks. He saw the centennial as a report on the first century of American independence, an accounting of which Americans should be proud—but with a realization that they still had far to go. He said, in part,

Figure 4-2. Smithsonian Secretary S. Dillon Ripley (*right*) and Chief Justice Warren Burger ride to the opening of *1876: A Centennial Exhibition.*

One hundred years ago our country was new and but partially settled. Our necessities have compelled us to chiefly expend our means and time in felling forests, subduing prairies, building dwellings, factories, ships, docks, warehouses, roads, canals, machinery, etc., etc. Most of our schools, churches, libraries, and asylums have been established within a hundred years. Burdened by these great primal works of necessity, which could not be delayed, we yet have done what this exhibition will show, in the direction of rivalling older and more advanced nations in law, medicine, and theology; in science, literature, philosophy and the fine arts. While proud of what we have done, we regret that we have not done more. Our achievements have been great enough however, to make it easy for our people to acknowledge superior merit wherever found.[145]

Following his remarks, national banners were hoisted all around, an organ and 800 singers intoned the "Hallelujah" chorus from Handel's *Messiah*, a chime of 13 large bells began to peal, and artillery fired a 100-gun salute.

Exactly 100 years later, down to the very hour, a much smaller procession pulled up to the Smithsonian's Arts and Industries Building. On 10 May 1976, the National Museum of History and Technology was opening the "largest and most colorful exhibit" ever staged by the museum, one of five it was mounting to celebrate the bicentennial of the American Revolution.[146] *1876: A Centennial Exhibition* was a unique recreation of the Philadelphia exhibition designed to commemorate the centennial. Here, visitors would see hundreds of objects that were the same as or similar to those seen by their predecessors a century earlier.

Smithsonian Secretary S. Dillon Ripley did not attempt to bring together the president, emperors, and other world leaders, enormous choirs, artillery, an organ, or crowds of thousands. However, he was determined that just as *1876: A Centennial*

Exhibition captured the spirit of the nineteenth-century exhibition, its opening would recall the pomp of the Centennial Exhibition's magnificent debut. His procession of five modest carriages was no match for the thousands of troops that had accompanied President Grant. The *1876* opening was graced with no royal presence. Chief Justice of the United States Warren Burger, chancellor of the Smithsonian, spoke in the president's place. The magnificent salute of banners, 800 singers, bells, and artillery were replaced by the much more modest National Presbyterian Church Choir and some 400 racing homing pigeons.[147]

Yet Ripley had something up his sleeve that only the Smithsonian could deliver. Though he and Chief Justice Burger donned borrowed top hats and coats, they rode to the opening in a true national treasure: the *very same* carriage that President Grant had used at the ceremony 100 years before.[148] Or at least, that is what the press was led to believe. It was definitely an authentic Grant carriage—a treasured museum object, and one in which Grant had ridden to his second inaugural. The museum's accession records make no mention of Grant riding in it to the Centennial Exhibition. But who knows?

What the ceremony lacked in grandeur, it made up in joy and whimsy: the gentlemen doffed their hats as they stepped from the carriage onto a red velvet stool that had been placed for their convenience, while their wives carried tiny parasols of black silk barely large enough to cover their heads. Newsboys dressed in period attire handed out the *Centennial Post* to the crowd, and two Smithsonian staffers arrived with tintype cameras to record the events of the day in true nineteenth-century style.

In his remarks, Secretary Ripley sought to recapture the exuberance of the American centennial and relate it to the nation's future. He said in part,

> I hope that what we have brought together here will give you at least a taste of the emotions of the time, the sense of earnest dedication to our task, the conquering of the continent, the expansion of America throughout its vast new territories and the preparation of the country for accepting its role in the world of manifest destiny.
>
> If your reactions are like mine, you will walk through this recreation of much of American life of a hundred years ago, finding little difficulty in imagining yourselves at Philadelphia in 1876 and in experiencing the same wonder and delight in American progress that so profoundly affected the visitors to Fairmount Park in that year.
>
> By looking backward we can refresh our spirits and take pride in the continuity of the Republic and in the style, vigor and ingenuity which persists in American life.
>
> And so we shall open, in a few minutes, perhaps the largest exhibit on a single theme that the Smithsonian has put together since 1876 in Philadelphia itself.[149]

Finally, the secretary and chief justice entered the building to turn knobs that started up the working machinery in the exhibition hall, just as the president and emperor had turned silver-plated cranks to start the famous Corliss engine of the Centennial Exhibition. Ripley's ceremony recalled the Philadelphia Centennial Exhibition with a special Smithsonian spirit. It made history vivid, personal, and linked to authentic objects from the past.

S. Dillon Ripley, Daniel Boorstin, and the Bicentennial

Government planning for the bicentennial began in the mid-1960s. Although this celebration would feature events and exhibits across the nation, Congress asked the Smithsonian—and especially the Museum of History and Technology—to play a central role. Smithsonian leaders saw this as both an important responsibility and an opportunity for funding to make necessary renovations, in both its new museum and the dilapidated Arts and Industries Building.

The exhibitions they planned were bold, innovative, and varied. The two most ambitious of the five the museum opened were *A Nation of Nations* and *1876: A Centennial Exhibition*. Both were huge—over 30,000 square feet—but they could hardly have been more different. With its copious red, white, and blue banners and bunting, *1876* was an experiment in immersion and nostalgic patriotism. It looked back to a time when the American growth and technological strength were astonishing the world. *A Nation of Nations*, in contrast, manifested a new kind of patriotism: one focused on American democracy, diversity, and inclusiveness. It was interpretive where *1876* was immersive, modern where *1876* was wistful.

Two Smithsonian leaders championed the Smithsonian's involvement in the bicentennial: Secretary S. Dillon Ripley and Director of the Museum of History and Technology Daniel Boorstin. Ripley had been appointed Smithsonian secretary soon after the opening of the Museum of History and Technology in 1964. He would serve in the position for 20 eventful years. Under his direction, the institution added eight new museums and five new research institutes.

Prior to his arrival at the Smithsonian, Ripley had spent nearly two decades as a professor of zoology at Yale University. He had a dramatic and eclectic past: he was a Renaissance man of learning, a renowned ornithologist and scholar, an ecological explorer, and an intelligence officer with the Office of Strategic Services (the forerunner to the CIA) during World War II.

Ripley came to the Smithsonian with grand goals for the whole institution and its history museum in particular. He was determined to bring increased dynamism and relevance to the museum. With his encouragement, the new exhibits of the late 1960s and early 1970s would become increasingly dynamic and theatrical, with complex, abstract ideas at their foundation.

In 1968, he wrote an impassioned call to action in the Smithsonian's annual report to Congress with the bicentennial in mind. He claimed that the Smithsonian had a "moral responsibility to consider its exhibits for the effect that they may have on all sorts and conditions of people."[150] Moreover, he criticized the National Museum of History and Technology for its lack of diverse representation of people of all ethnicities. "Far too little has been done to delineate the history of the ethnic minorities of our country or to single out and describe their achievements," he said. "If our Institution is to play a valid role in the Bicentennial of the American Revolution in 1976, we should be prepared to correct what is in effect a series of oversights in history, the history of our country and of the multiplicity of our people."[151]

A year later, Ripley hired Daniel Boorstin to help him achieve his goals. Formerly a renowned scholar and professor at the University of Chicago and at that time writing a popular trilogy on American history, Boorstin arrived at the Smithsonian with no curatorial experi-

Figure 4-3. Daniel Boorstin became director of the museum in October 1969.

ence but with an approach to American history that echoed Ripley's vision. Not incidentally, he was already a member of the American Revolution Bicentennial Commission. The secretary called his appointment "a milestone in the history of the Smithsonian" and expressed his hope that the Museum of History and Technology would "come of age … as a national center for the study of our Nation's history and for the diffusion of knowledge in new and imaginative ways."[152]

Boorstin's 1969 acceptance speech revealed his desire to combat what he saw as a disturbing national tendency toward self-criticism, pessimism, and apology. His solution was to direct the museum to emphasize the collaborative achievements of American society. He said, "And with the approaching Bicentennial, the 200th birthday of our nation, we have a special obligation to help the nation assess its whole achievement. This, then, must be a place of patriotism—of enlightened, *un*chauvinistic but still impassioned patriotism."[153]

In April 1970, Boorstin penned a report to the Bicentennial Commission that outlined the Smithsonian's expansive plans at that point. Ripley sent it not only to the commission, but also to the Smithsonian secretary and bureau directors. Boorstin wrote,

> The nation's approaching 200th birthday—like other national celebrations—gives the whole nation an occasion to recall its achievement and to renew its self-confidences. The Smithsonian Institution will use its vast resources, and enlist the resources of others, to help rediscover our national achievements. …
>
> We aim to help Americans and the world see the American Experience as a grand experiment of man. We aim to explore and assess the ways in which the life of man here has been shaped by the peculiar resources of our continent, and so help us see how we have shaped (and misshaped) the landscape of a New World. We aim to help Americans discover the meanings of the American Experience for the world. We aim to help the world discover

the meanings of the American Revolution and the American Experience for man everywhere. We aim to draw overall American Experience to illuminate the unfolding problems and promises of the late 20th century—and to help us draw hopeful prospectuses for the 21st century. We aim to help set new knowledge in the context of history.[154]

The Bicentennial Exhibitions

A Nation of Nations (1976)

A Nation of Nations, although the last of the bicentennial exhibitions to open, was the first to be envisioned. The original idea came from Boorstin, who wanted to use the exhibition to recontextualize the museum as a whole. In line with his passionate acceptance speech, he hoped to frame American accomplishments in relation to the rest of the world.

His ambitious plan would add two glass pavilions to the outside of the museum building, one representing the contributions of other nations to the formation of America and the other representing its subsequent influence on them. Between the two pavilions would be the museum itself, which would "continue to show the achievement of the whole manifold American community."[155] In Boorstin's view, the exhibition would promote a positive, patriotic synthesis of American history. In addition, it would pay tribute to Secretary Ripley's desire for the museum to recognize the diversity of the American people.

Although the idea of the glass pavilions was "new and imaginative," as Ripley wanted, it was also unrealistic and faced harsh criticism from the museum staff. Curators questioned the safety of a structure made of glass and pointed out the damage to objects that could be caused by weather and sunlight. Recently, the museum had suffered leakage and broken glass from other large windows in the building.

Curators also criticized the content of the proposed exhibition. Boorstin's proposal spoke only of ideas, not objects. He expected that curators would offer suggestions for appropriate artifacts from their collections or would acquire them once they understood his vision. Boorstin saw this process of "selecting objects to tell our story" as an advantage, but it was radically different from the standard method of exhibition development at the museum.[156] Curators were used to formulating their plans based on their existing collections. They struggled to find artifacts that would represent Boorstin's abstract ideas.

By the end of 1971, practical considerations had triumphed and a revised exhibition plan had emerged. While it was still structured around Boorstin's ideas, it included concessions to the concerns of the curators. The new plan was far more grounded in the museum's existing artifacts. Moreover, the exhibition would no longer consist of two new pavilions, but instead would occupy an existing space in the building: the second floor of the west wing. However, the exhibition script remained unfinished.

In 1973, four years after planning started, the exhibition team changed dramatically. Boorstin had decided to step down from his position as director and become the museum's senior historian. He had come to realize that he was more suited to working as a scholar than as a museum director. While he had brought a grand intellectual vision, he struggled with the responsibilities of administration and translating his ideas into objects-based exhibits. He much preferred to write. In 1973, he completed *The Americans: The Democratic Experience*, which won a Pulitzer Prize in 1974. In 1975, he left the museum to become the twelfth librarian of Congress, a position he would hold until 1987.

Brooke Hindle, another academic historian who had worked previously with the museum as an advisor, became its new director. Working closely with a team of curators, he supervised the completion of the bicentennial exhibits. For *A Nation of Nations*, he quickly named a formal curatorial team, which had not previously existed. They began collaborating more effectively with the design firm Chermayeff & Geismar, which had been hired under Boorstin's leadership. Together, the group finally completed the detailed work of choosing the objects and graphics, reformulating the themes, and writing the final script.

Boorstin's original plan for *A Nation of Nations* had been an attempt to understand all American history through the relationship between America and the rest of the world. He had wanted to explain what immigrants brought to America and what the nation in turn gave back to the rest of the world. As the curatorial and design teams developed the exhibition, they gave up on trying to be so expansive. They emphasized only how immigrant groups brought their distinct talents and traditions to America and how this changed the United States.

A Nation of Nations became the museum's blockbuster bicentennial exhibition. It did not tell the traditional story of the American Revolution and the signing of the Declaration of Independence, as might have been expected. Instead, curators chose to focus on the premise that all Americans are descended from immigrants. Whether they had crossed into North America in 22,000 BC or passed through Ellis Island in the twentieth century, these diverse peoples ultimately mixed their cultures and shared experiences in ways that shaped the "one nation" that is America.[157]

To reach *A Nation of Nations*, visitors walked through a new west-terrace entrance. Chermayeff & Geismar had designed this opening, along with the wide paths and directed flow, to accommodate the huge crowds anticipated during the bicentennial celebration. Their innovative design mixed a wide variety of period settings with collages of artifacts that appealed as much through their visual presentation as through their interpretation. A nine-foot-high "tube"—that is, a raised platform and dropped ceiling—allowed objects to be displayed both above and below eye level. This single path wound its way through the whole exhibition, revealing a unified story unfolding through four chapters. In addition, many objects were labeled with colored dots showing their country of origin. Visitors could follow along, tracing their own ethnicity by using the color key on the back of the exhibition brochure (Figure 4-4).

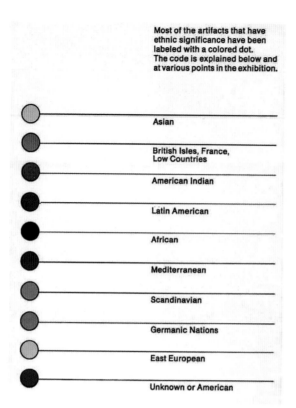

Most of the artifacts that have ethnic significance have been labeled with a colored dot. The code is explained below and at various points in the exhibition.

Figure 4-4. Code on exhibition brochure indicating ethnic origin of artifacts.

Asian

British Isles, France, Low Countries

American Indian

Latin American

African

Mediterranean

Scandinavian

Germanic Nations

East European

Unknown or American

A Nation of Nations presented a perspective of America at its bicentennial that visitors found nowhere else. Although it highlighted the traditional story of English settlement during the colonial era, it quickly displayed a broader intention: to show the balance between cultural diversity and unity in the budding nation.

The first section, People for a New Nation, opened with prehistoric America.[158] In displaying an array of Native American tools and other artifacts, the exhibit made the thematic point that there was no such thing as truly "Native" Americans, as these peoples, too, were originally immigrants. Visitors then passed through a long hallway displaying objects that represented the everyday lives of ordinary colonists. Artifacts associated with settlers from England were to the right, while those from other nations were to the left.

To represent the Revolutionary War, this section used famous national treasures such as George Washington's military uniform and Thomas Jefferson's writing desk. However, its surprising centerpiece was a 1695 colonial kitchen from Massachusetts.

The second section, Old Ways in the New World, presented a vast collection of tools, means of transport, and religious objects to show how immigrants brought their traditions, culture, and skills with them to America. It focused particularly on objects of work and travel, suggesting that these two activities were common to all immigrants. Featured objects from the nineteenth century included a Jewish peddler's wagon, a Mexican ox cart, a Spanish mill, and a Chinese gateleg table, emphasizing the cultural diversity and pluralism of that period. However, it also showed

Figure 4-5. Jewish peddler's wagon.

negative aspects of cultural diversity, displaying symbols of oppression and prejudice such as doorways labeled "Whites Only" and a cross burned by the Ku Klux Klan.

The third section, Shared Experiences, explored ways that immigrants integrated their traditions into American culture while still maintaining their ethnic identity. In addition, it called attention to institutions and environments that encouraged national unity, from the military to public schools.

One particularly memorable section of the exhibition featured a recreated period setting of a 1925 Italian American kitchen. It showed how standardized houses and mass-produced goods made it possible for immigrants to rise from poverty to the middle class, while still preserving elements of their ethnic heritage. Another was a military barracks, which illustrated how military service molded Americans of various ethnic backgrounds into standardized GIs through a unifying American experience.

The final section of the exhibition, called A Nation Among Nations, ushered visitors into the modern era. Focusing on mass-production technology and globalization, this section attempted to represent America's role as a global leader. It featured an eye-catching display of neon signs from immigrant-owned restaurants and stores around America.

Other displays included satellite communication technology, foreign advertisements for American products, and even a working machine that mass-produced pencils embossed with the Smithsonian name—which were conveniently available for purchase in the gift shop.[159] Although visually appealing, the section failed to

Figure 4-6. Italian immigrants' kitchen.

Figure 4-7. Military barracks illustrate how life was standardized for all soldiers.

Figure 4-8. Commercial neon signs showing ethnic influence on American business.

convey the exhibition's larger point about America's contributions to other nations. Visitors found it confusing and somewhat heavy-handed. It became the first section of the exhibition to close when *A Nation of Nations* was restructured to make way for the exhibition *Field to Factory*, discussed in the next chapter.

Reviewers frequently commented on the groundbreaking character of *A Nation of Nations*, compared both to previous exhibits mounted by the museum and to the rest of the bicentennial celebration across the nation. The *Washington Post* praised the exhibition's inclusion of some of America's defects, such as slavery and prejudice.[160] The London *Times* took note of what it saw as a unique perspective on American history—that the nation was more of a "tossed salad" than a melting pot. It stated that "the theoretical underpinning of this worthy educational show is a Catalogue Raisonné which sets out to be a history of immigration and a serious work of scholarship."[161] Above all, reviewers and visitors alike said that they saw their lives and families reflected in *A Nation of Nations*. One commentator wrote in *Washington Calendar Magazine*,

> Bicentennial celebrations may have given you the same vaguely uncomfortable feeling, too. Most tended to ignore the fact that for millions of Americans, the "land where my father died" lies somewhere across the ocean, and not in Great Britain, either. But take heart. There is one patriotic show that tells the story as you knew it to be all along. In an elegant, witty, and tremendously affecting exhibit, the Smithsonian's Museum of History and Technology triumphantly demonstrates that to be American is really to be foreign too; that our "one nation" is really a "nation of nations."[162]

We the People (1975)

After winding their way through the near acre of space that *A Nation of Nations* occupied, visitors could cross the floor to explore another newly opened bicentennial exhibition. *We the People* made effective use of the wide hallways that Taylor had championed. It spilled out into the east hall with an effusion of symbols of the United States, such as flags and eagles, decorated posters, chinaware, quilts, and even weather vanes.[163]

Behind the escalators, the rest of the exhibition awaited, separated into three sections inspired by President Lincoln's Gettysburg Address: Of the People, By the People, and For the People. Visitors were invited to explore the nature of the relationship between Americans and their government by examining over 6,000 objects from the museum's extensive political history collections.

The exhibition's first section, Of the People, illustrated who the American people were. Beginning with the display of national symbols, the section continued with examples of the U.S. census, contrasting the single slender volume that made up the 1790 census with the 60 volumes needed for the 1970 census. The section also contained notable gifts that the United States had received from other nations. These were shown to illuminate how foreigners perceived the American character, although this point was too abstract for many visitors.

The second section, By the People, was meant to highlight the participatory nature of the American government. Visitors saw posters and objects related to the

Figure 4-9. This section of *We the People* was installed in a hallway, in front of the escalators.

right to petition and the right to vote. Finally, they could peruse, according to the *Washington Star*, "more political and 'cause' buttons and banners and ribbons and badges and posters than one would care to look at."[164]

The final section, For the People, covered government services. Its objects were intended to represent demands that the American people have made to their government, either directly or through representatives. Its six subsections took their names from phrases in the preamble to the Constitution. Although this seemed like a clever idea, it became forced in execution. To Form a More Perfect Union showcased a panoramic painting and objects related to Lewis and Clark, to demonstrate the role of the government in westward expansion. It also included the table and chairs from Appomattox to represent the Union victory in the Civil War. "To Establish Justice" covered the court system, "To Insure Domestic Tranquility" focused on law enforcement, and so on. The largest and busiest subsection was "To Promote the General Welfare," which addressed food, housing, health, and education services, among others. For many visitors and reviewers, this area of the exhibition was simply too conceptual and too crowded with miscellaneous objects.

In contrast, one area of the exhibition was extremely successful and well received: the "protest wall" featured in the By the People section. A painted view of the east Capitol steps acted as a backdrop for life-sized protestors from various periods of American history. They ranged from Vietnam War demonstrators to women's rights advocates to abolitionists. Visitors seemed to appreciate the overall point of the display: as a *Washington Post* reviewer said, "What was most striking about this section, however, is the contemporaneity of the right to petition portion," noting that although the banners spanned centuries of American history, many of the issues were still relevant.[165]

This exhibition technique was so successful that the museum used it again in 2017, in a new exhibition on political history, *American Democracy: A Great Leap of Faith*. The later iteration retained the Capitol backdrop and the mix of historical and modern protest signs, featuring some of the original banners and adding

Figure 4-10. Comparison of the "protest walls" in *We the People* (left) and *American Democracy* (right).

twenty-first-century examples. But it removed the lifelike figures that curators in the 1970s used to make the "visitors feel a part of the historical protest movement." Instead, the modern version included a larger number of posters across the political spectrum, then dramatized them with spotlighting, videos, and interactive displays.

Even more than *A Nation of Nations*, *We the People* faced the new challenge of adapting abstract historical concepts to an exhibition comprising objects already in the museum's collection. The *Washington Star* criticized the layout of the exhibition, saying, "Often the abstract ideas get completely lost in a dizzy maze of trivial memorabilia reminiscent of the old museum way of displaying things by tossing everything into a showcase until the viewer's head was set to spinning."[166] On the other hand, the reviewer acknowledged the breadth of the topic that was being attempted. An exhibition that explored "the relationship between the American people and their government," though perhaps overly ambitious, was certainly "new and imaginative," just as Secretary Ripley wanted.

Suiting Everyone (1974)

On the basement level of the building, occupying a recently established exhibition space next to the cafeteria, was the very first bicentennial exhibition to open: *Suiting Everyone*. When it debuted in 1973, it was a pioneering example of the museum's trend toward conceptual exhibitions and away from collections-based exhibitions like the museum's earlier costume display, *American Costume*.[167] Chronologically organized into "Four Centuries of Costume in America," the previous exhibition's primary purpose had been merely to show examples of historical clothing.

Figure 4-11. Entry to *Suiting Everyone*.

Figure 4-12. Professionally made clothing "for somebody."

Suiting Everyone, in contrast, took an innovative approach by structuring the exhibition around a theme: the democratization of clothing in America. The result was a multidisciplinary display that weaved social and technological history together. Ultimately, in the words of the *Washington Star*, the exhibition was intended to "examine the clothing industry's origins in the Industrial Revolution and trace its growth before 1850, the expansion through 1920, and the beginnings of the sophisticated ready-to-wear industry that has made Americans among the best-dressed people in the world."[168]

The first section of the exhibition, entitled Clothing for Somebody, drew on the museum's collection of colonial-era costume. Visitors were able to contrast the clothing belonging to the wealthy—custom pieces made of expensive, imported fabric—with clothing belonging to everyday people. The latter was made by hand in private residences, with homespun materials or cheap, imported fabric. The exhibit emphasized the differences in appearance between these classes of people, arguing that the eighteenth century was a time when "the clothing a person wore told his station in life and added a visual dimension to the separation of classes."[169]

The next two sections, Clothing for Anybody and Clothing for Everybody, covered the nineteenth century and traced the development of ready-made clothing through the Industrial Revolution. These sections emphasized the interplay between the technical history of textiles and the social impact of its development, illustrating the strength of the museum's collections in both technology and history. Clothing for Anybody began with a display of industrial machines used to produce yarn and fabric, including the cotton gin patent model made by Eli Whitney and a model of

Figure 4-13. An array of men's suits showed mass production and conformity in American dress.

Samuel Slater's spinning machine. It continued with an array of men's ready-made clothing options from the early nineteenth century, showing how tailors began to use the extra time freed by more efficient machinery to design clothing out of leftover fabric, with no specific customer in mind. This section also covered the influence of the military in ready-made clothing: a setting of the U.S. Army Clothing Establishment represented the beginning of standardized sizing.

The Clothing for Everybody section spanned 1860 to 1920 and focused on the increased efficiency of textile machinery and the spread of ready-made fashion to women's clothes. This section included an original Elias Howe sewing machine, a Singer sewing machine patent model, and a 1920s factory setting. One of the most striking displays conveyed the advances in standardized sizing with a series of 18 identical men's suit coats in sizes from 34 extra-short to 60 extra-long.

The final section of the exhibition was the most memorable. Called Something for Everybody, it featured a large display of over 50 outfits from the 1920s to the 1970s. This section conveyed the ultimate thesis of the exhibition: that by 1920,

Figure 4-14. Clothes for everybody.

clothing had become "democratized." No longer could a person's class, background, or profession be identified simply by looking at his or her clothing.

Besides conveying its ambitious conceptual theme, a major goal of *Suiting Everyone* was to encourage familiarity and recognition.[170] Although *American Costume* had featured a small section on modern fashion trends (highlighting the emergence of the "little black dress"), this exhibition offered the museum its first chance to expand its collection of modern clothing. To this end, the museum sent out multiple requests to the public for donations of clothing from after 1920, asking specifically for pieces created by certain designers or items that highlighted particular trends. Around 1,500 garments were chosen from these donations and added to the collection.

Although clothing exhibitions in other museums of this era typically showcased only famous items made by famous designers, *Suiting Everyone* focused on clothing worn by ordinary people. The curators emphasized that they wanted the exhibition to feel relatable, saying, "We want viewers to say 'I had a gown like that,' or 'Good heavens! There's my old Kimberly pant suit.'"[171] To this end, although the final section of the exhibition did feature many designer pieces, none was identified by either designer or donor. Only an alphabetized list of designers at the end of the exhibition allowed fashion-savvy visitors to guess the origins of the various outfits.

1876: A Centennial Exhibition (1976)

Across the mall, the venerable Arts and Industries Building served as the location for *1876: A Centennial Exhibition*. What had been the source of this surprising idea? To those who knew the history of the Smithsonian, it was only natural. As discussed in chapter 2, the Smithsonian's first museum was in many ways an offshoot of the Centennial Exhibition in Philadelphia. The Smithsonian had accessioned into its collection many of the objects originally exhibited there. What could be easier than just dusting them off and putting them back on display?

Unfortunately, the Centennial Exhibition collection, though mythical in its size and significance to the history of the Smithsonian, was an eclectic assortment of leftovers. The most noteworthy and valuable pieces from the original exhibition—the fine furniture, the impressive engines, the priceless musical instruments—had not been given to the institution.[172] This was an unpleasant surprise to curators, who found their job much more challenging than expected.

As a result, four types of objects were ultimately displayed in *1876*, objects that the Smithsonian had inherited from the Centennial Exhibition, objects displayed there that the Smithsonian borrowed or acquired, nineteenth-century objects similar to those that had been at that exhibition, and replicas. When purists later criticized the use of replicas and the amount of restoration the Smithsonian made to original objects, curators snapped back: "[Our] philosophy is that the show is meant to give a feeling of the way it all was when the machines, and the country, were brighter and newer."[173]

Unlike the other bicentennial exhibitions, *1876* had no grand message or abstract theme. Rather, it was simply designed to immerse visitors in a memorable and

Figure 4-15. *1876* installed in the Arts and Industries Building.

Figure 4-16. The center of the *1876* exhibition.

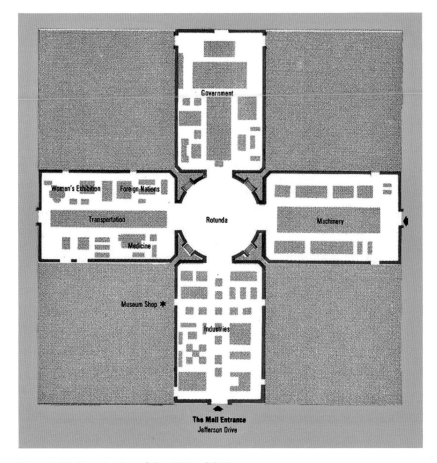

Figure 4-17. Organization of the *1876* exhibition.

significant event of a century earlier. The setting of the Arts and Industries Building, which had been constructed in the late nineteenth century, the old-fashioned and cluttered exhibit style, and the lack of exhibit labels or other explanatory material all contributed to giving them the experience of walking back into a period when the nation was immensely proud of its progress.[174]

The Arts and Industries Building featured four large exhibition halls arranged in a cross around the central rotunda. For *1876*, the rotunda was decorated in nineteenth-century style: patriotic bunting celebrated the centennial, flowers and greenery suggested the Horticultural Hall in Philadelphia, and an original fountain from the exhibition replaced the *Statue of Freedom*. A mechanical organ, rescued from the remains of a demolished exhibition building in Philadelphia, was restored and nestled into an alcove in the rotunda, where it played seven and a half hours' worth of historical music. Besides the decoration, the building itself had been renovated in preparation for the new exhibition. A large portion of the funds set aside for the exhibition paid for the installation of air-conditioning: no more heat and humidity in the summer. Even the elaborate pattern of tiles on the floor was reproduced and reinstalled by the same company that originally made them—quite a challenge for modern workmen.

Figure 4-18. A view from the balcony to the floor of the *1876* exhibition.

The four halls were loosely based on buildings at the Philadelphia exhibition: the North Hall was a replication of the main exhibition building at Fairmount Park, the South Hall was modeled after the Government Building, and the West Hall was based on the Machinery Hall. The East Hall featured a miscellany of displays, including exhibits from the Women's Pavilion.

Visitors entering the Arts and Industries Building from the National Mall through the north entrance were immediately plunged into the past; there was no gradual transition. The North Hall was devoted to displays of all kinds of American-manufactured products: ceramics and glass, silverware, furniture, musical instruments, axes, knives, shovels, and more, all intended to show the United States' prominence in the practical arts.

Detail was important to the success of the exhibition. Of particular appeal, especially in the North Hall, were the elaborate wooden cases designed for the show. Featuring expert wood carving and hand-painted lettering, the cases were almost an attraction in themselves.

Passing through the rotunda, visitors could choose among the three remaining halls. On the left, the East Hall, one of the more eclectic collections of objects, featured the steam engine *Jupiter*, which had been recovered from Washington, D. C.'s own Kennedy Playground and restored. *Jupiter* would later be moved to the National

Figure 4-19. The *Jupiter* locomotive on display in *1876*. Behind on the left are carriages, temporarily covered in plastic.

Museum of American History, where it was featured in the 2003 transportation exhibition, *America on the Move*.

The East Hall also contained displays from the Centennial Exhibition's Women's Pavilion. Designed and managed by women, this had featured examples of female accomplishment and had been a veiled form of lobbying for women's suffrage. Finally, the East Hall contained objects that represented a great many American states and foreign nations: Liberty Bell replicas made of materials ranging from tobacco to salt, Chinese carved furniture, and French scientific and electrical equipment. Of all the sections of *1876*, this was the one most criticized. Not only was it cramped and cluttered, but the lighting, kept purposefully low for verisimilitude's sake, made it difficult to see many of the displays.

The South Hall's main attraction was the enormous model of the USS *Antietam*, measuring about 54 feet long and 26 feet tall. One of the original displays at the Centennial Exhibition, it had been subsequently donated to the Naval Academy in Annapolis and used to train midshipmen. To represent the Government Building, which had included Smithsonian objects, the hall included 30-foot-tall totem poles from the Haida tribe, clockwork machinery, two lighthouse lenses and lamps, and a great deal of ordnance, including a Gatling battery gun mounted on a life-sized camel.

Figure 4-20. Many of the steam engines on display were operated using compressed air.

Many visitors thought that the final section, representing the famous Machinery Hall in Philadelphia, was the highlight of the exhibition. Here was a grand collection of painted, candy-colored steam engines, many of which moved with the aid of compressed air. Although these towering machines took up much of the center of the room, wider aisles around the edges allowed visitors the opportunity to gawk at the Otis steam elevator, the Nasmyth steam forging hammer, and a Corliss steam engine. Purists were sad that this was not actually the same Corliss engine that famously powered many of the machines at the Centennial Exhibition itself. It was instead a much smaller engine that had powered a George Pullman factory.

Overall, *1876* was a huge success. Visitors were enchanted by the many unusual sights and enjoyed the experience of stepping into the past for a few hours. Instead of staying open for just two years, the exhibition lasted for two decades. Nonetheless, it did receive its fair share of criticism. It was deliberately intended to be the exact opposite of modern exhibitry. It was neither conceptual nor interpretive. Many visitors and reviewers objected to the sparse labels. They noted that although nineteenth-century visitors might have been able to recognize the significance of these, modern visitors were often baffled. They had no introduction or even a main label to give background or orientation. Finally, low light levels made it hard to read what few labels there were, and cluttered and crowded rooms could be more claustrophobic than awe-inspiring.

Still, the enduring popularity of *1876* during its 20-year life testifies to its success in celebrating the bicentennial. As the exhibition brochure expressed,

> The Centennial introduced ten million visitors to exotic peoples and their culture—and it impressed upon every one of those visitors an indelible image of the United States as a nation come of age. Nothing else so gloriously captured the American spirit of '76. We were a proud people as we celebrated our one-hundredth birthday.[175]

While the Centennial Exhibition was a grand celebration of where America was headed, *1876* reminded Americans of their past. Its poignant nostalgia was not just

Figure 4-21. This artist's concept drawing of *1876*, done before it was built, captures the spirit of what the museum hoped to achieve.

for steam engines and booming industries, but for an era of uncomplicated pride and easy hope that Americans had since lost.

Although the exhibition is long gone, its chief designer, Ben Lawless, captured aspects of its story in a film he wrote about the original Centennial Exhibition entitled *Celebrating a Century*. Produced by the Smithsonian Office of Telecommunications, much of it was filmed in the *1876* exhibition. Moreover, most of the individuals featured in the film were Smithsonian staff dressed up in period costumes, including Secretary Dillion Ripley, Frank Taylor, and Ben Lawless himself. The film aired on PBS and won an Emmy award. As of 2020, it can still be viewed on the Internet Archive.[176]

Bicentennial Park

Does it seem surprising that none of the bicentennial projects above—those that the museum produced—related directly to the American Revolution itself? After all, the museum had a large military history collection and staff who knew the subject well. This seeming oversight was not a case of ignoring the obvious, but rather the result of a plan that failed. The museum had indeed attempted to create a new display that celebrated the military history of the American Revolution, and it was intended to be its most ambitious bicentennial effort of them all.

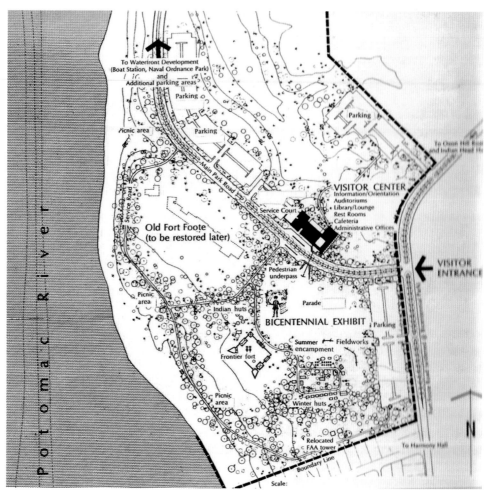

Figure 4-22. Layout of the proposed Bicentennial Park on the east bank of the Potomac River, south of Washington, D.C.

The goal was a Bicentennial Park that would be a joint project of the Smithsonian and the National Park Service, with assistance from the Department of Defense. It was to be located on the Maryland shore of the Potomac River, just south of Washington, D.C., on the site of Fort Foote. The fort had been a Civil War–era earthwork that was part of the defense of the capital. The National Park Service now maintained the area. The earthworks, however, had deteriorated and were overgrown. The entire area was little used and mostly forested. It seemed the perfect location for something new.

The plan was to recreate a Revolutionary War military encampment "where Americans of all ages can explore their country's fascinating past in an inspirational environment designed to bring history alive."[177]

The planners wanted to help visitors experience the spirit of '76 that had empowered Americans to win the nation's freedom. They wrote

Figure 4-23. Concept drawing of the proposed Bicentennial Park.

In the rural atmosphere of Fort Foote, emphasis will be placed on the everyday camp life of the patriot man-at-arms, on the long and patient labor, the sacrifice, and the self-reliance demanded in the struggle to bring forth the first modern republic.[178]

The park was to include a visitor center that showed an "inspirational and educational film," a living history encampment, a parade ground, and a primitive fort made of timber and lumber. Along the riverbank was to be a Naval Ordnance Park, where visitors could see an array of Revolutionary War naval guns, reconstructions of shipboard settings, and related tools and artifacts.

All the areas would be enlivened by dozens of volunteers who would wear period dress and reenact the work of soldiers and sailors of the era. This was to include cleaning and firing weapons, drilling, cooking food, standing guard, making and mending clothes, and other related activities. There would be national competitions of fife and drum corps, among other events. And although the bicentennial theme would be predominant, the park would also "serve as an arena for performances by modern-day bands and marching groups as well as a restful environment in which to enjoy concerts in the park."[179] The preliminary budget was $2.5 million, but more was likely needed to accomplish all that was intended—especially if, as planned, the park expanded after the bicentennial celebration ended to include the full sweep of American military history.

This project itself had a long history that stretched back to the concluding years of World War II. In the euphoria of victory, several proposals were advanced for a new military museum in Washington. In 1946, the Army and Navy jointly created a commission to study the idea. Several government institutions, including the Smithsonian, were consulted. The Bicentennial Commission first proposed a separate museum, but it failed to get a plan approved by Congress. In part, this was because the Smithsonian wanted no competition to its own expansion plans and the creation of the planned National Air Museum.

Another attempt followed in the late 1950s. In 1958, President Eisenhower established a Presidential Committee on the American Armed Forces Museum, headed by Chief Justice Earl Warren, to develop a consensus plan. The secretary of the Smithsonian was now integrally involved. The president wrote that he wanted it to be a "dynamic educational venture rather than limiting itself to the collection and cataloging of materials from the armed forces."[180]

Over the following years, the committee created a proposal that led to Public Law 87-186, which was enacted in 1961. It established "A National Armed Forces Museum Advisory Board of the Smithsonian Institution, to authorize expansion of the Smithsonian Institution's facilities for portraying the contributions of the Armed Forces of the United States." The bill also charged the Smithsonian with the responsibility to, among other things,

> commemorate and display the contributions made by the military forces of
> the Nation toward creating, developing, and maintaining a free, peaceful,
> and independent society and culture in the United States of America. The
> valor and sacrificial service of the men and women of the Armed Forces
> shall be portrayed as an inspiration to the present and future generations
> of America. The demands placed upon the full energies of our people, the
> hardships endured, and the sacrifice demanded in our constant search for
> world peace shall be clearly demonstrated.[181]

The law authorized the Smithsonian to find land and create museum buildings necessary to accomplish these tasks. The preferred site was on the banks of the Potomac, between the Lincoln and Jefferson memorials.[182]

Extensive efforts were made during the next several years to move the project forward. These ultimately led to a proposal for a new Smithsonian unit, a National Armed Forces Museum Park. It was described in a detailed study and plan published by the Smithsonian in 1966.[183]

The plan was much broader and bolder than the later Bicentennial Park proposal of the 1970s. The earlier institution, too, was to be located at Fort Foote, but it was to use more of the area and was to cover military history from the colonial era to the present, focusing on four major themes: land operation, naval and amphibious

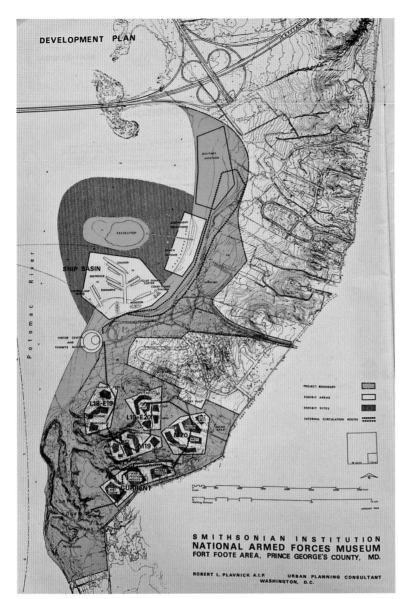

Figure 4-24. Map of the large National Armed Forces Museum proposed in 1966.

actions, coast defense, and military aviation. The estimated total cost was a little over $36.5 million, roughly what it had cost to establish the entire Museum of History and Technology.

Surprisingly, the new museum was not intended to absorb the military history units of the existing museum. The report stated:

> It is assumed that the Museum of History and Technology will continue to concentrate on uniforms, insignia and heraldry, small arms, models, and biographical displays while presenting a general summary of the role played by our armed forces in the Nation's history. The proposed National Armed Forces Museum Park, on the other hand, would be concerned with documenting more specifically the broad contributions made by the Armed Forces

in war and in peace and in tracing the technological evolution of warfare. In brief, the small arms, the historic flags, the epaulets, and the personal mementos of our military and naval leaders will continue to be housed on the Mall; the machines of war the fortifications, the guns, the vehicles and the ships that these leaders commanded would be displayed at the Armed Forces Museum Park.[184]

The timing of this grand new proposal could hardly have been worse. Over the next several years, the Vietnam War heated up and sparked increasing public opposition to the American military and its involvement in world affairs, especially among America's youth—the principal audience for the proposed park. Outside advisors and critics increasingly questioned whether the United States should now create what was essentially a National War Museum on the edge of the capital. By 1970, even the Nixon administration was expressing "major reservations" about the project. So was the National Bicentennial Commission.[185]

In response, the advisory board revised the plan described in the legislation and instead proposed creating the more limited Bicentennial Park outlined above. It focused only on the Revolution, not the general history of the armed forces, and was designed only to foster patriotism, not provide a comprehensive overview of American military history. However, the commission now ran into problems securing the Fort Foote site, due to local opposition, and the Bicentennial Commission still found the new plan of "limited relevance and significance."[186] By 1973, this plan too had died. Commemoration of the American Revolution itself was eliminated from the Smithsonian's bicentennial projects. In retrospect, planning a variety of exhibitions had been an extremely wise choice.

The Communications Exhibitions

Although the museum focused primarily on bicentennial exhibitions in the 1970s, it did make other significant changes. On 30 September 1970, a fire broke out early in the day on the third floor of the museum. It appeared to have started in a $50,000 IBM interactive computer display where visitors, particularly children, could challenge a computer to a game of tic-tac-toe. This included a computer terminal, typewriter, and television screen. The computer was programmed so that though it might end up with a draw, it could never lose. (Was there a lesson there somewhere?) The fire also wiped out a puppet theater where visitors could see productions of "Pinocchio." Finally, smoke from the fire filtered into the stamp, coin, graphic arts, ceramics, and glass exhibitions and even to storage rooms on the upper floors. Fortunately, no artifacts were destroyed or seriously damaged.[187]

Instead of just lamenting this tragedy, the museum turned it into an opportunity to revise a series of exhibitions.[188] They were able to gain support to upgrade the graphic arts, photographic history, numismatics, and philately exhibitions as well as to link them together under a general theme of communications. In addition to new federal funding, they secured a grant from the Henry R. Luce Foundation to create a new Hall of News Reporting. Finally, by working together with the U.S. Post Office, they were able to acquire a historic country store and post office building and install it as an operating post office next to the entrance on Constitution Avenue on the first floor. The revised exhibitions debuted between 1971 and 1973. They were the first major modifications in the museum since it had opened in 1964.

The Headsville Post Office (1971)

The Headsville Post Office exemplified a new approach for the museum. Boorstin's efforts to make it "a more total and more vivid, a more personal, a more participatory and a more communal recapturing of man's experience" had led curators to find ways to display the museum's artifacts as parts of everyday life.[189] Carl Scheele, the curator of postal history, believed that a post office would be the perfect personal and familiar object to fulfill these purposes. After a search of roughly 10,000 miles through 13 different states, he found the post office and general store he sought in the small town of Headsville, West Virginia. The Smithsonian purchased the store (including its selection of nonperishable goods) for $7,500, disassembled it, transported it 130 miles, and reassembled it in the museum.[190]

Figure 4-25. Front of the Headsville Post Office.

Figure 4-26. Inside the post office and general store.

The post office acted as a middle ground between public space and exhibit space. With no object labels or descriptions, it was not attempting to educate visitors about the past, but to immerse them in it. It was staffed by real postal service employees who sold all currently available U.S. commemorative stamps. Visitors could mail letters and postcards (conveniently sold in the museum shops) to their loved ones. The stamps would be hand-canceled with the museum's signature postmark. This active setting, beloved by visitors and staff alike, would stay open until the museum closed for renovations in 2006.

Hall of Photography (1973)

The updated Hall of Photography included new dioramas such as the one in Figure 4-27, showing one of the first photojournalists, Roger Fendon, documenting the Crimean War.[191] Other scenes showed photographers exploring and taking pictures of scenes in the American West and the interior of the first darkroom. Visitors could enjoy sampling an early penny arcade or see how their portrait would have looked if made using the tintype process.

The Luce Hall of News Reporting (1973)

The new Luce Hall on the third floor surveyed the history of news reporting from the colonial era to the present. It opened on 1 May 1973.[192] It was the museum's first attempt at an interactive multimedia exhibition. The artifacts were chosen to show how advancing technology continually made reporting the news more current and impactful. This subject lent itself well to an eclectic collection of objects and many new styles of exhibitry. At the entrance, visitors saw a replica of a 1910 Charles Ludwig news wagon, which had sold newspapers from around the world. Old-fashioned

Figure 4-27. Photographic documentation of the Crimean War.

Figure 4-28. Display of different forms of tintypes.

television sets broadcast news clips, newspapers papered the walls, and a small movie theater played newsreels.

Although the exhibition quickly became a hit with visitors, it had a somewhat rocky debut. Museum Director Daniel Boorstin had invited a small group of special guests to an intimate dinner in the hall just prior to the opening. Since the new hall was all about quick access to news, thought Boorstin, why not bring in some live news? He arranged for a color-TV hookup, so that they could all watch President Richard Nixon deliver his first public speech on the Watergate scandal. Together the guests, including Nixon appointees, heard the president try to distance himself from the affair, saying that there could be "no whitewash at the While House," and that he was "determined that we should get to the bottom of the matter, and that the truth should be fully brought out—no matter who was involved."[193] The speech drew laughs from some attendees, gasps from others, but no comments on the record for a *Washington Post* reporter who had been invited.

Figure 4-29. Entry to the Luce Hall of News Reporting.

Figure 4-30. The *Television News* display.

Figure 4-31. A printing demonstration in the updated Hall of Graphic Arts.

Figure 4-32. The job printing shop and type foundry.

Hall of Printing and Graphic Arts (1972)

Next to the Luce Hall was the revamped Hall of Printing and Graphic Arts.[194] It still featured the Japanese printmakers, but now there were also four reconstructed eighteenth- and nineteenth-century shops with printing equipment that could be used for demonstrations by museum docents and staff.

These were an eighteenth-century print shop that included the Franklin press and a similar common press that museum staff operated, a mid-nineteenth-century type foundry showing how lead type was cast, a job printshop of about 1860 with four specialized hand presses, and a newspaper shop of ca. 1885. The display also featured a selection of 20 patent models that illustrated improvements in nineteenth-century press design.

Hall of Postal History (1973)

Like the other revised halls, the Hall of Postal History benefited by the addition of more settings, including this nineteenth-century store counter where the postmaster-storekeeper sorted mail.[195] These settings helped visitors visualize how mail delivery changed dramatically over time. A new section, Stamps and the Mails, explored the constant search for speed in moving mail by using major national transportation systems and mechanical mail-handling devices.

Figure 4-33. Recreation of a nineteenth-century postmaster's office.

Hall of Money, Medals, and Medallic Arts (1972)

The Hall of Money, Medals, and Medallic Arts, which opened in July 1972, added new settings illustrating stages in coin-making. Near the entry was a reproduction of a coin stamper designed by Leonardo da Vinci and a geometric lathe. Of great interest to numismatists were gold coins from the Josiah K. Lilly collection that had been donated to the Smithsonian in 1968.[196] It included 6,125 coins valued at over $5 million and was thought to be the largest collection of gold coins ever amassed by an American collector.

Figure 4-34. The revised entry to the Hall of Money, Medals, and Medallic Arts.

Other Notable Exhibitions

Do It the Hard Way: Rube Goldberg and Modern Times (1970)

Do It the Hard Way was a temporary exhibition personally conceived by Director Daniel Boorstin. It celebrated the work of American cartoonist Rube Goldberg.[197] Goldberg was famous for his outrageous imaginary inventions: amusingly complicated machines for solving simple problems. In 1970, displaying the works of a cartoonist was unusual for the Museum of History and Technology, but Boorstin had made a career out of focusing on the seeming minutiae of American life. As he said at the exhibition opening,

> There have been exhibits of Einstein and Dr. Salk and Isaac Newton, but the exhibits here show us not only how to enrich and deepen man, but now how to amuse him. This show is about the ways we've discovered to give ourselves a headache. It tells us where technology leads us and misleads us, and touches the life of every American.[198]

Do It the Hard Way featured hundreds of Goldberg's original cartoons, as well as sculptures and even two full-sized functioning Goldberg machines: one that would snap a visitor's picture for a dollar, and another that stamped out copies of Goldberg's signature. Of course, these machines could not be true representations of Goldberg's ideas, which usually featured live animals and people, or materials unsafe for a museum, such as fire or explosives.

Here's how the picture-snapping machine supposedly worked:

> As you sit on pneumatic cushion (A), you force air through tube (B) which starts ice-boat (C), causing lighted cigar butt (D) to explode balloon (E). Dictator (F), hearing loud report, thinks he's been shot and falls over backward on bulb (G), snapping picture![199]

Figure 4-35. The Rube Goldberg exhibition.

Figure 4-36. The unusual display style of *If We're So Good, Why Aren't We Better?*

The version on display used a three-foot-tall model of a dictator and a pin for the lighted cigar. It didn't work very well on a regular basis, but fortunately it did manage to snap a photo of Goldberg himself, who attended the exhibition preview.[200]

Critics complained that the devices, even when they were working, were gimmicky, with one stating that the picture-snapping machine was "no more whimsical than any four-for-a-quarter bus station photography machine."[201] Ultimately, *Do It the Hard Way* faced the same struggles that many exhibitions from this era did: clever ideas, but more difficult to implement than anticipated.

If We're So Good, Why Aren't We Better? (1972)

If We're So Good, Why Aren't We Better? was an unusual temporary exhibition in that it was suggested by the Nixon administration to support a political agenda.[202] In the early 1970s, President Nixon appointed a National Commission on Productivity to address an approaching economic depression. Administration officials contacted the museum and offered to pay for an exhibition that addressed the topic of productivity. The exhibition focused on articulating the concept and examining its advantages and disadvantages.

The resulting display became controversial. Besides contradicting the policy that the museum should not involve itself in politics, the exhibition was unlike any other in the museum: it was neither historical nor technological. It did not even contain many historical objects. Instead, exhibit designer Ivan Chermayeff (from the design firm Chermayeff & Geismar, which later designed *A Nation of Nations*) created enormous props to act as metaphors for economic processes. Visitors found a life-sized cutout of a homemaker baking a pie, along with her tools and materials;

an eight-foot-wide apple pie; fiberglass Paul Bunyan boots as tall as the ceiling; and a "hazard wall," where simulated steel balls fell down a wall-sized pinball machine. These were all intended to represent different parts of the story of productivity in America. In retrospect it was deemed an inappropriate endeavor. The museum never produced another exhibition of this sort.

Edison: Lighting a Revolution (1979)

One exhibition mounted a few years after 1976 should be included in this era because of its longevity and its focus on the nation's best-known inventor. In 1979, for the 100th anniversary of Thomas Edison's invention of the lightbulb, the museum opened an addition to its *Electricity* exhibition.[203] *Lighting a Revolution* traced the development of electricity through the nineteenth century, with a focus on the work of Edison. Most significantly, it included an original Edison light bulb, used by the inventor himself as part of a public demonstration of his new lighting system. Indeed, *Lighting a Revolution* argued that Edison should be remembered more for creating this system than for simply inventing a light bulb. It further showed how electrical power was later applied to industry, homes, and transportation. The installation of the hydroelectric power plant at Niagara Falls, the world's first large-scale generating plant, was used as a concluding example.

Another section of the exhibition highlighted how electricity was used in the home. The toasters, electric fans, and waffle irons on display added whimsy and familiarity to the more technical sections. Although the original Hall of Electricity has long since been closed, *Lighting a Revolution* stayed on display for more than 40 years and remains open as this book goes to press.

New Visitor Experiences

Early exhibitions at the U.S. National Museum and the Museum of History and Technology were designed to be instructive. They were intended to lead visitors through history, showing examples of how clothing or ceramics or electrical equipment have changed over time. But the new exhibitions of the bicentennial era had additional goals. They were designed to give audiences emotional as well as intellectual experiences. Curators hoped that visitors walking through the museum would feel recognition, nostalgia, familiarity, awe, and wonder.

This aim of making history feel personal and relevant was directly tied to the museum's overall emphasis on a new form of patriotism. In earlier years, its exhibitions had focused simply on technological prowess and advancement, presenting a view of America as a successful world power. The patriotism of the bicentennial exhibitions, however, was rich and complex: *1876* prompted reflection on the past and nostalgia for the "golden years" of America, while *A Nation of Nations* promoted diversity, inclusion, and triumph over adversity. Most of all, the museum now sought to make visitors from across the country feel that they belonged in America and America belonged to them.

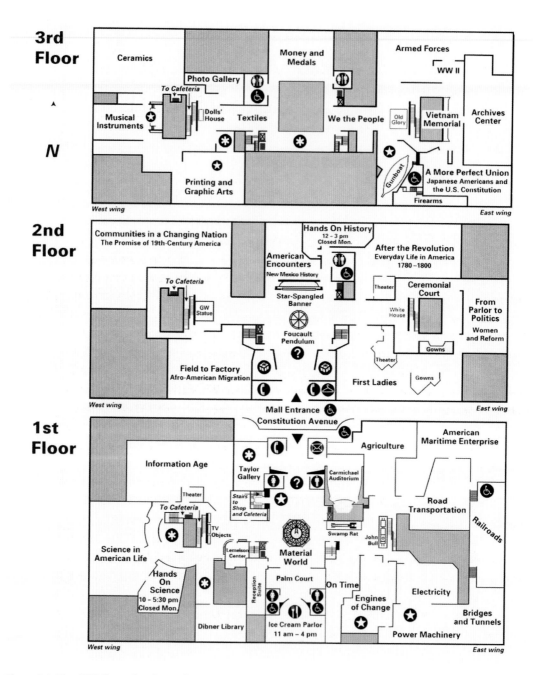

Figure 5-1. The 1999 floor plan shows the major exhibitions visitors would find in the museum in that year.[204] Although some had been inherited from earlier periods, the array was the culmination of trends and changes made during the 22 years when Roger Kennedy and his deputy director and successor, Spencer Crew, served sequentially as museum directors.

CHAPTER 5

A National Museum of American History (1979–2001)

The Era

In 1980, the National Museum of History and Technology was renamed the National Museum of American History (NMAH). This signaled a major shift in its exhibitions. They would now focus more on social and cultural themes than on the "increase of knowledge." This was true even in technology exhibitions, which now focused less on innovations that had increased American productivity, efficiency, and capacity, and more on social change.

During this era, which extended from 1979 to 2001, the museum worked to make its exhibitions more visitor-friendly and inclusive, by devoting greater attention to diverse communities, women, African Americans, Latinos, and Asian Americans. The new exhibitions gave visitors more opportunities for involvement, by using audiovisual components and interactive elements. Finally, displays on popular culture and entertainment were added to the museum's traditional subjects, following the introduction of this topic to the museum in A Nation of Nations. The popular-culture artifacts and exhibitions quickly became some of the most beloved displays.

The floor plan we chose to epitomize the era dates from 1999, when all these changes were in place. We organized our discussion of the new exhibitions by type, and then by opening date. Besides new exhibitions, the museum now had an ice-cream parlor, a bookstore, a hands-on history center, a hands-on science center, and a recreated setting from the 1912 White House. Such revisions had become increasingly expensive, even as the federal government reduced support for cultural institutions. Like other Smithsonian museums, the National Museum of American History had to raise millions of dollars of private funds during this era to pay for the design and construction of large exhibitions with their increasingly expensive components. Developing productive, ethical relations with private sponsors brought a range of new opportunities, but also many challenges.

Prelude: Collecting Popular Culture

On 13 February 1980, actor Henry Winkler came to the National Museum of American History to donate a leather jacket he wore as Arthur Herbert "Fonzie" Fonzarelli (or "the Fonz") in the popular television show *Happy Days*. A nostalgic sitcom about teenage life in the mid-1950s through 1960s, it ran on the ABC network from 1974 to 1984, peaking as the number-one television show in 1976 to 1977.

Teenage girls at the donation ceremony went wild and screamed when they saw the Fonz in person, reported the *Washington Post*. A sixteen-year-old even "announced the event would inspire her for life."[205] When asked about adding Fonzie's jacket to the collection, Roger Kennedy, the new director of the museum, said, "The history of this country is everybody's history, not just fancy people's history. And the Fonz is part of America's history."

Fonzie's jacket soon went on display in the exhibition *A Nation of Nations*. In subsequent years, donations of similar popular-culture items, including Jerry Seinfeld's puffy shirt from *Seinfeld* and Halle Berry's Storm costume from *X-Men*, became regular events at the museum and always drew both a local crowd and nationwide publicity.

GIFT FROM THE FONZ . . . *Henry Winkler, the cool dude of TV's "Happy Days" sitcom, was anything but cool when he donated his leather jacket to MHT's history of entertainment collection. It was, he said, one of the "truly thrilling moments" of his life. Curator Carl Scheele was solemn about the jacket, which he said "evokes the spirit of the 1950s."*

Figure 5-2. Winkler's donation was featured in the March 1980 *Smithsonian Torch*, the institution's in-house newspaper.

Figure 5-3. The Fonz's jacket became a visitor highlight when it went on view in *A Nation of Nations*. The label links the actor's family background to the exhibition's theme of immigration.

Another popular-culture object that visitors found displayed in *A Nation of Nations* in 1980 was a pair of the ruby red slippers that Judy Garland wore in the 1939 film *The Wizard of Oz* as the character Dorothy Gale. Unlike Fonzie's jacket, however, the slippers had arrived quietly in the museum a year earlier. They were given by a donor who wished to remain anonymous. The individual had written the museum saying simply, "if the Smithsonian is interested in receiving [the Ruby Slippers] as a gift...please contact me."[206] It was a substantial gift! The slippers had been purchased at an MGM auction nine years

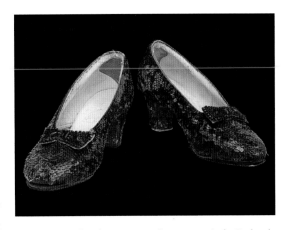

Figure 5-4. Ruby slippers worn by actress Judy Garland in *The Wizard of Oz*.

earlier for $15,000 and had increased in value since then.[207] The museum was delighted to obtain them.

Fonzie's jacket gradually lost its visitor appeal as the TV show ended and reruns became somewhat less popular. Dorothy's slippers, in contrast, proved to have an enduring place in public memory. They had not come to the museum until 40 years after *The Wizard of Oz* first appeared in theaters. Even in 1980, however, many visitors thought they rivaled—if not exceeded—the Star-Spangled Banner as the objects they most wanted to see. Why did visitors find them so meaningful? Dwight Blocker Bowers, longtime curator of the museum's entertainment collections, gave this answer:

> First of all, the slippers are bathed in the nostalgia generated by shared memory; for the innocence of youth and a deep appreciation of the film's central message, "There's no place like home." Second, they represent the Technicolor glamour of the golden age of the Hollywood studio system, where the best actors were turned into glittering stars and the production values were the best money could buy. Third, they are part of the bittersweet biography of the actress who first wore the shoes, the legendary Judy Garland; in fact, Garland's career and life often seemed to parallel Dorothy's elusive pursuit of the happiness envisioned in the dreamland her character imagined over the rainbow, where "troubles melt like lemon drops away above the chimney tops."[208]

Ellen Roney Hughes, another curator who later exhibited the slippers, saw them as objects that exemplified the broader transformation of the museum as it changed its name to the National Museum of American History and sought to follow new trends in American historical studies.

> This new social and cultural history promoted the study of events, artifacts, and cultural expressions closer to ordinary Americans' experience in both the distant and more recent past... [The museum's name change] reflected the

new trend in museums, academia, and the history profession at large away from focusing exclusively on customary subjects such as political, military, and technology history toward opening up to the examination of issues of immigration, community life, work, education, sports, and entertainment.[209]

Roger Kennedy, Spencer Crew, and Transforming the Museum

Changing the museum's name was the idea of Roger Kennedy. He became director in October 1979 and remained in the position for 13 years, longer than any other leader in the museum's history except the founding director, Frank Taylor. He was also the second and last director to be chosen by S. Dillion Ripley, who himself served as secretary for 20 years. Kennedy had an extremely varied background: lawyer, politician, banker, newsman, television producer, historical author, and vice president of the Ford Foundation. However, he had never previously worked in a museum or created an exhibition.[210]

Changing the name required not only approval of the secretary and regents of the Smithsonian, but also an act of Congress. The law authorizing it was signed by President Jimmy Carter on 13 October 1980.[211] Kennedy stated, "Our new name clarifies rather than changes what has always been the museum's basic mission—to illuminate, through collections, exhibitions, research, publications and educational programs, the entire history of the United States, including the external influences that have helped shape our national character."[212] As Figure 5-6 shows, Kennedy did not replace the marble where the original name, "Museum of History and Technology," was inscribed. He just covered it with printed banners—which stayed in place for decades.

Many staff at the museum were concerned that the change signified far more than a "clarification." Rather, they thought it signaled a reduced emphasis on science,

Figure 5-5. Roger Kennedy, who changed the name of the museum to the National Museum of American History.

Figure 5-6. Banner indicating the new name of the museum.

technology, and engineering history and an increased focus on social and cultural history. Despite denials by Kennedy, this concern was well founded and was ultimately reflected in the new exhibitions that populated the museum in the 1980s and 1990s.

The name change itself was not the only cause of this transition. Equally, if not more important, was the new generation of curators Kennedy hired who brought with them commitment to a "new social history" that was becoming standard in American universities. Increased focus on social context, racial and ethnic diversity, and social construction of American history were growing trends in the historical profession in general. This was true not only in areas such as political history and American studies, but even in the growing discipline of history of science and technology. New curators in this field focused less on studying scientific and technical methods and innovations and more on the social context and societal significance of technical change. Their research and thinking flowed into the exhibition designs and choices of artifacts that museum visitors would now see.

Before Kennedy arrived, the acting director, Otto Mayr, had sent him a detailed 10-year plan for revitalizing the museum's exhibitions. The museum's curators had labored over it for many months.[213] In their minds, the bulk of what the museum should continue to display was "halls" of its major collections, not topical thematic exhibitions. Kennedy succinctly thanked them for the plan, but then largely ignored

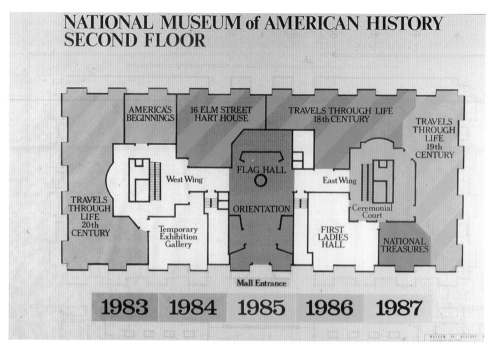

Figure 5-7. Roger Kennedy's second-floor exhibition plan, early 1980s.

it. He was determined not only to rename the museum, but also to follow an entirely different approach. The most important elements of this involved a complete overhaul of the second floor of the museum, where the principal bicentennial exhibitions had been located. Figure 5-7 shows an early working diagram of what he hoped to create.

The essence of the plan was a series of chronological exhibitions or "travels" through centuries of American life: America's beginnings, then the eighteenth, nineteenth, and twentieth centuries. The ever-popular first ladies gallery would be included here, as well as a changing exhibit space. Moreover, this bold revamping was to take only five years—not ten.

Kennedy was an architectural historian. Besides planning changes in the museum's exhibitions, he aimed to make major alterations in its central spaces, beginning with the iconic Flag Hall.[214] In 1981, the museum initiated a two-year conservation project in which the flag was carefully examined and cleaned. Kennedy contracted a New York designer to develop a dramatic new way to show the flag that would help protect it from dust, dirt, and prolonged light exposure. Beginning in June 1983, instead of being able to see the Star-Spangled Banner on view at any time, visitors had to schedule their stop there during a five-minute period every hour on the half-hour to see an opaque screen slowly drop and reveal the flag, then cover it back up. While watching, they heard two nineteenth-century renditions of "The Star-Spangled Banner" played on period instruments, reminding them of the flag's long history.

Equally surprising was the new location of the Foucault pendulum, whose bob now traced its daily course directly in front of the flag. For the first 23 years of the museum's history, the pendulum had swung dramatically on the first floor. The logic

Figure 5-8. The new Star-Spangled Banner installation, with the cover down. Note the changed location for the Foucault pendulum.

Figure 5-9. Entry to the *Material World* exhibition. In the foreground (*left*) is a 1912 Liberty-Brush Runabout.

behind this design was that the pendulum represented technology, the principal subject of the first floor, while the flag represented history, the subject of the second floor.

Now these two symbols were together, presumably symbolizing the new unity of the museum—yet they never worked as effectively in this configuration. The pendulum in its new location lost its impact, and in a few years was removed. Ever since, the flag alone has been the signature object in the museum.

On the first floor, visitors now saw an introductory exhibition entitled *A Material World*. Its goal was to challenge them to consider the importance of materials developed throughout history and used to make everyday objects, such as automobiles, tools, and building materials. As Director Kennedy told the *Washington Post*,

> We were sure that we needed a different kind of introduction to the museum.... An introduction that said, "Wait. Stop. Don't think first about association with great people and don't even think first about the new social history. Think first about *it*, the *thing*. Look at the thing."[215]

Other sections showed how the same type of object changed in both form and structure over time as materials and technology changed. One popular illustration of this was a juxtaposition of washing machines, made first with wood and iron, and later with plastics, alloys, and electronics.

Overall, the exhibition was a fascinating and eclectic array of stuff that perhaps only the Smithsonian could have pulled together. Yet many wondered whether it really served effectively as an introduction to the museum, and whether it was too dense and packed with objects for display in a central area.

Figure 5-10. Comparison of materials used in washing machines.

Figure 5-11. The palm court on the first floor, with artificial skylights above.

Visitors seeking a respite from this intensity could go behind the exhibition, where Kennedy had installed the recreation of an early twentieth-century palm court, complete with a Horn & Hardart automat from Philadelphia and the interior of Stohlman's Confectionary Shop from Washington, D.C., which previously had been displayed in *Everyday Life in the American Past*. In this nostalgic setting, visitors could sit and listen to period music or eat ice-cream treats.

The Major New Exhibitions

After the Revolution: Everyday Life in America, 1780–1800 (1985)

After the Revolution was the first of Roger Kennedy's attempts to provide an overview of the history of the nation through a series of chronological exhibitions. It was the only one of the four he planned that would be completed during his tenure.

Visitors began in an introductory theater, where a film briefly summarized the scope of the exhibition. Its goal was to provide "new views on the range of cultures and ways of life in the United States during the last 20 years of the 18th century." Three themes dominated: diversity, conflict, and everyday life.[216]

This was not the story of the political elite, or rich planters and merchants, or even the middle class, but a broad sweep of the population. It explored how four cultural groups struggled to maintain old traditions while adapting to new ways of life: Anglo-Americans, African Americans in the Chesapeake region, the Seneca Nation of the Iroquois Confederacy, and the citizens of Philadelphia, including craftsmen and free Black people. As the curatorial team wrote, "The installation discusses conflicts over goals as the result of choices people made and how these decisions affect their lives in an uncertain world. Their choices, conflicts, and aspirations are the foundation for the America we know today."[217] The exhibition overall displayed more than 1,000 artifacts.

In many respects, it was a revamping and expansion of *Everyday Life in the American Past*, which it replaced. After viewing the introductory film, visitors exited into one period room and then walked past two more. All these had been displayed in

Figure 5-12. The home of Thomas and Elizabeth Springer.

the earlier exhibition, but they had now been reinterpreted to share details of the families who lived in them and how they related to broader society. First came the log cabin of Delaware farmers Thomas and Elizabeth Springer; then the home of Tidewater, Virginia, planters Henry and Ann Saunders; and finally, the home of a merchant in Longmeadow, Massachusetts. New research showed that this third, previously thought to be the home of a joiner named Reuben Bliss, more likely was from the residence of merchants Samuel and Lucy Colton. This research itself indicated the growing trend in the museum toward greater attention to social history.

In *Everyday Life*, these homes had been presented as examples of how "ordinary" middle-class Americans lived in the early years of the republic. Now, however, they were relabeled and supplemented with displays on the lives of African Americans and Native Americans in these same years. Curators struggled to find detailed narratives of their histories, or objects that had been used by identifiable individuals, but they were determined to include their stories. This was a significant step forward in making the museum more inclusive.

The largest area of the display focused on Philadelphia, the leading city in America in this period and the nation's capital from 1790 to 1800. Highlighted were the diversity of peoples, trades, crafts, professions, and ways of life in the city. Visitors saw imported goods, objects from the new American government, religious artifacts, and tools used by skilled artisans. This section also included an operating print shop and a tavern area. Two study galleries were devoted to "British Ceramics in Maryland," and "Getting Dressed: Fashionable Appearance."

Figure 5-13. Examples of African American material culture.

Figure 5-14. Material culture from America's largest city at the time, Philadelphia.

Figure 5-15. Artifacts related to Richard Allen's African American Methodist Episcopal Church.

Particular attention was devoted to the story of Richard Allen, a highly accomplished enslaved man who had been able to purchase his freedom and had gone on to establish the Bethel African American Methodist Episcopal Church in Philadelphia. For this story, visitors could see objects on loan from the church and from the museum's own collection that related specifically to Allen's dramatic journey from enslaved individual to free man to church leader.[218]

Figure 5-16. Visitors enjoying the expanded Hands on History Room.

A new museum feature in the exhibition was the Hands on History Room. Here visitors, especially young people, could try on replicas of colonial clothes, touch and explore reproductions of artifacts of the period, and engage in a range of planned activities, such as ginning cotton. As the museum soon learned, this form of visitor amenity required a much higher level of staffing than it had devoted to exhibitions previously. However, the room was so popular with visitors that it was later expanded and remained in operation when *After the Revolution* closed.

Engines of Change: The American Industrial Revolution, 1790–1860 (1986)

New technology exhibitions in this period, like political and social history exhibitions, reflected the museum's movement from collections-based to theme-based presentations. *Engines of Change* explored how the Industrial Revolution transformed American lives.[219] Here, visitors began with a display of American technology similar to that shown at the famous 1851 Crystal Palace Exhibition in London's Hyde Park. This had been the first of the many world's fairs that would occur periodically over the next century and a half in Europe and America. The original Crystal Palace Exhibition included over 100,000 objects from 15,000 contributors. Britain was by far the largest exhibitor. Yet, for the first time, American technology gained international recognition, and Americans received a high number of prizes for their level of participation. How had the still-young nation developed to the point where it could compete with its European rivals?

Visitors learned that the answer was complicated. Instead of focusing simply on industrial progress, *Engines of Change* explored how technological development was

Figure 5-17. Entry to *Engines of Change*.

also shaped by social and cultural change. In addition to presenting the machines themselves and how they functioned, it discussed the people who invented, built, owned, and operated them.

Having sampled American achievements in 1851, visitors jumped back to 1790 to follow ways the new American nation had fostered technological progress. They learned that Americans had an abundance of land and resources, but also a labor shortage. Inventors and entrepreneurs had to create efficient tools to help a sparse population accomplish more with less. These included new manual devices for craftsmen and also powered machinery to grind grain, cut wood, spin cotton and wool, and shape wood and metal. The water and animal power that initially drove these machines was subsequently replaced by more reliable engines propelled by steam. On view were Samuel Slater's spinning frame and the John Bull locomotive, both of which helped transfer English technology to the United States.

Visitors saw the recreated machine shop of Augustus Alfred, a Connecticut clockmaker and machinist; a pin-making machine; and a scale model of a locomotive works in Philadelphia. Videos let them see these machines in operation. Periodically, the museum even operated some of the historic machines, using compressed air to run them instead of steam. Displaying machines in operation had long been a hallmark of the museum. However, this became the last major exhibition to try to keep such large artifacts operational. Ultimately, the maintenance cost led to these operations being scaled back long before the exhibition closed.

One display showed how the arms industry was a leader not only in creating specialized machinery and using interchangeable parts but also in establishing rules and regulations that helped make workers more efficient.

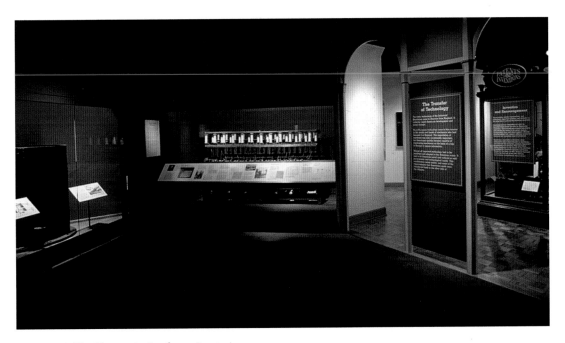

Figure 5-18. The Slater spinning frame (*center*).

Figure 5-19. The machine shop.

Figure 5-20. Concluding case display showing a cornucopia of new American industrial products.

The exhibition concluded with a case showing the cornucopia of manufactured objects that were flowing into American society in 1860. The display also highlighted a description of the changing American working class and a discussion of the human, social, and environmental costs of industrial development. Whereas the earlier Museum of History and Technology had trumpeted American growth and progress, this exhibition claimed only that industrialization brought change, with its many dimensions.

Field to Factory: Afro-American Migration, 1915–1940 (1987)

Visitors to *Field to Factory* found an exhibition that had no precedent at the museum: a display focused entirely on experiences of one racial minority group, African Americans. Kennedy, as well as many others, thought that their history been neglected for too long.

The display summarized the Great Migration, the movement of hundreds of thousands of African Americans from the rural South to northern cities in the quarter-century before World War II.[220] They went north for many reasons. Most sought increased economic opportunities in factories, businesses, or shops. Others were fleeing Southern prejudice and the oppression of Jim Crow laws. The exhibition was laid out so that as visitors saw it, they would retrace this historic journey for themselves.

In the first major section of the exhibition, they saw a tenant farmhouse as it

Figure 5-21. Setting taken from a real home of African American tenant farmers in Maryland in the 1920s.

would have appeared in rural Maryland in 1920. Its basic elements were taken from a real home. Although some tenants might have had a few luxuries, such as a phonograph player, they generally lived a life of back-breaking work and poverty. Exhibition designer Jim Sims drew on his background in theatrical set design to make the settings in the exhibition compelling and provocative.

Another setting, which was recreated, focused on the significant role of the church in shaping the lives of African Americans in the South.

Many of those who went north traveled by train. Visitors followed this same path. Along the way, they had a memorable experience that was common in the segregated South, but which many of them had never felt. To go into the train station setting, they had to choose between a doorway marked "White" or one marked "Colored." This made segregation personal and experiential.

Having arrived in the North, visitors learned about urban life in this period and what sort of jobs were available to African Americans, such as working on the line at a Ford Motor Company plant. Many women could find jobs only in domestic service. Although in their new environments they had escaped the worst of the Jim Crow laws, African Americans still often ended up living in ghettos in large cities such as Chicago or Philadelphia. They created their own robust political and social organizations, but often found that life in the North was not all they had hoped. The conclusion of the exhibition asked visitors, "Was it worth it?" The answer was indefinite, because it depended on individual circumstances.

Figure 5-22. Recreated setting of an African American church in the South.

Figure 5-23. Life in the North for African American migrants.

The curator behind this pathbreaking exhibition was Spencer Crew, whose scholarly expertise was in African American urban history. He began at the museum as a research fellow in 1981 and later became a curator and department chair. Kennedy named him deputy director in 1991.[221] Upon Kennedy's retirement in 1994, Crew became acting director and later succeeded Kennedy as director of the museum, the first member of any minority community and the first African American to fill the position. He later went on to head the National Underground Railroad Museum in Cincinnati, Ohio, and to assist with the creation of the Smithsonian's National Museum of African American History and Culture.

Figure 5-24. Spencer Crew with African American artifacts.

A More Perfect Union (1987)

On 1 October 1987, the museum opened what would become one of the most celebrated, but controversial, exhibitions in its history: *A More Perfect Union: Japanese Americans and the U.S. Constitution*. It was mounted as a surprising yet thoughtful commemoration of the bicentennial of the U.S. Constitution in 1987. It explored constitutional guarantees for legal protection of American citizens through a case history of the approximately 120,000 men, women, and children of Japanese ancestry who were relocated to internment camps[222] during World War II. Of these, 75,000 were Japanese American citizens, and another 45,000 were Japanese nationals who had long been denied citizenship because of their race.[223]

The exhibition resulted from three developments. For several years, the museum had been planning a major exhibition on the history of citizen soldiers in America, from the American Revolution to the present. The plan was to explore how traditional American resistance to standing armies had led to a continuing reliance on militias and conscription, and how that shaped the character of the military and the nation.

In the course of research on this topic, curators in the Division of Armed Forces History had devoted focused attention to the U.S. Army's 442nd Regimental Combat Team in World War II, which was composed almost entirely of Japanese Americans, many of whom had been sent with their families to internment camps. Roger Kennedy was aware of this research and was particularly interested in the story.[224]

During the same period, Kennedy was in contact with leaders of the Japanese American community who were seeking support for legislation that would include both a formal apology for the wartime internment and compensation for the surviving detainees. These leaders included Mike Masaoka, an influential lobbyist and former head of the Japanese American Citizens League; Norman Mineta, who represented California's thirteenth district in Congress and was a Smithsonian regent; and Robert T. Matsui, who represented California's third district. Masaoka had served in the 442nd Regimental Combat Team during the war, and the latter two, who were younger, had been youths detained in the camps.

Finally, the museum was considering what exhibitions it should mount to recognize the bicentennial of the United States Constitution, which would be celebrated in 1987.

The intersection of these three circumstances led to a plan to focus the new exhibition solely on Japanese American internment during the war as an example of how the U.S. Constitution had been tested by this action. It would not only tell the story of their suffering, but also of how many Japanese American men had come out of the camps and willingly served in the military with great distinction and valor. The planned exhibition was initially called *With Liberty and Justice for All*.

Japanese American groups, including the Japanese American Citizens League, were anxious to help museum staff acquire or borrow artifacts as well gain access to numerous Japanese Americans who had been interned and had stories to share. Kennedy and other museum staff determined that linking an exhibition on this topic to the bicentennial of the Constitution would make it particularly timely and significant.

In March 1987, the museum publicly announced that it was planning the exhibition. This elicited some critical responses, particularly from veterans of the Pacific theater during the war, who were concerned that it would be overly negative, too focused on the contributions of one group, and inappropriate for the occasion. Some opponents were also decidedly racist in their criticism. Newspaper stories, on the other hand, largely applauded the museum's decision. In the museum's press announcement, Director Kennedy stated,

> The Constitution isn't a costume drama of the past upon which the curtain went down in 1789.... The major criticism that we anticipate comes from people who regard the Constitution as a closed book—those people who are fearful of any suggestion that this is an evolving culture and that it wasn't ever perfect and isn't and we've got to keep working awfully hard by admitting our errors.[225]

Even more important, the announcement stimulated interest and anticipation. Producing the exhibition required around $1 million of outside funding. With Mineta's and Matsui's help in the House of Representatives, and Senator Daniel Inouye's leadership in the Senate, the museum obtained the bulk of that funding from Congress. The rest came from private sources. Although the museum stayed out of lobbying for reparations legislation, the congressmen knew that a Smithsonian exhibition on the subject could help their cause, and they later used it to gain additional support.

Figure 5-25. Curator Tom Crouch in the first section of *A More Perfect Union*, showing a store closed due to the Japanese American owner's relocation.

When the exhibition opened in October, curator Tom Crouch discussed what it was designed to communicate in a museum press release:

> This is a story of grave injustice done to a group of Americas who, by virtue of their ancestry were denied basic civil rights guaranteed to all Americans. The irony of their plight is underscored by the participation of some 25,000 Japanese Americans in the U.S. armed forces during the war...
>
> Despite having suffered great hardship and trauma at the hands of their government, these people have worked within the system to remove the old barriers of racial prejudice. Our concern is that all Americans understand the importance of extending the safeguards and protections of the Constitution to every citizen, regardless of race, color or creed.[226]

The exhibition included six sections: Introduction, Issei: East to America, The Decision to Imprison a People, Life Behind Barbed Wire: The Internment Experience, Japanese Americans in the War: The Battlefield Connection, and The Quest for Justice. The final section, which related directly to an issue actively being debated in Congress, was highly unusual for a Smithsonian exhibition.

Figure 5-26. Artifacts and images from the relocation camps.

On display were more than 1,000 photographs and artifacts and two large reconstructed settings: a deserted Japanese American neighborhood following the evacuation, and a barracks in an internment camp, complete with furniture, dishes, clothing, and other original objects. Also included was artwork produced by camp residents. Five audiovisual programs provided first-person accounts from Japanese Americans who either lived in the camps or fought in the war. A combat scene focused on the exploits of the 442nd Regiment. This unit saw very heavy combat in Italy and became the most decorated unit of its type in the war.

Visitors found the exhibition powerful and emotional. They empathized with the pain of the forced relocation of Japanese Americans without due process, their hard life in remote internment camps, and the heroic contributions of many of them to American victory in Europe. The exhibition dramatically raised the question of whether interned Japanese Americans ever received justice from the government in the years following the war. Few visitors left unmoved.

Press response after the opening of the exhibition was generally positive. Elizabeth Kastor wrote in the *Washington Post* review, "'A More Perfect Union' may be the most sobering and intriguing—and certainly the most controversial—event to come out of the Constitution's anniversary."[227]

Japanese Americans were attracted by the thousands. Many other visitors learned about this episode of American history for the first time, as it was rarely covered in textbooks or American history classes in this period.

The following year, Congress passed and President Reagan signed the Civil Liberties Act of 1988, which officially apologized for the internment and granted each surviving internee about $20,000 in compensation. It stated that the government

Figure 5-27. Audiovisual program of interviews with World War II Japanese American soldiers.

action had been based on "race prejudice, war hysteria, and a failure of political leadership," not legitimate security interests.[228] The exhibition likely played some part in stimulating its passage. *A More Perfect Union* stayed on display for over 16 years, until January 2004—far longer than originally planned. It unquestionably helped stimulate greater attention to the story of Japanese American internment in history books and American classrooms.

The United States government had established a National Commission on the Bicentennial of the United States Constitution in 1983, just as it had previously done for the American Revolution. The latter had been instrumental in the museum's transformation in the mid-1970s.

The Constitutional Bicentennial Commission spent millions of dollars on education programs across the nation Ironically, it played no part in the *A More Perfect Union* exhibition. However, it did fund a small political history exhibition at the museum entitled *The Blessing of Liberty*, which opened in September 1987, a month before *A More Perfect Union*.[229] This earlier exhibition focused on political institutions and voting-rights laws and included a selection of museum artifacts and a dozen posters developed jointly with the American Historical Association and the American Political Science Association. These were circulated to classrooms across the nation. While the legacy of *A More Perfect Union* lives on at the museum, this exhibition and poster series have largely been forgotten.

After *A More Perfect Union* opened, NMAH continued to collect artifacts related to the internment story and developed one of the richest collections on this topic in

Figure 5-28. Entry to 2017 Japanese American exhibition.

the nation. Years later, from February 2017 through March 2019, it opened a new, smaller exhibition to commemorate the 75th anniversary of Executive Order 9066, which President Franklin Roosevelt issued to authorize the internment. Like its predecessor, this second exhibition shared this important American story with millions of visitors.[230]

From Parlor to Politics: Women and Reform in America, 1890–1925 (1990)

Along with pioneering exhibitions exploring African American and Hispanic history, Kennedy mandated the museum's first broad exhibition on women's history: *From Parlor to Politics: Women in the Progressive Era, 1890–1925*. (The exhibition title was later changed to *From Parlor to Politics: Women and Reform in America, 1890–1925*.)[231] Originally intended as merely a temporary exhibition, it was soon extended indefinitely, just as *Field to Factory* had been. When announcing the extension in November 1990, Kennedy stated,

> This exhibition tackles two subjects we need to understand better—gender and race—matters which are not going away. . . . Because we have found that our audience is engaged by the way this exhibition deals with them, we've found the money to keep it going—indefinitely.[232]

The 4,500-square-foot exhibition focused on the role women played in motivating political action and demanding social reform in America in the late nineteenth and early twentieth centuries. Visitors saw over 700 objects and 275 photographs

Public Health: "Better Mothers, Better Babies, Better Homes"

Figure 5-29. The public health display.

focused on topics such as education, the women's temperance movement, women's suffrage, the home economics movement, public health, labor reform, social work, and peace activism. Among them were Frances Willard's traveling tea set, Susan B. Anthony's desk set and gavel, and Jane Addams's Nobel Peace Prize. The exhibition traced women's activities in the United States from talking politics at tea ceremonies to crusading for improved healthcare to fighting for voting rights.

One striking large object was Lucy Stone's suffrage wagon. Suffragists painted it with slogans and used it in rallies and to sell the *Woman's Journal*. It would be featured again in the *American Democracy* exhibition of 2017.

Near the conclusion, visitors passed through an area used for public programs that was based on Chicago's famous Hull House, where they saw textiles and furniture that had been created there. Jane Addams and Ellen Gates Starr founded Hull House in 1889, and it became nationally known as a community center for neighborhood poor and later as a center for social reform activities. Addams, a suffragist and a founder of the League of Women Voters, was awarded the Nobel Peace Prize in 1931.

The exhibition stressed that although the women it portrayed were idealistic, they were also shrewd realists. As curator Edith Mayo stated,

Figure 5-30. The women's suffrage wagon. The background mural was repurposed from the earlier *We the People* exhibition.

What distinguished these women was that they were very astute at lobbying, very effective at fundraising.... They were not going against the grain. Look at what they had to overcome. To win the right to vote, they had to get a constitutional amendment passed by not just a simple majority but a super majority of three-quarters of the states ratifying the amendment.... Women today are not aware of the relevance, the link between historic visibility and present political empowerment.[233]

Information Age (1990)

As the United States increasingly became an information society, Smithsonian leaders determined that the museum should replace its limited display of computers and communications with something far broader. *Information Age: People, Information, and Technology* was designed to be a bold new form of exhibition. Here, visitors were to experience the most interactive exhibition the Smithsonian had ever mounted. The exhibition team was challenged to employ advanced information technology to help tell the story of this dynamic sector of American life.[234]

In the resulting exhibition, visitors could use more than 40 computer or video stations to explore topics of interest to them, or often to see how a story related to themselves personally. Behind the scenes, over 50 computers, several dozen video disk players, and three computer networks ran the show. The museum had never tried anything like it before—nor, indeed, has it since.

Figure 5-31. A rotating carousel at the entry to *Information Age*. Some museum staff were shocked that the exhibition began with a humorous cartoon-like sculpture rather than a historic artifact.

As visitors entered the exhibition, they could scan an "interactive brochure," do it again at many locations, then create a personalized souvenir printout summarizing their visit when they left. At the display stations, they could find out what their life might have been like in 1890 (based on census data from that year), encode their name with the secret World War II Enigma machine, and scan their own fingerprint next to the very computer the FBI first used for analyzing prints of suspected criminals. They could even talk to volunteers who ran a live ham radio station.

Along with these new interactive experiences, the museum built an extensive traditional display of objects, images, and environments that explored both the historical causes of the information age and its social as well as technological effects. The exhibition featured over 700 artifacts from the museum's rich historical collection, including Samuel Morse's first telegraph, Alexander Graham Bell telephones, early radios and tubes, and a range of digital computers from mainframes to PCs. It included a street scene from New York in 1939, a World War II combat information center, and a multiscreen video-wall theater.

Chronologically, the first section of the exhibition stretched from the 1840s to the 1930s. Visitors learned that during this period, information *processing*—collecting and manipulating data, tabulating, calculating, and filing—involved both manual work and a range of electromechanical devices, such as typewriters and punched card machines.

Information *communication*, in contrast, was becoming electrified, and therefore instantaneous, through the advent of the telegraph, telephone, radio, and television.

Figure 5-32. Information processing before World War II.

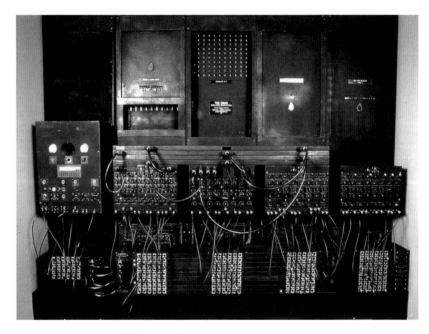

Figure 5-33. A section of the ENIAC computer.

Technological change accelerated during World War II, and visitors to the next section of the exhibition saw displays on mobile radio, radar, the first digital computers, and the atomic bomb. One of the highlights was the recreation of the ENIAC computer at the University of Pennsylvania, the machine that launched the computer industry in America. Visitors could not only see a large section of the machine, which originally filled a room 30 by 50 feet, but also hear descriptions of it from a video interview with J. Presper Eckert, the chief engineer on the project.

Pundits of this era predicted that after World War II, Americans would enter the atomic age, dominated by peaceful uses of the atom. Instead, the exhibition claimed, it became the information age, in which the processing power of digital computers and the speed of electronic communication created information networks that revolutionized society. This occurred in virtually all areas of American life, including science, education, business, entertainment, warfare, law enforcement, healthcare, and retail.

In the final section of the exhibition, visitors walked through examples of all these areas and were challenged to think not only about the power of the new technologies, but also how they affected issues such as privacy, security, automation, and individual identity. Were computers becoming too powerful and pervasive? Concluding displays focused on the development of personal computers, which brought the information age onto the desktop and into the home, and on the advent of the internet, which was just beginning to become widespread in American society.

In the press release for the exhibition, Smithsonian Secretary Robert McCormick Adams described the new display as

> one of the largest and most important exhibitions we have ever done.... Here, for the first time, we attempt to come to grips with fundamental changes going on all around us, transforming our lives with our own active involvement.... Behind many of the challenges we experience... the Information Age is probably the driving force in what has already differentiated us sharply from our grandparents.[235]

Figure 5-34. Post–World War II information technology applications.

Figure 5-35. Display of personal computers and associated marketing materials.

The exhibition was widely reviewed, and most reviews were positive. *Time* magazine reporter Eugene Linden wrote

> With 20/20 hindsight, it is tempting to view today's networked and digitized world as the inevitable culmination of [Samuel] Morse's breakthrough technology [of the electrical telegraph]. That would be a mistake, however. Technological change has been marked by fits, starts and left turns, and the clues to the future have often been hidden in the clutter of the present. That is the message of a new $10 million permanent exhibit at the Smithsonian Institution.[236]

Washington Post reporter Ken Ringle, however, found the interactivity in the exhibition problematic, in several ways.

> The exhibit…is very much an example of the phenomenon it tries to explain—or some might say, part of the problem.… [It] is a kind of mesmerized, gee whiz look at the hailstorm of data bytes increasingly pelting us (to which the exhibit, of course, contributes) and an almost total absence of reflection on the increasingly Orwellian aspects of our resulting society. One wonders if skepticism has come unplugged at the Smithsonian. Or been bought off.[237]

Marsha Mercer, a reporter from the *Richmond Times Dispatch*, wrote of the exhibition that she didn't just see it, she "interacted with it. The Information Age is a trip through time, a magical mystery tour of technology. It's also work, in the sense that a child's play is work."[238]

Heartwarming to the curators was the sort of comment that was submitted by a museum visitor a year later,

> I did not come to see your show, but to buy a gift. I was seduced in, and as a working computer professional since 1962, I must commend you on both a great job, and…a service to the history of our time. It gives me great pleasure to think my tax dollars are spent this way.[239]

Creating an exhibition of this size and scope had required over $10 million of financial donations and in-kind support. This was the most extensive fundraising the museum had ever done for an exhibition. Sponsorship had been part of the planning from the outset.

The idea for the display originated in a visit by Lewis Branscomb, chief scientist of IBM, to Smithsonian officials representing Secretary Dillion Ripley in January 1984.[240] IBM wanted to encourage the Smithsonian to develop a major new exhibition—or perhaps even a new museum—on the history of information technology. Branscomb indicated that IBM was willing to help pay for it. Smithsonian officials were keenly interested in the idea of an exhibition, but believed a new museum was unlikely.

Secretary Ripley responded to Branscomb's visit with a letter on 13 February 1984. He thanked Branscomb for his interest and committed the Smithsonian to work together with IBM on an exhibition on "the effects of the changes in information technology upon American society and the culture of the world." He stated further, "We are enthusiastic about working with you and with IBM toward a more ambitious program than that which we could ask the Congress alone to support."[241]

Initially the Smithsonian hoped that IBM might be its sole outside sponsor. However, the corporation was unwilling to take on this responsibility, not only because of the cost involved, but also because it believed that the exhibition should cover the broad information technology industry and should have a range of sponsors. The Smithsonian agreed. Ultimately, it received support from over 30 corporations, most notably IBM, Electronic Data Systems, Digital Equipment Corporation, Unisys, Hewlett Packard, Apple, and all the regional Bell telephone companies.[242] In addition, Electronic Data Systems volunteered a team of staffers to help program the interactive displays that museum staff had designed and to integrate the equipment that would run them. The team worked on site for several months before the exhibition opened and assisted operations for 10 years thereafter.

This fundraising approach set the pattern for all large displays that would follow in subsequent years. Indeed, both the U.S. Congress and Smithsonian leaders began to require it. Never again would the costs of major exhibitions at the museum be paid with federal funds alone. As later history would show, the museum had been wise to pursue the idea of having a variety of outside sponsors rather than just one. Single sponsorship inevitably raised the issue of who truly determined themes and content.

Figure 5-36. The entry to *American Encounters* reflected the architecture of New Mexican homes.

American Encounters (1992)

The year 1992 was the quincentenary of Columbus's "discovery" of America. Numerous commemorations were planned for this historic event in both North and South America. Yet, by the 1990s, many North Americans increasingly questioned whether Columbus's legacy should be celebrated. In retrospect, was the arrival of Europeans progress or a tragedy for native peoples? If NMAH were to mount an exhibition to commemorate this anniversary, what should it be?

Museum staff decided on a surprising answer. They would create an exhibition that would explore the history of New Mexico as a microcosm of Columbus's enduring impact on American history, focusing on the interactions of three groups: American Indians, Hispanic people, and Anglo-Americans. Not only would the exhibition present contrasting points of view of three distinct cultures, it would also bring to the museum a focus on the history of the American west, which had received scant attention in the building.[243]

Thus in 1992, visitors to the museum found the 3,800-square-foot display *American Encounters* to the left of the iconic Star-Spangled Banner. It included more than 500 examples of sculpture, weaving, and jewelry, as well as photographs documenting the diverse history of New Mexico.

The museum's new direction was clear in the main label:

This exhibition looks at some of the ways American Indians and Hispanics have interacted with each other and with Anglo-Americans in New Mexico

Figure 5-37. Interior of a Pueblo home in New Mexico.

Figure 5-38. Video theater focused on Pueblo resistance and self-determination.

for nearly 500 years. Often, these people's lives together have been shaped by fear, intolerance, and misunderstanding. They have suffered repression, discrimination, bloodshed, and loss of land, life, and liberty at each other's hands. They have also changed, adapted, and maintained their traditions, merged with one another, and forced others to acknowledge their right to exist. Today, they still struggle to retain their distinct identities and yet live side by side. Their story is not yet over; it is not just theirs, but ours as well.[244]

The exhibition included settings of family lives of the contrasting cultures, artifacts representing their faith traditions, and historic and contemporary craft objects. It juxtaposed the architectural styles of their homes and buildings.

Visitors could watch videos explaining historic events and varying perspectives, including the controversial role that Christianity had played in the development of the state.

Figure 5-39. One exhibit section focused on the role of Christianization in cultural interactions in New Mexico.

One section illustrated how distinctive New Mexican cultural objects had, in recent years, become popular souvenirs used to boost tourism to the "Land of Enchantment." A final display included a sampling of video interviews with individuals representing varied perspectives on the complex history of cultural integration in the state.

Speaking to the press after the opening of the exhibition, Director Kennedy stated that it had been among the most difficult and ambitious the museum had ever mounted, because it focused as much on human struggle as it did on cultural adaptation and coexistence. He noted, "It's not an altogether pleasant story, but life is not a pleasant story."[245] Like many "temporary" exhibitions mounted in this era, this one stayed on display for much longer than originally intended. It did not close until 2004.

First Ladies: Political Role and Public Image (1992)

The First Ladies Hall that had opened in 1964 ran for 22 years with only minor revisions and upgrades. For many years, it was the most popular exhibition in the building. As curator Edith Mayo, who would plan the subsequent 1992 exhibition, remarked, "For half the population who visited the Smithsonian... this was the only place they ever saw themselves as actors in American history."[246]

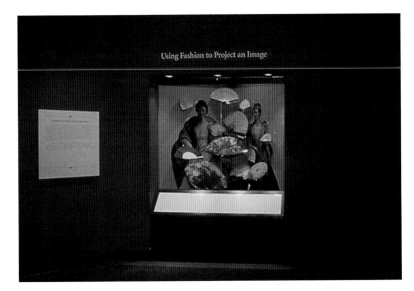

Using Fashion to Project an Image

Figure 5-40. A key theme of the exhibition was that fashion could be used politically.

By 1986, the exhibition needed a complete overhaul for both maintenance and object conservation, and it was closed. A year later, responding to popular demand, the museum opened a small temporary display showing gowns worn by Jacqueline Kennedy Onassis, Lady Bird Johnson, Patricia Nixon, Betty Ford, Rosalynn Carter, and Nancy Reagan. That closed in 1990, while a comprehensive new display was being completed.

Roger Kennedy's choice of Mayo as curator demonstrated his strong desire for the exhibition to be a radical change from its predecessor. The two wanted to make it a broad exploration of social and cultural history, not merely a collections-based display about fashion design and associated objects.

The resulting 8,000-square foot exhibition, entitled *First Ladies: Political Role and Public Image,* opened on 29 March 1992.[247] The 1964 exhibition had included a comprehensive set of dresses, one representing each of the first ladies from Martha Washington through Lady Bird Johnson. The minimal labeling focused on the dresses as objects, not the women who wore them. However, long exposure to light and hanging in fixed positions on mannequins had damaged the fabric on many of the dresses, and they needed extensive treatment.

In contrast, visitors would now find only 20 dresses on display, and they would be rotated over time. Eleven of them had not been shown before. The exhibition had a distinctively different organization—it was thematic rather than chronological. Moreover, it focused on the first ladies as political figures and social leaders. There were three broad sections: First Ladies: Political Role, The First Ladies Gown Collection, and Shaping the Public Image. Within these were six subsections that highlighted the diverse roles of first ladies as important leaders in American national life: Social Partner and the Nation's Hostess, Advocates of Social Causes, Promoters of Culture and Historic Preservation, First Ladies as Campaigners, Widowhood and National Mourning, and Capitalizing on the First Family. In the museum's press release about the project, Roger Kennedy said of the exhibition, "What we present is beautiful, but the story behind the beauty is sobering and provokes a lot of thought about power and people."[248]

To supplement the dresses, the exhibition included hundreds of photographs, memorabilia, and supporting artifacts such as china, silver, jewelry, furniture, buttons, campaign souvenirs, invitations, and White House menus.

The cases shown in Figures 5-40 to 5-42 illustrate the conceptual and design approach of the new exhibition.

The central display of the first ladies' dresses by themselves was simple and straightforward. It highlighted not only their design, but also issues of care and preservation.

Reviewers of the exhibition lauded the significance of the new approach. No one said it better than Michael Kilian of the *Chicago Tribune*:

> The Smithsonian Institute [sic] no longer treats America's first ladies like a bunch of dummies. From 1964 to 1987, its much visited First Ladies Hall exhibit…amounted to little more than a collection of mannequins wearing inaugural gowns.…A visitor [to the new exhibition] emerges with a feeling of knowing these women, at least as human beings. One also comes away with the sense that the pressures and burdens of their long-houred, unpaid job have, with few exceptions, served to make stronger and better human beings of them.[249]

In contrast to the bold new conceptual approach to the topic, the exhibition's design was less visually appealing to most visitors than the earlier presentation. They found no elaborate environments or settings. There were only flat wall displays of

Figure 5-41. First ladies became important figures in presidential campaigns.

graphics, traditional casework, and occasional cutout figures. Likely, this resulted primarily from funding limitations. The museum was able to raise only around a million dollars to help pay for the exhibition, from a private group, Friends of the First Ladies. This paled in comparison to the funds for other large exhibits of the era that had more elaborate presentations, such as *Information Age* and *Science in American Life*.

In part, the design strategy and content of the exhibition were also shaped by an adjacent display that had opened in 1989, *Ceremonial Court*. This installation reflected Kennedy's deep fascination with architectural history, the subject of many of his own historical writings. His director of design, Michael Carrigan, shared this interest and managed the production of this compelling space. It also served as an elegant new entry to the second-floor east wing.

Ceremonial Court provided a glimpse of the White House and objects associated with lives of American first families.[250] It was designed to resemble the cross hall of the White House after it was renovated in 1902 during Theodore Roosevelt's administration. It featured two trompe l'oeil paintings—one depicting the Roosevelt children at play on the Grand Staircase in the White House and the other depicting the State Dining Room. Original artifacts included plasterwork, mantels, giant mirrors, and crystal chandeliers that had come to the Smithsonian after a complete reconstruction and renovation of the White House during the 1950s. Also on view were examples of White House china, glassware, and tinware.

Dresses of the eight most recent first ladies were included in this exhibition and were not relocated to the new first ladies display when it opened three years later. Visitors who couldn't arrange a private tour of the White House could come to

Figure 5-42. Here, the First Ladies collection was addressed more from the perspective of preservation than fashion.

Figure 5-43. The opening section of *Ceremonial Court*.

Figure 5-44. The interior of *Ceremonial Court*.

Ceremonial Court to see presidential artifacts and to get an impression of the nation's most famous home. The exhibition also became an excellent location for intimate private events with museum friends and supporters.

In many ways, this linkage between *Ceremonial Court* and *First Ladies: Political Role and Public Image* foreshadowed the pairing, in the 2000s, of the presidency and first ladies exhibitions.

Figure 5-45. Laboratory of chemist Ira Remsen in the first section of the *Science in American Life* exhibition.

Science in American Life (1994)

Adjacent to *Information Age: People, Information, and Technology*, visitors in the late 1990s found the museum's newest and most extensive science exhibition, *Science in American Life*, which opened in 1994. Like other recent exhibitions, this was devoted to exploring social and cultural perspectives as well as technical ones. The museum's initial displays on physical science and technology had sought to illuminate and celebrate the growth of knowledge and the people who were responsible for it. In contrast, this presentation explored how science was affecting everyday life in America, and ways in which its role was increasingly being challenged.[251] The main theme of the exhibition was clearly stated in the introductory panel:

> Like politics, business, or religion, science is right in the thick of American history. Today, science and technology permeate American culture and daily life.
>
> Over the past 125 years, most Americans came to believe science and technology inevitably brought progress. As the 20th century ends people are less sure of this. They realize science can entail hazards as well as benefits. *Science in American Life* explores Americans' changing views of science and progress since 1876.[252]

The exhibition was divided into six historical sections, presented in chronological order, plus a separate learning center. The sections were Laboratory Science Comes to America, 1876–1920; Science for Progress, 1920–1940; Mobilizing Science for War, 1940–1960; Better than Nature, 1950–1970; Science in the Public Eye, 1970–Present; and Looking Ahead.

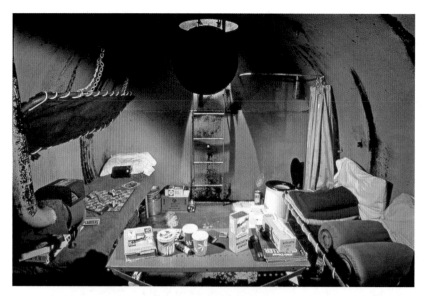

Figure 5-46. Interior of a backyard fallout shelter.

Figure 5-47. Birth-control pill display.

The content of the exhibition was broad and complex. On display were more than 900 objects, 600 historical photographs, and 20 computer and mechanical interactives. It included many examples of what anyone would consider triumphs of American science, among them the development of nylon, penicillin, microwave radar, plastics, and biotechnology products.

But much of the focus, particularly in the later sections, was on controversial aspects or products of modern science, including nuclear weapons, fallout shelters, insecticides, the birth-control pill, chlorofluorocarbons, and genetic engineering. The design and size of these latter sections emphasized these controversial subjects and how they had led Americans to question the role of science in society.

Figure 5-48. Superconducting Super Collider section.

One of the largest displays focused on the Superconducting Super Collider, a huge basic science research effort that Congress had canceled due to spiraling cost. Smithsonian curators saw this story as a compelling example of how the public was increasingly realizing that big science had to be closely scrutinized.

As the museum's press release stated, the exhibition was documenting "the shifts in American attitudes toward the idea of scientific and technological progress.... Judging the benefits and hazards of science and technology is no longer left to scientists. Science is a matter of public debate."[253]

Supplementing the main historical exhibition was the staffed Hands on Science Center where visitors—especially junior and senior high-school students—could conduct facilitated experiments or explore scientific principles through a range of activities. This continued and expanded a new approach to engaging visitors that had begun with the Hands on History Room associated with *After the Revolution*.

The learning center proved to be the most popular and successful section of the exhibition. In contrast, the historical section became one of the most controversial exhibitions the museum ever displayed. The controversy centered on the dissatisfaction felt by the American Chemical Society (ACS), which had donated $5.3 million to the museum and was the principal sponsor of the display. Unlike support arrangements before or after this point, the Smithsonian and the ACS had negotiated a contract that promised the ACS a major role in planning the exhibition, even while reserving final decisions on all content to the Smithsonian alone. At the outset, the goal was for the partnership to provide continuing support from the ACS to operate and maintain the exhibition during its lifetime, particularly the Hands on Science Center.

Over the four-year planning period, however, it became clear that the two organizations did not agree on what the historical sections should display and how

Figure 5-49. The Hands on Science Center.

the content should be presented. The process was trying for everyone. The exhibition team at the Smithsonian went through several reorganizations and leadership changes, and the original design firm planning it was replaced by internal designers.[254] Arthur Molella, head of the Department of Science and Technology, eventually took charge of the planning and successfully led the show to completion. He was assisted by curator Carlene Stephens, who served as codirector of the project. Throughout the process, the Smithsonian retained control over content decisions, but after the exhibition opening, the ACS spent several years lobbying the director of the museum and the Smithsonian secretary for significant changes.[255] While Smithsonian officials agreed that some alterations were appropriate, after long deliberation the two sides ultimately did not agree on what they should be.

In an 11 March 1996 article in the ACS *Chemical and Engineering News*[256], Joan E. Shields, who was chairman of the Special Board Committee on the Smithsonian Exhibition as well as chairman of the ACS Board of Directors, angrily announced that the ACS was giving up. She wrote that ACS representatives had ultimately submitted 40 changes they believed should be made, highlighting the top 10. They museum countered with a list of 35 changes, including many the ACS had not suggested. But the museum wanted ACS to help pay for them all, at a cost of $400,000. ACS refused, stating that the final changes were "trivial, nonsubstantive, and outrageously expensive."

Concluding the article, Shields summarized how the ACS now regarded the exhibition and the partnership with the Smithsonian:

> ACS did not expect a politically correct, revisionist historical display of
> science as a litany of moral debacles, environmental catastrophes, social

injustices and destruction by radiation, while at the same time ignoring the many triumphs, achievements, and contributions of science to our lives. This deconstructionist view of history seems to be pervading the Smithsonian and many other history museums today.

She also felt compelled to warn other potential donors to be careful in trying to work with the Smithsonian: "As one of the largest single donors to the Smithsonian, ACS feels an obligation to alert other potential private and corporate donors to the problems they will confront."

The highly negative conclusions of the ACS about the exhibition were shared by some reviewers, but others found the exhibition a refreshingly honest appraisal of the intersection of science and society, a welcome corrective to the overly positive ways that science had generally been presented at both the Smithsonian and most other museums in the past. In a thoughtful review of the exhibit, sociologist Thomas Gieryn concluded that the goal of achieving "balance" in an exhibition was often unattainable,

> curators and critics alike claim to seek balanced exhibitions, where sufficient materials are displayed for visitors to reach their own informed judgments about the place of science in society or the justifiability of dropping atomic bombs. But it is a precarious balance, undermined rather easily by counter-assertions that one is really using History to push a party line, squelching multiple interpretations in order to legitimize a reading that advances political interests.[257]

Surprisingly, little of the bitter debate over the exhibition seemed to affect how visitors to the exhibition responded to it. In 1995, the Smithsonian's Institutional Studies Office did an assessment of visitors to *Science in American Life*. Their findings stated:

> We found that the 16 minutes, on average, that visitors spent in the *Science in American Life* exhibition did not change their strongly positive attitudes towards science and technology nor their opinions on the key issues presented by the exhibition.[258]

The Smithsonian referenced this finding repeatedly when defending the exhibition to the ACS, but on closer scrutiny, it was a weak defense. Most visitors simply spent far too little time in the exhibition for it to affect views they held about science in society before they came.

Zahava D. Doering and Andrew J. Pekarik, who were involved in the study of the exhibition, used it in part to support an arresting 1996 article that provided important new insight about visitor behavior at the Smithsonian. They explained that no visitor enters an exhibition with a completely open mind, and in fact, many visitors don't primarily come to learn—the traditional assumption among exhibition planners at the museum. They wrote,

The internal story line that visitors enter with, which we can call their "entrance narrative," has three distinct components:
- A basic framework i.e. the fundamental way that individual construe and contemplate the world
- Information about the given topic, organized according to that basic framework
- Personal experiences, emotions, and memories that verify and support this understanding.

This model suggests that the most satisfying exhibitions for visitors will be those that *resonate with their experience and provide information in ways that confirm and enrich their view of the world.*

Assessing the implications of this notion, they concluded,

Instead of leading us toward questioning that will, in turn, bring about an adjustment in and engagement with what we know, *the interesting object can just as easily move us toward a rigid simplified understanding that may ultimately be more satisfying precisely because it requires less of us.*[259]

The fact that visitors had the freedom to move through exhibitions in any way they chose, and read only what interested them, made this possibility of reassurance rather than learning even more likely, especially if their visit was short.[260]

Communities in a Changing Nation:
The Promise of Nineteenth-Century America (1999)

This exhibition was the second of the set of broad chronological exhibitions that Roger Kennedy had imagined in his museum renovation plan of the early 1980s. Because development stretched over many years, *Communities* was completed under his successor, Spencer Crew. Kennedy's remaining chronological exhibitions, on the colonial era and the twentieth century, never became viable projects.

Funding this exhibition required raising private money, and this proved extremely difficult and time consuming. One surprising way the museum ultimately helped pay for it was by sending a traveling exhibition, *The Smithsonian's America: An Exhibition on American History and Culture* to the American Festival in Chiba, Japan, in 1994. It was priced to return a profit to the museum that was used to support creating this long-term display. Even with such creative external fundraising, however, the budget of the exhibition had to be slashed from the original $5 million to $1.2 million, its size was scaled back, contract designers were replaced with internal designers, and the audiovisual components of the display were drastically reduced.

This exhibition followed the model of *After the Revolution* and focused on select communities as representative of broader historical patterns. Likewise, it sought to balance treatment of both positive and negative aspects of the history of this era and include extensive coverage of minority groups.

In the exhibition, visitors learned about three communities: industrial workers

Figure 5-50. The factory gates from Dobson Textile Mills. Companies erected gates to establish greater control over employees, not just to protect their property.

and managers in Bridgeport, Connecticut; Jewish immigrants in Cincinnati, Ohio; and enslaved and free Black people in the low country of South Carolina.[261] This was a surprisingly limited perspective on nineteenth-century American history. It is explained in part by the fact that two major sections of the exhibition were postponed late in the planning and never ultimately completed.

The first of these two focused on the Cherokee Indians and their lives before and after their removal along the "Trail of Tears" from the eastern United States to Oklahoma Territory. It highlighted the community of Tahlequah, Oklahoma, which was established as the nineteenth-century capital of the Cherokee Nation in 1839.[262] The section was to show "how the Cherokee people dealt with confrontation as well as with Anglo-American efforts to change their way of life."[263]

The second uncompleted section was to focus on westward expansion by European Americans and the central role of railroads. It highlighted the community of Los Angeles and explored the interactions of White Americans with Hispanic and Indian populations.

Figure 5-51. This reproduction Jewish peddler's cart shows the type of goods itinerant salesmen sold as they traveled among towns and homesteads. It was previously displayed in *A Nation of Nations*.

Figure 5-52. This recreated setting depicts a market at Charleston, South Carolina, which was a hub of African American life throughout the nineteenth century.

It included topics such as the Mexican War and the resulting acquisition of huge tracts of western lands, the many Indian wars and related peace treaties, homesteading, the advent of cattle ranching, and the California gold rush.

Both these sections were put on hold late in the planning at the direction of Smithsonian Secretary Michael Heyman. The scripts for both were complete, objects had been identified and staged, and construction was underway. But after reviewing the script and exhibition layout, Heyman decided that the Cherokee section was too controversial, and delayed installation of both sections until an unspecified later date. That day never came.

This decision appears to have been solely political, to avoid public controversy about what Heyman considered sensitive historical issues. It was not related to the quality of the historical scholarship or design of the sections. Heyman made the decision in the aftermath of the turbulent controversy during the mid-1990s over the *Enola Gay* exhibition at the National Air and Space Museum[264] as well as the controversy at the National Museum of American History itself over *Science in American Life*.

Even with the deletions, *Communities in a Changing Nation*, like *After the Revolution*, portrayed a complex story that examined struggles and challenges as well as growth and economic development as the United States spread across the continent. As the main label stated:

This exhibition introduces some of the people who believed in and fought for the promises of America—promises of freedom, equality, abundance, land, democracy, independence, progress and opportunity.[265]

In the 5,000-square-foot exhibition that followed, visitors saw dynamic panoramas and settings, over 200 artifacts, and hundreds of photographs. They were led to question the extent to which the American "promises" were realized for different groups of people. As the exhibition demonstrated, realities tempered Americans' dreams and aspirations. Class, ethnic, and racial divisions often led to frustration instead of fulfilment. Some groups, such as Jewish immigrants, succeeded against the odds through hard work, useful skills, and community solidarity. Others, including African Americans, had their promises of freedom and opportunity deferred.

Lonnie Bunch, who later would become both the founding director of the National Museum of African American History and Culture and secretary of the Smithsonian, curated the African American section of the exhibition. He noted,

As the exhibition reveals, not all the promises became reality for everyone. But in seeking a better life, ultimately these 19th-century Americans defined, re-shaped and formed the United States we live in today.[266]

On Time (1999)

Throughout this era, curators explored different ways to develop exhibitions around themes rather than collections. In *On Time*, which was sponsored by the Timex Corporation, the trend reached its highest level of abstraction. Timekeeping objects had been on display in collections-focused galleries since the museum's earliest days. The multidisciplinary core team planning the new exhibition included curator Carlene Stephens, educator Howard Morrison, and designer Ann Rossilli. They chose to concentrate not on timekeeping artifacts but on the human experience of time. As their 1996 concept brief for the exhibition explained,

Although *On Time* will exhibit clocks and watches, it is not *about* clocks and watches in the traditional sense—that is, how timekeepers evolved through history. Instead, the exhibition will use timekeepers in combination with a surprising array of everyday objects and images to examine how we came to rely on clock time in place of environmental cues and our internal body rhythms.... *On Time* will use an interdisciplinary approach to present the history of these changes through the interpretation of material culture in its social context.[267]

As illustrated in the exhibition brochure below, the display was broken into five sections, each organized around a question and a representative timepiece.

Although the largest number of artifacts in the exhibition were timekeeping devices, the planning team strove to include a wide variety of objects that visitors would not expect to see in an exhibition about time, such as a horse skeleton (racing

required better timekeeping), a cocktail shaker (happy hour), and a refrigerator (time-saving technology).[268]

The exhibition opened on the 116th anniversary of the adoption of standard time in the United States, highlighting the degree to which this regimentation had become a controlling factor in the lives of every American. As Museum Director Spencer Crew noted in the press release, "Whether we think about time in large units, like the millennium, or small units, like nanoseconds, the bottom line is that American society is driven by time."[269] In this era, the museum wanted visitors to ponder what this meant historically, and not just follow the evolution of timekeeping devices.

Figure 5-53. *On Time* brochure. This format of this brochure was originally a linear foldout of six panels, not a vertical array.

Figure 5-54. Inside the *On Time* exhibition.

The Temporary Exhibitions

During the Kennedy and Crew years, the museum was far more active than it had been before—or would be thereafter—in mounting temporary displays. Because these did not appear on printed museum maps, visitors tended to find them by serendipity. Hundreds were created and shown for periods ranging from a few days to several years. For many visitors, these small temporary displays could be as memorable as what they saw in major exhibitions.

The temporary exhibitions illustrated the broad interests, diversity, and expertise of the staff and the vast range and somewhat quirky nature of the museum's collection of over 1.8 million objects. During their careers at the museum, not all staff members had opportunities to work on teams that created large, multifaceted major exhibitions, which could take years to complete. Fewer still had the chance to lead such efforts. For most curators, temporary displays became the best opportunity to present their personal research and perspectives to the museum's huge audiences.

To give greater attention to temporary exhibitions in following years, the museum opened the Taylor Gallery in 1989. Named for Frank Taylor, the museum's founding director, it was prominently located next to the Constitution Avenue entrance on the first floor, in a space that previously had been used for a bookstore. It remained until the museum closed for renovation in 2006, when it was replaced by a café.

Figure 5-55. Director Roger Kennedy (*right*) shows Founding Director Frank Taylor (*left*) the certificate naming the Taylor Gallery in his honor.

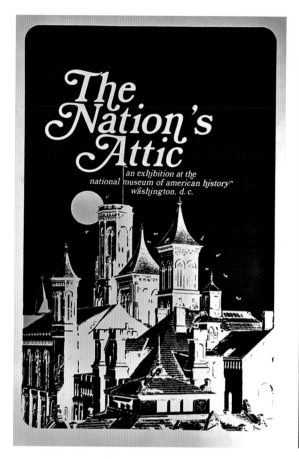

Figure 5-56. Poster for *The Nation's Attic.*

Figure 5-57. *Yesterday's Tomorrows* poster.

Temporary exhibitions were located throughout the building during this period. Some reflected the new social trends in the museum, while others were unabashedly collections-based. This list of a few illustrates their diversity[270]:

- *The Nation's Attic* (1981): One hundred surprising or weird things from the collections, including a real silk purse made from a sow's ear and a glass replica of the U.S. Capitol (Figure 5-56).
- *Black Baseball: Life in the Negro Leagues* (1981): Uniforms, baseballs, bats, shoes, and tickets related to this little-known story.
- *Hair, 1800–1899* (1981): Objects related to hairstyling or made from hair that illustrate the symbolic significance of hair in society.
- *Mathematical Teaching Aids* (1982): Cipher books, geometric models, slide rules, and calculators.
- *G. Washington: A Figure Upon the Stage* (1982): Over 650 artifacts together with related documents and artwork to commemorate Washington's 250th birthday.
- *Franklin Delano Roosevelt: The Intimate Presidency* (1982): Recreation of the White House broadcast room used for "fireside chats," plus artifacts and images to commemorate Roosevelt's 100th birthday.

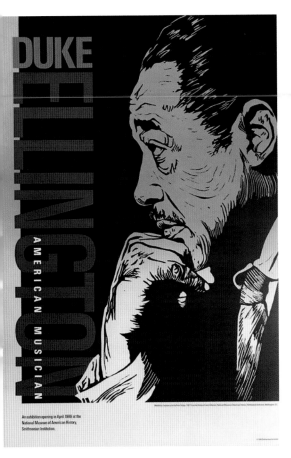

Figure 5-58. *Duke Ellington* poster.

Figure 5-59. Poster for the exhibition of the Teodoro Vidal collection.

- *E. C. Segar's Popeye—American Culture Hero* (1983): Popeye and Olive Oyl compared to George Washington, Abe Lincoln, and other traditional American heroes.
- *Vitamin Technology* (1984): A "capsuling" machine and other inventions of Casimir Funk and colleagues, who made vitamin pills standard.
- *Eleanor Roosevelt: First Person Singular* (1984): Objects, photographs, memorabilia and excerpts from radio and film to recognize Roosevelt's 100th birthday.
- *Yesterday's Tomorrows—Past Visions of the American Future* (1984): Toys, models, drawings, prototypes, and dreams from world's fairs and other efforts to predict the future (Figure 5-57).
- *Getting Dressed—Fashionable Appearance 1750–1800* (1985): Clothing and drawings showing fashion trends.
- *Business of Black Beauty—Early Development of Afro-American Beauty Culture, 1900–1950* (1986): Cosmetics, hair care items, packaging, and advertisements characteristic of this ethnic group.
- *Noses by Design* (1986): Graphics and instruments developed for nasal plastic surgery.

- *Rome at War as Seen through Coins* (1988): Showing conflicts among Celts, Dacians, Parthians, and others in antiquity.
- *Duke Ellington, American Musician* (1989): Music, awards, images, bandstand, and video related to this legendary composer and performer (Figure 5-58).
- *Typewriters—The Case Against QWERTY* (1989): Alternative typewriter keyboard designs that tried to compete against the dominant but inefficient QWERTY standard.
- *From Frying Pan to Flying V—The Rise of the Electric Guitar* (1996): Eight vintage guitars and their inventors, manufacturers, and players.
- *Masters of Their Trade—Slave Potters in the South* (1997): Five stoneware pots and jugs made by skilled enslaved artisans in South Carolina.
- *The Family Car* (1997): Three popular cars, a tent trailer, car models, memory books, and nostalgic objects reflecting the role of the automobile in American family life.
- *America's Clothespins* (1998): The entire museum collection of 41 clothespin patent models (1852–1887), along with books, illustrations, and a related Norman Rockwell poster.
- *Ella Fitzgerald: First Lady of Song* (1998): Costumes, awards, photographs, recordings, scrapbooks, sheet music, and personal memorabilia documenting the 60-year career of jazz singer Ella Fitzgerald.
- *A Collector's Vision of Puerto Rico* (1998): Teodoro Vidal's collection of carnival masks, costumes, art, jewelry, and toys that represented 500 years of Puerto Rico's history (Figure 5-59).
- *History in a Vacuum* (1999): An array of devices for cleaning carpets, from carpet beaters and brooms to electrical vacuum cleaners, plus toys and advertisements.
- *Photographing History: Fred J. Maroon and the Nixon Years, 1970–1974* (1999): A collection of 121 images showing how a news photographer remembered the Nixon years.

Three temporary exhibitions during this era were particularly significant and had a lasting influence on the museum.

M*A*S*H (1983)

Commentators who later assessed Kennedy's influence on the museum often highlighted his unabashed addition of popular-culture exhibitions. Objects he put on view included Archie and Edith Bunker's chairs from *All in the Family*, a red cardigan sweater from *Mr. Rogers' Neighborhood*, Fonzie's jacket from *Happy Days*, Dorothy's ruby slippers from *The Wizard of Oz*, and sets from *M*A*S*H*.[271] Although Kennedy did indeed support and encourage this trend during his tenure, much of its emergence was accidental. That was certainly the case with the *M*A*S*H* exhibition, the most popular of all these displays.

The *M*A*S*H* series ran on CBS from 1972 through 1983. It was a widely viewed comedy-drama that used a setting in a Korean War mobile hospital to provide oblique

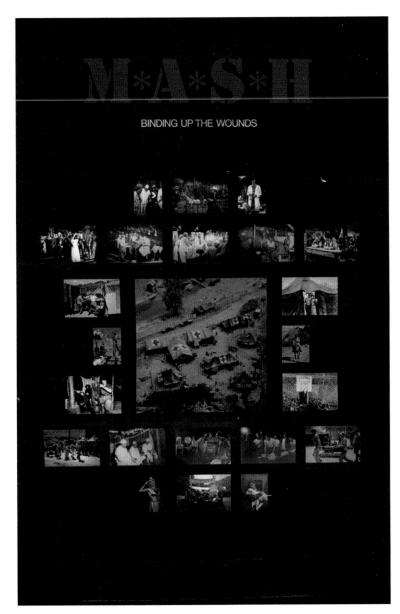

Figure 5-60. Poster for the exhibition.

commentary on the Vietnam War, which was ongoing when the series began. The final episode of this show in February 1983, entitled "Goodbye, Farewell and Amen," was viewed by 125 million viewers, a record audience at the time for a single TV series program.

The previous year, Michael Harris, a specialist in the Division of Medical Sciences, thought that the Smithsonian should collect several items related to the show. Perhaps, for example, the museum might acquire a Hawaiian shirt or stethoscope used by Alan Alda, who portrayed lead character "Hawkeye" Pierce.[272] Harris was going on vacation to California and suggested that while he was there, he might contact 20th Century Fox to see if the company would be willing to consider a donation.

He began consulting with Carl Scheele, curator in the Division of Community Life, about the idea. Surprisingly, staff members at 20th Century Fox were

Figure 5-61. The Swamp and operating room settings in *M*A*S*H*.

independently thinking along the same lines, and they too contacted Scheele to start a discussion. Plans quickly developed, and a third curator, Ed Ezell, head of military history, was added to the planning group. If the museum was going to mount an exhibition about *M*A*S*H*, they wanted to involve curators in all the subject areas related to it.

Working with the Museum Advisory Committee and Director Kennedy, the team came up with a proposal to do a temporary display during the summer after the show ended. They expected that this would become a popular "summer sizzler."

Fortunately, 20th Century Fox agreed with the idea and was willing to donate two stage sets, additional objects, images, video, and staff support. They also agreed to provide roughly $42,000 to help defray the cost of designing, mounting, and publicizing the exhibition.[273]

The result was entitled *M*A*S*H: Binding Up the Wounds* and was on display from 30 July 1983 through 3 February 1985 in the west corridor area of the museum's second floor. This was a six-month extension of the originally planned 14-month run. It had three sections: a photographic essay comparing 15 photos from the series with photos of actual events in Korea and Vietnam, the sets of the surgeon's tent ("the Swamp") and the operating room, and a selection of 30 costumes, props, documents, and objects that illustrated the show's significance in entertainment history.[274] The museum published a catalog for the exhibition and, to capitalize on its expected popularity, also sold a poster, T-shirts, patches, dog tags, teddy bears, and scale models of vehicles.

Audiences loved the exhibition and lined up for hours to see it. More than 17,000 came in the first week alone, the largest turnout for a single exhibition in the history of the museum.[275] An internal museum memorandum proudly noted that the millionth visitor came through on 1 December 1983.[276]

Kennedy knew that critics, not to mention some staff, were likely to scoff at the notion that this exhibition was really American history. He addressed the issue in a brochure for the exhibition. He said the museum invited audiences to "draw your own conclusions from this exhibit: about the museum that now celebrates a TV series, about the people who created that series, and about the events the series depicted." He continued,

> M*A*S*H was, like all human products, flawed and erratic. But it tackled serious subjects boldly, and, at the same time with a fit sense of the absurd. It carried within it the kind of reexamination which, among historians, is often called "revisionism," but it did so with a straightforwardness and good humor which is sometime found wanting in historical writing.[277]

Following the enormous popularity and success of the M*A*S*H exhibition, popular-culture displays became enduring additions to the museum floor, while some older subjects, such as civil engineering and petroleum, faded away.

Pain and Its Relief (1983)

While M*A*S*H used an operating room as a forum for comedy and satire, an exhibition on the first floor opening the same year treated it as a landmark historical setting. This display too was also only possible through financial support from an outside sponsor, in this instance, the American Society of Anesthesiologists.[278]

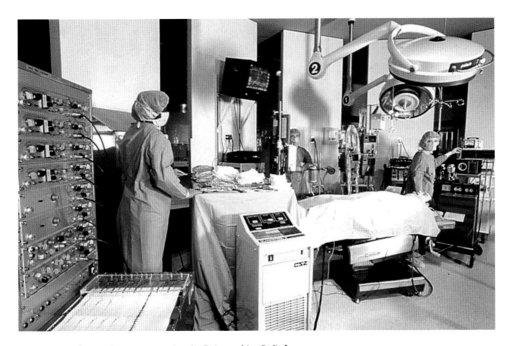

Figure 5-62. Operating-room setting in *Pain and Its Relief*.

Figure 5-63. Poster for *Pain and Its Relief.*

Pain and Its Relief moved beyond technical explanations of medical equipment to exploring the personal dimensions of pain. Although experiencing pain is common to everyone, different societies have understood, explained, and treated it very differently. The exhibition guided visitors to compare broad historical patterns, then followed the story to twentieth-century scientific developments in surgical anesthesia. It culminated in an operating-room setting that showed a broad array of equipment to administer anesthesia as well as devices to monitor its effects on the health of the patient.

The scene featured an empty bed—were they waiting for you, the visitor, to be wheeled in? Few other exhibitions in this period were able to connect history as directly to visitors' own life experiences. The exhibition also produced a highly popular poster (Figure 5-63), still remembered as a museum classic.

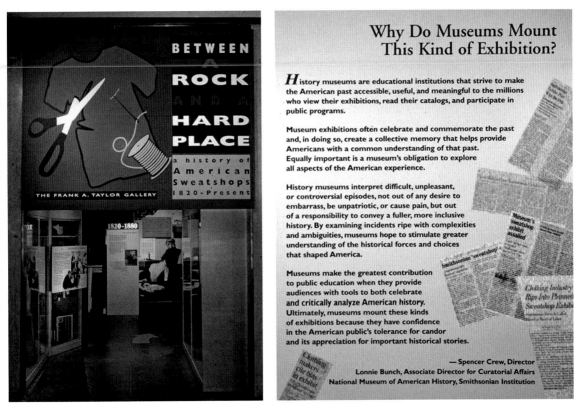

Figure 5-64. Entry to the *American Sweatshops* exhibition.

Figure 5-65. Directors' explanatory label.

Between a Rock and a Hard Place: A History of American Sweatshops, 1820–Present (1998)

In the wake of the controversy over the *Enola Gay* exhibition at the National Air and Space Museum in the mid-1990s, curators at the American History Museum were concerned that they might be prohibited from taking on controversial topics, even having been reassured that it was appropriate to do so if Smithsonian guidelines were followed and multiple perspectives were addressed. Curators Harry Rubenstein and Peter Liebhold tested this policy when they planned and produced an exhibition on American sweatshops.

In the press release announcing the exhibition, Liebhold summarized its purpose, "Sweatshops are often discussed as good versus evil, but the issue is much more complex. This exhibition uses historic material to explain the complexity of the issues, and the concerns and pressures experienced by those in the garment industry."[279]

The 3,000-square-foot exhibition included historic clothing, photographs of sweatshops from 1900 to the 1990s, union posters, material from the 1911 Triangle Shirtwaist Company fire, and objects from law enforcement agencies. A highlight was material from the 1995 raid of a sweatshop in El Monte, California, which illustrated that sweatshops were still present in America. To ensure that the exhibition explored multiple contrasting perspectives, the curators included statements from six national figures involved with the subject.[280]

Although the exhibition generated considerable controversy in the press and in Congress, throughout its development museum leaders cautiously stood behind the project. The final exhibition was generally regarded as a well-balanced treatment. Just days after the opening, the Smithsonian Institution decided to put the entire exhibition online, and it became one of NMAH's first digital exhibitions.

Museum critic Jacqueline Trescott, in her review in the *Washington Post*, would have preferred more advocacy. She wrote, "the show treads the line between hot-button advocacy and cold, precise historical facts. Outrage, which should be the heartbeat of a show about human exploitation and illegality, is present only in the weighty collection of details."[281] But a museum is not a newspaper. To make clear what they wanted the exhibition to convey, museum leaders Spencer Crew and Lonnie Bunch took the unusual step of including their perspective on the approach and significance of the exhibition in a signed label (Figure 5-65).

New Visitor Experiences

Few visitors to the museum in the 1980s and 1990s would have grasped the full range of the changes that were making it broader and more inclusive. Yet all would have seen some of the new subjects and artifacts now on display. There were now objects made by Japanese Americans in internment camps during World War II and products being sold by African Americans in beauty shops in Northern cities where they had moved to seek a better life. There were personal computers and electronic games that were ushering in an information age, birth-control pills that had expanded women's reproductive choices, Puerto Rican art objects, and stage props associated with television programs that were reshaping American culture.

Some visitors also enjoyed new activities and programs. They could try on colonial-era clothes, gin cotton, or conduct chemistry experiments. At interactive computers, they could hear personal perspectives of Japanese American war heroes, computer pioneers, and scientists debating genetic engineering. They could walk through settings of a market in nineteenth-century Charleston, an early-twentieth-century Horn & Hardart automat, a room in the 1912 White House, and a robotic automobile assembly station. They could compare the design and construction of everyday objects such as washing machines, bicycles, and hairbrushes as they had changed over time due to innovations in technology and materials.

Visitors could also interact with the museum remotely. They could find Smithsonian materials on its forums on America Online (AOL), or explore the Smithsonian's rapidly expanding website, which within a decade of its debut in 1995 (Figure 5-66) would attract more visitors than the number who came to its museums. Across the

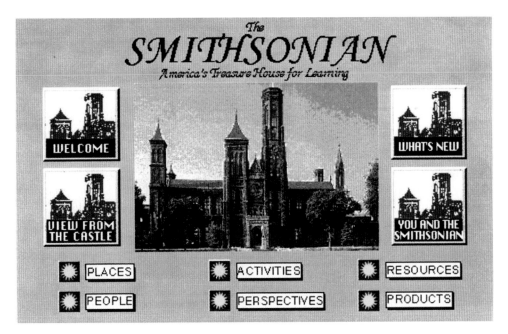

Figure 5-66. The Smithsonian's first website home page, 1995, which linked to pages about individual museums.

county, they could find NMAH curriculum materials in their schoolrooms or traveling exhibitions in regional museums.

As the museum had expanded its scope and offerings, visitors must increasingly have wondered how they would ever have enough time to experience it all. But there was an exhibition even for that! *On Time* could help them understand the history behind how and why Americans had come to be in such a hurry.

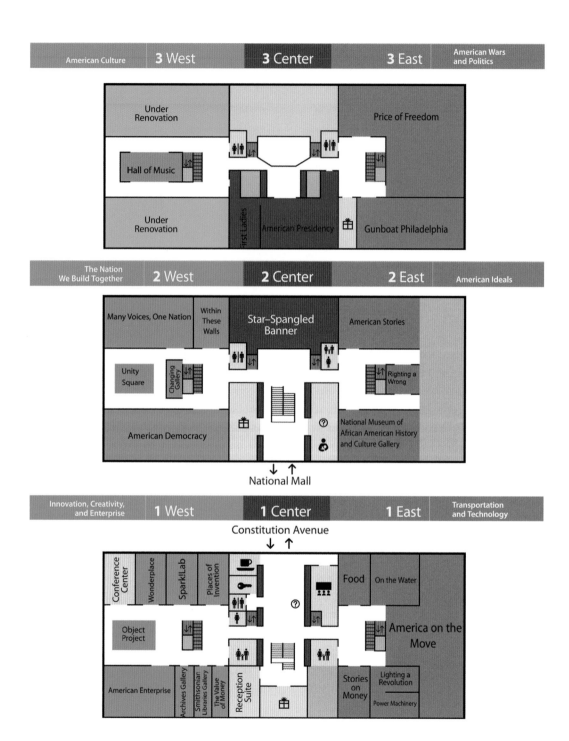

Figure 6-1. The 2018 floor plan shows the major exhibitions visitors would find in the museum in 2018.[282] All the exhibitions except the gunboat *Philadelphia*, *Lighting a Revolution*, and *Power Machinery* were renovated in the first two decades of the twenty-first century.

CHAPTER 6

What Does It Mean to Be American? (2001–2018)

The Era

In the early twenty-first century, the museum entered an extended period of "public space renewal" that will continue through the 2020s. Heating and air-conditioning systems were replaced, elevators, escalators, and bathrooms renovated, restaurants revamped, and additional space was allocated to educational programs and activities. Taking advantage of this opportunity, the museum decided to renovate all its exhibitions as well. This comprehensive effort was the most extensive change in the museum since it opened in 1964. While federal funding paid for the building renovations, private sponsorship had to cover much of the cost for the new exhibitions.

The era we cover extends from 2001 to 2018. The floor plan we chose to epitomize it dates from 2018, when the first three phases of the renovation were nearly complete. We organized our discussion of the new exhibitions by museum section and then by date of their opening. Of note is that the renewal project forced the museum to adopt a new approach to orienting its visitors. Previously, the exhibits had been themed by floors, but as the map indicates, they now were themed in vertical sections: center core, west wing, and east wing.

During this period, the museum also modified its focus. While it still strove to celebrate American innovation and tell inclusive community stories, it now challenged visitors to explore American national identity by pondering the question "What does it mean to be American?"

Prelude: Americans by Choice

On 24 May 2012, the National Museum of American History held a naturalization ceremony in its spacious Flag Hall, in front of the new display of its most revered artifact, the Star-Spangled Banner. Twelve individuals from 12 different countries were there to become naturalized citizens—Americans by choice.[283] Unlike those who were Americans by birth, these 12 all had to think deeply about what it meant to be an American and why they wanted to become one.

Madeleine Albright, the first female secretary of state of the nation, was an honored guest. She had been born in Czechoslovakia, immigrated to the United States, and herself became a citizen while a college student. She was donating objects to

Figure 6-2. Former Secretary of State Madeleine Albright and new American citizens take their citizenship oaths.

the national collection that documented her extraordinary career in public service. They included the red dress she wore when being sworn in as secretary of state, a briefcase she used while U.S. ambassador to the United Nations, a white beaded pin with an AIDS ribbon from an AIDS clinic in South Africa, and a badge from the July 2000 Middle East peace summit at Camp David.

When the director of the U.S. Citizen and Immigration Services, Alejandro Mayorkas, asked the new citizens to stand and take the oath, Albright stood up too, raised her right hand and joined them. Family members and guests in the audience were deeply moved. Albright later said she never wanted to forget how the act of becoming an American had changed her life.

The updated Flag Hall, the setting for this memorable ceremony, opened in 2008, marking the end of the first phase of the museum's multi-year public space renewal project. The area was designed to be a monumental space that featured an inspirational display of the museum's most symbolic object. It was also extensive enough to be suitable for a wide range of events, including artifact donations, concerts, dinners, receptions, and public presentations—like this one.

Renewing the Museum

The scope and timing of public space renewal, the transformation of the building and all the museum's exhibitions, were determined by a complex set of events. In the late 1990s, strategic planning led by Director Spencer Crew, Deputy Director Martha Morris, and Associate Director of Curatorial Affairs Lonnie Bunch refocused the museum's mission on a new goal: exploring what it means to be American. As explained in the museum's "Vision for Transforming the National Museum of American History" of 2001,

> We want visitors to come away from their Museum experience thinking about the simple yet complex question, "What has it meant to be an American?" That question is at the heart of "American Identity," the thematic focus for our new exhibitions, programs and other activities.[284]

The 1999 exhibition *Communities in a Changing Nation* had been the first one to explore this theme specifically.[285] However, even as the museum committed to the new approach, it was reluctant to provide specific answers to the question of what American identity meant, leaving it instead as a subject for exploration. In their book *Legacies: Collecting America's History at the Smithsonian*, also published in 2001, curators Steven Lubar and Kathleen M. Kendrick wrote this about the new theme:

> When do Americans consciously think of themselves as American? Times of conflict—war, economic crisis, increased immigration, political protest—can trigger expressions and redefinitions of national identity. . . . In deciding to include stories of conflict and inequality in its story of America, the National Museum of American History has sparked some conflicts of its own. . . . Why do curators seem to focus on issues and events that divide Americans rather than pull them together? At the heart of these conflicts lie different ideas about the role history should play in Americans' lives and thus the kind of place a national history museum should be. . . . Only by fostering dialogue about the collective and complex legacy inherited from this nation's past can the museum help people truly understand what it means to be American.[286]

Although encouraging visitors to explore American identity on their own was a noble goal, it did not provide an effective way to orient visitors to the museum's exhibitions. Could the theme of American identity be used in that way?

Years later, under the leadership of John Gray, curators developed a pragmatic response to the question "What does it mean to be American?" that gave the museum a new means of organizing its exhibitions that related them to each other and the museum. That answer was that American identity was defined by citizens of every race, gender, class, and ethnicity striving—often against prejudice and adversity—to reach the ideals set forth in the founding documents of the nation, including democracy, opportunity, and freedom. This chapter follows the circuitous path to reaching this new understanding of the museum's national role, and how this evolving approach shaped the exhibitions museum visitors would see.

Larry Small and the Blue Ribbon Commission

On 13 September 1999, the Smithsonian announced that its board of regents had unanimously chosen Lawrence M. Small as the institution's new secretary, to replace I. Michael Heyman. Unlike all his predecessors, Small was neither a scholar nor a university administrator. He was a professional banker, albeit also an avid art collector and a proficient flamenco guitarist. However, it was his management expertise and potential as a fundraiser that attracted the regents most. Aged 59, Small was the president and chief operating officer of the Federal National Mortgage Association ("Fannie Mae"), a position he had held since 1991. He also had the reputation of being an effective administrator.[287]

The regents believed he would be just the individual to bring a new sense of order and discipline to the sprawling institution, which had recently gone through much public turmoil, had an aging infrastructure, and desperately needed a large infusion of outside funding. Congress was increasingly unwilling to pay the full cost of new exhibitions, new museums, and large research initiatives. Its view was that the Smithsonian had to reenergize its "public–private partnership" and increase the percentage of private funding to balance what the government was contributing, which at that point was around 70 percent of the total.

In taking the job, Small clearly understood what was expected of him. As he told Jackie Trescott of the *Washington Post*, "Am I going to devote a huge amount of my time to fund-raising? You bet I am. Do I think it is tremendously important? Yes, I do. Do I think the flow of money to the Smithsonian needs to be increased by $1 billion? Yes."[288]

After assuming his new position in January 2000, Small took a particular interest in the National Museum of American History. Among his first initiatives was commissioning a major new exhibition on the American presidency, which he required to be completed in seven months, not the three-to-five-year cycle that large exhibitions usually required. He simply couldn't understand why the museum didn't already have such an exhibition, since it had displayed the first ladies' gowns for decades. And he was determined to raise the money to redress this imbalance. As will be discussed in detail later in the chapter, NMAH Director Spencer Crew grudgingly accepted the daunting assignment to create the new exhibition and agreed to lead the team personally. Meanwhile, Small got moving on fundraising. In August, he managed—in a remarkable turn of events—to secure the largest pledge in the Smithsonian's history.

In 1997, real estate developer turned philanthropist Kenneth E. Behring had donated $20 million to the National Museum of Natural History for refurbishing the museum's rotunda, supporting a traveling exhibition, and endowing a large new exhibition: the *Kenneth E. Behring Family Hall of Mammals*. Unfortunately, this gift became problematic. Behring, who was a big-game hunter, also wanted to donate some of his private collection of hunting trophies. The museum agreed to accept them, but soon learned that they included the remains of highly rare endangered sheep. When this fact became public, controversy erupted. "Big-Game Hunter's Gift Roils the Smithsonian" blared the *New York Times*[289], "A Big Gun with Big Bucks," countered the *Washington Post*.[290] Behring claimed he had killed the sheep legally in Kazakhstan, but for the museum, which prided itself on its devotion to conservation, the symbolism became unacceptable. The controversy also was unpalatable to Behring, who felt falsely accused and then abandoned by the institution he was trying to help.

In walked the new secretary, who had arrived in the middle of this affair. He proposed a surprising resolution to it. Behring should move his philanthropy from Natural History across the street to the National Museum of American History. While the original gift would still pay for the Hall of Mammals, Behring could now do even more at American History and salvage his good name. The scheme worked. Behring was impressed with Small and became intrigued with the possibilities for new history exhibits.

In August 2000, he pledged to give the museum $80 million. That, together with his gift to Natural History, brought his total to $100 million, the largest gift in the history of the Smithsonian Institution.[291] Five million dollars would help pay for the new presidency exhibition Small had previously mandated, due to open in November 2000. This would be followed by a series of other exhibitions, each of which would highlight a "particular aspect of American history and accomplishment." Next would come an exhibition of approximately 18,000 square feet focused on the military's role in "preserving and protecting freedom and democracy." It was to open in 2004. After that would be a hall devoted to deceased Americans who had "truly epitomize[d] the 'American Spirit.'" It was due to open in 2006. Plans for other exhibitions would be made and agreed upon later. The gift was scheduled to be payable through 2010.[292]

To recognize Behring's generosity in perpetuity, the museum agreed to change its name to the National Museum of American History, Kenneth E. Behring Center. This title would be inscribed on both entrances to the building and also used on all official stationery, signs, educational programs, and other communications. Announcing the gift, Secretary Small gushed,

> A gift of this magnitude is unprecedented. We are delighted to honor this great benefactor to the Smithsonian Institution by establishing the Behring Center. Mr. Behring's generous contribution will allow us to begin a complete

Figure 6-3. Secretary Small (*left*) and Ken Behring discuss his major gift, September 2000.

transformation and modernization of The National Museum of American History, the only museum of its kind in the world. It is private philanthropy such as this gift from Ken, combined with our Congressional support, that will move the Smithsonian Institution into the 21st century.[293]

Within months, in May 2001, Small had secured another major donor. She was Catherine Reynolds, who pledged $38 million to fund a permanent "Hall of Fame of American Achievers."[294] This seemed duplicative of the biographical exhibition that Small had already agreed to let Ken Behring fund, but the secretary expected that he could work out the overlap between the two donors, who knew each other. He was successful. Behring later agreed for his funding to be used instead on a general introductory exhibition to the museum.

Like the deal that Small had made with Ken Behring, this new gift had been secured with almost no involvement by leaders at NMAH. Although in the 1960s, the museum had once included a Hall of Historic Americans (see chapter 3), it had enjoyed limited success, and the museum had not intended to reprise the idea of a major biographical exhibition.

Reynolds created her charitable foundation, the Catherine B. Reynolds Foundation, in 2001 with proceeds from the sale of Servus Financial Corporation, which she chaired. The corporation had been enormously profitable through marketing student loans, and Reynolds had created the foundation to "give back" to society. In contrast to Ken Behring, Reynolds already had quite definite ideas of what should be included in the exhibition she planned to support. As she told a *New York Times* reporter, who later published an article entitled, "Smithsonian Is Promised $38 million, With Strings," she hoped that the people honored might include

…the Rev. Dr. Martin Luther King, Jr., Michael Jordan, Jonas Salk, Steven Spielberg, Oprah Winfrey, Martha Stewart, the home fashion guru, Dorothy Hamill, the ice skater, Frederick W. Smith, the founder of Federal Express, and Steve Case, chairman of AOL Time Warner.[295]

The article noted that Reynolds understood and accepted that the Smithsonian would make the final decision of who would be profiled, but she clearly expected to have deep involvement in the process. Although many NMAH curators were already expressing concerns about the exhibition before the gift was announced, Director Spencer Crew chose to emphasize the positive, saying, "If you can highlight how people are successful and give kids the sense of possibility, that's a good thing."[296]

As museum staff assigned to work on the exhibition came to understand, Catherine Reynolds' ideas had much deeper roots than her own personal views. Her husband was Wayne Reynolds, the youngest son of acclaimed sports photographer Brian Blaine Reynolds (also known as Hy Peskin). In 1961, Brian Reynolds had established the American Academy of Achievement, in order to bring together accomplished people from diverse fields to network and encourage young leaders. He initially funded its work with proceeds from his photography. Each year the academy held an International Achievement Summit, where aspiring students met with recognized leaders who were honored for their achievements.

In 1985, Wayne and Catherine Reynolds took over management of the academy, which was now a nonprofit organization, and moved its headquarters to Washington, D.C. The Reynolds Foundation had now become its primary sponsor. Ken Behring was honored by the academy in 1989, so he had come to know the Reynolds well. Although the academy was widely recognized for its program and annual summit, it had no permanent display space. That led the Reynoldses to think that they could include a Hall of Achievement related to the academy inside the National Museum of American History.

Over the coming months, NMAH curators and the Reynoldses struggled to find a way to make the partnership work without the museum sacrificing its integrity and control of the exhibition. Unquestionably, the Academy of Achievement had recognized many people who might be appropriately included in a Smithsonian exhibition, but the Smithsonian insisted that it could not be limited to them. And the display would have to be truly independent from the academy, not an extension of it.

In January 2002, the *Washington Post* published an extensive exposé by reporter Bob Thompson entitled "History for $ale," about the museum's new donors and staff reaction to them.[297] By this point, many staff members had utterly lost confidence in Secretary Small and his high-handed approach to fundraising, done without the museum's involvement. They were happy to share their views with a *Washington Post* reporter. Thompson's article captured the spirit of the disagreement. He quoted longtime NMAH curator Bernard "Barney" Finn, who explained to him, "We're not a great man/great woman place. This museum is about context, about putting people and events in place within the social fabric." Contrasted to that was Wayne Reynolds's perspective,

> Well, they've certainly done such a *wonderful* job of exhibiting all those light bulbs and drag racers and ceramic pots…I think it just frustrates those curators and "scholars"—I use scholar in quotes, because I don't *know* what their

credentials are—who for 30 years have been there collecting movie posters and coins and ceramic pots. That there's somebody who comes in there who really doesn't have the emphasis on collecting things, but on inspiring kids, it freaks them out.[298]

It is hardly surprising that the relationship continued to deteriorate. By February, Catherine Reynolds had decided to give up, and canceled her pledge. The museum had already spent $1.5 million of her planned gift, which would not be returned, on the initial planning and contracting of what they had dubbed *The Spirit of America*. At this point, Reynolds claimed she was disappointed less with her loss of control than with how the museum was handling the exhibition process, which included hiring contractors whose prices she found exorbitant.

By this time, Spencer Crew had left the museum to become chief executive officer of the Underground Railroad Freedom Center in Cincinnati, Ohio. His replacement, Marc Pachter, who was also director of the National Portrait Gallery and was only at American History on a temporary detail, sadly concluded, "I thought [the Reynoldses] were in it for the long haul and we would get it right. Call me an optimist. I am disappointed that we couldn't work it all out. In the end these exhibitions are Smithsonian exhibitions and the Smithsonian is responsible for them. But yet I thought some of the things they were hoping for would happen."[299]

Watching from the sidelines during these controversies was the museum's advisory board, which had been created in 1996. Its establishment grew out of a broad institutional study by a Commission on the Future of the Smithsonian Institution. It had been convened in 1993 to provide outside perspective on how the Smithsonian should chart its future in the twenty-first century. The commission issued its final report, *E Pluribus Unum: This Divine Paradox* in May 1995.[300] Among the many subjects it addressed was governance of the growing set of museums and research centers that constituted the institution. The report noted,

> Museums in general, and the Smithsonian in particular, are increasingly flash points in the debates that characterize our nation's transition from a society that depends for coherence on a single accepted set of values and practices to one that derives its strength and unity from a deep tolerance of diversity. This happens because museums, to fulfill their missions, must prepare exhibitions that record and illuminate this transition. Museums have responded by providing a broad range of interpretive approaches to exhibitions and encouraging deeper examination and debate of issues. This sometimes results in acrimonious and contentious debate on controversial subjects. The Smithsonian has hardly been immune. Its position is especially challenging because it is a national institution with large and complex collections and missions. These challenges can be better understood by recognizing that the Smithsonian is an educational forum rather than a cultural or scientific authority or even a home for congratulations.[301]

To help guide museums through the changing public environment in the coming years, the commission recommended that all of them either revitalize or establish strong advisory boards. They concluded,

> By strengthening all the advisory boards, the Institution would gain several important advantages: enhanced external expert advice, especially for the establishment of policies and assessment of programs; increased contacts with similar institutions nation-wide, thereby facilitating the formation of partnerships; and attraction of outstanding citizens from all over the nation to nurture the Institution at the grassroots, including through private fund-raising. To ensure an important role in governance by the advisory boards, we recommend that the Board of Regents adopt a statement of their roles and responsibilities. These should include substantive tasks such as reviewing and monitoring program priorities; annual budgets and strategic plans; participating in the selection and evaluation of directors; recommending proposed new board members to the Regents; fund-raising for the unit; participating in outreach and representational activities as appropriate; participating in and reviewing the results of external evaluations; and reporting to the Regents on a regular basis.[302]

The Smithsonian accepted the commission's recommendations and issued Smithsonian Directive 123, "Regents' Guidelines for Smithsonian Advisory Boards," in October 1995. It established policies and procedures for both existing and new boards.

At the time, the National Museum of American History did not have a board. The Smithsonian asked Ivan Selin to help establish it and serve as its chair. Selin was chief executive officer of Phoenix International, a private investment firm specializing in technology and energy. He had previously served as chairman of the U.S. Nuclear Regulatory Commission and assistant secretary for systems analysis for the Department of Defense. Under the bylaws that he largely created, the museum's board was to have three functions: advising and supporting the director and board of regents, advocating for the museum to the nation and broader constituencies outside the academic world, and helping build the financial base of the museum by identifying and securing private funds.

In Selin's mind, although the third role was critical to the success of the museum, the first two functions were even more important. This was reflected in the board's composition. It was to have up to 31 members. One was to be a representative of the board of regents. Four were to be professionals in American history from academia, not-for-profit organizations, or other scholarly organizations. The other members should be Americans who broadly represented social, geographic, and ethnic diversity across the nation and had a strong interest in the museum and its mission.[303]

In 2001, reacting to the public controversy that had recently surrounded the museum, and the chaos it created, the new NMAH advisory board, together with the secretary and the board of regents, concluded that the National Museum of American

History needed a thorough outside review. It was also a provision of the gift agreement with Ken Behring. The document promised, "...the Smithsonian Institution, in consultation with Mr. Behring, will with all due diligence establish a blue ribbon panel of historians, commentators, and scholars, that will consult with NMAH staff and Board of Directors on the design and content of future exhibitions."[304]

On 29 June, the regents announced the creation of the Blue Ribbon Commission to study the situation and make recommendations on strategic exhibition planning. Nothing like it had previously occurred in the history of the organization, nor has there been a similar external review since. The press release explaining its purpose stated,

> The advisory group will assist the museum director and his staff in planning exhibitions for the museum and offering recommendations on the most timely and relevant themes and methods of presentation for the museum in the 21st century. The members will study the museum's own strategic plan, review existing topics and exhibitions, and examine the strength of the National Museum of American History's three-million object collection.[305]

Composed of 24 individuals, the commission included notable historians and archivists, among them Ellsworth Brown, president of the Carnegie Museums of Pittsburgh and Carnegie Library; David Donald, emeritus history professor at Harvard University; Eric Foner, history professor at Columbia University; Richard Norton Smith, executive director of the Gerald R. Ford Foundation; Laurel Ulrich, history professor at Harvard University; and Don Wilson, former archivist of the United States. However, like the regents themselves, it also included many notable Americans. Among them were Tom Brokaw of NBC News, Senator Daniel Inouye, Roger Mudd of the History Channel, Hall of Fame basketball player Bill Russell, and Charles Townes, physicist and winner of the 1964 Nobel Prize for research in quantum mechanics.

Although all the commission members were accomplished and well-known public figures, few had any experience in conceiving, planning, or producing major exhibitions, such as the ones on which their advice was now being sought. Moreover, the group did not include any exhibition designers or fabricators.

This commission was chaired by Richard Darman, a partner in the Carlyle Group investment firm, professor of public management at the John F. Kennedy School of Government at Harvard University, and former head of the Office of Management and Budget under President George H. W. Bush. Darman was also an active member of the NMAH Advisory Board and would succeed Selin as its chairman in 2003. He led the study with a strong hand. While other commission members reviewed the final report and provided input, it was largely Darman's product and presented his perspective.[306]

Following an approach often found in management reviews, the commission's final report began on a positive note. It outlined the museum's major cultural importance as the "only *national* museum of American history." Then it summarized the exciting opportunities that could allow the museum to become a recognized leader in interpreting and explaining the American experience. Next, it turned to the difficult topic at hand. It provided a frank and detailed assessment of the many issues the museum currently faced that were preventing it from achieving its full potential. Its difficulty with recent donors was only one example, and, in the commission's assessment, not the most important one. Finally, it detailed a set of 20 recommendations on how the museum should work to resolve these issues and become the institution the nation needed and that it wanted it to be.

The report's analysis of the issues the museum faced was thoughtful and perceptive. These included problems with the building's architecture and aesthetics; choice of topics and themes; the challenge of achieving fairness, accuracy, and inclusiveness in presentations; effective use of information technology; and attending to diverse visitor demands. Discussing the last of these, the report noted,

> Interpretations can help shape history. And this reality presents a serious challenge for NMAH management. Advocates inclined to emphasize the role of heroic individuals vie with those who would concentrate on less powerful figures and the larger historical forces that shape their lives. There is a tension between those inclined to celebrate American achievement and those inclined to focus on America's failure to meet her declared aspirations. There is a related tension between those who see American history as a series of leaps from triumph to triumph and those who see the history as a more difficult and troubled journey. And there is a basic difference of perspective between those who see American values and experience as in some positive sense "exceptional" and those who do not.... The challenge for NMAH is to attend fairly to divergent frameworks—and to use legitimate arguments about interpretation to help make exhibits more interesting and engaging. That is more easily said than done.

Overall, the commission found that the museum was disorganized and incoherent. The report argued,

> As it is now, the Museum does not seem to meet any obvious test of comprehensibility or coherence. Indeed, in the most basic physical sense, visitors frequently have difficulty orienting themselves.... Many serious observers and most members of the Commission believe that the problem has to do, more fundamentally, with the Museum's content and the organization of its presentation.

The commissioners thought the institution needed a much clearer focus and a detailed process for selecting what exhibitions would be displayed. The report strongly endorsed the museum's recent decision to make the overarching theme of the museum "American identity," and using its exhibitions to explore the question "What has it meant to be an American?" It endorsed continuation of the major exhibitions that were already underway, but also highlighted topics that it thought were troubling holes in the museum's coverage, including immigration, slavery, ethnic diversity, business history, regional history, religion, and public education.

On the issue of donors, the commission was coldly realistic. The museum simply could not achieve its potential without large amounts of outside funding, and it had to find better ways to manage its fundraising effectively and tactfully, while still maintaining full control over exhibition content as well as public trust. This was far from a new issue. The museum had dealt with donors or sponsors who had agendas from its earliest days. The pledges from Ken Behring and Catherine Reynolds were larger in size than in earlier years, but not different in kind. The commission noted:

> Both public sector and private sector donors are capable of attempting to impose views that, in some cases, may not be fairly representative or academically responsible. On the other hand, donors may have the ability to provide valuable conceptual contributions (in addition to financial contributions). The Museum does not have a monopoly on good ideas. What the Museum does have is a responsibility to assure that the content of its exhibits meet certain standards of scholarship, quality, and integrity.

As the size of donations grew across the Smithsonian, managing donor relations effectively was becoming increasingly difficult everywhere, not just at American History. Indeed, the institution had recently issued new policies on gift agreements, naming opportunities, and corporate sponsorship. The commission attached these as an appendix to its report, believing that careful adherence to them would resolve most of the museum's fundraising issues.

To help the museum become more coherent, the commission strongly recommended a large new introductory exhibition. In the commission's assessment, it was critical that this exhibition be chronological in organization and comprehensive in scope. It should be organized around "a few central theme lines for the examination and interpretation of American history—themes widely recognized to be of defining importance for America: like freedom, democracy, opportunity, and enterprise." In size, the exhibition should be around 22,000 square feet, the second largest in the building, and located prominently on the second floor.

Surprisingly, the commissioners seemed unaware of the three previous attempts at this same museum to do something similar to what they were now recommending. Furthermore, if commission members had in mind exhibitions in other museums that were successful models of what they envisioned, they chose not to share them.

Brent Glass and Renovating the Center Core

In addition to making its recommendations, the commission was deeply concerned that they be fully implemented. In that respect, its report came at a favorable time. The Smithsonian was in the process of selecting a new director to replace Spencer Crew. The commission specifically advised that the individual chosen should promise to accept the guidance it had provided in its report.

Figure 6-4. The museum's founding director, Frank Taylor (*left*), meeting with Brent Glass (*right*) in July 2003.

In their choice of a new director, Smithsonian leaders did indeed heed the guidance of the Blue Ribbon Commission. After a nationwide search, they hired Brent Glass, former director of the Pennsylvania State Historical Commission.[307]

Glass began his tenure as director in December 2002. He had previously had extensive experience in public history. He held a PhD from the University of North Carolina and had served for 15 years as executive director of the Pennsylvania State Historical Commission. During this period, he managed the largest and most comprehensive state history program in the country, which included a staff of 350 full-time and 150 part-time employees. He oversaw 25 historic sites and museums, the state Historic Preservation Office, varied public history programs, and history publications. Earlier, he had served as executive director of the North Carolina Humanities Council.

During his nine years at the Smithsonian, Glass focused on implementing the recommendations of the Blue Ribbon Commission, including the renovation of the center core of the museum and the conservation and reinstallation of the Star-Spangled Banner. He accepted the prevailing theme for the museum, that its goal was to "have visitors come away from their Museum experience thinking about America, American history, and the simple yet complex question, 'What has it meant to be an American?'"[308] However, he further articulated his interpretation of the goal of the museum as showing how Americans have always been a people who have sought to achieve the American Dream. As he told the *Washington Post* in 2003,

> You don't read about a Brazilian Dream or a French Dream or a Chinese Dream. It doesn't resonate with people the same way. [The American Dream means] freedom. It means economic opportunity. It means education. There is belief in progress for the individual and a respect for the individual....

You can talk about how we came to be the nation we are now through those themes with the arching theme being the American Dream.[309]

Glass saw the situation at the museum as a huge opportunity. He believed that the Blue Ribbon Commission's report and recommendations set forth the fundamental agenda for his leadership. Moreover, the Behring donation, in spite of the issues related to it, meant that most of the fundraising needed to accomplish major projects during his tenure was already done.

Ken Behring's original gift was initially intended to support only new exhibitions. But by 2001, Secretary Small began talking to him about devoting part of his money to renovating the museum building. As it approached its fortieth anniversary, it needed an overhaul, like many other Smithsonian buildings. Its basic systems for heating and air-conditioning needed replacing, electrical and plumbing systems needed upgrading, and elevators and escalators needed modernizing. Moreover, all the public exhibition spaces needed restructuring. However, to move this effort to the top of the Smithsonian's extensive priority list, the museum would need private money to match government funding.

Behring, who had made much of his fortune in real estate, agreed that if his name was to be on the building, it should be modernized, and was willing to help pay for the transition. His support was the essential catalyst that stimulated the Smithsonian to initiate a broad-ranging public space renewal project at the museum. It began in 2002 with the center core of the building and ultimately would extend to the west and east wing exhibition galleries. Originally, the Smithsonian thought the entire process would take around 15 years, but as of the writing of this book, it is projected to extend into at least the late 2020s.

A major decision in planning the center core renovation was how to redisplay the Star-Spangled Banner, the museum's most important single artifact. This had become a complicated issue.

As discussed in chapter 5, the museum had taken a major step in conserving the flag in 1981, when a protective screen was installed in front of it that dropped to reveal the flag for only five minutes every hour. By 1994, however, one of the mechanisms that operated the screen failed and it was taken down. Once again, the flag was constantly on display.

Recognizing that the protective mechanism, while helpful, had not prevented further degradation of the flag, the museum commissioned a major new study that included leading conservators, historians, curators, and scientists to determine how best to preserve and display it in perpetuity.[310] Based on its recommendations, the museum took the flag off display completely in 1998. In 1999, it was moved to a 2,000-square-foot conservation treatment facility built specifically to allow public viewing. There visitors could see the careful work to save the flag for future generations. Conservators painstakingly removed 1.7 million stitches that tied the flag to a linen backing that had been added in 1914 to allow it to be displayed vertically. Then they gently cleaned the flag and sewed it to a lightweight Stabitex synthetic silk

Figure 6-5. Star-Spangled Banner on display in the conservation laboratory in 2005.

backing for support. They determined that it should never again be shown vertically. In the future it had to be displayed flat on a table at a 10-degree angle.

Meanwhile, the museum development staff began a public campaign to raise money to support the preservation and future display of the flag. They first obtained a grant of $10 million from Polo Ralph Lauren through First Lady Hillary Clinton's Save America's Treasures fund. Over the next few years, additional gifts came from the Pew Charitable Trusts, the John S. and James L. Knight Foundation, and the U.S. Congress, for a total of $18 million.[311]

Parallel to the conservation work and fundraising, museum curators deliberated the question of how the museum's central object should be interpreted and exhibited in the future, when it would be moved out of the conservation laboratory. The debate began in earnest in 2000. Some staff now questioned whether displaying the flag by itself was effective, especially if it had to be shown horizontally at a 10-degree angle, which required extensive floor space. In the past, they noted, visitors who saw it vertically had not learned much about the flag from the brief label text. Many didn't even realize it was a real historical object, much less the item the museum considered its most important artifact. Curator Steve Lubar, who then headed the division that bore responsibility for the flag, was among them. He said,

> I believe that American history is too complex—too interesting—to be repre-
> sented by any single object. As a Museum, we stand for the idea that Amer-
> ica is a multicultural country, with "many peoples," many ideals; a complex

identity. We've done our best to move beyond a simple history of America to tell a more true, and more interesting, story. A single object tends to tell a simple story. It can be made to tell a more complex story, true, but the Flag Hall space is not conducive to the sort of labeling that would be required.[312]

Instead, he suggested the museum might better display a selection of objects representing more collections and themes.

Soon, the museum formed an exhibition planning team to explore new ways to display and interpret the flag. Over the next year, they conceived an exhibition entitled *For Which it Stands*, in which the flag would be moved to a new location in the museum featuring a large surrounding display that would situate it in historical context. In May 2000, they presented their proposal to the museum's board for review. They said:

> The main body of the [planned] exhibition, rich with artifacts and images, [will be] a chronological look at how Americans have used and thought about the flag, from the Revolutionary era to the post-Cold War period. Organized into approximately eight time periods, *For Which It Stands* considers the flag in historical context, in connection to major events and issues—westward expansion, immigration, the Civil War, the Civil Rights Movement, etc.—and as a part of people's daily lives.[313]

The Star-Spangled Banner itself would be in the rear of the exhibition, where visitors would experience it after learning about its historical context. This plan was put on hold while the project to renovate the center core took shape.

Center core renovation opened a wide range of new possibilities for restructuring the building and redisplaying its most important artifact. To plan this major initiative, the museum hired the architectural firm Skidmore, Owings, & Merrill (SOM) to be responsible for overall planning and design.[314] Turner Construction would manage structural changes. The design firm Chermayeff & Geismar, which earlier had designed *A Nation of Nations*, was engaged to plan a new permanent gallery for the Star-Spangled Banner.

SOM proposed many intriguing ideas for the renovation, including even encasing the entire museum building in a "glass box" that would allow visitors to move from floor to floor outside the museum walls, while being able to see the city around them (Figure 6-6).

This bold change proved impractical. However, the museum did decide to make a less drastic alteration in the building by

Figure 6-6. Artist's concept drawing of the museum surrounded by a glass box, 2003.

Figure 6-7. Design concept showing the skylight, opening of third-floor balconies onto the Flag Hall, and the grand staircase leading down to the first floor.

opening a skylight from the Flag Hall in the center of the second floor up to the roof of the building three stories above (Figure 6-7).

Although this required major changes in the upper three floors of the building and considerable loss of storage space for collections, the change achieved the benefit of bringing natural light into the heart of a building that had been widely criticized for being too dark and uninviting. Associated with that change was the removal of walls on the third floor that flanked the center hall. This created broad vistas across the museum. A new grand staircase connected the museum's first and second floors, and the Nina and Ivan Selin Welcome Center opened next to the second-floor Mall entrance to enhance visitor orientation. Together, these alterations made the museum much brighter, more open, and easier to navigate.

The changes in the structure of the center core opened new possibilities for how the Star-Spangled Banner could be displayed. By the time the Blue Ribbon Commission report was issued in 2002, Smithsonian leaders had overruled the earlier curatorial plans and decided that the flag must remain at the center of the building. Sufficient space could now be configured to display it there at the required 10-degree angle. The report stated: "The Commission affirms the museum's intention to treat

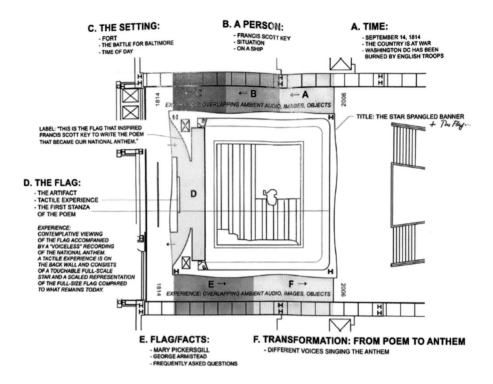

C. THE SETTING:
- FORT
- THE BATTLE FOR BALTIMORE
- TIME OF DAY

B. A PERSON:
- FRANCIS SCOTT KEY
- SITUATION
- ON A SHIP

A. TIME:
- SEPTEMBER 14, 1814
- THE COUNTRY IS AT WAR
- WASHINGTON DC HAS BEEN
  BURNED BY ENGLISH TROOPS

TITLE: THE STAR SPANGLED BANNER

LABEL: "THIS IS THE FLAG THAT INSPIRED
FRANCIS SCOTT KEY TO WRITE THE POEM
THAT BECAME OUR NATIONAL ANTHEM."

EXPERIENCE: OVERLAPPING AMBIENT AUDIO, IMAGES, OBJECTS

D. THE FLAG:
- THE ARTIFACT
- TACTILE EXPERIENCE
- THE FIRST STANZA
  OF THE POEM

EXPERIENCE:
CONTEMPLATIVE VIEWING
OF THE FLAG ACCOMPANIED
BY A "VOICELESS" RECORDING
OF THE NATIONAL ANTHEM.
A TACTILE EXPERIENCE IS ON
THE BACK WALL AND CONSISTS
OF A TOUCHABLE FULL-SCALE
STAR AND A SCALED REPRESENTATION
OF THE FULL-SIZE FLAG COMPARED
TO WHAT REMAINS TODAY.

EXPERIENCE: OVERLAPPING AMBIENT AUDIO, IMAGES, OBJECTS

E. FLAG/FACTS:
- MARY PICKERSGILL
- GEORGE ARMISTEAD
- FREQUENTLY ASKED QUESTIONS

F. TRANSFORMATION: FROM POEM TO ANTHEM
- DIFFERENT VOICES SINGING THE ANTHEM

Figure 6-8. Design plan for the new Star-Spangled Banner gallery, 2004.

the restored Star Spangled Banner as a central icon—to return it to the visible core of the museum and present it in conjunction with an interpretive exhibit on the flag's meanings and uses throughout American history."[315] Chermayeff & Geismar worked with the staff to explore different ways this could be accomplished. By 2004, they had settled on the design shown in Figure 6-8, which provided some historical context for the flag.

The final plan for the center core renovation required such extensive changes to the building that the museum had to close to the public for two years to implement it. During the closure, an exhibition of over 150 objects entitled *Treasures of American History* was shown at the National Air and Space Museum so that visitors to Washington could still see at least a sample of some of the best-known objects in the museum's collections.[316] It included such favorites as the ruby slippers from *The Wizard of Oz*, Thomas Edison's light bulb, Lewis and Clark's compass, Abraham Lincoln's top hat, George Custer's buckskin coat, sections of the ENIAC computer, Prince's guitar, and Kermit the Frog.

The museum reopened to the public on Friday, 21 November 2008, under the theme "Shining New Light on American History," which highlighted the architectural changes to the building.[317] President George W. Bush was there to dedicate the new Star-Spangled Banner gallery, the most important new attraction. Concluding

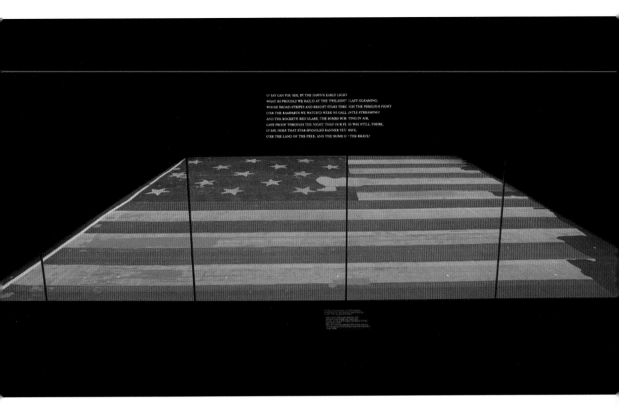

Figure 6-9. The Star-Spangled Banner installed in its new location.

his remarks, he said, "The Museum of American History is a wonderful place to begin your journey as an American. These halls reflect both the duties and privileges of citizenship. They remind us that America's highest ideals have always required brave defenders. They remind us that our liberty is a precious gift from God."[318]

The flag, which measured 34 by 30 feet, was now housed in a protective case that the museum claimed was "one of the largest display environments ever designed for a single object." Visitors could see it up close and examine its detail. The controlled atmosphere inside the case maintained constant heat and humidity and protected the flag from dirt, dust, and even fire, as the controlled, nitrogen-rich atmosphere would not support combustion. The flag was shown tilted at a 10-degree angle in very low light, below the first stanza of Francis Scott Key's poem "The Defence of Fort M'Henry." All these provisions were required to preserve the large and fragile 200-year-old textile and "ensure that future generations will have the opportunity to view one of the most potent symbols of our national identity." A companion interactive display allowed visitors to explore a wide range of facts about the flag.[319]

As planned, the exhibition surrounding the artifact explained its history as an object, told how and when it came to the Smithsonian, summarized how it had been displayed over time, and concluded with a video sampling the many ways Americans have historically used their flag, from celebrations to rallies to protests. On the outside wall where the flag had once hung, the museum mounted an "abstract flag" sculpture that signaled what was in the exhibition behind. Although purists in the museum lamented that this central location no longer displayed a real object, the size and scope of the sculpture gave the location definition and purpose.

Initially, the museum still planned to mount a separate exhibition elsewhere in the building to trace a more extended history of the Star-Spangled Banner as a national symbol, but funding was not readily available, and soon, the principal curators who had planned *For Which It Stands* left the museum for other jobs. This was unfortunate, because it meant that the opportunity to provide an extensive, thoughtful historical analysis of the role of the flag as symbol as well as a material artifact in American history was lost.

The major architectural changes in the center core were successful. Navigation around the building was greatly improved. Visitors were less likely to become disoriented. The relation of the three exhibition floors to each other was visible from one space. Flag Hall became the clear center of the building, and the location for major events and ceremonies. These included naturalization ceremonies for new citizens (as discussed previously), inaugural parties, Fourth of July celebrations, concerts, and many dinners and parties for sponsors.

Perhaps only historians noted a dark circle of terrazzo that is surrounded by stars in front of the "abstract flag." This marked where earlier visitors once peered through an opening to the floor below and watched the Foucault pendulum slowly demonstrate the diurnal rotation of the earth. While the museum had changed its name to National Museum of American History back in 1980, this architectural change finally finished the symbolic restructuring of the center of the building to match it.

The public space renewal plan led to a fundamental shift in the organization of museum exhibitions. From the time the museum building opened in 1964, exhibitions had been structured by floors. The renovation, however, was planned to proceed by vertical sections of the museum: first the center core, then the west wing, and finally, in future years, the east wing. This in turn meant that the floor plan of the museum took on a new form (Figure 6-1). Unlike the plans for earlier periods, each floor was now divided into three zones: West, Center, and East. Themes were listed for each wing of each floor: 3 West, American Culture; 3 East, American Wars and Politics; 2 West, The Nation We Build Together; 2 East, American Ideals; 1 West, Innovation, Creativity, and Enterprise; and 1 East, Transportation and Technology.

This organizational structure developed from the realities of the building renovation, not a conceptual restructuring. It was a marked contrast to the clarity and coherence—introduced by a large, chronological exhibition—that the Blue Ribbon Commission had sought.

The Major Exhibitions: East Wing

A Team Approach to Exhibitions

By the 2000s, exhibition development—especially for large exhibitions—increasingly depended on extensive teams of professionals. Content was usually shaped not by a single curator but by a group of them, often representing different areas of the museum. Likewise, design was becoming more complex and often required multiple designers rather than just one. Because of this, designs for larger exhibitions were now often contracted to outside firms, which could draw on specialists in a wide variety of areas more easily than the in-house design staff. Collections specialists, exhibit developers, image researchers, conservators, media specialists, interactive exhibit designers, lighting specialists, and others all became involved in developing the final exhibition products that museum visitors came to see. The number of people involved could range from a handful to dozens of individuals. The successes, as well as the failures, of exhibitions depended on all of them. More than in the past, the museum's major exhibitions were broad institutional products involving a wide range of contributors, not the work of individual curators or small curator-and-designer pairs.

The American Presidency: A Glorious Burden (2000)

As noted earlier, creating an exhibition on the American presidency was the highest priority Secretary Small had for the National Museum of American History when he took office in 2000, and he secured major funding for it from Kenneth Behring. Other support came from the U.S. Congress and a group of 10 private individuals and corporations. Museum Director Crew, Head of Curatorial Affairs Lonnie Bunch, and Curator of Political History Harry Rubenstein led the extensive team that collaborated on this crash project, which had to open shortly after the presidential election that year.[320] Created in only 10 months, it was the fastest project of this size and scope the museum had ever done.

All three men were aware of the strengths and limitations of the museum's political history collection as it related to presidential history. They shrewdly developed a plan for the exhibition that made it comprehensive but also selective in ways that would showcase the museum's most important presidential artifacts. The exhibition included a photographic timeline listing every president and including an image of him, but overall, it was thematic, not chronological. It was not organized as a march through every administration, or the standard eras of American history as presented in textbooks.

The resulting exhibition was divided into 11 sections and spread across 9,000 square feet. As noted in the title, it focused not only on the power and significance of the office, but also on the trials and difficulties faced by American chief executives.[321]

Visitors entered through a section focused on presidential campaigns, which was the broadest area of museum holdings in political history. These highlighted the freedom Americans had to participate directly in selecting their national leader,

Figure 6-10. George Washington's uniform displayed at the entrance to the presidency exhibition.

a defining characteristic of American democracy. Next came Swearing In, where visitors could hear voices of recent presidents reciting the oath of office. The Creating the Presidency section displayed objects dating from the earliest days of the republic. Next were the two sections Celebrating Inaugurations and Presidential Roles. The latter was particularly clever, as the various roles were illustrated by objects from those eras and presidential administrations where the collection had strengths. The roles presented were Chief Executive, Commander in Chief, Chief Diplomat, Manager of the Economy, National Leader, Party Leader, and Ceremonial Head of State.

The exhibition continued with The White House as Symbol and Home, Limits of Presidential Power, and Assassination and Mourning, again an area where the museum had important collections, especially related to President Lincoln's death. Finally came Communicating the Presidency, The Presidency in Popular Imagination, and Life After the Presidency.

Initially standing at the entrance of the exhibition was one of the museum's greatest national treasures, George Washington's military uniform. Later, this would be moved to the *Price of Freedom: Americans at War* exhibition when it opened in 2004. It was replaced by the carriage in which President Ulysses S. Grant rode to his second inaugural in 1873 (and in which Secretary Dillon Ripley rode to the opening of *1876* during the bicentennial—see chapter 4). The desk on which Thomas Jefferson drafted parts of the Declaration of Independence was also originally a highlight, but it too was later moved to a newer exhibition, *American Democracy: A Great Leap of Faith*, when it opened in 2017. Other important objects included a "Teddy" bear inspired by Theodore Roosevelt, radio microphones used by Franklin D. Roosevelt

Figure 6-11. Section on assassination and mourning in the presidency exhibition.

for fireside chats, testimony from the Watergate hearings, and Bill Clinton's saxophone.

A section called Assassination and Mourning contained many important objects associated with President Lincoln, including the top hat he wore the night of his death.

The History Channel produced more than a dozen videos as a donation for the exhibition, and it included a range of interactive displays. One of the most popular, for visitors of all ages, was an interactive podium and teleprompter, where visitors could deliver an excerpt from a famous presidential speech and see their image projected into a historical setting. Chief Justice William Rehnquist, whose robe was on display in the exhibition, enjoyed the interactive so much that he performed Franklin Roosevelt's first inaugural address several times for his family and his clerks.

Figure 6-12. A visitor tries delivering a presidential address.

In the press release announcing the exhibition, Secretary Small focused on the wide-ranging expectations that Americans have of their president. "We take for granted that the same person who has the qualities to command armies and deploy an arsenal of awful force will also be able to launch a baseball season. This exhibition shows all these aspects of the job."[322]

What Does It Mean to Be American? (2001–2018)   255

The exhibition was extremely popular with the public, and initially required timed tickets. It also received generally favorable press coverage. Many wondered, as had Secretary Small, why an exhibition on the subject had never been mounted before. No director since has considered eliminating it.

America on the Move (2003)

In the mid-1990s, the museum began working to modernize its transportation exhibitions. Except for the Maritime Hall, which had been updated in 1978, they had changed little since the 1960s. In 1997, the museum received $3 million in seed money from the Department of Transportation to begin planning a new exhibition. It allowed the museum to hire staff, contract with a design firm, and bring in outside advisors. By 1999, a conceptual design was complete.

In contrast to the previous transportation exhibitions, which had focused on tracing the development of technology, the new exhibition would concentrate on the social, economic, and cultural changes related to transportation. Americans were a mobile people, and freedom to move was among the defining qualities of what it meant to be American. As the museum reported to the Blue Ribbon Commission in 2001,

> For the first time, visitors will be able to see these artifacts as they once were: moving people and products from place to place, a vital part of the nation's transportation system, a vital part of our business, social and cultural history. *America on the Move* will tell of immigration and migration, cars and culture, the importance of cars, trucks and trains in the nation's economy—as well as the pleasures of hitting the road for a summer vacation.[323]

With the plan in hand, the museum initiated a fundraising campaign that eventually raised a total of $22 million. The principal sponsor was General Motors Corporation, which donated $10 million. Additional major funding came from the State Farm Companies, the American Automobile Association, and ExxonMobil, while five other companies donated $1 million. The History Channel donated $3 million, including production of video elements for the show.[324]

The exhibition opened on 22 November 2003.[325] At 26,000 square feet, it was the largest in the building at the time, and second only to *A Nation of Nations* in the history of the museum. It included 340 objects, among them trains, cars, a bus, a streetcar, motorcycles, a subway car, a camping trailer, and a piece of U.S. Route 66, the "People's Highway." The largest artifact was the 199-ton, 92-foot-long 1401 locomotive that had been installed in the museum building before it opened (Figure 6-13). The new exhibition was planned around it, but it was painstakingly moved back 30 feet to provide more usable exhibit space. It was now interpreted not from a technical perspective, but to tell a story of expanding national markets and the role of African American porters and firemen in the railroad industry.

The exhibition included 19 sections and more than a dozen historical settings. These were brought to life by large mural backdrops, 73 cast figures, and carefully

Figure 6-13. The 1401 locomotive in the 2003 exhibition.

constructed soundscapes. Among the settings were the coming of the railroad to a California town in 1876 and the role of the streetcar and automobile in creating suburbs—and traffic jams.

The exhibition concluded in Los Angeles, a "global city," and the related port of Long Beach. This section focused on the multimodal containerized shipping that standardized movement of goods around the world and made life both more hectic and more efficient. Multiple video screens, music, voices, and a large satellite image of Los Angeles gave this section a frenetic character that was a marked contrast with the other settings. A book, *On the Move: Transportation and the American Story*[326], accompanied the exhibition.

America on the Move attracted media coverage from around the nation, most of it positive. The *Baltimore Sun* gave the exhibition extensive coverage, concluding that "visitors to *America on the Move* will feel like they're on a road, in a rail depot, wandering a car dealership, seeking shelter for the night or riding a streetcar. The word 'museum' rarely comes to mind."[327] Often reporters featured objects in the exhibition that related to their local communities. The *Santa Cruz California Sentinel*, for example, focused on the *Jupiter* engine that had been built for the Santa Cruz railroad in 1876. The *Indianapolis Star* in Indiana featured a 1939 Indiana school bus that was on display.[328]

The *Washington Post* was more wary. Its article "The Wheel Thing,"[329] was written by Bob Thompson, who in 2002 had penned the long exposé "History for $ale," about the impact of major donors on the museum, discussed earlier in the chapter. Now he was back, seeking to discern whether General Motors, the main exhibition

Figure 6-14. Coming of the railroad to Santa Cruz, California.

sponsor, had unduly influenced the content of this large new show. He didn't mention the many other sponsors.

Although he noted that curators told him the initial planning was done under a grant from the Department of Transportation and the content was largely decided before General Motors even got involved, Thompson continued to probe. He didn't find much to expose, other than that the exhibition had not devoted much space to political or environmental issues related to transportation, which of course had not been its subject. His article also provided a general, if opinionated, overview of the show. He concluded, a bit grumpily, "The museum has mounted a rich exhibition, in both senses of the word, and there's much more to it than the question of a few pulled punches."

More interesting was the study that the Smithsonian's Office of Policy and Analysis did of behavior of visitors to the exhibition in the spring of 2005, a year and a half after it opened. They tracked 151 visitor groups.[330] Surprisingly, 46 percent went into the exhibition through the intended exit, not the entrance. Visits ranged from less than a minute to 55 minutes. The average visit tracked was 11.5 minutes. Visitors spent the most time in sections near where they entered, and many turned around and left before walking through the entire large display.

Comments generally indicated that most visitors understood and appreciated the new focus on the social history of transportation rather than on transportation technology. Many older visitors felt nostalgic at seeing cars or buses like those they had used in earlier years. Some liked the soundscapes and interactives, while others

Figure 6-15. Coping with traffic jams.

were interested only in objects, and wished they could read the labels in silence without distracting sounds.

Was the exhibition ultimately too big? Most visitors said they wanted more, not less, even though almost no one saw everything. Ninety-eight percent of visitors rated the exhibition either superior (19%), excellent (58%), or good (21%), and only two percent rated it fair (1%) or poor (1%). Moreover, the longer they stayed, the more they liked it.

The Price of Freedom: Americans at War (2004)

From the late 1960s until the early 2000s, the museum's Armed Forces Hall had not had a complete renovation. Its large permanent exhibition did not extend beyond the history of the Civil War and it was filled with cases of uniforms, equipment, and guns presented with antiquated designs and labels. These focused more on object descriptions than historical interpretation. Indeed, as it aged, museum leaders toyed with the idea of eliminating a large exhibition on military history altogether.

As an alternative, the museum had been mounting topical temporary exhibitions. These included *Personal Legacy: The Healing of a Nation* (1992), showing objects left at the Vietnam Veterans Memorial; *World War II GI* (1993) on the experience of the common soldier; *WWI, All May Apply: Women in the Navy, The Yeoman (F)* (1997) on the first women to serve in the U.S. Navy; *Fast Attacks and Boomers: Submarines in the Cold War* (2000); and *West Point in the Making of America, 1802–1918* (2002), on the role of West Point graduates in reshaping America's infrastructure as well as fighting its wars.

Ken Behring's pledge put mounting a large military history exhibition back at the top of the museum's agenda. His commitment to this topic was deeply personal. Although he had never served in the military himself, he strongly believed that those who had fought and died for the nation had guaranteed him the freedom that had made it possible for him and his family to prosper. As he would say about his gift to the Smithsonian in his 2004 autobiography, *Road to Purpose*, "I . . . knew I owed a debt of gratitude to the country that had allowed me to achieve my dreams. I was inspired to show the history, opportunity and future that can be attained with the freedom we have in America."[331]

Planning began in early 2002 and, like the presidency exhibition, this was put on a fast track—scheduled to open in late 2004. To lead the effort, the museum hired Robin Reed, former director of the Museum of the Confederacy in Richmond, Virginia, and several support staff. Although Behring was kept apprised of exhibition progress, he was not involved in planning it. Because the exhibition was to be large and complicated, the museum hired the firm of Christopher Chadbourne & Associates of Boston to design it. The company had extensive experience in creating exhibitions related to military history.

By July 2002, the exhibition team had selected its main theme: "*The Price of Freedom* investigates the dynamic relationship between American society and its military." The exhibition was to examine four major wars, the American Revolution, the Civil War, World War II, and the Vietnam War.[332] As the team developed their plans, they convened a group of leading military historians to review and comment on them. The group include Allan Millett of Ohio State, Russell Weigel of Temple University, and Richard Kohn of Duke University, among others.

The outside experts concluded that focusing on just these four wars gave a distorted picture of America's military history. They advised that the exhibition also had to cover, at least to some degree, conflicts between White Americans and Native Americans, the Seven Years' War, the War of 1812, the Mexican War, the Spanish-American War, the Korean War, and perhaps even recent conflicts. Although this made creating the exhibition much harder, especially since the space allocated to it did not change, the team agreed and modified the plans accordingly. The initial four wars would be "pillar conflicts," and the other wars would be covered in connecting sections between them.

By January 2003, the project had reached 35 percent design, a major milestone. However, it was also moving into troubled waters. When the Smithsonian team saw how Chadbourne & Associates had developed their initial ideas into a full floor plan and sample elevations, they recognized that it would need fundamental revision. Moreover, they were behind in identifying objects and images to support the plan and in drafting a workable script. Particularly problematic was that the museum had not identified a Bell UH-1H "Huey" helicopter to put on display in the section on the Vietnam War, even though it was designated to be the largest single object in the exhibition. Topping off the crisis was the fact that project director and chief curator Robin Reed had decided to leave the museum to take a position with Colonial Williamsburg.

At the same time, Ken Behring was becoming concerned about the costs of the outside staff being hired to do the project. He had expected that only existing museum staff would plan it. He told the Smithsonian that he would not pay for hiring a replacement for Reed from outside the museum. Behring was also upset about other costs being charged to the exhibition budget, such as artifact storage and development expenses. Indeed, he became so upset that he demanded his support for the exhibition be cut from $20 million to only $16 million, and said that henceforth, he would reimburse the museum only for expended costs that he approved, not give them a free hand in spending his gift. Although this was contrary to Smithsonian practice, Smithsonian leaders reluctantly agreed to the restrictions rather than cancel the project.

To replace Reed in the spring of 2003, the museum chose curator David Allison (this book's author). He had experience with large exhibitions, having been project director of *Information Age* and served on the curatorial team for *Science in American Life*. He also had a background in naval history. He warily accepted the assignment. Although he knew the exhibition was having difficulties, he also recognized the importance of the project to the museum, especially in the wake of the failure of the Reynolds-funded exhibition. Finally, he thought his experience might help put things back on track. To save additional money after he took the lead, he soon had to lay off other temporary project staff, scale back expensive audiovisual programs, and slash planned maintenance funds.[333]

The revised exhibition team reviewed the major theme for the exhibition.[334] They decided that instead of trying to focus on the very broad topic of the interaction of the military with society at large, a subject not well supported by the museum's collections, they should narrow the theme to focus directly on American wars. The decision to expand exhibition coverage from four wars to over a dozen made this even more imperative. This revised theme became "Wars have been defining episodes in American History." Linked to it were two subthemes, "American wars were fought on the home front as well as the battlefield," and "Wars have demanded great sacrifice by both soldiers and civilians." The exhibition then became a sequential survey of American wars, focusing on ways they reflected the major themes.

The team benefitted greatly from the results of focus groups held to explore ideas and themes related to the topic. Results indicated that visitors wanted to see the reality of war, including images of causalities and destruction, and not just artifacts such as weapons and uniforms. Visitors were also interested in having the exhibit extend to the present to cover current conflicts that were affecting them and their families.

The title of the exhibition also became an issue. After expanding the display's scope, the team became convinced that the title needed to be replaced. They pointed out that many American wars were not, in fact, fought to defend American freedom. These included the Indian Wars, the Mexican War, the Spanish-American War, the Korean War, and the Vietnam War. They also said that it tacitly made a claim that the substance of the exhibition was not designed to support. Their recommendation was supported by surveys of museum visitors. The team proposed that the name be changed simply to "Americans at War" or "Fighting for America."

After much discussion within the Smithsonian, Secretary Small personally

Figure 6-16. Entry to the *Price of Freedom* exhibition.

decided that the title could not be changed. He professed that he made this decision because he thought it was the best title, but he certainly also knew that Ken Behring continued to favor it. The team was allowed only to add a subtitle, making the full exhibition name *The Price of Freedom: Americans at War.* As the team predicted, when reviews of the exhibition came out, the title became a frequent point of criticism.

Creating the exhibition became an exciting challenge. Curator Dik Daso led the effort to acquire a Huey helicopter from the Texas Air Command Museum. Artifacts from the museum's extensive military history collection were identified. Hundreds of images were acquired, and personal stories collected from books, diaries, memoirs, and websites. Chadbourne & Associates demonstrated their experience and skill with military topics, especially their ability to create large graphic murals and image panels that would serve as backdrops for many sections. The History Channel produced and donated 10 videos shown throughout the exhibition, plus a concluding film, *Fighting for America*.

The resulting 18,200-square-foot exhibition opened on schedule: Veterans Day, 11 November 2004. It was organized chronologically in 10 sections: an introduction, the Revolutionary War, the Wars of Expansion (including the Indian Wars, the Mexican War and the Spanish-American War), the Civil War, World War I, World War II, the Cold War and Korean War, the Vietnam War, recent conflicts (including the 1991 Gulf War and the wars in Afghanistan and Iraq), and a concluding section focused on Medal of Honor recipients.[335]

On display were more than 850 artifacts. Among them were George Washington's uniform and camp kit, the buckskin coat worn by George Custer while he

Figure 6-17. Siege of Yorktown, 1781, turning point in the American Revolution.

was stationed at frontier army posts in the west during the western Indian War, the chairs on which Civil War generals Robert E. Lee and Ulysses S. Grant sat during the surrender ceremony at Appomattox Court House in Virginia, a Willys Jeep used for transporting troops and supplies during World War II, General Colin Powell's uniform from Operation Desert Storm during the Gulf War, twisted steel girders from the World Trade Center attack on 11 September 2001, and a PackBot robot used in Afghanistan to help troops explore compounds and caves from a safe distance. The Bell UH-1H Huey helicopter, which had been deployed to Vietnam in 1966, included a video display on which visitors could hear a selection of war stories (Figure 6-18). The exhibition was the first time the Smithsonian had mounted an interpretive display on the Vietnam War.

Numerous "My View" panels throughout the exhibition were an innovative feature. These provided perspectives of historical actors, in their own words. The team's goal in using this device—indeed in the exhibition as a whole—was to invite visitors to reflect more deeply for themselves on how wars had shaped American history. In addition, visitors could also use touch-screen computers to select among "My Story" first-person accounts of men and women who had been eyewitnesses or participants in the nation's conflicts. As an introductory video in the exhibition advised, "As you visit this exhibition, consider how wars have affected the nation, how they have influenced American society, and how they have touched you and your family." Accompanying the exhibition was an extensive website, a catalog, and an education packet that was distributed to every school district in the nation.

Announcing the exhibition in a museum press release, Director Glass stated,

Figure 6-18. The Huey helicopter, largest artifact in the exhibition. A video station located inside the Huey let visitors hear related war stories.

This exhibition—the only one of its kind in a U.S. museum—gives visitors a sweeping and memorable overview of America's military experience and the central role it has played in our national life. Visitors will experience the impact of war on citizen soldiers—average men and women who serve their country—as well as on their families and communities.[336]

As the museum had anticipated, response to the exhibition was mixed. Smithsonian studies confirmed that visitor response was highly positive: 78 percent of visitors rated it as either superior or excellent, a figure matched only by the *Star-Spangled Banner* exhibition. The overall experience rating was 25 percent, compared to the average exhibit rating of 20 percent.[337] It quickly became one of the museum's most popular exhibitions. Not surprisingly, veterans and their families deeply appreciated it. Vietnam veterans in particular were glad the museum was finally exhibiting something that recognized their place in American history. Some left memorabilia about their units and service with the museum staff, and some of these were later added to the display of the Huey. Families of victims of the 11 September 2001 attack on the United States were also moved by the inclusion of a display covering that event.

On the other hand, others disliked the exhibition or found it disturbingly positive. They included visitors who found some or all of the wars depicted, including the ongoing conflicts in Afghanistan and Iraq, to be horrifying, tragic, costly, and unjust.

This mixed response was mirrored in the extensive press coverage the museum received. Thomas Ricks, military correspondent at the *Washington Post*, for example, gave the exhibition a largely positive review.

Showing unusual courage, the Smithsonian has charged onto the controversial battleground of America's wars—and generally done well.... [Its]
exhibition opening today to mark Veterans Day is the first overview of U.S.
military history the Smithsonian has ever mounted...Some might be put off
by the loaded title, "The Price of Freedom: Americans at War." But behind
that red-state rubric is a well-balanced show, with enough combat gear to
please the warriors, enough emphasis on casualties and Indians and blacks
and women to comfort the loyal opposition, and enough balance to satisfy
most historians.[338]

Press coverage outside Washington frequently focused on the theme of sacrifice and
on the objects and stories of common soldiers in the display. An article in the *Austin
American Statesman*, for example, stated,

Battlefield veterans remember these artifacts of American wars. The tiny
folding can opener that was kept on a chain necklace with dog tags and used
to rip through the round green tops of C-rations in the boonies of Vietnam.... "It's important for kids to see all this and know that war is not like
the video games they play," said Vietnam veteran Clarence Sasser of Texas,
who won the Congressional Medal of Honor as a 20-year-old medic who
struggled to save those around him after his legs were shot.[339]

In contrast, Carole Emberton wrote in the *Journal of American History*,

"The Price of Freedom" ignores the cost of war, both on the home front
and abroad.... The exhibit's title suggests an interpretive stance that assumes
freedom is, and has always been, the objective of American military engage-
ments. But freedom is a problematic term, and in failing to recognize how
the meaning of freedom has been contested historically, the exhibit takes the
viewer on a whiggish stroll through American social and political history,
conveniently indulging any desire he or she might have to rely on a facile
belief in the mythic march of progress and democratic expansion.[340]

Whatever visitors felt about their experiences in the exhibition, it gave them the
opportunity to walk through a comprehensive overview that highlighted the significance of war in shaping America history, from the colonial era to the present. In its
earlier displays of military history, the museum never had either the aspiration or the
resources to attempt anything so ambitious.

On the Water (2009)

Since the opening of the Museum of History and Technology in the 1960s, the
transportation exhibitions at the museum had always included a section on maritime
history. When *America on the Move* was being planned in the 1990s, the museum also
planned to renovate its maritime exhibition and keep it linked to the new exhibition
on land transportation. In fact, the new General Motors Hall of Transportation
included the space for both.

Figure 6-19. Entry to the maritime exhibition.

The maritime exhibition had already been updated once, in 1978. The original exhibition had mostly been ship models that illustrated changes in watercraft design. The 1978 display blended models with other artifacts and settings that linked technological with economic and social history. Favorites included a towboat pilothouse, a tobacco warehouse, and a tattoo parlor.

Planning for the new maritime hall was led by project director Paula Johnson.[341] Initially the exhibition was to be produced at the same time as *America on the Move*, but the museum did not have enough money to build and open it on that schedule. Attracting the necessary support took years of making proposals. Finally, in 2007, the museum made a pitch to Mærsk Mc-Kinney Møller, a 93-year-old Danish businessman who ran A. P. Moller–Maersk, the world's largest shipping conglomerate. Møller was delighted to learn that the Smithsonian was planning to do an exhibition on maritime history and particularly interested in the section on American shipbuilding in World War II. He credited this effort to being critical not only to winning the war, but also to saving the company that he inherited. The A. P. Møller and Chastine McKinney-Møller Foundation soon pledged $4.5 million to the exhibition and became its principal sponsor. Final design and construction of the exhibition could now be completed.

On the Water: Stories from Maritime America opened on National Maritime Day, 22 May 2009.[342] The goal of the 8,500-square-foot exhibition was to go beyond traditional sea stories and displays of ship models to demonstrate that maritime history had a broad relevance to American history and all museum visitors. This meant

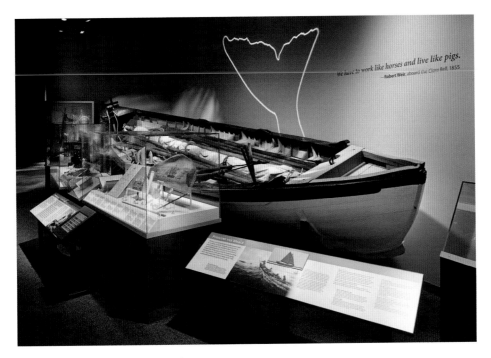

Figure 6-20. Exhibit section on whaling.

including stories about women as well as men, ethnic and racial diversity, and shipboard and waterfront life of average maritime workers as well as famous sea captains.

The exhibition included more than 360 objects, supporting images, video, and interactives. It had seven chronological sections: Living in the Atlantic World, 1450–1800; Maritime Nation, 1800–1850; Fishing for a Living, 1840–1920; Inland Waterways, 1820–1940; Ocean Crossings 1870–1969; Answering the Call, 1917–1945; and Modern Maritime America.

Visitors could walk through a two-story display of a 1920s engine room from a buoy tender. The passage led directly into *America on the Move*. As Paula Johnson, curator of the exhibition explained,

> In addition to covering familiar topics such as fisheries and ocean commerce, [*On the Water*] also addresses important themes in American history: the transatlantic slave trade, migration and the California gold rush, the exploitation of natural resources, immigration, and the role of maritime activity in modern globalized commerce. This integrated and expanded treatment of American maritime history inspires visitors to recognize the relevance of the maritime past and present.[343]

The First Ladies (2011)

The exhibition that opened in 2011 entitled simply *The First Ladies* was the eighth version of the museum's display of first ladies' gowns since the first one in the Arts and Industries Building in 1914. No other artifact collection had been reinterpreted so many times. New versions were done for different reasons, sometimes because dresses had to be changed for conservation, other times because exhibit areas were being refurbished. Throughout its history, however, the museum always endeavored to keep some portion of the collection on view, due partly to its popularity, and also because the exhibition was one of the few displays in the museum that focused explicitly on an area of women's history.

Curator Lisa Kathleen Graddy and designer Clare Brown led the team that planned this new version. They were well aware of the earlier exhibitions and aimed to include their best features. These were blended together in the most sophisticated and balanced presentation of the subject that the museum had ever achieved.[344]

Outside the exhibition were life-sized photographs of notable first ladies, creating a photo opportunity for visitors, as had been done for *First Ladies: Political Role and Public Image* (1992). Featured in the first section inside, The Fashionable First Lady, was a large case with dresses of 12 first ladies from different eras, reminiscent of a previous short-term exhibition, *The First Ladies at the Smithsonian* (2008) (Figure 6-21).

Now, however, the team used fiber-optic lighting that allowed the display to be much brighter and more dramatic than in earlier exhibitions (Figure 6-22). More-

Figure 6-21. *The First Ladies at the Smithsonian* short-term exhibition from 2008.

Figure 6-22. *The First Ladies* (2011).

Figure 6-23. *First Ladies* case studies from 2011.

over, the presentation was modular, so different examples could easily be rotated. Also here were china and silver from different eras in the White House, echoing displays included in *Ceremonial Court* (1989).

In the next section, the dress of the current first lady stood alone in a central case, as in *A First Lady's Debut* (2010), another short-term presentation.

Nearby were dresses of other recent first ladies. Now the team wisely added video, donated by the Lifetime channel, a component of A&E Networks, showing first ladies dancing in their dresses, accompanied by a screen highlighting specific details of their dress designs. This was the first time the museum had shown the dresses in motion. The exhibition concluded with case studies of four first ladies from different eras, summarizing their political roles and personal agendas during their tenures, reminiscent of *First Ladies: Political Role and Public Image* (1992).

This section also was modular, so individual examples could be changed without affecting the design. Overall, the exhibition displayed 26 dresses and more than 160 other objects, including artifacts belonging to first ladies ranging from Martha Washington to Michelle Obama.

Looking to the future, a prominent exhibition panel explicitly raised the issue of what would happen if the nation elected a woman as president. It pointed out that the role of first lady was essentially to be the official hostess for the White House and president. The role had sometimes been filled by family members who were not the president's wife. Should the first female president so desire, the function could easily be filled by her husband or some other family member. No matter what she decides, it is likely that the museum will need to respond by producing a ninth version of its first ladies exhibition.

Food: Transforming the American Table, 1950–2000 (2012)

In August 2001, popular television chef Julia Child announced that she was leaving her home in Cambridge, Massachusetts, and moving back to California, her home state.[345] Curators at the museum who were interested in food history saw this as an exceptional opportunity. They contacted Child to see if she would be willing to donate a selection of objects to the Smithsonian. She agreed. Then, when the curators arrived to survey possibilities, they came up with a much bolder idea. Would she be willing to donate the entire kitchen, including all the objects? Once again, she said yes. Over the next seven months, a team from the Smithsonian surveyed, cataloged, and packed some 1,200 objects to come to the Smithsonian. Not since the acquisition of the Headsville Post Office in 1971, with its 306 associated objects, had the museum acquired a setting so extensive.

In August 2002, the museum opened *Bon Appétit! Julia Child's Kitchen at the Smithsonian* on the first floor of the west wing.[346] Child, who was 90, came to the opening. The small display featured the beloved kitchen with its original objects and video from Child's PBS television program. Originally planned for a run of six months, the display stayed on view until the west wing closed for renovation in 2012.

Realizing that the closure was coming, the food history group proposed a new exhibition that included, but did not focus exclusively on, Julia Child's kitchen. Instead, they used it as a point of departure for a broader exploration of changing American food ways. This 3,800-square-foot exhibition was approved and in 2012 the museum opened *Food: Transforming the American Table, 1950–2000.*[347]

The exhibition had four sections: Resetting the Table, which explored how foods and flavors from nations around the world were integrated into American life; Wine for the Table, which traced the growth and expansion of American wine and wine-making after 1950; New and Improved, which explored new technologies and increased food production, processing, and distribution; and Open Table, a

Figure 6-24. Inside Julia Child's kitchen.

Figure 6-25. Display of fast-food artifacts.

22-foot-long communal table where visitors could share their thoughts and experiences about food in American history.

Curator Paula Johnson said of the exhibition,

> The second half of the 20th century was a time of rapid change in America. This exhibition taps into the widespread and robust interest in food-related topics and encourages dialogue about food and the forces and factors that influenced how and what we eat.[348]

American Stories (2012)

A principal recommendation of the Blue Ribbon Commission had been that the museum create a large introductory exhibition that was chronological in organization and comprehensive in scope. In the tentative floor plan included in its report, this exhibition was to be 22,000 square feet in size and occupy the majority of the second floor of the west wing. Renovation of three public floors of this wing were to follow renovation of the center core. Principal funding for the exhibition was to come from the Behring gift. Planning for the exhibition began in 2003, but it moved at a slow pace while the center core renovation and the presidency and military history exhibitions in the east wing took priority.

By the spring of 2005, the exhibit team had developed their preliminary plan. At this point, following the guidance of Director Glass, the exhibition was entitled *American Dreams: A new exhibition about life, liberty, and the pursuit of happiness.* The concept proposal further explained,

> For centuries, people have imagined America as a land of opportunity, a place to pursue dreams of a better life for themselves, their families, and their communities. This exhibition tells the story of how this vision first emerged during the colonial era, how it was established as a founding principle of the nation, and how it has been expressed, pursued, claimed, and contested by diverse groups over the course of American history.[349]

The team proposed two ways the exhibition could be organized: chronological, as had always been intended, or thematic. Following the thematic structure, which the team preferred, topics such as religion, upward mobility, and the frontier would be explored across time. Alternatively, the chronological structure would consider the themes in each period.

To move from concept to design, the museum hired Christopher Chadbourne & Associates, recently finished designing *The Price of Freedom: Americans at War.* Over the next several years, while the museum was closed for renovation, the plan matured. The space allocated for it was reduced to around 8,000 square feet. The title also changed to *Explore American History—Discover American Dreams.*

In developing the revised content, the curators sought to provide a more balanced view of American history. They wanted to convey that, in fact, there was not one American dream, but that Americans differed in their aspirations. They wanted to show that American history included much conflict and failure as well as realization of ambitions. Stories they planned to cover, for example, would include creating the Declaration of Independence, the Constitution, the transcontinental railroad, electric lighting, and personal computers. But they also must include the Trail of Tears, slavery, persecution of Mormons, Chinese exclusion, the Scopes trial, and protest movements.

In September 2007, the team presented its revised concept for review to a group that included the director, Ken Behring, and David Behring, Ken's son. Just prior to the meeting, David had sent to the museum a list of notable Americans that he and his father thought should be candidates for the exhibition.[350] It seemed like a return to their initial idea of an exhibition on American achievers. The museum did not have time to respond to this input.

The meeting was a disaster. Ken Behring despised the museum's new plan. Meeting notes reported that he believed it was only approaching American history from a negative perspective and that it was not about "the people who made this country." When told that the plan intentionally struck a balance between positive and negative aspects of history, he countered "50/50 is fine for the *Washington Post*, but not for me." He concluded "I'm not going to fund something that is negative.... It is time we had something that makes this country look great."[351]

In the weeks following the meeting, the director and museum board members calmed the situation down with Behring, and planning continued. Yet over the following months, it became clear that basic issues remained. The museum would not accept the donor dictating content and was unwilling to present only a rosy view of the nation's past. Behring, for his part, was not willing to sponsor an exhibition that did not emphasize what, in his mind, were the achievements of past leaders that had made America exceptional. Without his funding, the large project petered out. The museum at this point was not willing to seek major funding from another source.

Three years later, in 2010, Glass launched an alternative chronological exhibition with a revised, more limited goal. Since the museum's entire west wing would be closing in 2012 for renovation, many objects favored by visitors would come off display. These included the ruby slippers from *The Wizard of Oz* and other popular-culture objects, musical instruments, sports artifacts, textiles, and technological artifacts. The museum would create a temporary gallery of around 6,000 square feet, *American Stories*, to feature these and other museum treasures on a rotating basis.[352]

Like the broad introductory exhibition it replaced, this display was to be organized chronologically and explore the theme of "a chronological orientation to American history." Scheduled to open in 2012, it was to remain in place until 2017, when the east wing was expected to undergo renovation. A long-term introductory exhibition might still come later. The new gallery was largely funded internally, partly by the Office of Facilities and Operations and partly by the museum. However, limited support was also raised from a few private individuals and the History Channel. In contrast to the earlier efforts, planning proceeded smoothly and the entire project was done by internal museum staff.[353]

Figure 6-26. Entry to *American Stories*. The ruby slippers were featured in the display case.

American Stories opened in April 2012.[354] It was organized with clusters of objects in five sections modeled on the historical eras defined in the national standards for history. These standards had been developed in the mid-1990s under the leadership of the National Endowment for the Humanities and the U.S. Department of Education. The sections were: Forming a New Nation, 1776–1801; Expansion and Reform, 1801–1870; Industrial Development, 1870–1900; Emergence of Modern America, 1900–1945; and Postwar and Contemporary America, 1945–Present. In the center of the space was an interactive timeline on a large electronic touch table. It included some 100 major events in American history that had been chosen by Director Brent Glass. (He stepped in because curators had been hesitant to identify the 100 most important events in American history. "Based on what criteria?" they asked.) The table was little used by visitors, who were more attracted to the physical displays. After experiencing maintenance problems during its first several years, it was removed.

The emphasis in the exhibition was on showcasing objects that were not only individually intriguing but also representative of both achievements and struggles in each period. Marc Pachter, interim director of the museum, who temporarily replaced Glass after his retirement in 2011, said

> This exhibition tells us many of the stories we share as individuals, communities and as a nation. Objects are witnesses to the past that lead you to the stories that shape our American experience.[355]

In addition to Dorothy's ruby slippers, the exhibition displayed pottery made by an enslaved American known only as Dave, Muhammad Ali's boxing gloves,

Figure 6-27. The section of *American Stories* on contemporary America.

Abraham Lincoln's gold pocket watch, Benjamin Franklin's walking stick, a Mormon sunstone, Jonas Salk's polio vaccine, Kermit the Frog, and many other treasures. Each section of the exhibition included a large glass case suitable for displaying costumes on forms.

American Stories ended the efforts to create a chronological introductory exhibition as recommended by the Blue Ribbon Commission. Since the museum opened in 1964, it had attempted several times to provide a comprehensive, chronological introductory overview. The first attempt, *Growth of the United States* (1964), included innovative and interesting displays but was never completed. *A Nation of Nations* (1976) was highly popular with visitors, but was limited in coverage, and made no attempt to summarize the general history of the nation. Just one of the four chronological exhibitions that Roger Kennedy had planned was fully realized, *After the Revolution* (1985). A second, *Communities in a Changing Nation* (1999), was only partially completed. The small *American Stories* (2012) exhibition succeeded in providing a broad sweep of American history and was organized according to the prescribed categories of the national history standards. But it was episodic at best, and far less ambitious than the Blue Ribbon Commission had envisioned. Nor did it claim to introduce the museum as a whole.

The museum made one last attempt at an introductory experience in 2015, when it collaborated with the Smithsonian Channel to produce an introductory film, *We the People*. Following the thematic structure developed under Director John Gray's leadership, the film provided a chronological overview of United States history, focused around historical aspirations and struggles related to three basic ideals: democracy, opportunity, and freedom. The film was initially shown hourly in a theater next to the entrance. Over time, however, experience showed that most visitors were not willing to begin their limited stay in the building with a 20-minute introductory film, and the showings became only occasional.

In retrospect, one must wonder whether a major introductory experience, which museum leaders had so often tried to provide, would ever succeed, no matter what its format. Were museum maps, or navigation signage, or—more recently—background on the museum's website that visitors could read before they came, enough? It is likely this question will continue to be debated in the future.

John Gray and Renovating the West Wing

Following completion of the center core renovation in 2008, the Smithsonian commenced the third phase of its Public Space Renewal Plan: renovation of the three public floors in the west wing. A new firm, Ewing Cole of Philadelphia was chosen to design the general floor plans, beginning in 2009. Grunley Construction of Rockville, Maryland, was later chosen to partner with them.

Planning, which took several years, was completed by 2012, when the museum closed the west wing to implement architectural changes. All galleries on the three exhibition floors were to be reconfigured as black-box exhibition spaces, with standard overhead lighting, electrical, and information grids that would make them easier and less expensive to update or change. In many ways, this idea harked back to the flexibility that the founding director, Frank Taylor, had worked to implement in the building from the beginning.[356]

West wing renovation was led by a new director, John Gray. He assumed the position in 2012, following the retirement of Brent Glass. Gray previously had served for 12 years as founding president of the Autry National Center of the American West. He had guided the establishment of the center by merging the Autry Museum of Western Heritage in Los Angeles with the Colorado Women of the West Museum and the Southwest Museum of the American Indian. Gray, who held a master's degree in business administration from the University of Colorado, had spent most of his career in commercial banking, rising to serve as executive vice president of First Interstate Bank of California. He had also worked for two years in the Small Business Administration in Washington, D.C. This business and governmental experience was instrumental in helping him work with the museum's board and raise the funds needed to complete the west wing.[357]

Near the beginning of his term at the museum, Gray oversaw the drafting of a new strategic plan for the museum and crafted a new mission statement:

> Through incomparable collections, rigorous research, and dynamic public outreach, we explore the infinite richness and complexity of American history. We help people understand the past in order to make sense of the present and shape a more humane future.[358]

Figure 6-28. *Left to right:* John Gray and his senior staff in 2018: Sue Fruchter, Priya Menzias, and Jay Kaveeshwar.

Committing the museum to the moral objective of shaping a more humane future was particularly important to him. Under his direction, the museum also refined its long-established goal of exploring "What does it mean to be American?" It now posited that the nation's distinction was its dedication to a set of "Ideals and Ideas." The *ideals* were national aspirational goals and values that Americans had adopted in their efforts to establish a more perfect union and build a more humane future for all. These included democracy, freedom, justice, knowledge, opportunity, and equality. The *ideas* were social, cultural, and institutional frameworks that characterized how Americans structured and managed their daily lives. These included capitalism, innovation, diversity, laws, religion, culture, and individualism, among others. The museum used this framework to determine themes for the three floors of the west wing. The first floor was devoted to innovation and creativity, the second floor to democracy and diversity, and the third floor to culture as a reflection of American ideals and ideas.[359]

In addition to his focus on the west wing, Gray and his deputy director, Sue Fruchter, made major strides in rebuilding the staff of the museum after years of decline. They devoted particular attention to hiring a diverse new generation of curators, most with a doctoral degree, who would lead the intellectual work of the museum in its next era. Most of these new curators were hired with expanded federal funding, but for the first time, the museum also added three endowed curatorial positions, in the histories of business, religion, and philanthropy.

When Gray took charge, the museum was in serious financial difficulty. Ken Behring was reneging on the remaining $45.7 million of his $80 million pledge to the museum. This had been the main source of outside funding expected to cover costs of the west wing exhibitions. The initial part of his pledge had been spent on *The American Presidency: A Glorious Burden* ($5 million), *The Price of Freedom: Americans at War* ($16 million), renovation of the rotunda ($13.8 million), and *American Stories*

($0.19 million). However, after the failure of the planned introductory exhibition, Behring and the Smithsonian could not come to agreement on allocating the remainder of the pledge. Behring refused to fund any project in the west wing. Although Gray, who had once been Behring's banker, tried many times to interest him in the west wing projects, none of his efforts succeeded.

Consequently, Gray worked quietly with other Smithsonian officials, including Secretary David Skorton, to implement a gradual but graceful termination of the relationship. In July 2017, the Smithsonian and Behring agreed to terms. Behring would make no further contributions to the Smithsonian. The National Museum of American History building would continue to include "Kenneth E. Behring Center" at both entrances and in signs, information catalogs, websites, and programs until August 2027. However, the museum could remove recognition of his support from the *American Presidency*, *Price of Freedom*, and *American Stories* exhibitions. Behring's bust was no longer displayed in the building. Less than two years later, on 25 June 2019, Ken Behring died.[360]

While carefully managing the termination of the agreement with Behring, Gray worked with his Director of Development Maggie Webster and her staff, to find new funding to support the west wing renovation. The cost of building renovation was being paid by the government under the Public Space Renewal Project. However, the costs of project staff, exhibition design, media development, and construction had to be covered with private funds. Most of this support came either directly or indirectly through Gray's and Webster's careful work with the central Smithsonian development office and the museum's own board. They worked hard to cultivate board members individually and make board meetings and activities far more interesting and appealing.

They set a planning goal of $120 million for the fundraising, and, at Gray's insistence, an aspirational goal of $150 million, which included not only support for the cost of exhibition development, but also funds for long-term maintenance and several endowed curatorial positions. In a few short years, they succeeded in securing $150.3 million from a wide range of new donors.[361]

The Gateways

The Blue Ribbon Commission had recommended removing object cases from hallways in the interest of cleaning up "clutter." In response, Ewing Cole had designed passageways that clearly distinguished between navigation space and exhibition space. Gray determined that this had been overdone. While he agreed with the need for clear orientation and navigation, he also wanted compelling objects in the entryways that intrigued visitors and reminded them that they were in a museum, not a hotel. He decided that space should be allocated for a featured object near the first-floor entrance, and that each floor in the west wing should have a "gateway" situated in the elevator lobby area. These areas would set the theme and context for what visitors would experience as they moved forward.

First-Floor Entry (2012)

Some members of the museum staff were concerned about locating a large object in the center of the first floor. It would restrict space often used for sponsored events, a significant source of revenue for the museum, and would break the view from the entrance to the staircase leading to the second floor. Gray insisted on trying his idea, and it proved to be appealing—even to most event sponsors. The first object placed there was the Conestoga wagon, which reflected Gray's own interest and background in western history, as well as being a well-

Figure 6-29. The Conestoga wagon as displayed in 2012.

known symbol of westward expansion (Figure 6-29). The wagon had previously been a favorite in *Growth of the United States* in the 1960s.

Objects later shown there included a Ford Mustang (which debuted in 1964) during the museum's celebration of its 50th anniversary in 2014; the carriage that took President Lincoln to Ford's Theater on 14 April 1865, in honor of the 150th anniversary of his death (it was on loan from the Studebaker National Museum); and in 2018, the Batmobile from the 1989 film *Batman*, directed by Tim Burton, to highlight the museum's exploration of American popular culture on the third floor of the west wing. (The vehicle was on loan from Warner Brothers.)

The First-Floor Gateway (2015)

The gateway to the first floor of the west wing was entitled Inventing in America.[362] It was a collaboration between the United States Patent and Trademark Office and the Smithsonian. Three large cases displayed more than 70 objects that represented how inventions shaped American history, through both major new technologies and incremental improvements. Among the objects were Samuel Morse's original prototype for the electrical telegraph, Alexander Graham Bell's experimental liquid transmitter telephone, and an original Apple I computer. Also included were Post-it notes and patent models for improvements in elementary-school desks. A display on trademarks highlighted the fact that not only logos but also colors, designs, and even sounds could receive legal protection from the government. "This exhibit will provide an exciting opportunity for the pubic to interact with and appreciate the role innovation has played in our country's history," noted Michelle K. Lee of the U.S. Patent and Trademark Office.[363]

The landmark at the end of the gateway was the home workshop of Ralph Baer, the inventor of the video game.[364] It was chosen to represent the myriad sanctuaries that inventors create in their attics, basements, and garages for conceiving and developing new ideas. Baer, who was Jewish, had fled Nazi Germany for the United States in 1938. After serving in the U.S. Army in World War II, he went to work for

Figure 6-30. Display of objects related to trademarks (*left*) and patents (*right*) in the first-floor gateway.

Figure 6-31. Workshop of Ralph Baer, inventor of the video game, the first-floor landmark setting, as it appears in the first-floor gateway.

a defense contractor and focused on potential military uses of the new technology of television. In the process, he determined that TV could be a great device for electronic games and secured broad early patents on the technology. He built his workshop in the basement of his home in Manchester, New Hampshire. The Smithsonian collected it specifically for display in this location (Figure 6-31).

The Second-Floor Gateway (2017)

The second-floor gateway centered on Horatio Greenough's statue of George Washington, created for Congress for the centennial of Washington's birth. The statue had been in this location since the building opened. It had previously been shown as a bare single object with only a simple label and no context (Figure 6-32). The new interpretation discussed how it had historically been a controversial portrayal of the first president. Was the statue a tribute or an embarrassment? One young visitor in the 1980s had reportedly asked, "What's he doing?" "Pointing to the escalator," quipped another passerby.[365]

Figure 6-32. The Greenough statue of George Washington before redesign.

In the renovation, in contrast, the statue became a symbol for the floor's theme, "The Nation We Build Together." While the statue's checkered history was still noted, the museum finally used it effectively to draw visitors to its new exhibitions (Figure 6-33).

Figure 6-33. The Greenough statue of George Washington after redesign.

Figure 6-34. America's Listening, the third-floor gateway.

The west wing of the second floor featured two new main exhibitions, *American Democracy: A Great Leap of Faith*, and *Many Voices, One Nation*. To represent them both, one case in the gateway displayed a nineteenth-century ballot box and the 1940s suitcase of a German immigrant who had survived the Holocaust. A case on the opposite wall included objects that represented "The Nation We Dream."[366] The label stated, "We aspire to make our own decisions, create homes and raise families, get an education, and help others. Our dreams are not always the same, but our efforts to see them realized shape the nation we share."

The Third-Floor Gateway (2018)

The gateway on the third floor was called America's Listening.[367] Its landmark object was a window from the tower of the historic Victor Company headquarters in New Jersey. It depicted the iconic advertising image of Nipper the dog, who presumably cannot distinguish between a recorded version of his master's voice and the real thing. Cases on the floor traced the history of recorded sound in America through five landmark innovations illustrated by original objects: Thomas Edison's phonograph, Alexander Graham Bell's graphophone, Emile Berliner's gramophone, Ray Dolby's noise reduction system, and Steve Jobs' iPod. In future years, this is slated to lead to *Entertaining America*, a long-term exhibition on the history of American culture, a rotating gallery, and a theater for musical performances.

The Major Exhibitions: West Wing

Within These Walls (2001)

As discussed in chapter 3, the Ipswich house had been acquired for and installed in the *Growth of the United States* exhibition. When that exhibition closed in 1976, the house became part of *Everyday Life in the American Past*. In turn, that exhibition closed in 1982, and the house was walled off. Numerous plans were proposed over the years to show it to the public again, including an effort by Roger Kennedy to put seats in front of it and install a sound-and-light show inside. However, no plan came to fruition until 2001, when the museum opened *Within These Walls*.[368] The new exhibition was supported by a major grant from the National Association of Realtors.[369]

The interpretation of the house in this new exhibition was dramatically different from the way it had been shown initially. The new display reflected both the trend in the museum to focus more on social and cultural history than on history of technology, and increased attention to the lives of common citizens. "Ordinary people, living their everyday lives can create extraordinary history," said Director Spencer Crew when the exhibition opened.

Years of meticulous research had revealed much about the roughly 100 people who had occupied the home. The museum chose to focus on five families who had lived there.

First was prosperous merchant Abraham Choate, his wife, and his eight children, for whom the house was built in the 1760s. Next came Abraham Dodge, a veteran of the Battle of Bunker Hill in 1775, who purchased the house in 1777. Chance,

Figure 6-35. Entry to *Within These Walls*, 2001.

Figure 6-36. Family stories in *Within These Walls*.

an African American man who formerly had been enslaved, remained in the household as Dodge's servant after slavery was abolished in Massachusetts. However, he was not listed as a free head of household until 1809. The war years left Dodge in debt, and after his death the family had to sell the house. Some years later, in 1822, Josiah and Lucy Caldwell bought it. They were virulent abolitionists and hosted meetings of the Anti-Slavery Society in their parlor.

In 1865, the wealthy Heard family purchased the home from the Caldwell estate and divided it into rental apartments. Among the Irish immigrants who lived there were Catherine Lynch and her daughter Mary. Mary worked in a hosiery mill, and Catherine earned money by taking in laundry.

A final family vignette of 1942 found Mary Scott and her family in the home during World War II. She was growing vegetables in those years, conserving fat and saving tin cans, while her two sons were fighting in the war. Her daughter, Annie Scott Lynch, was working in a factory making war materials.

Visitors to the exhibition loved learning the stories of the people who lived there, but the new interpretation had a limitation. It all was presented on panels and labels opposite the house. Viewing and reading them tended to take visitor attention away from looking at the extraordinary house itself.

In August 2018, the museum supplemented its earlier display with computerized theatrical projections using soundscapes, animated shadows, historic images, and scene-setting text projected on objects inside the home.[370] This was reminiscent of the sound-and-light show that Roger Kennedy had wanted to create several decades earlier. At times, this was further supplemented using costumed interpreters (Figure 6-37). The Ipswich House finally came back to life.

Figure 6-37. Animation and a costumed interpreter in the Ipswich House exhibition.

American Enterprise (2015)

Prior to the opening of *American Enterprise* in 2015, the museum had never mounted an exhibition on American business history, even though engaging with business and commerce was one of the distinctive qualities of being an American. Instead, it had treated business topics from the perspective of the history of technology and industry.

The Blue Ribbon Commission had criticized the museum for not covering the role of capitalism and the "incentives for enterprise and innovation" in American history.[371] Members of the museum's board also believed this was a serious deficiency. Brent Glass, who had become director in 2002, agreed there should be an exhibition on business history and commissioned a team to begin work on one. An initial plan was approved in 2004 for a 14,000-square-foot display to be located on the first floor in the east wing of the museum. Initial fundraising took several years, as the focus of the museum during this period was renovation of the center core, but by 2008 the museum had seed money to hire design firm Haley Sharpe and assemble an exhibition team.[372]

A preliminary plan was completed in February 2009. However, just as it was finished, Glass determined that the exhibition needed to be moved from the east wing of the first floor to the west wing, primarily because that area was slated to be renovated next, following the reopening of the center core in 2008. Unfortunately, the space available in the west wing was only 8,000 square feet, around 60 percent of the earlier plan, so the exhibition had to be completely redesigned.[373]

Between 2009 and 2014, a new version of the exhibition was conceived and planned for the west wing location. During this period, John Gray had become director of the museum and assumed responsibility for overseeing management and funding for the west wing. *American Enterprise* was the largest, most expensive, and most complex of the exhibitions that opened together on the first floor in June 2015.[374]

The curators planning the exhibition knew that traditional business history, focused on topics such as the rise of corporations, capital formation, business plans, management, and labor, would likely make for a dull display for most visitors. They looked for a different approach.

In part, they drew on a theory that had been developed by researchers in the Smithsonian's Office of Institutional Studies. Years of research had revealed that the elements of exhibitions that most interested visitors could be summarized in four "typologies": ideas, people, objects, and participation, or IPOP. They summarized, "The evidence suggests that exhibitions that strongly appeal to all four visitor typologies—that leave out no one, in effect—will be highly successful with visitors."[375]

Taking this into account, the team decided not to focus solely on producers of goods and services, but also on consumers of business products—that is, everyone—as well as the advertising and marketing that connected producers and consumers. The plan included interactive displays that allowed visitors to do self-guided, participatory exploration of topics in depth. Finally, it included over 100 profiles of business people—well known and unknown, successes and failures, women as well as men, and representative of the diversity of the American people. One notable display focused on the business of slavery (Figure 6-39), which was central to early American economic development.

For each historical period, the exhibition also profiled leading figures "debating enterprise," or comparing fundamentally different ideas about business and society.

Figure 6-38. The entry to *American Enterprise*, which included a large touch-screen video wall. Here visitors could playfully interact with the objects, people, and ideas they would encounter in the exhibition.

Figure 6-39. Display on the business of slavery, with an interactive terminal for in-depth exploration.

The first of these contrasted the perspectives of President George Washington, Secretary of State Thomas Jefferson, and Secretary of the Treasury Alexander Hamilton, about how the new United States should develop its economy.

The resulting exhibition included more than 600 objects, hundreds of images, hands-on activities, and video. The display traced the nation's development from a small, dependent agricultural nation to one of the world's most vibrant economies. In announcing the exhibition, Director John Gray said, "*American Enterprise* chronicles the tumultuous interaction between capitalism and the common good, which is fundamental to understanding our history and our global role."[376]

The center of the exhibition traced select topics in four chronological eras: the Merchant Era, 1770s–1850s; the Corporate Era, 1860s–1930s; the Consumer Era, 1940s–1970s; and the Global Era, 1980s–2010s. Displays showed achievements of American business, including innovations in agriculture, manufacturing, and electrical technology, but also the brutality of American slavery, the challenges of the Depression, and government efforts to break up monopolies.

An introductory section across the front of the exhibition presented a captivating collage of American advertising from the eighteenth century to the present.

Personal stories of businesspeople were presented on a faceted biography wall that stretched along the back of the exhibition. Interactive and video stations were spread throughout.

Figure 6-40. Corporate Era section, including units on the Depression, the New Deal, and Prohibition.

Figure 6-41. Section of the biography wall for the 2010s.

Among the noteworthy artifacts were the eighteenth-century business desk of William Ramsay, a colonial merchant; a Native American wooden cart used in the fur trade; an early Thomas Edison electric light bulb, contrasted with an Edison talking baby doll—a product that failed; a 1918 Fordson tractor; a 1960s home refrigerator stocked with TV dinners, Jell-O, and other favorites of the era; equipment from a 1950s African American radio station; a section of a 1999 prototype Google server; and Michael Bloomberg's own Bloomberg terminal from 2008.

Reviews of the exhibition were generally favorable. As an article in the *Economist* stated,

> [The United States] is both unusually business-minded and prone to ferocious debates about how capitalism should be organized and regulated. That record is explored by "American Enterprise".... The exhibition is the Smithsonian's first to focus on America's business history. It asserts that commerce was, from earliest time, bound up with ideas of democracy and individual rights.[377]

On the other hand, Ed Rothstein, in a review of the exhibition in the *Wall Street Journal*, found that the exhibition focused too much on lesser figures in American business and not enough on major innovators and leaders and the essence of their success.[378]

Major support for the exhibition came from Mars, Inc., the Wallace H. Coulter Foundation, and the S. C. Johnson Company. Additional support came from a range of other companies and individuals. The History Channel donated video and interactive content production. Besides covering the costs of design and production, the funding supported the endowment of a permanent curator for business history and maintenance for the exhibition during its anticipated 20-year lifespan. This was unprecedented for major exhibitions and set a high standard for future projects.

Places of Invention (2015)

Places of Invention was developed by the Jerome and Dorothy Lemelson Center for the Study of Invention and Innovation. The center was established in 1995 to engage, educate, and empower the public to participate in technological, economic, and social change. It undertakes historical research, develops educational initiatives, creates exhibitions, and hosts a variety of public programs.[379] Although the center raises money from multiple sources, including the National Science Foundation, its funding has primarily come from the Jerome and Dorothy Lemelson Foundation, which has donated more than $40 million to support it. This sum was greater than the amount ultimately donated by Kenneth Behring, and made the Lemelson gift the largest the museum has ever received. Unlike the relationship with Behring, that between the museum and the Lemelson family and foundation has remained free from major disagreements and conflict. It became a model for other fundraising efforts. Much of the success of this arrangement was due to Arthur Molella, the founding director of the center, who led it from 1995 to 2015, and the staff he hired to help him manage it.

Figure 6-42. *Invention at Play* after being reinstalled at the museum.

Places of Invention was the second major exhibition that the center created. The exhibition team was led by project director and historian Monica Smith. The center's first exhibition was *Invention at Play* in 2002.[380] It explored how play connects to the creative impulse of both historical and contemporary inventors. It had five thematic sections: Recognize the Unusual, Borrow from Nature, Jump the Tracks, Keep Making it Better, and Many Heads Are Better than One. It highlighted a diverse range of inventors, famous and little-known, whose habits of mind and skills began in their childhood play. Its goal was to show how children's play parallels processes used by inventors.

Invention at Play opened at the museum for a six-month period, then traveled to nine museums around the country before returning and being reinstalled (Figure 6-42). It remained on display until 2011.

The second exhibition, *Places of Invention*, explored how particular physical locations fostered the inventive process. Again, the exhibition team was led by project director and historian Monica Smith.[381] The display examined six distinct communities in different historical eras, focusing on how each had a mix of people, resources, and inspiring surroundings that made them hotbeds of invention and innovation. These six were stories of precision manufacturing in Hartford, Connecticut, in the late 1800s; technicolor movies in Hollywood, California, in the 1930s; cardiac health technology in Medical Alley, Minnesota, in the 1950s; the birth of hip-hop music in the Bronx, New York, in the 1970s; the personal-computer revolution in Silicon Valley, California, in the 1970s to 1980s; and clean-energy innovations in Fort Collins, Colorado, in recent decades.[382]

Near the entry of the exhibition was a large interactive map, which featured text, images and video highlighting innovative communities across the country and around the world. It was designed to become fuller over time as visitors, both on-site and online, contributed additional stories. Highlighted on the map were materials

Figure 6-43. Personal-computer innovation in Silicon Valley.

Figure 6-44. Clean-energy innovation in Fort Collins, Colorado.

from 12 Smithsonian Affiliate museums and their community partners. Summarizing the significance of the exhibition, Lemelson Center Director Molella said, "Understanding America's rich invention history is key to inspiring the next generation of inventors and innovators. After visiting and participating in *Places of Invention*, we hope Americans will not only appreciate this history, but will also come to see themselves and their communities as inventive."[383]

The Value of Money (2015)

The Smithsonian's numismatics collection, which holds an estimated 1.6 million coins and pieces of currency, is by far the museum's largest. In number of specimens, it constitutes between 40 and 50 percent of the museum's total holdings. Although not officially recognized as such, the collection is essentially the monetary reference collection of the United States government, as it includes the historic holdings of both the United States Mint and the Bureau of Engraving and Printing.

Despite the size and significance of the collection, however, displaying it had not been among the top priorities of the museum when it planned renovation. As discussed in the previous chapter, in the 1960s the new museum featured a sizeable exhibition on *Monetary History and Medallic Art* on the third floor. Although sections of this display were updated several times, it was never fully modernized. It finally closed in August 2004, after 40 years. This was in anticipation of the renovation of the museum, as the numismatics display area was directly above the chamber being reconfigured for the new Star-Spangled Banner exhibition.

Coin collecting is among the most popular hobbies in America. It is the focus of several large and very active professional organizations, among them the American Numismatic Association and the American Numismatic Society, as well as major publications including *Coin World* and *Numismatic News*. When the exhibition closed, the museum was very concerned that the action might alarm leading American numismatists and generate negative publicity in the numismatics press. Instead of catching the numismatic community by surprise, the museum turned to it for assistance. It challenged the community to support revitalizing the display in the coming years.

Leaders of the community responded positively. They agreed that the old hall, which was out of date and poorly maintained, needed to be closed. They promised to work with the museum to support temporary displays of coins until a new exhibition could be opened as part of the overall museum renovation. The most active was Jeff Garrett, president of Mid-American Rare Coin Galleries. He later became a member of the museum's board.

The first temporary exhibition was *Money and Sovereignty: Selections from the National Numismatics Collection*, which went on display at the International Monetary Fund Center from April to October 2005. It was followed in December 2005 by *Legendary Coins and Currency*, an exhibition in Schermer Hall in the Smithsonian Castle.[384] This included 56 extraordinary treasures from the collection organized in five specially built cases with specific themes: Legendary Firsts, Legendary Beauties, Unexpected Legends, Golden Legends, and Legends of the Human Spirit. The

Figure 6-45. The *Stories on Money* exhibition, which opened in 2009.

display was supplemented by a website where visitors could zoom in to see the details of the coins. The Numismatic Guaranty Corporation of America and Numismatic Conservation Services were sponsors for the exhibition. It stayed on display until 11 February 2008, several years longer than expected.

On 9 June 2009, the museum finally opened a new numismatics gallery in its own building, less than a year after completing the center core renovation. Although the gallery was small, it was prominently situated on the first floor. Entitled *Stories on Money*, the exhibition showed the interplay among people, money, and history, from the earliest times to the present (Figure 6-45). It included objects from colonial America, the gold rush era, the Great Depression, and current times. One case, The Power of Liberty, highlighted how feminine personifications of Liberty had been standard on nineteenth- and early-twentieth-century American coins.[385] This too depended on outside sponsorship, from the Numismatic Guaranty Corporation of America, Numismatic Conservation Services, and Monaco Rare Coins.

Finally, on 1 July 2015, the museum presented *The Value of Money*, a major gallery in its new first-floor, west wing exhibitions. Originally, this was not part of the plan for the floor. The space had a low ceiling and had been designated to become a storage area. However, curators convinced Director Glass that the numismatics community would likely be willing to donate the cost of creating the gallery if the museum would use the space for that purpose. Glass agreed, and the numismatics community, again following the leadership of Jeff Garrett, provided the funds needed to create the gallery. Numismatics now had a permanent home in the museum, in prime real estate on the first floor.

The 1,000-square-foot exhibition showcased more than 400 objects and was organized into five sections: The Origins of Money, Numismatic Art and Design, The Practice of Collecting Money, Political and Cultural Messages Money Conveys, and New Monetary Technologies.[386] The curatorial planning team was led by project director Jennifer Jones and curator Ellen Feingold. The exhibition design was done by the firm of Haley Sharpe and the museum's in-house staff completed the production. To prevent visitors from being visually overwhelmed by seeing too many objects at once, some were shown in lit cases while others were accessed through pull-out drawers. Featured objects included a rare 1933 20-dollar gold piece, a $100,000

Figure 6-46. The entrance to the *Value of Money* exhibition in the Gallery of Numismatics.

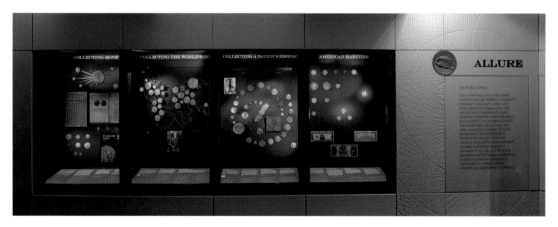

Figure 6-47. The Allure section featured coins collected for their rarity and beauty.

note, a 465 BC decadrachm coin from Siracusa, Sicily, a 168-pound stone ring monetary artifact from the Island of Yap in Micronesia, and a personal check signed by President James Madison in 1813.

The massive bank-vault door that opened into the exhibition was intended to highlight the unique significance of the collection (Figure 6-46). As curator Ellen Feingold said at the opening ceremony,

> When visitors look through the gallery's vault door, we hope that they will feel as though they are looking into the collection's vault—a space that secures one of the Smithsonian's most valued collections.[387]

American Democracy: A Great Leap of Faith (2017)

From the early years of the museum, curators of the political history collection had emphasized collecting objects related to the fundamental characteristic of American democracy: popular participation in the federal government. In recent decades, curators went to the Democratic and Republican national conventions every four years and collected buttons, hats, signs, pins, and other objects that represented ways in which delegates expressed their support for candidates. They also collected voting machines and examples of ballots and voting ephemera. In addition, they gathered artifacts from major demonstrations in the national capital, including antiwar protests, women's rights marches, antiabortion rallies, veterans' rallies, and gay-rights parades. Over the years, these wide-ranging artifacts of democracy had been displayed in a series of museum exhibitions, including *Historic Americans* (1964), *We the People* (1975), *We the People: Winning the Vote* (1982), and *From Parlor to Politics* (1990).

By the time the American presidency exhibition opened in 2000, however, it and the first ladies exhibition had become the museum's only political history displays. They focused on executive leadership of the government, not citizen participation in the nation's politics. The floor plan in Figure 6-48, from the Blue Ribbon Commission's report of 2002, shows how at that point, these two exhibitions, which were to occupy a major section of the third floor, were planned to be expanded and to remain the only political history stories the museum presented.

Compare this to the floor plan that actually emerged as depicted in Figure 6-1, where the presidency and first ladies exhibitions occupy a much smaller portion of the third floor and are supplemented by an additional political history exhibition on the second.

In the early 2010s, the museum realized that Ken Behring would no longer support the huge chronological introductory exhibition that the Blue Ribbon Commission had recommended. The abandonment of this plan, and the substitution of the much smaller *American Stories* exhibition (2012), opened new opportunities on the west wing of the second floor to mount several new exhibitions. One of these became *American Democracy: A Great Leap of Faith*. The others became *Many Voices, One Nation* (see below), and changing exhibitions in the Taubman Gallery.

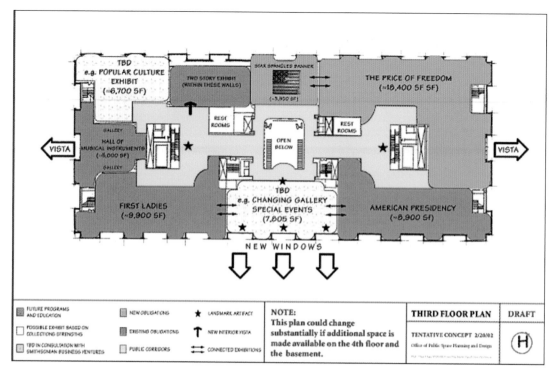

Figure 6-48. Third-floor plan proposed by the Blue Ribbon Commission.

The democracy exhibition was a return to the earlier tradition of political history that focused on the fundamentals of American democracy. In many ways, it was a refinement and simplification of *We the People* (1975). The earlier exhibition had attempted to cover the full range of ways that the American people interacted with their federal government, including its provision of goods and services. *American Democracy* explored only the involvement of the American people in national politics.

The exhibit team was organized and led by project director Harry Rubenstein.[388] The exhibition they planned addressed a simple question: "What happens when the people of a nation decide to govern themselves?"[389] It had five sections. First was The Great Leap, which explored the issues American colonists addressed as they established their new national government. Next was A Vote, a Voice, which examined both the continued expansion and contraction of voting rights throughout American history, including the fight for women's suffrage (Figure 6-50).

Third was The Machinery of Democracy, which focused on how political parties and campaigns sought to motivate citizens to participate in their government and vote. Fourth was Beyond the Ballot, which reviewed ways other than voting in which Americans have sought to influence government actions, including petitioning, protest, and lobbying. Finally, Creating Citizens explored contested ways that America has fostered a citizenry that could support its democratic ideals (Figure 6-51).

The exhibition included over 900 objects, six video presentations, and five electronic interactives. Among its outstanding objects were the desk that Thomas Jefferson used to draft the Declaration of Independence, Susan B. Anthony's iconic

Figure 6-49. Entry to *American Democracy*.

Figure 6-50. Exhibit section on voting rights.

red shawl, and a historical array of voting machines and campaign paraphernalia. Particularly noteworthy was the extensive display of historic campaign materials. It began with buttons and ribbons from the early republic and ended with a cloud of media on screens that extended overhead and surrounded visitors with a cacophony of moving images and sound (Figure 6-52).

In announcing the exhibition, Director Gray said, "Democracy is still a work in progress, but it is at the core of our nation's political, economic, and social life. We invite visitors to explore our distinctive American democracy and to participate in creating a more perfect union."[390]

Figure 6-51. Section on creating citizens.

Figure 6-52. The campaign media cloud.

Many Voices, One Nation (2017)

Like *American Democracy: A Great Leap of Faith*, *Many Voices, One Nation* revisited the theme of an earlier major exhibition—in this case, *A Nation of Nations* (1976). The exhibit team planning it was the most diverse the museum had ever assembled to create a large exhibition. It was led by project directors Nancy Davis and Bonnie Campbell Lilienfeld.[391]

The new exhibition provided a distinctly different interpretation of American immigration and diversity than had *A Nation of Nations*, one that was far less positive and celebratory.[392] The earlier exhibition had highlighted ways that immigrants assimilated themselves into America while still maintaining aspects of their own culture and identity. *Many Voices, One Nation* focused on the struggles that immigrants had endured in their efforts to become American, and their need to negotiate for their rights as citizens. It also emphasized that although most had come to America voluntarily, others were incorporated into the nation when their lands had been assimilated through war or diplomacy. Enslaved peoples had been brought to the nation against their will. As the exhibition's main label stated, "As the population grew, the people who lived in the United States found ways to negotiate, or work out, what it meant to be American. That negotiation continues. This exhibition explores how the many voices of people in America have shaped our nation."[393]

Figure 6-53. Entry to *Many Voices, One Nation*.

Figure 6-54. Display exploring the annexation of Hawaii in 1898.

The outer sections of the exhibition traced case histories of diverse American populations in four chronological periods. The first covered from 1492 to 1776, and included stories not only of European colonists, but also of Native Americans and enslaved Africans. The second period extended from 1776 to 1900 and explored population growth as the nation expanded across the continent and to overseas territories. New populations included European immigrants, Hispanic people in territories taken from Mexico during the Mexican War, and native Hawaiians, who became Americans when the United States annexed Hawaii in 1898.

The third period, focusing on creating new communities, ran from 1900 to 1965. It explored case histories of two cities, Chicago and Los Angeles. The final section, covering the years from 1965 to 2000, presented stories of new Americans who arrived after the landmark Hart–Celler Act of 1965. It had allowed increased immigration from Africa, Asia, Latin America, and the Middle East, significantly changing the makeup of the American population.

The center sections of the exhibition examined how Americans with varied backgrounds negotiated their identities in shared communities: workplaces, playing fields, schoolrooms, houses of worship, and the military. Here, they had to resolve

Figure 6-55. Display of objects related to immigrants from Latin America, including a section of border fence and the uniform of a border patrol agent.

with each other what basic American promises would mean for them. The exhibition asked: Who is free? Who is included? Who is equal? Audiovisual presentations in the exhibition dramatized ways their struggles played out historically.

A final section traced a growing new trend in immigration: people who led transnational lives, maintaining strong family and business ties to their countries of origin even as they also identified, in part at least, as Americans.

The exhibition included pictures of hundreds of diverse Americans from all historical periods. It displayed over 250 artifacts, both from the museum's collection and on loan from other institutions. Many of these had symbolic significance in defining American identity, such as a statue of Uncle Sam, a bald eagle, a statue of Columbia, and various renditions of the Statue of Liberty.

Figure 6-56. Immokalee Statue of Liberty.

The most arresting of the last was the Immokalee Statue of Liberty, which was carried by agricultural workers in Immokalee, Florida, in 2000 when they were demonstrating for higher wages (Figure 6-56). The statue's original pedestal proclaimed the simple but powerful message, "I, too, am America."

In many ways, the exhibition was an in-depth exploration of the traditional American motto, *E pluribus unum*, "Out of many, one," first adopted by an act of Congress in 1782. As curator Margaret Salazar-Porzio wrote in the companion book to the exhibition, the real opportunity of the phrase *E Pluribus Unum* is its simultaneous flexibility and tension: "one" and "many" are not fixed and neither is dominant. Reconciling the inherent tensions between "one" and "many" is not an easy task, but the phrase can tie together the strands of migration, race, and nation.... Our history is messy, complex, and multifaceted.... The presentation of our seemingly disparate pasts inspires possibilities for a shared future as we constantly reinterpret our *E Pluribus Unum*—our nation of many voices.[394]

In sum, the exhibition answered the question "What does it mean to be American?" by showing that many, if not most new Americans had to struggle and negotiate in their attempt to find freedom, opportunity, and justice in their new home. Support for the exhibition came from a variety of sources, many of them recent immigrants or organizations founded by immigrants.

The Temporary Exhibitions

The museum's ongoing exploration of what it means to be American shaped its temporary exhibitions as much as it did its longer-term displays. Because the former tended to be more focused, they allowed the museum to highlight significant people, events, and trends in ways that were not possible in larger exhibitions with broader scope. The following are a few of the most important during this era.

September 11: Bearing Witness to History (2002)

The terrorist attacks on the United States on 11 September 2001 were a shock and an assault felt by all Americans. To curators at the National Museum of American History, they were also a call to action. The staff immediately realized that they had witnessed an event that would dramatically shape American history and cause citizens to rethink what it meant to be American.

Within several weeks of the event, curators began building a collection of artifacts at the nation's history museum that would document the tragedy. This was done in coordination with other institutions, including the New-York Historical Society, the City University of New York, and George Mason University. In January 2002, Public Law 107-117 designated the museum as the official national repository of September 11 collections. The museum's collecting efforts were broad ranging. Stories of some of them were later documented on the museum's website.[395]

Whether the collection should lead to an exhibition on September 11 was hotly debated among the staff, but ultimately, they decided to mount a display to commemorate the attack on its first anniversary. Never before—or since—has the museum responded to a major historic event so rapidly and intentionally.

September 11: Bearing Witness to History opened on 11 September 2002, and remained open until 5 July 2003, six months longer than originally planned.[396] The large curatorial team that planned it came from many areas of the museum, including work and industry, photographic history, information technology, graphic arts,

Figure 6-57. The flag that had been unfurled at the Pentagon on 12 September 2001.

armed forces, home and community life, and education and public programs. All agreed that the exhibition should not be interpretive. It was too soon to try to examine the historical background and context, or to evaluate the historical consequences of this seminal event.

The result was a 5,000-square-foot exhibition located in the center of the second floor. Ironically, this space was available only because the exhibition on the nineteenth century, *Communities in a Changing Nation,* had remained unfinished, leaving prime space conveniently vacant.

The new exhibition was adjacent to the Flag Hall, where the Star-Spangled Banner had traditionally hung. It had been taken down in 1998 for conservation, as discussed earlier in this chapter. When the exhibition opened, the museum decided to display in this vacant location the flag that had been unfurled at the Pentagon on 12 September 2001, to symbolize America's resilience after the attack the day before. That flag hung outside the Pentagon for a month. The museum now borrowed it from the U.S. Army Center of Military History and unfurled it again on 11 September 2002. It was extremely popular with visitors, and would hang in the Flag Hall until 7 September 2006, when the museum closed for renovation.

The museum's goal in *September 11, 2001: Bearing Witness to History* was, as the title indicated, to share witness stories and objects that documented the events. Most

Figure 6-58. Entry to the September 11 exhibition.

Americans had learned of the attacks only through media reports: on television, in newspapers, or on the internet. The exhibition would allow visitors to see artifacts that were directly related to the attacks in New York, Washington, and Pennsylvania and to read and hear personal accounts of individuals who had been directly involved.

The entry to the exhibition presented dramatic images of people witnessing aspects of the attacks, at the World Trade Center in New York, at the Pentagon in Arlington, Virginia, and in Shanksville, Pennsylvania, where United Airlines Flight 93 had crashed (Figure 6-58). This was followed by a photo gallery that included photographic equipment and both still and motion pictures from photographers who documented the events. Among them were images and the cameras of Bill Biggart, who lost his life in the World Trade Center collapse, and the digital movie camera and video of Jules and Gédéon Naudet, who captured the only moving images of the first plane that slammed into the World Trade Center.

Next, visitors moved into an objects gallery that displayed around 50 objects representing all three sites as well as nationwide responses. Among the most dramatic were a burned and tattered American flag, twisted steel from the World Trade Center, a New York firefighter's protective clothing, and a charred limestone fragment from the Pentagon facade.

Showing in an adjacent theater was a gripping 10-minute video presentation produced by ABC News that traced the experiences on September 11 of news anchor Peter Jennings, who reported much of the day live. Next to it were a series of five touch-screen multimedia stations where visitors could choose among 25 witness stories of individuals who had been directly involved. These included reflections of a New

Figure 6-59. Gallery showing artifacts from the September 11 attacks. Objects from the Pentagon are to the right.

York father who had lost two sons—one a policeman and the other a firefighter—in the recovery effort, a woman who had been severely burned in the attacks, and an American Muslim woman who feared that she and her family would be ostracized because of what had happened.

In the final section, visitors were invited to share their own stories of September 11 by answering two questions: "How did you witness history on September 11?" and "Has your life changed since September 11?" A selection of these was posted in the exhibition, and the entire collection was digitized and preserved by George Mason University in its September 11 Digital Archive.

September 11, 2001: Bearing Witness to History was the most emotional exhibition the museum has ever mounted. Museum staff realized that it would deeply affect visitors and included seating where they could sit and reflect, as well as boxes of tissues for those who were reduced to tears. Both were needed and regularly used.

At the opening of the exhibition, Joseph Pfeifer of the New York Fire Department recalled his sad memory of sending another firefighter up into the burning towers:

> I told him to go up, go up with his company, but not to go any higher than 70....After I told him, he stood there and in the silence we looked at each other, and he turned around and he walked over to his men and took them upstairs. That was the last time I saw that lieutenant. The lieutenant was my brother, Kevin.

Secretary Larry Small noted the unique character of the role the Smithsonian was playing by mounting the exhibition:

Figure 6-60. Visitors view September 11 artifacts on open display in 2011.

We realize we are on new ground. We realize that we are challenged to fulfill a particular responsibility to the American people in unprecedented ways— to collect and interpret history in the making and to acknowledge the heroes for making that history.[397]

In addition to the exhibition, the museum mounted a related website and produced and distributed educational materials.

Since this initial presentation, the museum has displayed selections of its September 11 collection in several ways. When *The Price of Freedom: Americans at War* opened in 2004, the museum included a selection of September 11 objects in its section on recent conflicts, showing how they were related to wars in Iraq and Afghanistan.

Ten years after the 2001 attacks, the museum determined that it should once again show a broad range of the objects in its collection. *September 11: Remembrance and Reflection* was not a traditional exhibition, but a presentation on open tables of objects from all three September 11 sites: New York, Washington, and Pennsylvania. Because the artifacts were not in glass cases, visitors could inspect them closely and connect to the human stories they represented. Museum staff were behind all the tables to protect the artifacts and answer visitor questions (Figure 6-60). The display was open for only eight days, from 3 September through 11 September 2011, from 11:00 a.m. to 3:00 p.m.[398]

The response was overwhelming. People lined up for hours to walk past the objects and see them in the open. Although photographs of every object were already available online, most visitors took their own images with cell phones or digital cameras, documenting their personal encounters with the objects.

Finally, five years later, in 2016, the fifteenth anniversary of September 11, the museum mounted a more limited open display of objects on tables in the Flag Hall for one day only. Response again was positive, but as memories had faded, so had desire to make a special effort to see artifacts related to the event.

Figure 6-61. Comparison of White and African American schoolrooms in the *Separate Is Not Equal* exhibition.

Separate Is Not Equal: Brown v. Board of Education (2004)

In 2004, to commemorate the historic Supreme Court decision of 1954 that outlawed racial segregation in public schools, the museum mounted *Separate Is Not Equal: Brown v. Board of Education.*[399] It was the last exhibition to be displayed in the Taylor Gallery for changing exhibitions on the first floor.

Using objects, graphics, photographs, and video presentations, the exhibition told the story of how dedicated lawyers, parents, students, and community activists fought to overcome legal racial segregation in America. Through personal stories and broad historical themes, the display traced the fight to bring the injustice of segregated schools before the United States Supreme Court. Their victory in *Brown v. Board of Education* transformed the nation.

The exhibition did not present a story of unalloyed triumph. The final sections showed that although the decision gave hope to millions for social justice, it also unleashed dramatic reactions among those who feared change. As Director Brent Glass said, "With this exhibition, the museum will lead its visitors to explore the question of what equal opportunity means in the diverse world of the 21st century."[400]

Bittersweet Harvest: The Bracero Program, 1942–1964 (2009)

The stories of migrant workers form an important but little-known area in American history. In 2005, the museum began a pioneering, multi-institutional collecting initiative to document and preserve the experiences of braceros. This was the name given to the 4.6 million Mexican nationals who were brought to the United States on short-term contracts to work in the agricultural fields and on the railroads between 1942 and 1964. This collecting encompassed hundreds of photographs, documents, artifacts, and over 700 oral histories with former braceros. These were shared online

Figure 6-62. Entry to the braceros exhibition.

by the Center for History and New Media at George Mason University. They also formed the basis for the temporary exhibition *Bittersweet Harvest: The Bracero Program, 1942–1964.*[401]

The exhibition was designed so it could easily travel to other locations. It included 15 freestanding banners with images and text about both the work the braceros did and the harsh realities many faced. It included only a few artifacts, among them a bunk bed from a labor camp, a well-worn straw hat, and farming tools. After closing at the museum in 2010, the exhibition traveled for years to other locations around the country.

In announcing the display, Director Brent Glass said,

> This exhibition allows us to explore complex issues of race, class, community and national origin while highlighting the irrefutable contributions by Mexican Americans to American society. "Bittersweet Harvest" is a unique opportunity to share an important but overlooked chapter in American history with visitors across the country.[402]

Abraham Lincoln: An Extraordinary Life (2009)

In contrast to the little-known story of the braceros, *Abraham Lincoln: An Extraordinary Life* reviewed the biography of one of the best-known and highly regarded American presidents.[403] The exhibition marked the 200th anniversary of Abraham Lincoln's birth by showing the remarkable collection of more than 60 Lincoln artifacts that the museum held in its collection. They had never before been assembled together in a single display. Among these were an iron wedge Lincoln used to split wood in the early 1830s, a model he used to secure his patent for a device to lift boats over shoals and obstructions in a river, his office suit, one of his wife's gowns, and the iconic top hat he wore the night of his assassination.

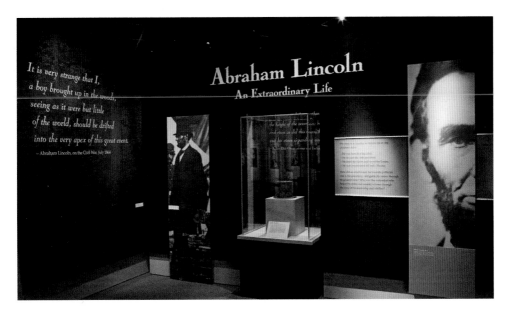

Figure 6-63. Entry to the Lincoln exhibition.

Figure 6-64. Life mask and cast hands of Lincoln.

A visitor favorite was a display of casts of a Lincoln life mask and of his large hands, including a reproduction that visitors could compare to their own (Figure 6-64).

Curator Harry Rubenstein, who developed the exhibition, described its purpose simply: "It reminds us that Abraham Lincoln, whose story has become so mythic, was a real individual. Through all his achievements, successes and tragedies, he led an extraordinary life."[404]

Giving in America (2016)

When curators were developing the exhibition *American Enterprise*, a question they were frequently asked was whether the exhibition would include a section on American philanthropy. Many of the business leaders and historians the curators consulted in their planning believed that the relation of American business to philanthropy was a defining quality of American enterprise.

While that exhibition touched on this subject, it did not explore it in detail. However, studying the topic spurred the curators to question whether the museum should do more to document and display American philanthropy, not only by business leaders, but other organizations and the public at large. For many Americans, the curators determined, giving back was an essential part of their American identity.

Growing interest in this subject led the museum to establish a philanthropy initiative in 2015. It was supported through a major grant from the Bill and Melinda Gates Foundation and a gift from David M. Rubenstein, cofounder of the Carlyle Group and a member of the Smithsonian Institution Board of Regents. This funding supported an annual symposium on a theme in philanthropy, a dedicated exhibition space for changing displays on philanthropy, the endowment of a curator of philanthropy, and the collection of artifacts and documents for a national collection in this subject area.

In 2016, the museum opened its permanent display related to the initiative, entitled *Giving in America*.[405] It was divided into two parts. The first, which changed little from year to year, included sections that addressed the questions Who Gives?,

Figure 6-65. *Giving in America* display, with the changing section to the left focused on Giving and the Arts.

Why do we Give?, What do we Give?, and How do we Give? The other part was designed to rotate in coordination with the theme of the annual symposium. The first three displays focused on philanthropy's impact on sustainability and the environment, culture and the arts, and health. Included in the exhibition and a related interactive display each year were letters from wealthy individuals from around the world who had signed the Giving Pledge, committing more than half of their wealth to philanthropy. The initiative had been started in 2010 by Bill and Melinda Gates and Warren Buffett. The letters displayed related to the specific theme for the year.

When announcing the philanthropy initiative in 2015, Director John Gray related it directly to the new mission of the museum proclaimed in its 2013 strategic plan, which stated that the museum helps people understand the past in order to make sense of the present and shape a more humane future. Gray said:

> Philanthropy has made a profound difference in defining who we are as individuals, a nation and how the world views us. These objects will help our visitors better understand the collaborative power of giving and how ordinary people contribute to the nation's well-being.[406]

The Changing Galleries

The Albert H. Small Documents Gallery (2008)

In 2008, the museum opened the 1,500-square-foot Albert H. Small Documents Gallery on the second floor, in the space formerly occupied by *Ceremonial Court*.[407] The new gallery was devoted to the display of rare and historically significant documents. Exhibitions were put on display there for periods of several months to a year.

Between 2008 and 2018, 18 exhibitions were displayed in the gallery. As with the temporary exhibitions of earlier eras, they reflected the diverse holdings of the museum and the broad range of interests among the staff. They provided many perspectives on notable Americans. Although only the documents are highlighted below, all the displays also included images and other objects that illustrated their context and significance. Notable among the exhibitions were:[408]

- *The Gettysburg Address* (2008): A display of the White House copy of the Gettysburg Address, on loan for the exhibition. It is the last known draft of this important document written in Lincoln's own hand.
- *Duke Ellington and Billy Strayhorn: Jazz Composers* (2009): Manuscripts of the most-recorded songs of the two legendary composers, Ellington's "Caravan" (1936) and Strayhorn's "Take the 'A' Train" (1941).
- *Earl Shaffer and the Appalachian Trail* (2009): The 1948 diary of Earl Shaffer, the first person to walk the entire Appalachian Trail in one continuous hike.
- *Keeping History: Plains Indian Ledger Drawings* (2010): Drawings done by Native American warriors of Northern and Southern Plains tribes in the late nineteenth century that document combat, ceremonies, and cultural life.

- *A Gateway to the 19th Century: The William Steinway Diary, 1861–1896* (2010): Selections from the nine-volume, 2,500-page diary that extend over 36 years and document the life of a famous American who rose from young immigrant to successful industrialist.
- *Have you heard the one about…? The Phyllis Diller Gag File* (2011): A sample of jokes from a 3 × 5 card file acquired by the Smithsonian that included more than 50,000 jokes and gags.
- *Thomas Jefferson's Bible* (2011): The original 84-page assemblage of passages from the first four books of the New Testament compiled by Thomas Jefferson in a collection he entitled "The Life and Morals of Jesus of Nazareth." Notably, he excised all the reported miracles.
- *Little Golden Books* (2013): A selection of original drawings done for the Little Golden Books series of children's books, begun in 1942, that were written for children ages three to eight.
- *Making a Modern Museum* (2014): A 50th-anniversary display of the authorizing legislation and other materials related to the creation of the Museum of History and Technology and its subsequent development.
- *Righting a Wrong: Japanese Americans and World War II (2017)*: Executive Order 9066, which authorized incarceration of 120,000 Japanese Americans during World War II.

National Museum of African American History and Culture Gallery (2009)

The National Museum of African American History and Culture (NMAAHC) was established in 2003 as the Smithsonian's nineteenth museum. In 2006, the Board of Regents decided to build the new museum on a five-acre site on the National Mall, across the street from the National Museum of American History. Some key staff members of the new museum, including its founding director, Lonnie Bunch, had previously worked at American History.

As a way of supporting the African American museum, NMAH agreed to allocate a gallery space that would allow the staff of the future museum to mount a series of exhibitions prior to its opening. In this gallery, they could test themes and ideas and gain publicity for the new institution.[409]

Between 2009 and 2017, eight different exhibitions were shown in the gallery.[410]

- *The Scurlock Studio and Black Washington: Picturing the Promise* (2009): More than 100 images created by a premier African American photographic studio in Washington, D.C., providing a vivid portrait of life in Black Washington from 1911 to 1994.
- *Ain't Nothing Like the Real Thing: How the Apollo Theater Shaped American Entertainment* (2010): Photographs and artifacts that traced the rich history of cultural significance of Harlem's Apollo Theater.
- *The Kinsey Collection: Shared Treasures of Bernard and Shirley Kinsey; Where Art and History Intersect* (2010): Over 100 artifacts including books, sculptures,

Figure 6-66. Entry to *Slavery at Jefferson's Monticello* exhibition.

paintings, and photographs that spanned 400 years and illustrated the hardships and triumphs of the African American experience.

- *For All the World to See: Visual Culture and the Struggle for Civil Rights* (2011): An examination of the historic role of visual images in shaping, influencing, and transforming the fight for civil rights in the United States. It explored how the struggle for racial justice was fought in the media as well as in the streets.
- *Slavery at Jefferson's Monticello: Paradox of Liberty* (2012): An exploration of slavery and the lives of enslaved people in America through the example of Thomas Jefferson's plantation at Monticello (Figure 6-66). The exhibition presented the stories of six enslaved families who supported plantation life.
- *Changing America: The Emancipation Proclamation, 1863, and the March on Washington, 1963* (2012): A commemoration and comparison of two seminal events in American history that occurred a century apart: the 1863 Emancipation Proclamation and the 1963 March on Washington. Both events were the culmination of decades of struggles by individuals, famous and forgotten, who believed in the American promise that all men are created equal.
- *Rising Up: Hale Woodruff's Murals at Talladega College* (2014): A series of murals painted for Talladega College, Alabama, one of the first colleges established

for Black people in the United States. The six murals portrayed noteworthy events in the rise of Black people from slavery to freedom.

- *Through the African American Lens: A Preview of the National Museum of African American History and Culture* (2015): A sampling of artifacts that would be shown in the new museum, demonstrating the richness and diversity of the African American experience.

The gallery would close soon after the National Museum of African American History and Culture opened in 2016.

The creation of this new museum raised difficult questions for the National Museum of American History. How should it display stories of African Americans in the future? Certainly, they would continue to be included in exhibitions of broad themes, such as *Many Voices, One Nation, The Price of Freedom: Americans and War*, and *America on the Move*. However, should the museum continue to create exhibitions that focused solely on topics related to African American history, such as *Field to Factory*, or leave such displays to its new sister museum? Equally problematic was whether it should now focus more on other ethnic groups that did not have their own museum, such as Asian Americans and Latinos. Should the national history museum be a place for helping such groups incubate their own museums? Or should it try to maintain the National Museum of American History as a comprehensive institution that tells the story of all the American people? Would such an idea even be acceptable to twenty-first-century Americans? None of these questions had easy or obvious answers, and they will continue to be debated in the future.

Nicholas F. and Eugenia Taubman Gallery (2017)

In redesigning the second floor of the west wing, the museum decided to create a new gallery for changing exhibitions. Measuring approximately 1,000 square feet, it was designed to include three permanent wall cases and a group of floor cases that could be used or not, depending on the needs of the specific exhibition. The general theme of the floor was "The Nation We Build Together," and its two long-term exhibitions were *American Democracy: A Great Leap of Faith*, and *Many Voices, One Nation*. The goal for the new space was to feature temporary exhibitions that explored themes directly related to these larger displays.[411]

In the first two years, two exhibitions were presented.

- *Religion in Early America* (2017): This exhibition explored the role of religion in America from the colonial era through the 1840s. It focused on the diversity of religious traditions during this period, the establishment of freedom of religion as a founding principle of the nation, and the growth of religion, especially evangelical denominations of Christianity, in the early republic. Objects on display, many of which were loans, included a copy of the Bay Psalm Book, the first book published in America; the Bible used in the inauguration of George Washington; and Thomas Jefferson's "The Life and Morals of Jesus of Nazareth."

Figure 6-67. Central case in the *Religion in Early America* exhibition.

Figure 6-68. Central case in the American Revolution exhibition.

- *The American Revolution: A World War* (2018):[412] This exhibition explored how the American Revolution grew from a domestic conflict between colonists and their king into a world war involving many nations and battles around the world. This expansion and the alliances the colonies formed were critical to the United States winning its independence. On display were a French cannon used at the Battle of Yorktown and original paintings of the battle created for the leading French general on the scene, the Comte de Rochambeau.

Both exhibitions were well reviewed and popular with audiences. *Religion in Early America* was the first thematic exhibition on religion that the museum had ever mounted. *The American Revolution: A World War* was a rare example in the museum of a display that focused on the degree to which United States history was shaped by international events.

New Visitor Experiences

Education and Program Areas

Among the most important changes that Brent Glass brought to the museum was increasing the attention it gave to public programs. Under his direction, the plans for west wing renovation included extensive new education and public programs spaces on all three floors. Working in close collaboration with him was Judy Gradwohl, under whose direction the Office of Public Programs was expanded and became independent from the Office of Curatorial Affairs. Although Glass retired four years before any of the west wing floors opened, the plans he pioneered brought major changes to all three floors. John Gray led the effort to complete planning and secure funding for them.

The most extensive changes were made on the first floor. It now included an education center that occupied the full north side and central sections of the floor. The new area had an exhibition gallery for the Jerome and Dorothy Lemelson Center for the Study of Invention and Innovation. Next to the gallery was a new home for Draper Spark!Lab, for children ages 6 to 12 (Figure 6-69).[413] It was the successor to

Figure 6-69. The Spark!Lab.

the Hands On Science Center first built for *Science in American Life*. It, too, was managed by the Lemelson Center. Spark!Lab offered a new approach to hands-on learning. Instead of giving visitors step-by-step instructions to follow, it challenged them to identify problems and challenges and come up with their own solutions, teaching them problem-solving skills and critical thinking. The idea was so successful that staff from the Lemelson Center helped create a network of spin-off Spark!Lab sites in additional locations in the United States and other countries.

Next to this was Wegman's Wonderplace, an early-learning center for children age six and younger that focused on learning with objects (Figure 6-70).[414] Beyond it was a conference center that could be used for meetings with outside groups, colloquia, museum staff and board meetings, and other gatherings.

In the center of the room was the Wallace H. Coulter Performance Plaza, which included a full demonstration kitchen (Figure 6-71), making it a

Figure 6-70. A young visitor enjoys Wegman's Wonderplace.

resource for programs related to the museum's growing interest in the history of American food ways. The museum offered programs such as "Cooking up History," which showcased guest chefs preparing food and talking about the history and traditions behind ingredients, culinary techniques, and food consumption. The space

Figure 6-71. Cooking demonstration in Performance Plaza.

Figure 6-72. Interactive civil rights program in Unity Square, 2017.

could also be configured for performances of the museum's jazz orchestra, lectures, exhibitions, and other events.

The museum decided it should include an innovative learning space in this central area for an interactive exhibition that would focus on "everyday things that changed everything," rather than a strictly historical display. Named the *Patrick F. Taylor Foundation Object Project*, it displayed innovative objects such as refrigerators, bicycles, and ready-to-wear clothing in ways that let visitors handle and experience the objects while learning things about their invention and history.[415] Planning for this was led by project directors and content developers Howard Morrison and Judy Gradwohl.[416] The combination of the performance stage, conference center, and open floor space for display tables or booths made this area ideal for special events such as the Innovative Lives presentations by leading inventors, the National Trademark Exposition, and Military Invention Day.

The second floor included the Wallace H. Coulter Unity Square. Here visitors were invited to participate in activities related to American civic life. One notable set of activities, American Experiments, had been developed in collaboration with The Exploratorium in San Francisco, California. Like the exhibitions in the new Taubman Gallery, the programs and activities in the square were designed to relate to the large exhibitions on either side, *Many Voices, One Nation* and *American Democracy: A Great Leap of Faith*. One of the museum's treasured artifacts, a section of a Woolworth's lunch counter from Greensboro, North Carolina, was now displayed here. At

Figure 6-73. Concert at the opening of the Taubman Hall of Music, 2019.

that lunch counter, in February 1960, a peaceful sit-in by four African American students helped spark the social movement that ended racial segregation in the South. It its new location, the artifact became a site for live educational programs that helped visitors understand the history of the Civil Rights Movement.

The third floor included the new Nicholas F. and Eugenia Taubman Hall of Music, designed specifically for small-group performances using instruments from the museum's collection. It became the resident home for performances by the Smithsonian Chamber Music Society, whose mission was "to use the priceless treasures of the Smithsonian's collection of musical instruments to offer the public unique experiences and insights into the Western classical music of the past 400 years."[417] Although the society had been performing since 1976, this was the first time it had a space specifically designed for its form of unamplified music.

These spaces dedicated to programs and interactive visitor experiences—particularly for younger visitors—added a new dimension to the museum's offerings. Besides allowing visitors to see historical objects, the new spaces let them get involved in activities related to the history around them. As Spark!Lab docents asked their visitors, "What will you invent today?"

By the time the renovated center core and west wing opened, the museum's website had expanded and matured. It included descriptions and additional information for almost every exhibition the museum mounted, including images and extensive information about objects. The printed curriculum kits of the past were superseded by the Smithsonian's History Explorer, which had been developed in partnership with the Verizon Foundation to offer free, innovating online resources to teachers, students, families, and individuals. As it grew over the years, it became a highly valuable resource for educators across the nation.

A New Graphic Identity

In the spring of 2016, John Gray asked for the assistance of board member John Adams in creating a new graphic identity for the museum.[418] Adams was the former CEO of The Martin Agency, an advertising agency in Richmond, Virginia, well known for its campaigns. (It developed the slogan "Virginia is for Lovers" and the GEICO Gecko.) The agency agreed to donate the time of some talented young staff members to work on the project. They toured the museum, studied planning and programming documents, met with staff members, and came up with a range of ideas. In January 2017, they presented their final recommendations. Gray and his senior staff were dazzled by the innovative and thoughtful suggestions.

The marketing team concluded that the museum's identity campaign should focus on indicating that "there are real stories behind every object, every exhibit, every idea within the National Museum of American History... stories that put people at the heart of history." Based on this principle, they believed the museum should aspire to help its visitors "find yourself in the American story."[419] (Figure 6-74)

This led them to suggest a new "logoform" that was dynamic and adaptable, and thus could be used in many variations to orient visitors to the museum, its exhibitions, and its services in a unified but flexible manner. The team demonstrated the flexibility of the idea by presenting an initial set of simple variations, shown in Figure 6-75. Besides images of artifacts, designs could also use images of images of people representing museum visitors., as in Figure 6-76.

The museum was excited about how it could employ the design strategy to reach its visitors and supporters in a fresh new way. In the months that followed, its own design staff gradually implemented the approach in its communication, marketing, fundraising, and museum navigation. Some examples can be seen in Figure 6-77 and 6-78.

Find Yourself in the American Story

An active journey anchored in the discovery of the new, familiar, unknown and surprising that can take people on many different paths

An always-evolving narrative using the real objects of the past and present to tell the stories of America's ideals and ideas

An experience that feels real, human and personal because it aims to put you at the center of an American story and connect you to America

Figure 6-74. Key ideas in the new graphic identity program.

The new signage (Figure 6-78) brought increased unity and coherence to the way the museum presented itself to its visitors. It clearly linked the topics of the museum's exhibitions to its original artifacts, visually conveying that this was an institution that told "real stories about the real stuff."[420]

Exhibiting What It Means to Be American

Beginning in the late 1990s, the museum devoted itself to encouraging visitors to think more deeply and profoundly about what it means to be American. Twenty years later, after massive investment totaling over $350 million, and fundamental restructuring, what was the result?

No formal evaluation has yet been done of the degree to which the museum has accomplished its strategic goal, and because these exhibitions are recent, it is perhaps too soon to tell how well they have succeeded with audiences. However, the new focus on American identity had brought fundamental changes to the museum's exhibitions. Comparing the floor map of 2018 that begins this chapter with the earlier map of 1999 shows that almost all the exhibitions had now been renovated.

Figure 6-75. Variations in the graphic identity program.

Figure 6-76. Personalizing the museum's identity.

Figure 6-77. Outdoor banners with the new graphic identity at the Constitution Avenue entrance.

The Star-Spangled Banner was still displayed in the center of the building, but now it was much more dramatically presented and it was much easier to see its details. Moreover, besides relating the story of this unique artifact, the museum also showed how Americans have used their flag to protest as well as celebrate, to demonstrate their anger with their government as well as commitment to its preservation.

Exhibitions now highlighted a set of ideals and ideas to which Americans aspired, including democracy, opportunity, equality, and freedom. Yet unlike *A Nation of Nations* in 1976, they no longer sought to foster an "unchauvinistic patriotism."[421] Besides showing growth in the American economy and increased participation in American politics, they explored the unequal distribution of American prosperity and the continuing struggle many had in attaining American ideals in their personal and family lives. Exhibitions showed many ways that citizens of different racial and ethnic backgrounds had contributed to American food, business, politics, and culture, but they also examined how racism and prejudice continued to plague American society.

Visitors learned that America continued to be a nation at war, as it had been for most of its history, defending its values and its position as the most powerful military force in the world. Yet they also saw that America's wars had been costly and controversial, and that they had required great sacrifice by the American people.

Figure 6-78. Floor navigation signage with the new graphic identity and thematic organization.

Exhibitions illustrated ways that Americans remain dedicated to invention and innovation as a national strategy, and capitalism as an economic system. They also addressed the unequal distribution of economic benefits and technological improvements and explored governmental efforts to address these issues. Visitors saw how Americans are continually on the move—on land and sea—and how they are fundamentally dependent on global trade. Yet they also learned how continued development has led to increased congestion, pollution, and climate change.

Finally, visitors who wanted to personalize their involvement with American history now had many new opportunities to engage more deeply through hands-on educational activities, programs, and postings on the museum's extensive website.

The museum had not achieved the Blue Ribbon Commission's goal of providing a comprehensive overview of American history, but in its fifth era, it was much more coherent and had provided a much more thoughtful, balanced, and dynamic presentation of the elements of American history.

Figure 7-1. Reverse side of an 1805 five-dollar coin showing the seal of the United States. Note that in this era, the eagle faced the arrows of war in its claw, not the olive branch of peace.

CHAPTER 7

Reflections

We have surveyed the National Museum of American History and its predecessors as they changed during five distinct eras, from 1881 through 2018. In relating this story, we focused on the museum's exhibitions and the differing ways they presented American history. Here we summarize our reflections on three important trends we discerned across the eras and on four challenges that we found in all of them—challenges that will continue in the future.

Trends

From Global to Nationalistic

Although it may seem surprising to twenty-first-century readers, when the Smithsonian's U.S. National Museum was created in 1881, its name did not mean that its mission was essentially nationalistic. It had not been established primarily to collect and display objects that documented the history and achievements of the American people. Its artifacts and exhibitions were global in scope. As James Smithson's bequest had mandated, they were dedicated to documenting and explaining "the increase and diffusion of knowledge among men" everywhere in the world. Even its historical collections were initially international, designed to document not only how the United States had developed, but how it related to and interacted with other nations, especially in fields of science and technology.

The museum was initially called "national" because it was designated as the repository of the federal government's national collections. These, too, were international in scope. As explained in chapter 2, they were principally specimens collected by government-sponsored expeditions, including the United States Exploring Expedition of 1838 to 1843, which was devoted to gathering artifacts from the Pacific Ocean and surrounding lands. The national collections also included objects from the Army, Navy, Coast and Geodetic Survey, and other agencies; donations to the government from private citizens; purchases; and what were called historic relics of notable Americans, including George Washington, Benjamin Franklin, and Ulysses S. Grant. In the late nineteenth century, the Smithsonian was the only official government repository for federal scientific and historical collections.

This responsibility slipped away in the twentieth century, as the federal government grew and numerous agencies, including the armed forces, began keeping their own research and culture collections and creating their own display centers and museums. Moreover, the Smithsonian has always collected objects on its own initiative, not simply served as a repository for those collected by other federal agencies. The first collection the institution purchased, in 1849, came from Vermont Congressman George Perkins Marsh, who had been involved in the debate over the creation of the Smithsonian and later would become a regent. It consisted of a large group of European engravings and related books on European art. The Smithsonian's interest in graphic arts was global: among the engravings were works by Albrecht Dürer, Rembrandt van Rijn, Leonardo da Vinci, and many other famous artists. Selections from the collection went on display in the Smithsonian Castle, which showed a mix of both printing technology and European and American prints.[422]

In the National Museum of American History of the twenty-first century, the only collection in the museum that could still be considered a systematic reference collection of a federal agency was the national numismatics collection. The museum aimed to include in it an example of every monetary product the U.S. Mint produced. The philately collection previously had a similar status, but it was transferred out of the museum in 1993, when it became the nucleus of the Smithsonian's National Postal Museum. It is jointly supported by both the Smithsonian and the U.S. Postal Service.

The National Museum of American History in recent decades has redefined the meaning of its role as a national institution. It now explicitly focuses on the nationalistic goal of building collections and presenting exhibitions that explore what is distinctive about being American. This redefined objective has led to its exploring many areas of national development, including not only political and social history but also scientific, technological, economic, and entertainment history. Whereas the museum of 1968 had numerous exhibitions that featured objects from around the world, the museum of 2017 had almost none. This is easily seen when comparing the floor plans in chapters 3 and 6 (Figures 3-1 and 6-1). This trend was found in many other national museums in this period. As anthropologist Sharon Macdonald noted in *The Politics of Display*,

> The [modern] museum is not…merely a product of or a site for displaying the narratives of modern developments; it is also one of the technologies through which modernity—and the democratic ideals, social differences and exclusions, and other contradictions which this has produced—is constituted.[423]

Vestiges of the earlier global perspective remain represented in many of its collections, including numismatics, physical science, music and entertainment, graphic arts, information technology, and work and industry. If, in the future, the museum broadens its focus again to explore the role of the United States history in a global context, these collections will provide a valuable place to start.

From Collections to Themes

Throughout the five eras we discussed, the broadest trend has been the museum's moving from simple displays of historical collections to complex presentations that use collections to explore historical themes. Case displays in the U.S. National Museum showed numerous objects lined up next to each other as concrete evidence of progress in design or technical expertise. Labeling was sparse. The same approach was used whether the subject was agricultural tools, automobiles, ship models, or ceramics. This began to change dramatically with the exhibits modernization program of the 1950s and 1960s.

When the Museum of History and Technology opened in the mid-1960s, the new exhibitions were a mix. Some, such as *Growth of the United States* and *Everyday Life in the American Past* were thematic and contextual, but still grounded in carefully chosen artifacts and historical settings. The goal was to help visitors see themselves or people like them reflected in the museum's displays. Other exhibitions, such as those in the Glass Hall, Philately Hall, and Graphic Arts Hall, remained primarily displays of collections with minimal contextual support. Here the focus was on the history of the objects themselves, not how they related to the visitors.

By the 1980s, thematic exhibits had become the dominant form of presentation. Examples included *Field to Factory*, *From Parlor to Politics*, *Information Age*, and *On Time*. This trend continued into the twenty-first century, as exhibition design became more elaborate, large-scale graphics more frequent, lighting more dramatic, and audiovisual or interactive components more common.

In most respects, this trend led to richer and more compelling exhibitions. For example, *The Price of Freedom* was a more coherent display than that of the earlier Armed Forces Hall. Rather than relating the internal history of the military services, it centered on explaining how American wars had been defining episodes in the history of the nation. *America on the Move* provided a broader view of how mobility changed America than did the Hall of Transportation. It explored ways in which changes in transportation had shaped the growth of the nation as it expanded across the continent.

Our study convinced us, however, that highly contextual and thematic presentations were not always improvements. Sometimes contextual materials such as graphics or video could overwhelm the experience of seeing unique, original objects. Sometimes an array of artifacts that allowed visitors to make their own determinations of what to compare and contrast was more valuable than giving them only one or two artifacts chosen to illustrate a curator's interpretation.

The series of first ladies exhibitions in the museum illustrates this point well. The first several versions in this series in the National Museum were simple collections displays with short descriptive labeling. Then, during the exhibits modernization program in the 1950s, the dresses were displayed in sumptuous contextual settings. The 1992 version, *The First Ladies: Political Role and Public Image*, was strongly thematic and interpretive. Visitors were encouraged to focus on the first ladies as political actors. The display minimized the significance of dresses as compelling objects in their own right. The most recent exhibition, *The First Ladies,* which opened in 2011, effectively blended collections and thematic presentation. It began with several large cases that focused visitors on examining the dresses and White House china as interesting artifacts that could be compared. These were then followed by cases that provided interpretive presentations about how four first ladies shaped their roles as important social and political leaders in the country. In this instance, the blend of the two forms of display worked better than an exhibition that was exclusively one type or the other.

We concluded that the museum's exhibitions benefitted from variety. We hope that the copious illustrations we included in this book show that displays in each era had their charms and triumphs as well as their disappointments. We also hope they reinforce the idea that museums should remain repositories where visitors find creative mixes of simple artifact displays as well as context and interpretation.

From Progress to Identity

From the 1880s through the 1970s, Smithsonian history exhibitions were largely devoted to documenting, explaining, and proudly displaying evidence of human progress. They were premised on the belief that progress resulted from new knowledge, and that Smithsonian exhibitions should show how the "increase and diffusion" of knowledge had continually changed the world for the better. To the museum leaders of this era, progress was most clear in science and technology, as revealing the secrets of nature led to new tools and machines that were ever faster, more powerful, and more efficient. In their minds, knowledge-based progress was also evident in the spread of democracy, the improvement of standards of living, and the increase of leisure and entertainment. Exhibitions showing material evidence of human progress not only educated visitors, but also made them more patriotic and informed citizens.

In the 1980s, this style of exhibitry changed dramatically. Responding to the new social history that had emerged in university history departments in the 1960s and 1970s, the museum sought to include more stories of ordinary Americans and groups that had not been widely represented before, including workers, women, African Americans, Latinos, and Asian Americans. Whether America's story was truly one of progress was now presented as problematic. Exhibitions included stories of struggles, oppression, exploitation, and the costs as well as benefits of technological change. By the 1990s, the museum had coalesced around a far different goal from knowledge-based progress: exploring what it meant to be American.

This fundamental change in mission led to challenging issues. Tracing the arc of human progress had been directly relevant to Smithson's bequest. Exploring American identity moved in a new direction that seemed less tied to it. Moreover, this new approach raised the troubling question of whether there truly was a unifying historical narrative that encompassed all Americans. Did the story of "what it meant to be American" differ fundamentally depending on one's race, gender, ethnic group, class, or community? Should the Smithsonian have only one National Museum of American History or should different institutions tell contrasting stories of different American communities?

The Smithsonian was not left to answer this question by itself. It became a charged political issue. The U.S. Congress and the president approved first the creation of the National Museum of the American Indian, which opened in 2004, and then the National Museum of African American History and Culture, which opened in 2016. Moreover, initial planning began for a National Museum of the American Latino, to be followed by a similar initiative for Asian Americans. Legislation for these two museums was introduced in 2013 and 2016 respectively.

What, in turn, did that mean for the National Museum of American History? The answer is still not clear. No one there wanted to embrace the notion that it should become what many critics thought, indeed, it had always been—a museum focused primarily on White Americans. But how should the establishment of these ethnically focused national museums affect the stated goal of the National Museum of American History to explore what it means to be American?

This study has provided no answer to this difficult question. What it does suggest is that as the museum has done at critical moments in the past, it should once again take a serious look at how it can best serve the people of the United States. In doing so, it should carefully examine the future significance of its existing collections and expertise, its past successes and failures, its relation to other new Smithsonian museums, and its role within the expanding Smithsonian Institution. It should remember that its past strength has always been its breadth: as a museum of both Arts *and* Industry, History *and* Technology. Rethinking how to interweave scientific and technological themes with social and cultural themes in compelling new ways is likely to be an important part of its future.

Perhaps, also, the museum of tomorrow might seek to broaden its perspective once again from national to global and seek to help its visitors understand how the history of the United States links to that of other nations. This remains a fruitful area where the National Museum of American History could take the lead within the Smithsonian.

Challenges

Plans and Realities

Much of this book has focused on the relationship between what exhibitions were planned in different eras and what was ultimately displayed on the museum floor. The differences between dreams and realities were most significant when the plans were broadest and grandest. The five distinct eras in the museum's exhibitions resulted from strong partnerships between museum directors and Smithsonian secretaries: George Brown Goode and Spencer Baird, Frank Taylor and Leonard Carmichael, Daniel Boorstin and S. Dillon Ripley, Roger Kennedy and S. Dillon Ripley, and Brent Glass and Larry Small. In each of the eras, projects begun under these initial partners were completed and often refined or fundamentally altered by successors at both the museum and secretarial level. Thus, for example, Director Brooke Hindle led the completion of the bicentennial exhibitions begun under

Daniel Boorstin, Spencer Crew the further articulation and completion of planning begun under Roger Kennedy, and John Gray the opening of the west wing of the museum as part of the twenty-first-century renovation.

All these leaders were dedicated to improving how the Smithsonian diffused knowledge about American history, and they all achieved significant results. Nonetheless, they never fully realized their ambitious plans. The National Museum of the 1880s fell far short of presenting George Brown Goode's comprehensive anthropological structure of all human knowledge. The Museum of History and Technology did not achieve a unified link between a comprehensive exhibition on the growth of the United States and collection halls on specific subjects. The bicentennial exhibitions did not provide a balanced review of the military, social, and technical history of the United States at its 200th birthday. In the 1980s and 1990s, the National Museum of American History failed to produce a complete series of chronological exhibitions on America in the colonial era, the eighteenth century, nineteenth century, and twentieth century. In the early twenty-first century, the National Museum of American History, Kenneth E. Behring Center produced neither a grand chronological overview of American history nor most other new exhibitions envisioned in the Blue Ribbon Commission's report of 2002.

Yet the fact that the grand schemes were only partly realized did not mean they had failed. They still inspired compelling exhibitions that millions of visitors found educational, inspirational, and enjoyable. Moreover, the incomplete results were hardly surprising. All exhibitions are custom-built, unique presentations. Especially when large, their production is always risky, and plans had to be adjusted and modified in response to unforeseen issues related to funding, scheduling, staffing, availability of artifacts, design problems, or issues with exhibition space. Sometimes modifications were done well; at other times they were poorly managed. Examples of how the museum adjusted to changes in plans are as revealing as the original plans themselves.

Chapter 2 reviewed George Brown Goode's plan to organize the U.S. National Museum around an anthropological structure of human knowledge. When this failed, museum leaders might have come up with a well-considered alternative structure, but they failed to do so. Thus, as can be seen from the floor plan of the National Museum in 1890, when the museum opened, there was no clear organization. For instance, the graphic arts displays were located among naval architecture, American history relics, and ethnology. When the natural history collections were relocated in 1911, the organization of the remaining arts and industries displays in the U.S. National Museum became equally random. In short, what was once envisioned as a museum devoted to telling the all-encompassing story of mankind in the universe had devolved into a disorganized "nation's attic."

When the Museum of History and Technology was being conceived in the late 1950s and early 1960s, Frank Taylor and his colleagues planned for the *Growth of the United States* exhibition to serve as an introduction to the rest of the museum. Although only some sections of the exhibition were completed, they were thoughtful, well designed, and effective. Yet the museum did not attempt to retitle or restructure the exhibition to deal with the realities of what it had become or reconfigure how it related to the displays around it. The adjacent *Everyday Life in the American Past* had effectively become a replacement for the introductory exhibition that *Growth of the United States* was supposed to be, but the museum never represented it as such. The closest it came was developing its "Rooms and Shops" tour described in chapter 3.

In contrast, when the original plans for *A Nation of Nations* proved too difficult[424], the museum extensively revised its goals and organization. Although the exhibition was less ambitious than originally planned, it became one of the most successful bicentennial exhibitions. Its specific focus on the role of immigrants in shaping the nation helped many visitors recognize the role of families like their own in the national story.

Communities in a Changing Nation: The Promise of 19th Century America, which opened in 1999, was truncated late in its development by Secretary Michael Heyman. Museum leaders initially hoped that its final sections would be installed later. Yet when it became clear that this would never happen, the exhibition was never revised to account for the missing pieces. Visitors were left to wonder how the stories of three communities in the eastern United States effectively represented the broad history of all of nineteenth-century America.

In the 2010s, in contrast, the first version of the *American Enterprise* exhibition was planned for installation in the east wing of the building in a space that measured around 14,000 square feet. Midway through planning, Director Brent Glass decided to move it to a new location on the other side of the building and cut it in half. He initially told the team they should keep the same basic plan and just reduce its size. However, the team convinced him that they must be allowed to re-envision the exhibition so that it worked in the new space and related thematically to the other displays that would be around it. Although this led to some cost escalation and schedule changes, it was critical to the success of the final display.

Making adjustments was not only important in planning new exhibitions but also in managing older displays. When exhibitions were planned, the museum always intended to keep them well maintained and up to date. However, in reality this tends to be the exception rather than the rule. In 2018, at the end of our story, sections of the *Power Machinery* exhibition that had been on display when the museum opened in 1964 were still on view. Although the style of the exhibition was now out of synch with the surrounding exhibitions, no attempt was ever made to recast it or make it fit effectively into a changed museum. Nor, indeed, was it deliberately presented as simply a historically interesting example of an earlier style of exhibition.

Coherence and Completeness

When surveying the state of the National Museum of American History in 2002, the Blue Ribbon Commission harshly concluded: "The Museum does not seem to meet any obvious test of comprehensibility or coherence....Many serious observers and most members of the Commission believe that the problem has to do...with the Museum's content and the organization of its presentation."[425] The commission strongly believed the museum had to find a way to become both more comprehensive and more coherent. This was not a new goal. As discussed in chapter 2, when George Brown Goode outlined what the National Museum should strive to present, he based his recommendations on a comprehensive anthropological view of human knowledge that would provide a context for "every object in existence which it is possible to describe."[426]

Although no museum director who followed Goode would ever be so expansive again, most sought ways to achieve the goals of comprehensiveness and coherence to some degree. For example, Frank Taylor, who gave a prominent place to the introductory *Growth of the United States* exhibition in the new museum, aimed to bring a coherence to it that had been lacking in the National Museum. In the 1980s, Roger Kennedy focused on having the museum include topics that had been omitted or minimized in the past, such as African American history or women's history, so that the museum would be more comprehensive. Yet the Blue Ribbon Commission found the results of these and other efforts to be sorely lacking. Why has it proved so difficult to achieve a seemingly obvious and appropriate goal?

The collections the museum inherited when it became a separate Smithsonian organization were very diverse. They included artifacts of national political and military history, but also physics, chemistry, engineering, numismatics, philately, graphic arts, music, costume, medicine, dentistry, textiles, mining, ceramics, metallurgy, electricity, telephony, underwater archeology, and many other subjects. Moreover, this diversity would grow over time. Curators in all areas worked to have their collections represented in the museum's exhibitions. Consequently, the range of topics the museum displayed has always been great, even while they have still fallen short of providing comprehensive coverage of all areas of American national life.

Several times, the museum sought to become more coherent by creating a chronological exhibition or timeline that would serve as an introduction to everything else on display. As the preceding chapters related, this approach failed multiple times. Other attempts focused on adopting broad organizational themes or categories and locating exhibits with similar subjects near each other. While this worked better, it would fall apart when important new exhibitions had to be installed in whatever space was available, whether or not the display related well to the topics of others in the area.

Perhaps the goals of being complete and comprehensive, as reasonable as they seem, were inappropriate. Certainly not everyone agreed that they were desirable. Perhaps diversity and surprise were the museum's strength, not its weakness. As John Fleckner, the longtime head of the museum's Archives Center, proposed during one laborious, multiyear cycle of master planning,

> GIVE IT UP—We can't create a systematic, comprehensive view of American History. Museums don't lend themselves to that—indeed, our strength is precisely in the opportunity for non-linear learning and for creating memorable experiences that expand our imaginations. If you want it *by* the book, *buy* a book.[427]

As we conducted our study, we frequently discussed the museum's many attempts to provide a more coherent and comprehensive perspective on American history to its visitors. History showed, we found, that achieving this goal through exhibitions was far more difficult than museum leaders ever imagined. We reasoned that the museum should unquestionably work to give its visitors coherent explanation of what is on display, why it is there, and how visitors could easily navigate through it all. However, the museum should aspire to be more like an exciting and dynamic shopping mall than a well-organized and comprehensive department store. It should present a mix of some exhibitions on major subjects of enduring importance such as American democracy, military history, transportation, and economic history, mixed with other surprising and provocative displays, such as *Yesterday's Tomorrows*, *M*A*S*H*, and *On Time*, that are based on the richness and diversity of the museum's vast collections and staff research. Finally, it should forthrightly admit that it is being thoughtfully selective, not comprehensive, and that its displays are an invitation to explore topics in American history in provocative ways, not a complete summary of the major events in the nation's development.

Past and Future

The future is always shaped by legacies of the past. Thus, we were led to ask, "In what important ways did the history of the museum and its predecessors shape what it presented in later eras?"

Most important, the museum was always shaped by being a "national" museum within the context of the Smithsonian. This established both responsibilities and boundaries that have guided its activities and its visitation. Its location on the National Mall guaranteed that the museum would always have large audiences. Yet this also meant that for many visitors, coming to it would be only one agenda item in a pilgrimage to the nation's capital. Only a small percentage come to see just this museum.

Directly related to this were the characteristics of the buildings that housed the museum: first the U.S. National Museum Building and later the custom-designed Museum of History and Technology. As chapters 2 and 3 detailed, the structures of the two buildings established physical conditions and limitations on what the museum could be. Once these conditions were determined, they shaped how exhibitions were presented in the buildings thereafter. New displays had to be tailored to fit existing halls in juxtaposition to other displays on topics that were often unrelated.

Equally important has been the influence of collections that museum staff at later periods of history inherited from earlier periods. As the preceding chapters have shown, some artifacts that have become national icons have been displayed repeatedly in different ways. The Star-Spangled Banner is the most obvious example, but the group also includes artifacts of George Washington, Abraham Lincoln, and Ulysses S. Grant; the Horace Greenough statue of Washington; the Jefferson desk; the first ladies' gowns; the gunboat *Philadelphia*; the 1401 locomotive; Samuel Morse's telegraph; Alexander Graham Bell's telephone; Thomas Edison's light bulbs; Eli

Whitney's cotton gin; the 20-dollar gold coin designed by Augustus Saint-Gaudens; the ruby slippers from *The Wizard of Oz;* and many others. A large percentage of the key objects visitors come to see in the twenty-first century have been in the museum's collections since the nineteenth or early twentieth centuries.

Curators planning major new exhibitions for the future knew that they must rely heavily on objects collected in the past. As Anthony Garvan learned when he tried to procure a large number of new artifacts for *Growth of the United States*, or Daniel Boorstin discovered when he sought to create a major exhibition section on a subject that had no basis in the museum's existing collections, it was very difficult to start from scratch, given the reality of budgets, schedules, and museum procedures. Displays of entirely new collections, such as Teodoro Vidal's collection of Puerto Rican cultural objects, acquired in 1997, have generally been small and limited. Usually curators must shape how they tell their stories so they can use a mix of existing and new objects. One good example is the exhibition *After the Revolution*, which repurposed historical settings previously used in *Everyday Life in the American Past*.

Throughout its five eras, the museum has produced over 1,000 exhibitions. Many subjects have come and gone, but others have persisted and been featured in a series of different displays. In some cases, the topics themselves were considered fundamental to the mission of the museum, such as American political history, military history, and transportation history. In other cases, the museum was committed to keeping specific objects or collections on display, such as the Star-Spangled Banner, the first ladies' gowns, the ruby slippers, and the national numismatic collection. In part, these choices were shaped by the museum's reputation and visitor expectations. For example, when in the 1980s the museum decided to remove the Foucault pendulum that had hung in the center of the building since it opened in 1964, the Public Affairs Office spent years responding to letters from angry visitors who fondly remembered seeing it there earlier and couldn't understand why it had been removed.

Finally, some exhibits remained and were updated because there was simply no compelling reason to put something else in that location, or because it was too costly to remove them. These are the principal causes of the long lives of *Lighting a Revolution* and *Power Machinery*.

In planning new exhibitions, the museum has always sought to be faithful to its heritage of having a mix of exhibitions presenting both social and cultural history, as well as the history of science and technology. Indeed, this mix was initially considered one of the distinct strengths of the museum. In many instances, such topics were treated in separate displays, but in recent decades, the museum has worked to produce exhibitions that demonstrated important ways that technological and social change were interrelated. Examples included *A Nation of Nations* in the 1970s, *Science in American Life* in the 1990s, and *American Enterprise* in the 2010s. In summary, our study showed that museum planning was most effective when it benefitted from its past successes, learned from past mistakes, and remained focused on shaping its mission with a clear understanding of how it related to other parts of the Smithsonian Institution.

Many or One

From the beginning, resolving tensions inherent in creating a unified nation from disparate parts has characterized American history. In 1782, the country chose as its motto the Latin phrase *E pluribus unum*—out of many, one. It became a central element in the national seal. The Star-Spangled Banner, the museum's most treasured artifact, represents this same thought in visual form: 13 stripes and 50 stars stitched together to make a unified whole.

In the country's early decades, tensions centered on whether common interests would be enough to hold together states that had divergent political and economic interests, particularly relating to the legalization of human slavery. These led to the nation's most divisive war. The union was saved, but at tremendous cost. In the years that followed, new tensions arose over tariffs, trade, internal improvements, and immigration. In recent decades, differences have focused on issues of class, race, ethnicity, gender, technological change, and economic inequality. When numerous exhibitions in the National Museum of American History have explored these challenges, they have focused more on the tensions and struggles than what held the nation together.

Should a major new goal of the National Museum of American History in the twenty-first century be relating what America's past teaches about efforts to preserve national unity in the face of differences and challenges? No other American museum is as well positioned to tell this story. One of the nation's founders, Benjamin Franklin, recognized its importance from the beginning. Aged 81, he was the oldest and most experienced delegate to the Constitutional Convention. When a woman asked him whether the delegates would make the new nation a monarchy or a republic, he replied, "A republic—if you can keep it."[428]

Appendix: NMAH Directors Timeline

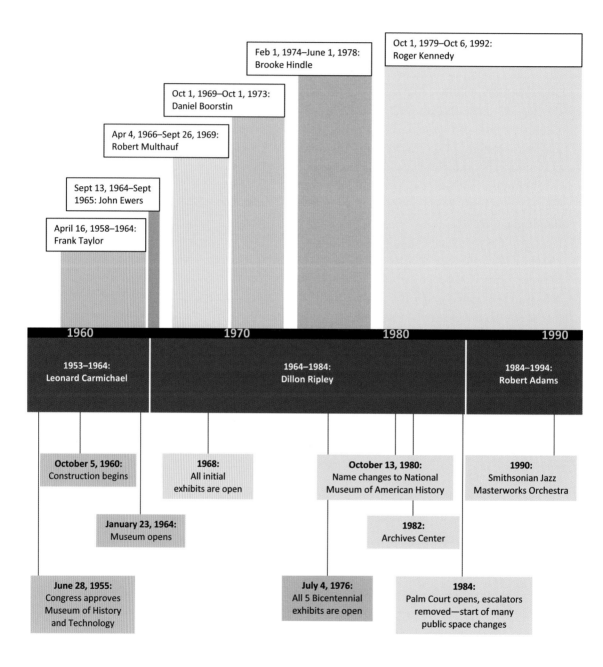

Figure A-1. Timeline of NMAH directors. Each Secretary of the Smithsonian since 1953 shown in dark gray.

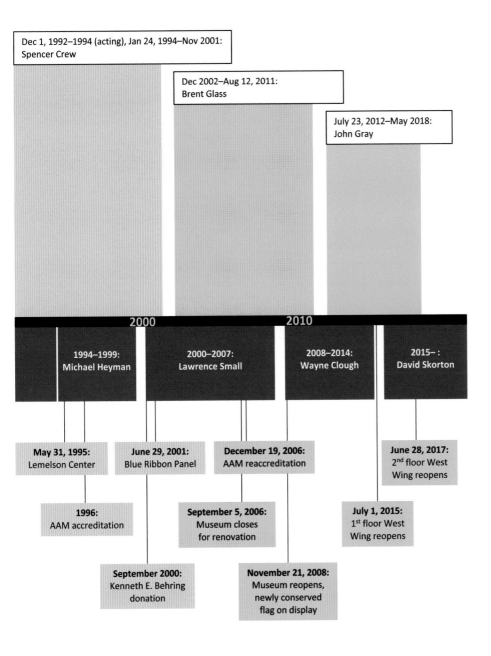

Dec 1, 1992–1994 (acting), Jan 24, 1994–Nov 2001:
Spencer Crew

Dec 2002–Aug 12, 2011:
Brent Glass

July 23, 2012–May 2018:
John Gray

2000

2010

1994–1999:
Michael Heyman

2000–2007:
Lawrence Small

2008–2014:
Wayne Clough

2015– :
David Skorton

May 31, 1995:
Lemelson Center

June 29, 2001:
Blue Ribbon Panel

December 19, 2006:
AAM reaccreditation

June 28, 2017:
2nd floor West
Wing reopens

1996:
AAM accreditation

September 5, 2006:
Museum closes
for renovation

July 1, 2015:
1st floor West
Wing reopens

September 2000:
Kenneth E. Behring
donation

November 21, 2008:
Museum reopens,
newly conserved
flag on display

Notes

1 George Brown Goode, "The Museums of the Future," in Annual Report of the Board of Regents of the Smithsonian Institution, 1889, 445, https://archive.org /details/annualreportofbo1889smith/page/444/mode/2up/search/%22A+ finished+museum%22 (accessed 28 June 2019).

Chapter 1 Notes

2 Details in this section are taken from Lonn Taylor, Kathleen M. Kendrick, and Jeffrey L. Brodie, *The Star-Spangled Banner: The Making of an American Icon* (Washington, D.C.: Smithsonian Books, 2008).

3 For other examples of this surprising practice, see William L. Bird Jr., *Souvenir Nation: Relics, Keepsakes, and Curios from the Smithsonian's National Museum of American History* (New York: Princeton Architectural Press, 2013).

4 Taylor, Kendrick, and Brodie, *The Star-Spangled Banner*, 108.

5 There have been surprisingly few studies of the museum's thousands of exhibitions, and no previous study has provided a comprehensive overview. Two of the broadest previous monographs are William S. Walker, *A Living Exhibition: The Smithsonian and the Transformation of the Universal Museum* (Amherst: University of Massachusetts Press, 2013) and Marilyn Sara Cohen, "American Civilization in Three Dimensions: The Evolution of the Museum of History and Technology of the Smithsonian Institution" (PhD diss., Georgetown University, 1980). The list of sources at the conclusion of this book includes numerous monographs or catalogs that discuss individual exhibitions or groups of them.

6 Goode, "The Museums of the Future," 445. Emphasis added by authors.

Chapter 2 Notes

7 Smithsonian Institution, *Brief Guide to the Smithsonian Institution*, Publication 4507 (National Publishing Co., 1963), inside cover.

8 Annual Report of the Board of Regents of the Smithsonian Institution, 1881, 1–3.

9 Joan Kapsch, "Education Congressman, Education President (Part II)," *The Garfield Observer: The Blog of James A. Garfield National Historical Site*, 2015, https://garfieldnps .wordpress.com/tag/gallaudet-university/ (accessed 28 June 2019).

10 Broadside for Garfield Inaugural Ball in U.S. National Museum, Smithsonian Archives, record unit 95, box 32, folder 10.

11 Inauguration Items, *Washington Post*, 6 February 1881.

12 "Inaugurated! Garfield and Arthur Sworn In as President and Vice President," *Washington Post*, 5 March 1881.

13 "U.S. National Museum Decorated for Garfield Inaugural Ball," Smithsonian Archives citation for image 44173, https://siarchives.si.edu/collections/siris_sic_9252 (accessed 2 November 2020).

14 George Brown Goode, "The Genesis of the United States National Museum," in *A Memorial of George Brown Goode* (Washington, D.C.: Government Printing Office, 1901), 85.

     Smithson's minerals were among the first scientific collections to come into the possession of the Federal Government. The earlier Lewis and Clark expedition of 1804 to 1806 had brought back extensive notebooks and botanical specimens. However, the government did not retain them. The bulk of the specimens were given to the American Philosophical Society in Philadelphia, where they reside today. (Lewis and Clark's Herbarium, The Academy of Natural Sciences of Drexel University website, https://ansp.org/exhibits/online-exhibits/stories/lewis-and-clark-herbarium/ (accessed 24 June 2019). Lewis's journals are at the American Philosophical Society and Clark's at the Missouri Historical Society.)

15 Proposed uses of the Smithson bequest are documented in William J. Rhees, *Smithsonian Miscellaneous Collections*, volume 17 (Washington, D.C.: Smithsonian Institution, 1880).

16 Rhees, Smithsonian Miscellaneous Collections, volume 17, 303.

17 This topic is discussed extensively in Goode, "The Genesis of the United States National Museum."

18 *Bulletin of the Proceedings of the National Institution for the Promotion of Science* (Washington, D.C.: The National Institution, 1841), https://www.biodiversitylibrary.org/bibliography/16039#/summary (accessed 26 June 2019).

19 Frederick William True, The United States National Museum, in George Brown Goode, ed., *The Smithsonian Institution: 1846–1896* (Washington, D.C.: Smithsonian Institution, 1897), 317.

20 True, The United States National Museum, 316.

21 William James Rhees, *The Smithsonian Institution: Documents Relative to its Origin and History, 1835–1899*, volume 1 (Washington, D.C.: Smithsonian Institution, 1901), 607.

22 Annual Report of the Board of Regents of the Smithsonian Institution, 1858, 40.

23 As Secretary Henry reported in 1861:

     "To advance original science, the duplicate type specimens are to be distributed as widely as possible to scientific institutions in this country and abroad in order that they may be used in identifying the species and genera which have been described…It must be distinctly understood that due credit is to be given to the Institution in the labeling of the specimens, and in all accounts which may be published of them since such credit is not only due to the name of Smithson, but also to the directors of the Establishment, as vouchers to the world that they are faithfully carrying out the intention of the bequest."

     Annual Report of the Board of Regents of the Smithsonian Institution, 1861, 41.

24 Goode, "The Genesis of the United States National Museum," 156.

25 True, "The United States National Museum," 326.

26 True, "The United States National Museum," 326.

27 Edward P. Alexander, *Museum Masters: Their Museums and Their Influence* (Nashville, Tenn.: American Association for State and Local History, 1983), 264.

28 Rhees, The Smithsonian Institution, 733.

29 Annual Report of the Board of Regents of the Smithsonian Institution, 1881, 36.

30 True, "The United States National Museum," 328.

31 Tanya Edwards Beauchamp, "Adolph Cluss and the Building of the U.S. National Museum: An Architecture of Perfect Adaptability" (master's thesis, University of Virginia School of Architecture, 1972) 33ff.

32 William J. Rhees, Visitor's Guide to the Smithsonian Institution and United States National Museum (Washington, D.C.: Judd & Detweiler, 1888), 13–16.

33 Alan Lessoff and Christof Mauch, *Adolf Cluss, Architect: From Germany to America* (Washington, D.C.: The Historical Society of Washington, D.C., 2005), 133.

34 Lessoff and Mauch, *Adolf Cluss, Architect*, 131.

35 National Register of Historic Places nomination form for the Smithsonian Institution Arts and Industries Building, 6 April 1971, at the National Portrait Gallery website, https://npgallery.nps.gov/NRHP/GetAsset/NHLS/71000994_text (accessed 1 July 2020).

36 Alexander, *Museum Masters*, 283.

37 Samuel P. Langley, "Memoir of George Brown Goode, in A Memorial of George Brown Goode, Together with a Selection of his Papers on Museums and on the History of Science in America" (Washington, D.C.: Government Printing Office, 1901), 54.

38 See, for example, Rhees, *Visitor's Guide*, 16.

39 Annual Report of the Board of Regents of the Smithsonian Institution, 1881, 89ff.

40 Annual Report of the Board of Regents of the Smithsonian Institution, 1882, 126.

41 Annual Report of the Board of Regents of the Smithsonian Institution, 1882, 10.

42 Annual Report of the Board of Regents of the Smithsonian Institution, 1884, part 2, Report of the National Museum, 14.

43 NMAH History Office files.

44 Rhees, *Visitor's Guide*, 24ff.

45 Annual Report of the Board of Regents of the Smithsonian Institution, 1903, part 2, Report of the National Museum, 12.

46 Annual Report of the Board of Regents of the Smithsonian Institution, 1903, part 2, Report of the National Museum, 13.

47 Annual Report of the Board of Regents of the Smithsonian Institution, 1911, 17.

48 Annual Report of the Board of Regents of the Smithsonian Institution, 1911, 30.

49 William S. Walker, "A Living Exhibition: The Smithsonian and the Transformation of the Universal Museum" (Boston: University of Massachusetts Press, 2013), 40.

50 Annual Report of the Board of Regents of the Smithsonian Institution, 1919, 27.

51 Annual Report of the Board of Regents of the Smithsonian Institution, 1919, 28.

52 Annual Report of the Board of Regents of the Smithsonian Institution, 1933, 78.

53 *Brief Guide to the Smithsonian Institution*, 2nd ed. (Washington, D.C.: Smithsonian Institution, ca. 1933).

54 Kimberly A. Hamlin, Free Thinker: Sex, Suffrage, and the Extraordinary Life of Helen Hamilton Gardener (New York: W. W. Norton, 2020), 282–284.

55 Annual Report of the Board of Regents of the Smithsonian Institution, 1948, 2.

56 Preliminary Report on Exhibition, Smithsonian Archives, record unit 190, box 76, folder "Exhibits Modernization."

57 Preliminary Report on Exhibition, Appendix A, "Examples of the Worst Exhibits," Smithsonian Archives, record unit 190, box 76, folder "Exhibits Modernization."

58 Carl Pfaffmann, *Leonard Carmichael, 1898–1873* (Washington, D.C.: National Academy of Sciences, 1980) , http://www.nasonline.org/publications/biographical-memoirs/memoir-pdfs/carmichael-leonard.pdf (accessed 3 July 2019).

59 Annual Report of the Board of Regents of the Smithsonian Institution, 1953, 2–3.

60 Lisa Kathleen Graddy and Amy Pastan, *The Smithsonian First Ladies Collection* (Washington, D.C.: Smithsonian Books, 2014), 6–7.

61 "Famous Gowns of First Ladies of the Land," *Washington Star* (Washington, D.C.), 8 March 1914, part 4, 2.

62 Justification for [Hall of First Ladies] Exhibit, Smithsonian Archives, record unit 275, box 44, folder "First Ladies, 1953–1955," written by Margaret Klapthor and others.

63 Justification for [Hall of First Ladies] Exhibit, Smithsonian Archives.

64 "White House Fashions," *Washington Post*, 25 May 1955, 31.

65 "Benjamin W. Lawless, Master Designer of Museum Exhibits, Dies at 88," *Washington Post*, 16 April 2013.

66 "The Man Behind the Exhibits: He's Become an Institution at the Smithsonian," *Washington Post*, 7 July 1978, B1.

67 "History's 'Fashion Parade' Is Reviewed by Eisenhowers," *Washington Post*, 25 May 1955.

68 "Exhibit to Show Miracle of Life," *Washington Post*, 27 October 1957.

69 Smithsonian Institution, *Brief Guide to the Smithsonian Institution*, Publication 4507, 24.

70 "Smithsonian Will Open Hall of Health on November 3," *Washington Evening Star*, 27 October 1957, 32.

71 Smithsonian Institution, *Brief Guide to the Smithsonian Institution*, Publication 4507, 24.

72 Annual Report of the Board of Regents of the Smithsonian Institution, 1957, 34.

73 This modernized exhibit opened a year after the floor plan included at the beginning of this chapter.

74 Annual Report of the Board of Regents of the Smithsonian Institution, 1957, 34.

75 "New Smithsonian Hall Tells Power Story," *Washington Post*, 25 March 1957.

Chapter 3 Notes

76 Museum of History and Technology, *Exhibits in the Museum of History and Technology,* Smithsonian Institution Publication 4720 (Washington, D.C.: Smithsonian Institution Press, 1968). This is the most thorough public guide to the museum's exhibitions published in any era, and the only one that was a collaborative effort of many of the museum's curators. It is the principal source for the discussion in this chapter of the content in the exhibitions. A secondary source of great value is Charlotte L. Sclar, *The Smithsonian: A Guide to Its National Public Facilities in Washington, D.C.* (Jefferson, N.C.: McFarland & Co., 1985).

77 "A New Museum of History and Technology," Smithsonian Institution brochure, n.d. (1953), back cover.

78 Remarks at the Dedication of the Smithsonian Institution's Museum of History and Technology, 22 January 1964, in *Public Papers of the Presidents of the United States, Lyndon B. Johnson, 1963–1964,* book I (Washington, D.C.: Government Printing Office, 1965), 218.

79 Wolf Von Eckardt, "Architects Goofed on Interior of Museum," *Washington Post,* 26 January 1964, G6.

80 Based on Dedication of the Museum of History and Technology of the Smithsonian Institution brochure, 22 January 1964, NMAH Public Affairs Office files.

81 Although in later years, audiences were not allowed to touch the 1401, in these years climbing into it was not only allowed but encouraged.

82 Hugh Wells, "Inside the New Museum," *Washington Star,* 29 March 1964, 4.

83 Arthur P. Molella, "The Museum That Might Have Been: The Smithsonian's National Museum of Engineering and Industry," *Technology and Culture,* 32(2) (1991):237–263.

84 As quoted in Arthur P. Molella, "The Museum That Might Have Been: The Smithsonian's National Museum of Engineering and Industry," *Technology and Culture,* 32(2) (1991):250.

85 Frank Taylor, *The Conceptual Planning of MHT,* March 1973, NMAH History Program files, 3.

86 Taylor, *The Conceptual Planning of MHT,* 2. Emphasis added by authors.

87 Fourth Oral History Interview with Frank A. Taylor Research Associate, Office of Museum Programs, 13 March 1974 in the Smithsonian Institution Building by Miriam S. Freilicher, interviewer for the Smithsonian Institution Archives, Smithsonian Archives, record unit 9512, 102.

88 Fourth Oral History Interview with Frank Taylor by M. S. Freilicher, 103.

89 "A New Museum of History and Technology" (brochure), 10.

90 Hearings Before the Committee on Public Works, 29 April 1955, Smithsonian Archives, record unit 334, box 81, 3–4.

91 Hearings Before the Committee on Public Works, 5.

92 Hearings Before the Committee on Public Works, 7–8.

93 Public Law 106 (H. R. 6410), 28 June 1955.

94 "Check List and Outline of Requirements for the Design of the Museum of History and Technology," 12 March 1956, Smithsonian Archives, record unit 190, box 20.

95 "A New Museum of History and Technology" (brochure), 10.

96 "A New Museum of History and Technology" (brochure), 10.

97 Frank Taylor, Talk on Museum of History and Technology, October 1960, Smithsonian Archives, record unit 360, box 20, 5.

98 "A New Museum of History and Technology" (brochure), 14.

99 Press release prepared by F. A. Taylor, 8 November 1960, Smithsonian Archives, record unit 190, box 72, 5–6.

100 "A New Museum of History and Technology" (brochure), 26.

101 Both quotations are from Herman Schaden, "Smithsonian Gets New Sculpture—You Name It," *Washington Evening Star*, 31 March 1967, C1.

102 "Carving Panels in New Museum is a Point of Pride for Stonecutter," *Washington Post*, 18 July 1964, 1.

103 Exterior inscriptions, Museum of History and Technology, NMAH Public Affairs Office files.

104 The museum's Foucault pendulum was built for it on contract in 1963 by the California Academy of Sciences, for which is was paid $2,622.40 (see Smithsonian Archives, record unit 276, box 94, folder "Foucault Pendulum, 1957–1970"). Although many visitors (and museum employees) thought that the pendulum rotated a full circle every 24 hours, its functioning and proof of the earth's rotation were much more complicated. Because the museum was frequently asked about this, the staff prepared a written description of its actual operation, which it shared with interested visitors. See "How the pendulum works," Smithsonian Archives, record unit 551, box 32, folder "Foucault Pendulum."

105 Herman Schaden, "New Smithsonian Unit to Be a Palace of Progress," *Evening Star*, 25 May 1962, A16.

106 "Check List and Outline of Requirements for the Design of the Museum of History and Technology," 3.

107 Museum of History and Technology, *Exhibits in the Museum of History and Technology*, Smithsonian Institution Publication 4720, 7.

108 Frank A. Taylor, "The Museum of History and Technology: The Smithsonian's Newest," *Museum News*, 42(10) (June 1964):11–18.

109 Fifth Oral History Interview with Frank Taylor, 20 March 1974, by Miriam S. Freilicher, Interviewer, Smithsonian Archives, record unit 9512, 150.

110 Handwritten notes on *Growth of the United States*, Smithsonian Archives, accession 03-070, box 1, 1.

111 Fifth Oral History Interview with Frank Taylor, 152.

112 University of Pennsylvania Archives, Anthony Garvan Papers, UPT 50 G244, box 37, John Ewers to Garvan, memorandum , 2 September 1960. Details in this section about Garvan's plans for the exhibition are based on his extensive records in this collection.

113 Fifth Oral History Interview with Frank Taylor, 153–154.

114 Gordon Harris, Choate-Caldwell House, 16 Elm St. (Now at Smithsonian), *Historic Ipswich*, 1 August 2015, https://historicipswich.org/2015/08/01/abraham-choate -house-16-elm-st-now-at-smithsonian/ (accessed 17 April 2019). See also "Museum Craftsmen Restore a Part of our Past," *Washington Post Potomac*, 27 February 1966, 8–10.

115 Silvio Bedini, Fair is Foul or Foul is Fair, 3 February 1969, Smithsonian Archives, record unit 360, box 16, 3.

116 A principal source for this section was the series of eight oral history interviews of Malcolm Watkins conducted by Pamela M. Henson and Susan H. Myers between 1992 and 1995, Smithsonian Archives, record unit 9586.

117 Oral History Interview with C. Malcolm Watkins, 17 January 1992, Smithsonian Archives, record unit 9586, 29.

118 C. M. Watkins to Richard Ahlborn, memorandum, Proposal for Introduction to Everyday Life, 26 February 1975, NMAH History Office files.

119 Oral History Interview with C. Malcolm Watkins, 14 May 1995, Smithsonian Archives, record unit 9586, 21–22.

120 More information on construction of the period rooms is in Smithsonian Archives, record unit 623, box 1, folder "Watson Period Rooms (2), 1960–1964."

121 Oral History Interview with C. Malcolm Watkins, 14 May 1995, 16.

122 Edna W. Wright to Frank Taylor and Daniel Boorstin, memorandum, 8 July 1970, Political History Division files.

123 The guide and summary of the visitor test, which is reported in a memorandum from Pater Marzio to Daniel J. Boorstin, 26 March 1970, are in Smithsonian Archives, record unit 334, box 1, folder "Brochures."

124 Museum of History and Technology, *Exhibits in the Museum of History and Technology*, Smithsonian Institution Publication 4720, 23.

125 Script for Historic Americans Hall, 25 April 1956, Smithsonian Archives, accession 03-070, box 1, 4.

126 Isaiah 2:4, King James translation of *The Bible*.

127 Museum of History and Technology, *Exhibits in the Museum of History and Technology*, Smithsonian Institution Publication 4720, 26–27.

128 Script for Historic Americans Hall, 9.

129 Fifth Oral History Interview with Frank Taylor, 156–157.

130 Smithsonian Institution, "Introduction," in *The First Ladies Hall* (Washington, D.C.: National Museum of History and Technology, 1976).

131 "Introduction" in *The First Ladies Hall*.

132 Hugh Wells, "Inside the New Museum," *Washington Evening Star Sunday Magazine*, 29 March 1964, 4.

133 Hearings before the Subcommittee on Buildings and Grounds of the Subcommittee on Public Works, Friday, April 29, 1955, Smithsonian Archives, record unit 334, box 81, 6.

134 Smithsonian to Re-Open Hall of Monetary History and Medallic Art on October 21; press release, 21 October 1964, Smithsonian Archives, record unit 360, box 14, folder "Hall of Monetary History."

135 Check List and Outline of Requirements for the Design of the Museum of History and Technology," 3.

136 Robert Vogel, "Assembling a New Hall of Civil Engineering," *Technology and Culture*, 6(1) (1965)59–73.

137 Diotima Booraem, "Steaming into the Future," *Smithsonian Magazine*, September 1998, https://www.smithsonianmag.com/science-nature/steaming-into-the-future -157045311/ (accessed 16 October 2019).

138 Museum of History and Technology, *Exhibits in the Museum of History and Technology*, Smithsonian Institution Publication 4720, 105.

139 Herman Schaden, "Smithsonian Displays March of Medicine," *Washington Evening Star*, 25 August 1966, B1.

140 Smithsonian Year, 1965, in *Annual Report of the Smithsonian Institution for the Year Ended June 30, 1965* (Washington, D.C.: Smithsonian Institution, 1965), 131.

141 "Smithsonian Gusher Land Depicts Oil from the Ground Up," *Washington Evening Star*, 20 July 1967, B1.

142 Smithsonian Year, 1965, 131; "Oil Painting," *Tulsa World*, 27 June 1998, https://www.tulsaworld.com/archive/oil-painting/article_b00df740-dc72-5db3-b2d2-4bd 742e02a1e.html (accessed 16 October 2019).

Chapter 4 Notes

143 This floor plan is from *Official Guide to the Smithsonian 1976*, 2nd ed. (Smithsonian Institution and CBS Publications, 1976), 22–23.

144 For detailed coverage in the press, see "Philadelphia World's Fair: Topics in Chronicling America," https://guides.loc.gov/chronicling-america-worlds-fair-philadelphia /selected-articles (accessed 2 November 2020). See also Robert C. Post, ed., *1876: A Centennial Exhibition* (Washington, D.C.: Smithsonian Institution, 1976), 11–25.

145 Text of the speech may be found on "President Grant's Philadelphia Speech," http://www.sonofthesouth.net/union-generals/ulysses-s-grant/president-grants -philadelphia-speech.htm (accessed 27 August 2019).

146 Post, *1876: A Centennial Exhibition*, 9.

147 The Centennial: 100 Years Later, Smithsonian Institution press release, 10 May 1976, Smithsonian Archives, record unit 360, box 8, folder "Press Releases."

148 "1876 Carriage Trade in Step with the Times," *Washington Evening Star*, 11 May 1976, 1.

149 The Centennial: 100 Years Later, Smithsonian Institution press release.

150 Statement by the Secretary, S. Dillon Ripley, in Smithsonian Year, 1965, in *Annual Report of the Smithsonian Institution for the Year Ended June 30, 1968* (Washington, D.C.: Smithsonian Institution, 1968), 1.

151 Statement by the Secretary, S. Dillon Ripley, in Smithsonian Year, 1965, 3–4.

152 Herman Schaden, "Smithsonian Taps Boorstin," *Washington Evening Star*, 27 January 1969, B2.

153 Remarks of Daniel J. Boorstin upon assuming the Directorship of the National Museum of History and Technology, 30 September 1969, *Daniel J. Boorstin Papers*, Library of Congress, box 199.

154 S. Dillon Ripley to Members of the Secretariat and Bureau Directors, memorandum, dated April 29, 1970, Smithsonian Archives, record unit 334, National Museum of American History, box 94, folders "Bicentennial of the American Revolution."

155 Bicentennial Pavilions for MHT: A Nation of Nations, 5 May 1969, *Daniel J. Boorstin Papers*, Library of Congress, box 45, 4.

156 Bicentennial Pavilions for MHT, 4.

157 *A Nation of Nations*: A Bicentennial exhibition at the National Museum of History and Technology, Smithsonian Institution, exhibition brochure, National Museum of American History, Smithsonian Archives, accession 06-163, box 3.

158 *A Nation of Nations*, Smithsonian press release SI-6-76, Smithsonian Archives accession 06-163, box 3.

159 *Why Pencils?* bulletin from the Pencil Makers' Association, Smithsonian Archives, accession 06-163, box 3.

160 Jean M. White, "'Nation of Nations' from 6,000 Perspectives," *Washington Post*, 9 June 1976, C1.

161 Patrick Brogan, "America: A Tossed Salad Rather than a Melting Pot," *Times* (London), 26 June 1976.

162 Beryl Benderly, July Spotlight, *Washington Calendar Magazine*, Smithsonian Archives, accession 06-163, box 3, 6.

163 *Official Guide to the Smithsonian 1976*, 35–36; Bicentennial Exhibit Looks at the American People and their Government, Smithsonian Institution press release, 3 June 1975, Smithsonian Archives, record unit 360, box 8, folder "Long Term Exhibits."

164 John Sherwood, "We the People on Exhibit," *Washington Star*, 4 June 1975, C1.

165 Hollie I. West, "Historic Reflections: A Bicentennial Array in the American Spirit," *Washington Post*, 4 June 1975, B1.

166 Sherwood, "We the People on Exhibit," C-.3

167 *Suiting Everyone* exhibit description, Smithsonian Archives, accession 15-185, box 1; *Suiting Everyone*: Smithsonian Exhibit Shows Democratization of American Dress over Two Centuries, Smithsonian Institution press release, 9 September 1974, Smithsonian Archives, record unit 360, box 13.

168 "They'll 'Suit Everyone' at the Smithsonian," *Washington Star*, 11 September 1973, B3.

169 *Suiting Everyone* exhibit description, 1.

170 Bernadine Morris, "Bicentennial Spirit at the Smithsonian; A History of Clothing," *New York Times*, 21 September 1974, 14.

171 "'Suiting Everyone'—200 years of U.S. Clothing," *Baltimore Sun*, 27 September 1974, 26.

172 Post, *1876: A Centennial Exhibition*, 24–25.

173 Sarah Booth Conroy, "Evoking the 1876 Centennial in a Bicentennial Extravaganza," *Washington Post*, 9 May 1976, F3.

174 *1876: A Centennial Exhibition* Opens at Smithsonian's Newly Renovated Arts and Industries Building, May 10, 1976, Smithsonian Institution press release, 9 May 1976, Smithsonian Archives, record unit 360, box 8.

175 "1876: A Centennial Exhibition," exhibition brochure, Smithsonian Archives, accession 16-343, box 1.

176 Smithsonian Institution, Office of Telecommunications Film, *Celebrating a Century*, 1976, https://archive.org/details/celebratingacenturythe1876philadelphiacentennial (accessed 2 November 2020).

177 "Bicentennial Park," Smithsonian Institution brochure, files of Armed Forces Division, NMAH, 1971, 5.

178 "Bicentennial Park" (brochure), 7.

179 "Bicentennial Park" (brochure), 7.

180 Joanne Gernstein London, draft of "A Modest Show of Arms: Exhibiting the Armed Forces, National Identity and the Smithsonian Institution, 1946–1976," files of the Armed Forces Division, NMAH, n.d., 143.

181 Public Law 87-186, https://www.govinfo.gov/content/pkg/STATUTE-75/pdf/STATUTE-75-Pg414.pdf (accessed 16 October 2019).

182 London, draft of "A Modest Show of Arms," 145.

183 This discussion is based on The National Armed Forces Museum Park: A Study Prepared by the National Armed Forces Museum Advisory Board, Smithsonian Publication 4692, October 1966.

184 The National Armed Forces Museum Park: A Study, 3.

185 London, draft of "A Modest Show of Arms," 182.

186 London, draft of "A Modest Show of Arms," 179.

187 "Blaze in Smithsonian Building Ruins IBM Computer Display," *Washington Evening Star*, 30 September 1970, A1.

188 Statement of the Secretary in Smithsonian Year, 1972, *Annual Report of the Smithsonian Institution for the Year Ended June 30, 1972* (Washington, DC: Smithsonian Institution, 1972), 20.

189 "A Prospectus for a Program for the National Museum of History and Technology," April 1970, *Daniel J. Boorstin Papers*, Library of Congress, box 46, 1.

190 Phil Casey, "Old Store, New Site," *Washington Post*, 28 September 1971, B2; Patrick Milhoan, "Neither Snow nor Rain: A West Virginia Post Office in the Smithsonian," Smithsonian Archives Blog, 13 September 2016, https://siarchives.si.edu/blog/neither-snow-nor-rain-west-virginia-post-office-smithsonian (accessed 16 October 2019).

191 *Official Guide to the Smithsonian 1976*, 40–41; draft Smithsonian Institution press release for the Hall of Photography, Smithsonian Archives, record unit 360, box 14.

192 *Official Guide to the Smithsonian 1976*, 41; Tom Shales, "Lucely Financed News Museum," *Washington Post*, 29 April 1973, F1.

193 "Instant Analysis in the Hall of News," *Washington Post*, 1 May 1973, B1. Also text of speech, https://watergate.info/1973/04/30/nixons-first-watergate-speech.html (accessed 16 July 2019).

194 *Official Guide to the Smithsonian 1976*, 42; David R. Legge, "Where Gutenberg Left Off in 1450," *Washington Post*, 14 July 1972, B8.

195 Official Guide to the Smithsonian 1976, 42; Smithsonian Year 1973, Annual Report of the Smithsonian Institution for the Year Ended June 30, 1973 (Washington, D.C.: Smithsonian Institution, 1973), 107.

196 Smithsonian Year 1973, 104.

197 Herman Schaden, "Prank Maker of American Jokelore," *Washington Star*, 22 November 1970, D1; Paul Richard, "Mad Gadgets on Exhibit," *Washington Post*, 25 November 1970, B1.

198 Israel Shenker, "Smithsonian Exhibit Resembles Goldberg Cartoon, Which It Is," *New York Times*, 25 November 1970, 38.

199 Paul Richard, "Mad Gadgets on Exhibit," *Washington Post*, 25 November 1970, B1.

200 Shenker, "Smithsonian Exhibit Resembles Goldberg Cartoon, Which It Is," 62.

201 Richard, "Mad Gadgets on Exhibit," B1.

202 Philip M. Kadis, "A Productivity Pie," *Washington Star*, 19 December 1972, D8; Jo Ann Lewis, "As a Show, It's Good, But It Could Be Better," *Washington Star*, 14 January 1973, G1.

203 Smithsonian Year 1980, *Annual Report of the Smithsonian Institution for the Year Ended June 30, 1970* (Washington, D.C.: Smithsonian Institution, 1980), 209.

Chapter 5 Notes

204 This floor plan is from a 1999 NMAH "Museum Guide for Visitors" brochure.

205 Elizabeth Bumiller, "Exhibit A-a-a-a-y: 'The Fonz' and His Jacket Make History," *Washington Post*, 14 February 1980, C1.

206 Dwight Blocker Bowers, "The 'Sole' Survivors: The Smithsonian's Ruby Slippers," in *Engaging Smithsonian Objects through Science, History, and the Arts*, ed. Mary Jo Arnoldi, pp. 257–265 (Washington D.C.: Smithsonian Institution Scholarly Press, 2016), 257.

207 "How Dorothy's Ruby Slippers Came to the Smithsonian," on the Smithsonian website, https://www.smithsonianmag.com/smithsonian-institution/how-dorothys-ruby-slippers-came-to-the-smithsonian-180960760/ (accessed 15 July 2019).

208 Bowers, "The 'Sole' Survivors," 259.

209 Ellen Roney Hughes, "The Amazing Ruby Slippers and Their Magical Travels," in *Engaging Smithsonian Objects through Science, History, and the Arts*, ed. Mary Jo Arnoldi, pp. 267–275 (Washington D.C.: Smithsonian Institution Scholarly Press, 2016).

210 Wolf Von Eckardt, "High on Tech: Roger Kennedy's Aim," *Washington Post*, 1 March 1980, B1; Smithsonian Announces Appointment of Roger Kennedy, Historian and Foundation Executive, as Director of Museum of History and Technology, Smithsonian Institution press release SI-289-79, 20 June 1979, NMAH Public Affairs Office historical files.

211 Public Law 96-441. The same act changed the name of the National Collection of Fine Arts to the National Museum of American Art.

212 Smithsonian Institution press release SI-444-80, 15 October 1980, NMAH Public Affairs Office historical files.

213 The 10-year plan and transmittal letter from the museum to Kennedy are in Smithsonian Archives, record unit 551, box 32, folder 1976–1979.

214 Smithsonian press release SI-203-82, 14 June 1982, NMAH Public Affairs Office historical files.

215 Elizabeth Kastor, "The Re-Creation of the 'Material World,' Confusing Smithsonian Exhibit Rethought, Revamped." *Washington Post*, 6 July 1988, C1.

216 *After the Revolution* media advisory and packet of exhibit materials, Smithsonian Archives, record unit 360, boxes 30 and 31.

217 *After the Revolution* media advisory and packet of exhibit materials.

218 Barbara Clark Smith, *After the Revolution: The Smithsonian History of Everyday Life in the Eighteenth Century* (New York: Pantheon, 1985).

219 *Engines of Change* Fact Sheet, Smithsonian press release SI-367-86, 21 November 1986, NMAH Public Affairs Office historical files; Bob Davis, "'Engines of Change' at the Smithsonian," *Wall Street Journal*, 23 December 1986, 18.

220 *Field to Factory: Afro-American Migration, 1915–1940* to Open at National Museum of American History in February 1987, Smithsonian press release SI-459-86, 12 December 1986, Smithsonian Archives, record unit 90-074, box 2, Folder 13; *Field to Factory* exhibit brochure, Smithsonian Archives, record unit 90-074, box 2, Folder 13; David Saltman, "Reaching Out to Minorities," *Washington Post*, 19 January 1987, D7.

221 Spencer Crew Named Director of Smithsonian's National Museum of American History, Smithsonian press release SI-27-94, 21 January 1994, NMAH Public Affairs Office historical files.

222 Whether the camps should be called "internment" camps or "incarceration" camps has long been a subject of historical debate. When the exhibition was mounted, the term generally used was "internment camps," but more recently historians have thought that "incarceration" camps is more accurate.

223 *A More Perfect Union: Japanese Americans and the U.S. Constitution* Exhibition Opens at American History Museum, October 1, Smithsonian press release SI-385-87, 10 September 1987, NMAH Public Affairs Office historical files.

224 Information in this section is based on documentation in files related to *A More Perfect Union* in the Armed Forces Division, National Museum of American History.

225 Mary Battiata, "Smithsonian's Constitution Controversy, Show on Japanese Americans' Internment Protested by Vets," *Washington Post*, 16 March 1987, B1.

226 *A More Perfect Union: Japanese Americans and the U.S. Constitution* Exhibition Opens at American History Museum, October 1, Smithsonian press release SI-385-87.

227 Elisabeth Kastor, "Remembrance of Sorrows Past, The Smithsonian's Hard Look at WWII Internment of Japanese Americans," *Washington Post*, 1 October 1987, C1.

228 100th Congress, S.1009—a bill to accept the findings and to implement the recommendations of the Commission on Wartime Relocation and Internment of Civilians, https://www.congress.gov/bill/100th-congress/senate-bill/1009 (accessed 17 October 2019).

229 *We the People, The Commission on the Bicentennial of the United States Constitution, 1985–1992: Final Report* (Washington, D.C.: Government Printing Office, 1992), 75, https://play

.google.com/books/reader?id=InsB_lHK4NYC&hl=en&pg=GBS.PA75 (accessed 17 October 2019).

230 Smithsonian Marks 75th Anniversary of Executive Order 9066, National Museum of American History press release, 17 February 2017, NMAH Public Affairs Office historical files.

231 *From Parlor to Politics: Women in the Progressive Era, 1890–1925*, exhibition booklet, Smithsonian Archives, record unit 551, box 30; Jene Stonseifer, "Women's Voices: Influencing Political Action," *Washington Post*, 28 June 1990, 26.

232 Women's History Exhibition Extended Indefinitely at the National Museum of American History, Smithsonian press release SI-477-90, 8 November 1990, NMAH Public Affairs Office historical files.

233 Edith Mayo, quoted in Peter Nye, "Moving from Parlor to Politics," *The National Voter*, April/May 1990, 12–14.

234 Smithsonian Opens Major Exhibition on the Information Age at the National Museum of American History, Smithsonian press release SI-115-90, 6 April 1990, included in a press package with a fact sheet and other documentation, NMAH Public Affairs Office historical files.

235 Smithsonian Opens Major Exhibition on the Information Age, Smithsonian Institution press release.

236 "Dashed Hopes and Bogus Fears," *Time*, 11 June 1990, 58.

237 "When More Is Less: The Smithsonian's Dazzling, Orwellian, 'Information Age,'" *Washington Post*, 6 May 1990, G1.

238 "Technological dunce visits Information Age," *Richmond Times Dispatch*, 13 May 1990.

239 Visitor Comment Form from Daniel B. Davis, 10 December 1991, NMAH History Office files.

240 David Challinor, memorandum for the record, 11 January 1984, Smithsonian Archives, record unit 613, folder 1 of "Information Revolution (IBM)."

241 Dillion Ripley to Lewis Branscomb, 13 February 1984, Smithsonian Archives, record unit 613, folder 1 of "Information Revolution (IBM)."

242 *Information Age: People, Information, & Technology* Fact Sheet, Smithsonian press release SI-25C-90, NMAH Public Affairs Office historical files.

243 Cesar G. Soriano, "Close 'Encounters' of the New Mexican Kind," *Washington Times*, 25 June 1992, E5; Hank Burchard, "On Exhibit: New Mexico's Travelogue and Souvenir Store," *Washington Post*, 3 July 1992, 45; Lonn Taylor, "American Encounters," *Washington Post*, 20 July 1992, A14.

244 Wording transcribed from photograph of the main label at the entry to the *American Encounters* exhibition, Smithsonian Institution photograph SI-92-15447.

245 Soriano, "Close 'Encounters' of the New Mexican Kind."

246 Hank Burchard, "First-Rate 'First Ladies,'" *Washington Post*, 3 April 1992, 63.

247 Paula Span, "Return of the Gowns," *Washington Post Magazine*, 1 March 1992, 27; First Ladies Exhibition at Smithsonian gives new Understanding and Insight to the Job, Smithsonian press release SI-148-92, March 1992, NMAH Public Affairs Office Historical files.

248 First Ladies Exhibition at the Smithsonian, Smithsonian press release SI-148-92, March 1992.

249 Michael Kilian, "Ladies First: Smithsonian takes a Serious Look at Lives of Presidents' Wives," *Chicago Tribune*, 12 April 1992.

250 Jo Ann Lewis, "Peeking in on the Presidents, Smithsonian's glimpse of White House Life," *Washington Post*, 6 April 1989, B1.

251 *Science in American Life* Exhibition Opens at the National Museum of American History, Smithsonian press release SI-488-93, 22 April 1994.

252 *Science in American Life* script, Smithsonian Archives, record unit 06-276, box 4, file "SAL Script."

253 *Science in American Life* Exhibition Opens, Smithsonian press release SI-488-93.

254 Documentation on the development of the exhibition can be found in Smithsonian Archives, record unit 06-276, 16 boxes, record unit 98-048, box 2, and the *Science in American Life* folders in the NMAH Public Affairs Office historical files.

255 For a summary of the debate over the exhibition, see Robert C. Post and Arthur P. Molella, "The Call of Stories at the Smithsonian Institution: History of Technology and Science in Crisis," *Icon*, 3(1997):44–82.

256 Joan E. Shields, "Science in American Life Revisited," *Chemical and Engineering News*, 11 March 1996, 40.

257 Thomas F. Gieryn, "Balancing Acts: Science, Enola Gay and History Wars at the Smithsonian," in *The Politics of Display: Museums, Science, Culture*, ed. Sharon Macdonald, pp. 170–196 (London: Routledge, 1998), 190.

258 Andrew J. Pekarik, Zahava D. Doering, and Adam Bickford, An Assessment of the *Science in American Life* Exhibition at the National Museum of American History, Smithsonian Institution Institutional Studies Office, report 95-5, https://repository .si.edu/bitstream/handle/10088/20921/95-5-Science.pdf?sequence=1&isAllowed=y (accessed 17 October 2019).

259 Zahava D. Doering and Andrew J, Pekarik, "Questioning the Entrance Narrative," *The Journal of Museum Education*, 21(3) (Fall 1996):20–23. Emphasis added by authors.

260 Several years later the same authors reported more broadly on the range of "satisfying experiences" in museums, drawing on thousands of visitor surveys over many years. The authors divided the experiences into four types:

Object Experiences
- Seeing "the real thing"
- Seeing rare/uncommon/valuable things
- Being moved by beauty
- Thinking what it would be like to own such things
- Continuing my professional development

Cognitive Experiences
- Gaining information or knowledge
- Enriching my understanding

Introspective Experiences
- Imagining other times or places
- Reflecting on the meaning of what I was looking at

- Recalling my travels/childhood experiences/other memories
- Feeling a spiritual connection
- Feeling a sense of belonging or connectedness

Social Experiences
- Spending time with friends/family/other people
- Seeing my children learning new things

This research and analysis shaped future exhibition development at the Smithsonian. (Andrew J. Pekarik, Zahava D. Doering, and David A. Karns, "Exploring Satisfying Experiences in Museums," *Curator*, 42(2) (April 1999):152–173.)

261 National Museum of American History Explores the Promise of America through Three 19th-Century Communities, Smithsonian press release SI-45-99, 11 February 1999, NMAH Public Affairs Office historical files.

262 The script for all sections of the planned exhibition is in Smithsonian Archives, accession 17-113, box 2, folder "Script 1996–1997." Other significant records related to the exhibit are in accession 03-091, box 7; accession 96-006, boxes 4–8; and accession 04-161, box 1.

263 Fundraising brochure for *Land of Promise: America in the 19th Century*, August 1994, MAH Public Affairs Office historical files.

264 A good place to start in the voluminous literature on this episode in Smithsonian history is Edward T. Linenthal and Tom Englehardt, eds., *History Wars: The Enola Gay and Other Battles for the American Past* (New York: Holt Paperbacks, 1996).

265 Smithsonian Archives, accession 17-113, box 2, folder "Script 1996–1997."

266 National Museum of American History Explores the Promise of America through Three 19th-Century Communities, Smithsonian press release SI-45-99.

267 Records of Howard Morrison, director of Museum Education and Interpretation, National Museum of American History.

268 *On Time* Opens at Smithsonian's National Museum of American History, Marks Anniversary of Standard Time in America, Smithsonian press release SI-358-99, 18 November 1999, NMAH Public Affairs Office historical files.

269 *On Time* Opens, Smithsonian press release SI-358-99.

270 Data on past temporary exhibitions is scattered through museum archival records and office files. The only systematic (but incomplete) record we found is maintained in a Smithsonian Institution central database and available for searching online at https://www.si.edu/exhibitions/past. It contains brief descriptions.

271 Emily Langer, "Roger Kennedy, Former Director of National Museum of American History, Dies," *Washington Post*, 30 September 2011, https://www.washingtonpost.com/local/obituaries/2011/09/30/gIQAJE2JAL_story.html (accessed October 18, 2019).

272 Susan Kalcik to Mary Dyer and Michael Harris, memorandum, 7 March 1984, Re: Smithsonian Women's Council Newsletter Article on M*A*S*H, Smithsonian Archives, record unit 360, box 32, folder "M*A*S*H Exhibition File."

273 Letter of Agreement between 20th Century Fox and the Smithsonian Institution, 9 June 1983, Smithsonian Archives, record unit 360, box 32, folder "M*A*S*H Exhibition File."

274 *M*A*S*H: Binding Up the Wounds* Opens July 30 at the National Museum of American History, Smithsonian press release SI-320-83, 21 July 1983, Smithsonian Archives, record unit 360, box 32, folder "M*A*S*H Exhibition File."

275 "M*A*S*H Again a Hit—at the Smithsonian," *New York Times*, 12 August 1983, C12.

276 Mary Steward to Mary Dyer, 3 December 1984, Smithsonian Archives, record unit 360, box 32, folder "M*A*S*H Exhibition File."

277 *M*A*S*H: Binding Up the Wounds* exhibition brochure, files of the Armed Forces Division, National Museum of American History.

278 Hank Burchard, "Mankind's Lot has been a Lot of Pain," *Washington Post*, 14 October 1983, Weekend Section, 43; Sandy Rovner, "The Ageless Ache," *Washington Post*, 13 October 1983, D8.

279 National Museum of American History Opens Exhibition on Sweatshops, Smithsonian press release SI-105-98, 20 April 1998, NMAH Public Affairs Office historical files.

280 Maria Echaveste, director of the White House Office of Public Liaison; Kathie Lee Gifford, Kathie Lee Fashions; Robert Haas, chief executive officer, Levi Strauss & Co.; Floyd Hall, chairman and chief executive officer, Kmart Corporation; Jay Mazur, Union of Needle trades, Industrial and Textile Employees (UNITE); and Julie Su, Asian Pacific American Legal Center, Los Angeles.

281 Jacqueline Trescott, "In 'Sweatshops,' Smithsonian Holds Back the Outrage," *Washington Post*, 22 April 1998, https://www.washingtonpost.com/archive/lifestyle /1998/04/22/in-sweatshops-smithsonian-holds-back-the-outrage/57b55552-1d01 -48f5-8df2-7ea02360c9b5/ (accessed 15 November 2019).

Chapter 6 Notes

282 This image of the floor plan was copied from the NMAH website in August 2018.

283 Smithsonian Citizenship Ceremony Welcomes a Dozen New Americans, Madeleine Albright Donates Objects from her Diplomatic Career, Smithsonian press release SI-250-2012, 24 May 2012, https://www.si.edu/newsdesk/releases/smithsonian -citizenship-ceremony-welcomes-dozen-new-americans (accessed 18 October 2019).

284 Report of the Blue Ribbon Commission on the National Museum of American History, Appendix F: NMAH's Initial Vision for Transforming the National Museum of American History (2001), March 2002, https://americanhistory.si.edu/reports /brc/4f1.htm (accessed 18 October 2009).

285 The National Museum of American History Explores the Promise of America Through Three 19th Century Communities; Exhibition Marks Museum's New Focus on American Identity, Smithsonian Institution press release, 10 February 10 1999, https://americanhistory.si.edu/press/releases/national-museum-american-history -explores-promise-america-through-three-19th-century (accessed 18 October 2019).

286 Steven Lubar and Kathleen M. Kendrick, *Legacies: Collecting America's History at the Smithsonian* (Washington, D.C.: Smithsonian Institution Press, 2014), 214–215.

287 Lawrence M. Small, Smithsonian Archives Profile, https://siarchives.si.edu/history /lawrence-m-small (accessed 18 October 2019); Jacqueline Trescott, "Smithsonian Picks Banker as New Chief: Fannie Mae President Takes Over in January," *Washington Post*, 14 September 1999, A1.

288 Jacqueline Trescott, "Team Player," *Washington Post*, 25 January 2000, C1.

289 Tim Golden, "Big-Game Hunter's Gift Roils the Smithsonian," *New York Times*, 17 March 1999, 14, https://timesmachine.nytimes.com/timesmachine/1999/03/17/791920.html?pageNumber=14 (accessed 18 October 2019).

290 Jacqueline Trescott, "A Big Gun with Big Bucks, Humane Society Takes a Shot at Smithsonian's Top Donor," *Washington Post*, 18 March 1999, C1.

291 Smithsonian Institution Announces Biggest Single Donation in Its 154-year History, 19 September 2000, Smithsonian press release SI-316-2000, NMAH Public Affairs Office Historical files.

292 Smithsonian Institution Gift Agreement with Kenneth E. Behring, 21 August 2000, Behring File, Director's Office, National Museum of American History.

293 Smithsonian Institution Announces Biggest Single Donation in Its 154-year History, Smithsonian press release SI-316-2000.

294 "Millionaire creating new Smithsonian Hall of Fame," *Chicago Tribune*, 10 May 2001, NMAH Public Affairs Office historical files.

295 Elaine Sciolino, "Smithsonian Is Promised $38 million, With Strings," *New York Times*, 10 May 2001, 19, https://timesmachine.nytimes.com/timesmachine/2001/05/10/246972.html?pageNumber=19 (accessed 18 October 2019).

296 Sciolino, "Smithsonian Is Promised $38 million, With Strings."

297 Bob Thompson, "History for $ale," *Washington Post*, 20 January 2002, https://www.washingtonpost.com/archive/lifestyle/magazine/2002/01/20/history-for-ale/3da8fdce-47ca-4155-8014-7151258179ec/ (accessed 18 October 2019).

298 Thompson, History for $ale.

299 Jacqueline Trescott, "Catherine Reynolds, The Giver Who Gave Up," *Washington Post*, 6 February 2002, https://www.washingtonpost.com/archive/lifestyle/2002/02/06/catherine-reynolds-the-giver-who-gave-up/208dd760-f8e0-48c9-98ff-f52904dedf66/ (accessed 18 October 2019).

300 *E Pluribus Unum: This Divine Paradox*, May 1995, Report of the Commission on the Future of the Smithsonian Institution, https://archive.org/details/epluribusunumthi00unse (accessed 15 November 2019).

301 E Pluribus Unum, 12–13.

302 E Pluribus Unum, 29–30.

303 Interview by David Allison with Ivan Selin, 29 October 2019; Board Bylaws, NMAH Director's Office historical files.

304 Smithsonian Institution Gift Agreement with Kenneth E. Behring, 21 August 2000, Behring File, Director's Office, National Museum of American History.

305 Smithsonian's National Museum of American History Names Advisory Commission for Long-term Exhibit Planning, Smithsonian press release SI-282-2001, 29 June 2001, NMAH Public Affairs Office historical files.

306 Report of the Blue Ribbon Commission on the National Museum of American History, March 2002, https://americanhistory.si.edu/reports/brc/index.htm (accessed 18 October 2019).

307 Brent D. Glass Named Director of the Smithsonian's National Museum of American History, Smithsonian Institution press release, 16 October 2002, https://american

history.si.edu/press/releases/brent-d-glass-named-director-smithsonian%E2%80%99s-national-museum-american-history (accessed 18 October 2019).

308 National Museum of American History 2005–2010 Strategic Plan, 3, NMAH Director's Office historical files.

309 Jacqueline Trescott, "American Dreamer, The Smithsonian History Museum's New Director Charts our Brilliant Past," *Washington Post*, 3 January 2003, C1.

310 The Star-Spangled Banner, State of the Flag Report, 2001, https://americanhistory.si.edu/reports/SSB2001report/html_version/home.htm (accessed 18 October 2019); see also Smithsonian Releases "State of the Flag Report" on Flag Day, Smithsonian press release SI-246-2001, 14 June 2001, NMAH Public Affairs Office historical files.

311 Smithsonian Completes Star-Spangled Banner Conservation Treatment, Smithsonian press release SI-134-2006, 12 April 2006, NMAH Public Affairs Office historical files.

312 Steve Lubar to Paula Johnson, memorandum, 21 March 2000, Smithsonian Archives, record unit 16-322, box 12, folder "FWIS and Flag Hall Scope of Work, 2000."

313 For Which It Stands, The Star-Spangled Banner, An Overview provided to the Board, May 5, 2000, NMAH Public Affairs Office historical files.

314 Smithsonian Selects Firm to Plan Renovation of its National Museum of American History Building, Smithsonian press release SI-282-2002, 5 June 2002, NMAH Public Affairs Office historical files.

315 Report of the Blue Ribbon Commission on the National Museum of American History.

316 Treasures of American History Coming to Air and Space on the Mall, Smithsonian Institution press release, 22 August 2006, https://airandspace.si.edu/newsroom/press-releases/treasures-american-history-coming-air-and-space-mall (accessed 18 October 2019).

317 National Museum of American History will Open November 21, Smithsonian Institution press release, 29 July 2008, https://americanhistory.si.edu/press/releases/national-museum-american-history-will-open-nov-21 (accessed 18 October 2019); *Shining New Light on American History, National Museum of American History Grand Reopening Year, November 2008–December 2009* reopening brochure, NMAH Public Affairs Office historical Files; Jacqueline Trescott, "America's Attic is Ready for its Public," *Washington Post*, 20 November 2008, http://www.washingtonpost.com/wp-dyn/content/article/2008/11/19/AR2008111901361_pf.html (accessed 18 October 2019).

318 President Bush Attends Reopening of the National Museum of American History, White House press release, 19 November 2008, https://georgewbush-whitehouse.archives.gov/news/releases/2008/11/20081119.html (accessed 14 April 2020).

319 Folder on design of the new flag chamber and presentation of the Star-Spangled Banner, NMAH Public Affairs Office historical files.

320 The exhibit team members were as follows: project directors Lonnie G. Bunch III and Spencer R. Crew; curators Lonnie G. Bunch III, Spencer R. Crew, and Harry R. Rubenstein, with William L. Bird Jr. and Shannon Perich; project managers Lynn Chase and Patrick Ladden; public programs and education: Harold Closter and Julia Forbes; collection managers Frances Dispenzirie, Lisa Kathleen Graddy, and Jane Fortune; video producer Selma Thomas; editor Joan Mentzer; graphic managers Laura Kreiss and Carrie Burns; research support William Eastman, Ian Cooke, Lisa

Kathleen Graddy, David Miller, and Sue Ostroff; object photography coordinator Kathryn Henderson.

321 The Nation's Flagship History Museum Explores a Uniquely American Office—the Presidency—in Exhibition of Unprecedented Size and Scope, Smithsonian press release SI-318-2000, 14 November 2000, NMAH Public Affairs Office historical files.

322 The Nation's Flagship History Museum Explores a Uniquely American Office, Smithsonian press release SI-318-2000.

323 Report of the Blue Ribbon Commission on the National Museum of American History, Appendix G.

324 The exhibition team was led by project director Steve Lubar, and included curators Bill Withuhn, Susan Tolbert, Paula Johnson, Peter Liebhold, Bonnie Campbell Lilienfeld, Roger White, and Peter Liebhold. Howard Morrison was the team's educator and manager of multimedia development, and Laura Hansen a project assistant. Andrew Heymann was the project manager, Ann Rossilli the design manager, and Shari Stout the collections manager. The exhibition was designed by Museum Design Associates. Communications and marketing were managed by Melinda Machado and Valeska Hilbig. John McDonagh led fundraising efforts. Contractor Second Story created an extensive exhibition website.

325 "America on the Move" Exhibition Opens November 22 at National Museum of American History, Smithsonian press release SI-556-2002, 18 November 2003, NMAH Public Affairs Office historical files.

326 Janet F. Davidson and Michael S. Sweeney, *On the Move: Transportation and the American Story* (Washington, D.C., National Geographic, 2003).

327 "Smithsonian Exhibit Explores America's Life on the Road," *Baltimore Sun*, 22 November 2003, 1D.

328 *America on the Move* press clips, NMAH Public Affairs Office historical files.

329 Bob Thompson, "The Wheel Thing," *Washington Post*, 22 November 2003, C1.

330 Multiple Perspectives on *American on the Move* at the National Museum of American History, Smithsonian Institution Office of Policy and Analysis, August 2005, https://repository.si.edu/bitstream/handle/10088/17225/opanda_AOTM.pdf?sequence=1&isAllowed=y (accessed 19 October 2019).

331 Kenneth E. Behring, *The Road to Purpose* (Blackhawk, Calif.: Blackhawk Press, 2004), 93.

332 Planning documents, *The Price of Freedom*, 2 August 2002, files of Lynn Chase, exhibition project manager, Armed Forces Division, NMAH.

333 The revised exhibition team had both breadth and experience. From the American History Museum it included Jennifer Jones as collections curator, supported by Kathy Golden, David Miller, and Jane Fortune as collections managers. Military history curator Barton Hacker contributed expertise on World War I. Educator Howard Morrison was the principal script writer. Dik Daso, curator at the Air and Space Museum and an Air Force veteran added both valuable expertise and a connection to collections of his museum. This type of collaboration between Smithsonian museums has been surprisingly rare. The exhibition depended on two talented photo editors, Laura Kreiss and Laurel Macondray. Seasoned project manager Lynn Chase managed budget and schedule, of which project assistant Ann Burrola handled myriad

administrative details. Stevan Fisher acted as design manager, coordinating relations between the museum and contract designers Chadbourne and Associates. The contractor Second Story, which had developed a website for *America on the Move*, now created one for this exhibition.

334 This discussion is based on records related to the exhibition in Smithsonian Archives, accession 05-180, boxes 1–6.

335 National Museum of American History's New Exhibition Examines 250 Years of American Military Conflicts, Smithsonian press release SI-370-2004, 21 October 2004. This is one element in a press kit that includes a fact sheet, a listing of select objects, biographies of key people involved with the exhibition, and further documentation, in NMAH Public Affairs Office historical files.

336 National Museum of American History's New Exhibition Examines 250 Years of American Military Conflicts, Smithsonian press release SI-370-2004.

337 Visitor Ratings of Exhibitions at the National Museum of American History, Smithsonian Institution Office of Policy and Analysis, July 2005, https://repository.si.edu /bitstream/handle/10088/17268/opanda_RATINGS_NMAHexit.pdf?sequence =1&isAllowed=y (accessed 19 October 2019).

338 Thomas E. Ricks, "Our Wars; The Smithsonian's New Military Exhibit, Choosing its Battles Well," *Washington Post*, 11 November 2004, C1.

339 Bob Dart, The Pieces that Form the Picture of War, *Austin-American Statesman*, 11 November 2004, NMAH Public Affairs Office Historical files.

340 Carole Emberton, "The Price of Freedom: Americans at War," *Journal of American History*, 92(1) (June 2005):163–165.

341 Other members of the team were curator Paul Johnston, historian Michael Harrison, and educators Howard Morrison and Heather Paisley-Jones. Shari Stout was the collections manager. Andrew Heymann served as project director and Ann Rossilli as design manager. Matt MacArthur managed development of the website.

342 National Museum of American History's New Exhibition Goes "On the Water," Smithsonian Institution press release, 19 May 2009, https://americanhistory.si.edu /press/releases/national-museum-american-history's-new-exhibition-goes-"-water" (accessed 19 October 2019).

343 From an unpublished article by Paula Johnson, Division of Work and Industry, National Museum of American History.

344 *The First Ladies* Exhibition Opens at National Museum of American History, Smithsonian Institution press release, 17 November 2011, https://americanhistory.si.edu /press/releases/"-first-ladies"-exhibition-opens-national-museum-american-history (accessed 19 October 2019).

345 Paula J. Johnson, "Growing Food History on a National Stage: A Case Study from the Smithsonian's National Museum of American History," in *Food and Museums*, ed. Nina Levent and Irina D. Mihalache, pp. 113–129 (London: Bloomsbury, 2016).

346 Bon Appétit! Julia Child's Kitchen on Display at the Smithsonian, Smithsonian Institution press release, 14 July 2002, https://americanhistory.si.edu/press/releases/bon -app%C3%A9tit-julia-childs-kitchen-display-smithsonian (accessed 19 October 2019).

347 New Exhibition Looks at Food, Wine and Eating in America, Smithsonian Institution press release, 8 November 2012, https://americanhistory.si.edu/press/releases /museum-satisfies-food-history-craving (accessed 19 October 2019). The team that developed the new exhibition was led by project director Paula Johnson and project manager Nanci Edwards. They were assisted in content development by Rayna Green, Steve Velasquez, and Cory Bernat. Howard Morrison was the exhibit developer and Frances Dispenzirie the collections manager. Clare Brown designed the exhibition and Matt MacArthur oversaw development of the website. Valeska Hilbig handled public relations and marketing.

348 New Exhibition Looks at Food, Wine and Eating in America, Smithsonian Institution press release.

349 American Dreams: Concept Proposal, 14 March 2005, Smithsonian Archives, record unit 11-064, box 9, folder "Concept Proposal C, American Dreams (Thematic)."

350 Draft Idea for *American Dreams* Exhibition, David Behring to Jim Gardner, by fax, 5 September 2007, Smithsonian Archives, record unit 11-063, box 8, folder "Meeting with Ken Behring, 2007."

351 Explore American History meeting notes, 12 September 2007, Smithsonian Archives, record unit 11-064, box 8, folder "Meeting with Ken Behring."

352 American Stories: An Exhibition at the Smithsonian's National Museum of American History Opening in 2012, and American Stories, 10% Conceptual Development, NMAH Director's Office historical files.

353 Leading the planning was project director William Yeingst. Bonnie Campbell Lilienfeld was the curator, Howard Morrison the exhibit developer, Ann Burrola the project manager, Stevan Fisher the designer, and Jane Fortune the collections manager.

354 *American Stories* Exhibition Opens at National Museum of American History, Smithsonian Institution press release, 12 April 2012, https://americanhistory.si.edu/press /releases/%E2%80%9Camerican-stories%E2%80%9D-exhibition-opens-national -museum-american-history (accessed 19 October 2019).

355 *American Stories* Exhibition Opens at National Museum of American History, Smithsonian Institution press release.

356 Ewing Cole website, National Museum of American History, West Wing, https:// www.ewingcole.com/portfolio_page/national-museum-american-history-west-wing/ (accessed 19 October 2019).

357 John Gray, Former President of Autry National Center of the American West, Named Director of National Museum of American History, Smithsonian Institution press release, 8 May 2012, https://americanhistory.si.edu/press/releases/john-gray-former -president-autry-national-center-american-west-named-director (accessed 19 October 2019).

358 *National Museum of American History Strategic Plan, 2013–2018*, https://amhistory.si.edu /docs/NMAH_StrategicPlan_2013.pdf (accessed October 19, 2019).

359 American Ideals and Ideas: A Thematic Framework for the National Museum of American History, May 2017, NMAH Director's Office historical files.

360 Behring Named Spaces and Recognition at NMAH for his $80,000 gift, in Behring Analysis, 10 July 2015 and Behring Agreement, 26 July 2017, NMAH Director's Office historical files.

361 Board minutes from East Wing Planning Board Meeting, 11 May 2018, NMAH External Affairs Office historical files, 7.

362 Smithsonian and USPTO Present "Inventing in America" Gateway to National Museum of American History's New Innovation Wing Opening July 1, Smithsonian Institution press release, 1 July 2015, https://americanhistory.si.edu/press/releases /inventing-in-america (accessed 19 October 2019).

363 Smithsonian and USPTO Present "Inventing in America" Gateway, Smithsonian Institution press release.

364 The Father of the Video Game: The Ralph Baer Prototypes and Electronic Games, NMAH object group, https://americanhistory.si.edu/collections/object-groups/the -father-of-the-video-game-the-ralph-baer-prototypes-and-electronic-games?ogmt _page=video-game-history (accessed 19 October 2019).

365 Elizabeth Slattery Clare, "The Presidents' Monumental Woes," *Washington Post Weekend Guide,* 12 February 1988.

366 Grand Opening Week: Experience The Nation We Build Together, Smithsonian Institution press release, 1 June 2017, https://americanhistory.si.edu/press/releases /June-2017 (accessed 19 October 2019).

367 Dolby Laboratories Founder Honored for Innovation at the Gateway to Culture and Future Entertainment Exhibition at Smithsonian: The "Ray Dolby Gateway to Culture" Opens Oct. 19 at the National Museum of American History, Smithsonian Institution press release, 10 October 2018, https://americanhistory.si.edu/press /releases/dolby-laboratories-gateway-american-culture (accessed 19 October 2019).

368 Smithsonian Tells 200 Years of History through One House, Smithsonian press release SI-170-2001, 20 April 2001, NMAH Public Affairs Office historical files; Coco McCabe, "Old House, New Home," *Smithsonian Magazine,* June 2002, https://www .smithsonianmag.com/history/old-house-new-home-64659339/ (accessed 19 October 2019).

369 The exhibition team was led by project director Susan Myers. The curators were Shelley Nickles, Lonn Taylor, and William Yeingst. Nanci Edwards was the project manager and Janet Rockenbaugh the collections manager. Nigel Briggs and Erin Galbraith were the designers, Howard Morrison and Tim Grove the educators.

370 *Within These Walls* Exhibit Uses Technology to Bring Stories to Life, Smithsonian Institution press release, 31 August 2018, https://americanhistory.si.edu/press/releases /within-these-walls-projections-enliven (accessed 19 October 2019).

371 Report of the Blue Ribbon Commission on the National Museum of American History, Recommendations, section IIID.

372 The core exhibition team, led by project director David Allison, included curators Peter Liebhold, Nancy Davis, and Kathleen Franz, as well as educator Howard Morrison, project manager Andrew Heymann, design manager Stevan Fisher, collections manager Jane Fortune, and project assistant Katharine Klein.

373 Extensive documentation on the early planning of the exhibition is located in Smithsonian Archives, accession 17-134.

374 Smithsonian's *American Enterprise* Explores Business History, Smithsonian Institution press release, 11 June 2015, https://americanhistory.si.edu/press/releases/american -enterprise (accessed 19 October 2018).

375 Andrew J. Pekarik, James B. Schreiber, Nadine Hanemann, Kelly Richmond, and Barbara Mogel, "IPOP: A Theory of Experience Preference," *Curator*, 57(1) (January 2014):5–27.

376 Smithsonian's *American Enterprise* Explores Business History, Smithsonian Institution press release.

377 "Capitalism in America," *Economist*, 27 June 2015, 44.

378 Edward Rothstein, "*American Enterprise* Review: A Skewed History of American Business," *Wall Street Journal*, 17 August 2015, https://www.wsj.com/articles/american -enterprise-review-a-skewed-history-of-american-business-1439847030 (accessed 19 October 2019).

379 About the Lemelson Center, NMAH website, https://invention.si.edu/about-lemelson -center (accessed 19 October 2019).

380 Gretchen Jennings, Invention at Play, exhibit files, 7 June 2007, http://www .exhibitfiles.org/invention_at_play (accessed 19 October 2019); *Invention at Play*, exhibition summary, https://americanhistory.si.edu/exhibitions/invention-play (accessed 19 October 2019).

381 Other content developers were Eric Hintz, Joyce Bedi, Laurel Fritzsch Belman, Chris Gauthier, and Tricia Edwards. Hal Aber was the design manager and Frances Dispenzierie the collections manager. Roto Group LLC designed and built the gallery.

382 *Places of Invention* Explores Invention Hotspots throughout American History, Smithsonian Institution press release, 18 June 2015, https://americanhistory.si.edu/press /releases/%E2%80%9Cplaces-invention%E2%80%9D (accessed 19 October 2019).

383 *Places of Invention* Explores Invention Hotspots throughout American History, Smithsonian Institution press release.

384 Smithsonian Showcases Never-before-seen Pattern Coins in Traveling Display, Smithsonian Institution press release, 30 November 2006, https://americanhistory.si.edu /press/releases/smithsonian-showcases-never-seen-pattern-coins-traveling-display (accessed 19 October 2019). Despite the press release title, the exhibition did not travel, but was only displayed in the Smithsonian Institution Building (the "Castle").

385 Money Talks at the Smithsonian's National Museum of American History: New Display of Numismatic Rarities, Smithsonian Institution press release, 9 June 2009, https://americanhistory.si.edu/press/releases/money-talks-smithsonian%E2%80 %99s-national-museum-american-history-new-display-numismatic (accessed 19 October 2019).

386 Measuring Worth at the Smithsonian's National Museum of American History: *The Value of Money* Exhibition to Showcase Numismatic Rarities, Smithsonian Institution press release, 29 June 2015, https://americanhistory.si.edu/press/releases/The-Value -of-Money (accessed 19 October 2019).

387 Steve Roach, "Smithsonian Opens New Exhibition of Its National Numismatic Collection," *Coin World*, 24 July 2015, https://www.coinworld.com/news/precious-metals /smithsonian-opens-new-exhibit-of-its-national-numismatic-collect.html (accessed 19 October 2019).

388 Other team members included curators William L. Bird Jr., Lisa Kathleen Graddy, Grace Cohen Grossman, and Barbara Clark Smith. Megan Smith was the exhibit developer. Kathryn Campbell was the project manager, Stevan Fisher the design

manager, and Sara Murphy the collections manager. The display was designed by Haley Sharpe Design.

389 *American Democracy* Exhibition Opens June 28 at the Smithsonian, Smithsonian Institution press release, 12 June 2017, https://americanhistory.si.edu/press/releases/democracy, (accessed 19 October 2019).

390 *American Democracy* Exhibition Opens June 28 at the Smithsonian, Smithsonian Institution press release.

391 Curators were Margaret Salazar-Porzio, Steve Velasquez, Tim Winkle, Lauren Safranek, Debbie Shaeffer-Jacobs, Barbara Clark Smith, Fath Ruffins, and Christopher Turner from the National Museum of the American Indian. Howard Morrison and Megan Smith were the exhibit developers. Christine Klepper and Molly Horrocks were the collections managers. Kathryn Campbell was the project manager and Heidi Eitel and Hana Kim the design managers. The firm Haley-Sharpe designed the exhibition.

392 *Many Voices, One Nation* Exhibition Opens June 28 at the Smithsonian, Smithsonian Institution press release, 12 June 2017, https://americanhistory.si.edu/press/releases/many-voices (accessed 19 October 2019).

393 *Many Voices, One Nation* Exhibition Opens June 28, Smithsonian Institution press release.

394 Margaret Salazar-Porzio, Joan Fragaszy Troyano, and Lauren Safranek, *Many Voices, One Nation: Material Culture Reflections on Race and Migration in the United States* (Washington, D.C.: Smithsonian Institution Scholarly Press, 2017), 19–21.

395 For further information, see the website https://amhistory.si.edu/september11/

396 Smithsonian's National Museum of American History to open September 11 Exhibition, Smithsonian press release SI-258-2002, 22 May 2002, NMAH Public Affairs Office historical files.

397 Both quotations are from Jacqueline Trescott, "Common Things with Uncommon Meaning," *Washington Post*, 11 September 2002, C1.

398 National Museum of American History to Commemorate 10th Anniversary of September 11 Attacks, Smithsonian Institution press release, 15 June 2011, https://americanhistory.si.edu/press/releases/national-museum-american-history-commemorate-10th-anniversary-sept-11-attacks (accessed 19 October 2019).

399 National Museum of American History Marks 50th Anniversary of Brown v. Board of Education, Smithsonian Institution press release, 11 May 2004, https://americanhistory.si.edu/press/releases/national-museum-american-history-marks-50th-anniversary-brown-v-board-education (accessed 19 October 2019).

400 National Museum of American History Marks 50th Anniversary of Brown v. Board of Education, Smithsonian Institution press release.

401 National Museum of American History Explores Bracero Story in New Exhibition, Smithsonian Institution press release, 8 September 2009, https://americanhistory.si.edu/press/releases/national-museum-american-history-explores-bracero-story-new-exhibition (accessed 19 October 2019).

402 National Museum of American History Explores Bracero Story in New Exhibition, Smithsonian Institution press release.

403 National Museum of American History to Open *Abraham Lincoln: An Extraordinary Life*, Smithsonian Institution press release, 30 December 2008, https://american history.si.edu/press/releases/national-museum-american-history-open-%E2%80 %9Cabraham-lincoln-extraordinary-life%E2%80%9D (accessed 19 October 2019).

404 National Museum of American History to Open *Abraham Lincoln*, Smithsonian Institution press release.

405 National Museum of American History Opens Philanthropy Exhibition, Smithsonian Institution press release, 23 November 2016, https://americanhistory.si.edu /press/releases/smithsonian-accepts-als-%E2%80%9Cice-bucket%E2%80%9D -philanthropy-exhibition (accessed 19 October 2019); Smithsonian Accepts ALS "Ice Bucket" for Philanthropy Exhibition, Smithsonian Institution press release, 29 November 2019, https://americanhistory.si.edu/press/releases/smithsonian-accepts-als -%E2%80%9Cice-bucket%E2%80%9D-philanthropy-exhibition (accessed 19 October 2019).

406 National Museum of American History adds Objects on #Giving Tuesday, Smithsonian Institution press release, 1 December 2015, https://americanhistory.si.edu /press/releases/national-museum-american-history-adds-objects-givingtuesday (accessed 19 October 2019).

407 National Museum of American History to Display Lincoln Documents from Abraham Lincoln Presidential Library, Smithsonian Institution press release, 30 December 2008, https://americanhistory.si.edu/press/releases/national-museum-american -history-display-lincoln-documents-abraham-lincoln (accessed 19 October 2019).

408 These exhibit descriptions come from the Smithsonian's EDAN database, which is available for searching online at https://www.si.edu/exhibitions/past

409 "The Scurlock Studio and Black Washington: Picturing the Promise" Photography Exhibition Opens at the Smithsonian, January 30, Smithsonian Institution press release, 29 January 2009, https://americanhistory.si.edu/press/releases/%E2%80%9C -scurlock-studio-and-black-washington-picturing-promise%E2%80%9D-photography -exhibition (accessed 19 October 2019).

410 Smithsonian Exhibitions database, https://www.si.edu/exhibitions/past

411 *Religion in Early America* Exhibition Opens June 28 at Smithsonian, Smithsonian Institution press release, 12 June 2017, https://americanhistory.si.edu/press/releases /religion-early-america (accessed 19 October 2019).

412 *The American Revolution: A World War* Exhibition Opens at the Smithsonian, Smithsonian Institution press release, 21 June 2018, https://americanhistory.si.edu/press /releases/"-american-revolution-world-war"-exhibition-opens-smithsonian (accessed 19 October 2019).

413 New Draper Spark!Lab Offers Hands-on Inventive Fun for Kids, Smithsonian Institution press release, 18 June 2015, https://americanhistory.si.edu/press/releases /draper-sparklab (accessed 19 October 2019).

414 Smithsonian Opens Wegmans Wonderplace for Young Historians, Smithsonian Institution press release, 9 December 2015, https://americanhistory.si.edu/press/releases /smithsonian-opens-wegmans-wonderplace-young-historians (accessed 19 October 2019).

415 "Object Project" Explores Everyday Things that Changed Everything, Smithsonian Institution press release, 18 June 2015, https://americanhistory.si.edu/press/releases/object-project (accessed 19 October 2019).

416 Nanci Edwards was the project manager and Hal Aber the design manager. Emma Grahn and Heather Paisley-Jones managed the collections and teaching objects. Fernanda Luppani worked as project assistant. Roto Group, LLC, designed and built the display.

417 For more about the Smithsonian Chamber Music Society, see its website: https://www.smithsonianchambermusic.org/about (accessed 19 October 2019).

418 NMAH Director's Office historical files on branding project.

419 The Martin Agency, *Style Guide for the National Museum of American History*, Version 01, 2017, NMAH Director's Office historical files.

420 See chapter 1 section "The Star-Spangled Banner: An American Icon."

421 See chapter 4 section "S. Dillon Ripley, Daniel Boorstin, and the Bicentennial."

Chapter 7 Notes

422 See Helena E. Wright, The First Smithsonian Collection: The European Engravings of George Perkins Marsh and the Role of Prints in the U.S. National Museum (Washington D.C.: Smithsonian Institution Scholarly Press, 2015).

423 Sharon Macdonald, "Exhibitions of Power and Powers of Exhibition: An Introduction to the Politics of Display," in *The Politics of Display: Museums, Science, Culture*, ed. Sharon Macdonald, pp. 1–20 (London: Routledge, 1998), 8.

424 See chapter 4 section "A Nation of Nations." The exhibition opened in 1964.

425 Report of the Blue Ribbon Commission on the National Museum of American History, chapter 6, https://americanhistory.si.edu/reports/brc/3b.htm (accessed 18 October 2019).

426 Annual Report of the Board of Regents of the Smithsonian Institution, 1881, 89ff.

427 New Blueprint Ideas, Smithsonian Archives, record unit 14-272, box 1, folder "The Blueprint Plan." Emphasis added by authors.

428 Library of Congress website, *Creating the United States* exhibition, https://www.loc.gov/exhibits/creating-the-united-states/convention-and-ratification.html#obj8%20?loclr=blogtea (accessed 18 November 2019).

Sources

This book focused on only one of the many activities of the Smithsonian's national history museum: its development and production of exhibitions. Thus, our research centered on identifying the goals, organization, design, and content of exhibitions at the museum in each of the five historical eras of that we identified.

Exhibitions have unquestionably been the museum products that have received the most attention by the institution over the years. They have been the most expensive and attracted the largest audiences. Despite this, institutional record-keeping on exhibitions has been haphazard and idiosyncratic. To discover the information we used for this book, we had to look far beyond official archival records.

In explaining and documenting our sources, we determined it was best to organize them under the topics we investigated rather than by type or repository. This allowed us to explain not only what materials we found to be the most valuable, but also where we were able to locate them and how they changed from one era to the next.

Exhibition Lists

To gauge the range and scope of history exhibitions the Smithsonian has done, we first looked for comprehensive lists. We found that the Smithsonian has no complete itemization of all the exhibitions it has produced, or even regular annual listings. The most extensive body of information we found was an institution-wide list of "Past Exhibitions" posted on the Smithsonian Institution website (https://www.si .edu/search?edan_q=past%2Bexhibitions). We were able to secure the data behind this list in August 2018, and at that time it identified 920 "exhibitions" that had been on display at the Museum of History and Technology and its successors from 1964 to 2018. The information originated in the Smithsonian's visitor services unit and was based on what had been shared with visitors over the years. Thus, the information had been reviewed and approved and was generally reliable. However, we determined that this listing was far from complete. Moreover, what constituted an "exhibition" ranged from small temporary displays to long-term exhibitions of 23,000 square feet. Nonetheless, this data was extremely useful because it included the exhibition names, opening and closing dates, locations, and brief descriptions. It became a highly valuable source.

The National Museum of American History's collections information system, Mimsy XG, included itemization of 893 exhibitions that date from the 1880s to the present. This information was gleaned by museum staff who sought to retrospectively identify the exhibitions in which individual objects had appeared. While helpful, this information was less systematic and less reliable than the information we found on the Smithsonian-wide site.

Finally, the National Museum of American History website included a past exhibitions listing, with similar data to that on the institution-wide site. This generally had reliable information, but it extended back only to 2003.

Based on these data sources, it is difficult to make any reasonable estimate of the total number of history "exhibitions" the Smithsonian has mounted since it opened the National Museum in 1881. Our best guess is that the number ranges between 1,000 and 2,000.

Exhibition Floor Plans

Just as it has no complete listing of its history exhibitions, the Smithsonian has no comprehensive set of floor plans for its history museums, as those plans changed over the years. During the initial eras of the museum, from the late nineteenth century through the 1980s, the Smithsonian as a whole, or the National Museum of American History and its predecessors, periodically published printed guides that included descriptions of exhibitions. These usually included floor plans, and they were the principal sources for those we found for the earlier eras. The last printed guide with descriptions that we found dated from 1988. Thereafter, the museum simply published floor plans without exhibition descriptions, presumably because there was no longer a market for the more detailed guides.

The floor plans were freely distributed to museum visitors at the information desks, (although in recent years they have been asked to make nominal donations to help pay for them). Printing of these plans was often paid for by donors; sometimes they were even designed by outside organizations. The museum made no systematic attempt to preserve copies of each edition of these in its official records. Fortunately, however, the manager of visitor programs at the museum kept a personal collection of many of them, which she made available to us.

In recent decades, exhibition floor plans were posted on the National Museum of American History website. However, when they changed, no archival record was kept of previous versions. In short, finding floor plans that documented changes over time turned out to be surprisingly difficult. Although we were not able to assemble a complete set, we were fortunate to find good representative examples for each of the five eras we identified.

Content of Exhibitions and Audience Responses

A major goal of this book has been to provide brief descriptions of individual exhibitions and representative images of what they displayed. The best sources of exhibition descriptions we found varied over time. For years when published museum guides were available, they were always the place to start. However, most of these were not written by curators or individuals who had been involved in creating the exhibitions, but rather by staff writers who might not always have reviewed their copy with those who created the exhibitions.

There were two notable exceptions to this pattern. In 1968, the museum issued Smithsonian Publication 4270, entitled *Exhibits in the Museum of History and Technology*, prepared by curators of the museum. This 128-page guide is the longest and most detailed ever published by the museum, and the only one written by multiple exhibit curators themselves. Two decades later, in 1987, curator of graphic arts Elizabeth Harris published a comprehensive *Small Guide to the National Museum of American History*, on which she consulted with other curators. It was a thoughtful and insightful presentation of her personal walk-through of the museum, well illustrated with diagrams and her careful choice of images.

Annual reports were a second valuable source. Every year since 1846, the Smithsonian has issued an annual report to Congress. For the years from the beginning until 1970, these reports were useful sources for information about the development and content of exhibitions. They are particularly valuable records for the years when S. Dillon Ripley was secretary, from 1964 through 1984. Since the 1970s, these reports have transitioned into public relations documents devoted more to recognizing sponsors and partners than providing substantive summaries of exhibitions and other museum activities, so they had little value to us.

Exhibition press releases were a third principal source. Beginning in the 1960s, the Smithsonian central Office of Public Affairs began issuing releases when it opened major exhibitions. We found many of them scattered among the museum's archival records of both the Director's Office and curators' files. By the 1980s, the National Museum of American History was issuing the releases on its own, and since 1982 it has kept a set of reference copies. Museum press releases since 1999 are also all available on the museum's website. Like the guidebooks, the releases are a systematic and reliable source for determining the museum's intent in its exhibitions. They were extremely helpful in determining the goals for exhibitions and providing a summary of their organization and contents when they opened. Although written by the Public Affairs Office, the releases were reviewed both by exhibition curators and the Director's Office to ensure that they faithfully represented the museum's perspective. At times, the Public Affairs Office supplemented press releases with more extensive "press kits" that included further background information.

Media coverage of exhibitions provided a contrasting perspective. Archives of the *Washington Post*, the *Washington Star*, the *Washington Times*, and the *New York Times* are all available online, and we found useful reviews in them of many of the museum's most significant exhibitions. In recent decades, the museum's Public Affairs Office gathered and preserved clipping files from press coverage around the nation for many exhibitions, especially for those that became controversial, such as *A More Perfect Union* and *Science in American Life*. Not all these files have been preserved, and many that have been saved are still held by the Public Affairs Office and likely will not be transferred to the Smithsonian Archives. Professional historical journals including *Technology and Culture*, *American Historical Review*, and *The Public Historian* also occasionally published reviews that were directed at scholarly audiences. Determining general audience reactions to exhibitions was very difficult. The most reliable and perceptive sources were the few systematic studies conducted by the Smithsonian's Institutional Studies Office. Using visitor tracking techniques and standardized questions for interviews, they provided the most objective analysis the Smithsonian has of what visitors did in exhibitions and the reactions they had.

Curators and exhibit teams frequently transferred records related to exhibition development to the Smithsonian Archives. These transfers generally came years after the exhibition opened, often when curators left, retired, or simply ran out of storage space in their offices. For major exhibitions with large teams, multiple groups of records related to an exhibition often ended up in the archives. Records related to exhibitions were also found at times in files from the director's office, or even the Smithsonian secretary's office if an exhibition required high-level attention. These dispersed materials remain scattered among multiple accessions and can be difficult to locate, especially if file headings, which are searchable, are not accurate. At times, archival files in outside repositories were particularly useful, for example the records of Daniel Boorstin in the Library of Congress and the records of Anthony Garvan at the University of Pennsylvania.

The archival collections tend to be very uneven in depth and coverage. There have never been museum guidelines on what should constitute an official archival record for an exhibition. This is an interesting contrast to records for museum artifacts, for which such standards have long been in place. Very few collections on exhibitions, for example, contain verified final scripts or final lists of objects included in the exhibition, in part because changes are often made late in the process of exhibition production, and the final script might be in the hands of a museum editor or production staff member rather than a curator. The museum's production unit has never had the responsibility of preserving definitive records of the floor plan, design, and script of exhibitions.

In general, we found official press releases and press coverage of what went on display more reliable summaries of the goals and final content of exhibitions than archival records from curatorial offices. They, on the other hand, were most useful when we sought to explore discussion or debates in the development of exhibitions, when major changes were being made or different opinions sorted out.

Many, but not all, exhibition teams have published catalogs or books related to their respective exhibitions. In some instances, these catalogs were valuable references of what was displayed, but more often, they became explorations of the subject of each exhibition rather than descriptions of the cases and displays that were physically present in the museum. While catalogs might include images of objects in the exhibition, they almost never include pictures of the exhibitions. Likewise, the narrative was generally more discursive than the exhibit text. This is particularly true for recent decades, because publishers have found that books with this broader perspective are more appealing to readers than detailed exhibition catalogs.

Oral histories conducted by the Smithsonian Archives, many by longtime Smithsonian Historian Pamela Henson, were extremely valuable in gaining insight into the thinking of some early museum leaders, including Frank Taylor, Malcom Watkins, and Roger Kennedy. Unfortunately, many of the more recent leaders of the museum have not been interviewed.

Exhibition Photographs

We were determined to include many illustrations of exhibitions in this book. For most people, visits to exhibitions are primarily visual and experiential activities. They come to "see an exhibition," after all, not to "read" or "contemplate" it. While the photographs we included are at best only a sample of how the museum appeared over the years, we think they are enough to illustrate trends in how displays changed visually as their goals and objectives evolved.

As we found with locating written records on exhibitions, finding images was surprisingly challenging. The museum never had a firm policy on what photographs of exhibits should be taken and how record sets should be preserved. In recent decades, the practice of visual documentation has become more standard for larger exhibitions, but many smaller ones may still not be photographed. Nor is there a set policy for what sections of exhibitions should be captured. There is almost never a complete set of images that includes every single display unit.

Most collections of Smithsonian photographs are held by the Smithsonian Archives. They are not in a single collection but are dispersed among multiple collections. A brief description of the majority of them is available at the Smithsonian Institution Archives website https://siarchives.si.edu/what-we-do/photograph-and-image-collections. The holdings of these collections are slowly being digitized and made available to the public through the Archives website and the Smithsonian comprehensive collections research site, the Collections Search Center on the main Smithsonian Institution website (http://collections.si.edu/search/index.htm). Since around 2008, the Smithsonian has developed a digital asset management system that has become the record repository for all images that Smithsonian photographers take. Those that are publicly available are released through the collections site mentioned above.

Unfortunately for our project, the thousands of Smithsonian photographs held in the archives that are not yet digitized were not readily available for research, because of the way they were being stored and processed. Thus, we had to find other caches of images outside the official records and digitize them ourselves. We found these in the form of both prints and slides.

Sometimes there were images in the archives, mixed in with print materials. One collection of particular note was accession 03-040, three boxes of "Color Slides circa 1962–1985 and undated," which had been deposited by Robert Harding of the museum's Archives Center. It included a wealth of color slides of exhibits that Harding had taken himself or that he had obtained from the museum's photo services unit. These provided crucial coverage of the first set of exhibitions in the Museum of History and Technology. For exhibits from the 1970s to 2000s, we found many valuable images in an extensive set of binders that the museum's Public Affairs Office had kept for reference and later stored away. Beyond these, we located collections stashed in the museum's design studio and many curatorial offices. Finally, we drew on the museum's Flickr site, https://www.flickr.com/photos/nationalmuseumof americanhistory/. It included a number of images we couldn't locate elsewhere.

While someday, most of these images that are not yet in the Smithsonian's comprehensive digital asset management system will end up being available there, it will at best require a process that will take many years. For us, finding the images was a challenging hunt through back rooms and dark corners.

Museum Planning and Management

Although our research focused primarily on the development and presentation of exhibitions, we discussed that process within the context of the museum's planning and management functions. Much of our story related to the relationship between the initial plans for exhibitions and the exhibitions that finally resulted.

Traditional archival practice privileges the preservation of records of planning and management, and we found records of strategic planning and museum management more readily identifiable and accessible than those for exhibition development. Annual Smithsonian reports to Congress from the time when compiling these was taken seriously were a valuable resource. Reasonably good records of museum directors over the years are available in the archives, although they are spread through a surprisingly large number of different accessions. We were able to locate copies of the formal strategic plans the museum compiled over the years. Many records, including oral histories, were available regarding the planning of the Museum of History and Technology in the 1950s and its initial set of exhibitions. Particularly valuable was the large body of documentation that the Director's Office compiled when it applied for reaccreditation by the American Association of Museums in 2005, which included useful historical background. We had access not only to the full Blue Ribbon Commission report of 2002, but also background materials, including Chairman Richard Darman's personal notes. For recent years, we were able to draw on the museum's "board books," or reports made to the museum board for its thrice-a-year meetings. Because of the lack of thorough annual reports to Congress, these documents contained some of the best records we found of the museum's annual plans and goals, as well as the resources it required to attain them.

As the records of museum work increasingly became digital and took the form of emails, PDFs, and electronic calendars, their preservation became more haphazard and less likely to happen. As part of this project, for example, we assisted in the transfer of Director's Office records to the Smithsonian Archives covering years from around 2002 through 2015. Many of these existed only in electronic form and accessing them in the Smithsonian Archives is likely to be more challenging than accessing traditional paper records, because effective procedures are still in development. Moreover, it is quite difficult with electronic files to retrospectively separate "temporary" records from "permanent" ones. So, in practice, either virtually all emails or files are preserved for an individual, or none are saved. In short, writing about the coming eras of the history of the museum may turn out to be more difficult than the periods we studied.

Secondary Sources

Although this book is written largely from primary source materials cited in the notes, we consulted many secondary sources for reference and context. However, we found no studies that attempted, as we did, to survey the development of exhibitions at the museum across its full history.

Abbott, Shirley. *The National Museum of American History.* 1st ed. New York: Harry N. Abrams, Inc, 1981.

Alexander, Edward P. *Museums in Motion: An Introduction to the History and Functions of Museums.* Nashville, Tenn.: American Association for State and Local History, 1979.

Alexander, Edward P. *Museum Masters: Their Museums and Their Influence.* Nashville, Tenn.: American Association for State and Local History, 1983.

Allison, David, and Larrie D. Ferreiro, eds. *The American Revolution: A World War.* Washington, D.C.: Smithsonian Books, 2018.

Allison, David, Peter Liebhold, Nancy Davis, and Kathleen G. Franz. *American Enterprise: A History of Business in America.* Ed. Andy Serwer. Washington, D.C.: Smithsonian Books, 2015.

America's Smithsonian: Celebrating 150 Years. Washington, D.C.: Smithsonian Institution Press, 1996.

Behring, Kenneth E. *Road to Purpose.* Blackhawk, Calif.: Blackhawk Press, 2004.

Bird, William L. *Holidays on Display.* New York: Princeton Architectural Press, 2007.

Bird, William L. *America's Doll House: The Miniature World of Faith Bradford.* 1st ed. New York: Princeton Architectural Press, 2010.

Boorstin, Daniel J. *The Americans: The Colonial Experience.* New York: Random House, 1958.

Boorstin, Daniel J. *The Americans: The Democratic Experience.* 1st ed. New York: Random House, 1973.

Boorstin, Daniel J. *The Americans: The National Experience.* New York: Random House, 1965.

Brodie, Jeffrey L., Lonnie G. Bunch, Ellen Roney Hughes, Steven D. Lubar, Smithsonian Institution, National Museum of American History, National Air and Space Museum, and Bijutsu Shuppan Dezain Sentā (Japan), eds. *The Smithsonian's America: An Exhibition on American History and Culture.* Tokyo: American Festival Japan '94 Organizing Committee, 1994.

Bunch III, Lonnie G. *A Fool's Errand: Creating the National Museum of African American History and Culture in the Age of Bush, Obama, and Trump.* Washington, D.C.: Smithsonian Books, 2019.

Bunch, Lonnie, Spencer Crew, Mark Hirsch, Harry Rubenstein, and Richard Norton Smith. *The American Presidency: A Glorious Burden.* Washington, D.C.: Smithsonian, 2000.

Chapelle, Howard Irving. *The National Watercraft Collection.* United States National Museum Bulletin 219. Washington, D.C.: Smithsonian Institution, 1960.

Cohen, Marilyn Sara. "American Civilization in Three Dimensions: The Evolution of the Museum of History and Technology of the Smithsonian Institution." Ph.D. diss., Georgetown University, 1980.

Conaway, James. *The Smithsonian: 150 Years of Adventure, Discovery, and Wonder.* 1st ed. New York: Knopf, 1995.

Corn, Joseph J., Brian Horrigan, and Katherine Chambers. *Yesterday's Tomorrows: Past Visions of the American Future.* New York: Summit Books, 1984.

Crew, Spencer R. *Field to Factory: Afro-American Migration 1915–1940.* Washington, D.C.: National Museum of American History, Smithsonian Institution, 1987.

Daso, Dik A., ed. *The Price of Freedom: Americans at War.* Seattle: Marquand Books Inc, 2004.

Davidson, Janet F., and Michael S. Sweeney. *On the Move: Transportation and the American Story.* Washington, D.C.: National Geographic, 2003.

Edwards, Nanci K., David Andrews, Smithsonian Institution, and National Museum of American History, eds. *Who's in Charge? Workers and Managers in the United States.* Washington, D.C.: Smithsonian Institution Traveling Exhibition Service, 1992.

Ewing, Heather. *The Lost World of James Smithson: Science, Revolution, and the Birth of the Smithsonian.* New York: Bloomsbury, 2007.

Friedel, Robert D., and Eric F. Long. *A Material World: An Exhibition at the National Museum of American History, Smithsonian Institution.* Washington, D.C.: National Museum of American History, 1988.

Gardullo, Paul, National Museum of African American History and Culture, and National Museum of American History, eds. *The Scurlock Studio and Black Washington: Picturing the Promise.* Washington, D.C.: National Museum of African American History and Culture, in collaboration with the National Museum of American History, 2009.

Graddy, Lisa Kathleen, and Amy Pastan. *The Smithsonian First Ladies Collection.* 1st ed. Washington, D.C.: Smithsonian Books, 2014.

Harris, Elizabeth. *Small Guide to the National Museum of American History.* Washington, D.C.: National Museum of American History, 1987.

Harris, Michael R., Carl H. Scheele, and Elsa M. Bruton. *M*A*S*H: Binding up the Wounds.* New York: G. Fenmore Associates, 1983.

Hellman, Geoffrey T. *The Smithsonian: Octopus on the Mall.* 1st ed. Philadelphia: Lippincott, 1967.

Henson, Pamela M., and Smithsonian Institution, eds. *From Smithson to Smithsonian: The Birth of an Institution.* Smithsonian Institution Libraries electronic ed. Washington, D.C.: Smithsonian Institution Libraries, 1998.

Hoes, Rose Gouverneur. *Catalogue of American Historical Costumes: Including Those of the Mistresses of the White House, as Shown in the United States National Museum.* Washington, D.C., 1915.

Hooper-Greenhill, Eilean. *Museum and Gallery Education.* Leicester Museum Studies Series. Leicester, UK: Leicester University Press, 1991.

Hoover, Cynthia A., Patrick Rucker, and Edwin M. Good. *Piano 300: Celebrating Three Centuries of People and Pianos*. Washington, D.C.: National Museum of American History, Behring Center, Smithsonian Institution and NAMM-International Music Products Association, 2001.

Hughes, Ellen Roney. *Sports: Breaking Records, Breaking Barriers*. London: Scala, 2004.

Jones, Jennifer Locke, Brad Johnson, and National Museum of American History, eds. *A More Perfect Union: Japanese Americans & the U.S. Constitution*. Virtual Exhibitions / Smithsonian. National Museum of American History, Behring Center, 2001. http://americanhistory.si.edu/perfectunion/experience/index.html

Jordan, David Starr. *Leading American Men of Science*. Biographies of Leading Americans, ed. W. P. Trent. New York: H. Holt and Company, 1910.

Kavanagh, Gaynor. *History Curatorship*. Washington, D.C.: Smithsonian Institution Press, 1990.

Kendrick, Kathleen M., and Peter Liebhold. *Smithsonian Treasures of American History*. 1st ed. New York: HarperCollins, 2006.

Kennedy, Roger G. *Rediscovering America*. Boston: Houghton Mifflin, 1990.

Kindlon, Audrey E., Andrew Pekarik, and Zahava D. Doering. *Visitors to History: A Report Based on the 1994–95 National Museum of American History Visitor Study*. Report 96-3B. Washington, D.C.: Institutional Studies Office, Smithsonian Institution, 1996.

Klapthor, Margaret Brown. *The Dresses of the First Ladies of the White House*. Smithsonian Institution Publication 4060. Washington, D.C.: Smithsonian Institution, 1952.

Klapthor, Margaret Brown, Howard Alexander Morrison, and Carole J. Jacobs. *G. Washington, a Figure upon the Stage: An Exhibition in Celebration of the 250th Anniversary of His Birth*. Washington, D.C.: Smithsonian Institution Press, 1982.

Knight, Nancy. *Pain and Its Relief*. Washington, D.C.: National Museum of American History, Smithsonian Institution, 1983.

Lubar, Steven. *Inside the Lost Museum: Curating, Past and Present*. Cambridge, Mass.: Harvard University Press, 2017.

Lubar, Steven D. *InfoCulture: The Smithsonian Book of Information Age Inventions*. Boston: Houghton Mifflin, 1993.

Lubar, Steven D., and Kathleen M. Kendrick. *Legacies: Collecting America's History at the Smithsonian*. Washington, D.C.: Smithsonian Institution Press, 2001.

Lubar, Steven D., and Eric F. Long. *Engines of Change: An Exhibition on the American Industrial Revolution at the National Museum of American History, Smithsonian Institution*. Washington, D.C.: National Museum of American History, 1986.

Macdonald, Sharon, ed. *The Politics of Display: Museums, Science, Culture*. London: Routledge, 1998.

Macdonald, Sharon, and Gordon Fyfe, eds. *Theorizing Museums: Representing Identity and Diversity in a Changing World*. Sociological Review Monograph. Oxford: Blackwell, The Sociological Review, 1996.

Manseau, Peter. *Objects of Devotion: Religion in Early America*. Washington, D.C.: Smithsonian Books, 2017.

Marzio, Peter C. *A Nation of Nations: The People Who Came to America As Seen Through Objects and Documents Exhibited at the Smithsonian Institution.* 1st ed. New York: Harper Collins, 1976.

Mayo, Edith, and Lisa Kathleen Graddy. *First Ladies: Political Role and Public Image.* London: Scala, Smithsonian's National Museum of American History, and Smithsonian Institution Traveling Exhibition Service, 2004.

Molella, Arthur P. "The Museum That Might Have Been: The Smithsonian's National Museum of Engineering and Industry." *Technology and Culture,* 32(2) (1991):237–263. https://doi.org/10.2307/3105710.

Molella, Arthur P., and Elsa M. Bruton. *FDR, the Intimate Presidency: Franklin Delano Roosevelt, Communication, and the Mass Media in the 1930s: An Exhibition to Commemorate the 100th Anniversary of the Birth of the 32nd President of the United States, January 1982.* Washington, D.C.: National Museum of American History, Smithsonian Institution, 1982.

Morrison, Howard Alexander. *American Encounters: A Companion to the Exhibition at the National Museum of American History, Smithsonian Institution.* Washington, D.C.: National Museum of American History, 1992.

Multhauf, Robert P. "A Museum Case History: The Department of Science and Technology of the United States Museum of History and Technology." *Technology and Culture,* 6(1) (1965):47–58. https://doi.org/10.2307/3100951.

Museum of History and Technology, ed. *Exhibits in the Museum of History and Technology.* Smithsonian Institution Publication 4720. Washington, D.C.: Smithsonian Institution Press, 1968.

Museum of History and Technology, ed. *Dedication of the Museum of History and Technology of the Smithsonian Institution, January 22, 1964.* Smithsonian Publication 4531. Washington, D.C.: Smithsonian Institution, 1964.

National Museum of American History. *Official Guide to the National Museum of American History.* Washington, D.C.: Smithsonian Institution Press, 1988.

National Museum of American History, ed. *On Time: An Exhibition at the National Museum of American History.* Virtual Exhibitions / Smithsonian, National Museum of American History. Washington, D.C.: National Museum of American History, 1999. http://americanhistory.si.edu/ontime/index.html (accessed 3 November 2020).

National Museum of American History, ed. *The Henry R. Luce Hall of News Reporting.* Baltimore: Ashton-Worthington, 1973.

National Museum of American History, Harry R. Rubenstein, William Bird, Lisa Kathleen Graddy, and Barbara Clark Smith. *American Democracy: A Great Leap of Faith.* Washington, D.C.: Smithsonian Books, 2017.

Noordegraaf, Julia. *Strategies of Display: Museum Presentation in Nineteenth- and Twentieth-Century Visual Culture.* Rotterdam: Museum Boijmans Van Beuningen: NAi Publishers, 2004.

Post, Robert C. *Who Owns America's Past? The Smithsonian and the Problem of History.* Baltimore: Johns Hopkins University Press, 2013.

Post, Robert C., ed. *1876: A Centennial Exhibition: A Treatise Upon Selected Aspects of the Great International Exhibition Held in Philadelphia....* 1st ed. Washington, D.C.: Smithsonian Institution, 1976.

Rhees, William Jones. *An Account of the Smithsonian Institution: Three Centuries of Science in America.* New York: Arno Press, 1980.

Rhees, William Jones. *An Account of the Smithsonian Institution: Its Founder, Building, Operations, Etc.* Washington, D.C.: T. McGill, 1857.

Rhees, William Jones. *James Smithson and His Bequest.* Washington, D.C.: Smithsonian Institution, 1880.

Rhees, William Jones. *The Smithsonian Institution: Documents Relative to Its Origin and History, 1835–1899.* Smithsonian Miscellaneous Collections 42–43. Washington, D.C.: Government Printing Office, 1901.

Rhees, William Jones. *Visitor's Guide to the Smithsonian Institution and National Museum, Washington. D.C.* Washington, D.C.: Judd & Detweiler, 1881.

Rubenstein, Harry R. *Abraham Lincoln: An Extraordinary Life.* 1st ed. Washington, D.C.: Smithsonian Books, 2008.

Salazar-Porzio, Margaret, Joan Fragaszy Troyano, and Lauren Safranek, eds. *Many Voices, One Nation: Material Culture Reflections on Race and Migration in the United States.* Washington, D.C.: Smithsonian Institution Scholarly Press, 2017.

Schwarzer, Marjorie. *Riches, Rivals & Radicals: 100 Years of Museums in America.* Washington, D.C.: American Association of Museums, 2006.

Sclar, Charlotte L. *The Smithsonian: A Guide to Its National Public Facilities in Washington, D.C.* Jefferson, N.C.: McFarland & Co, 1985.

Shayt, David H.; National Museum of American History, Association of Museum Specialists, Technicians, and Aides; and Smithsonian Institution; eds. *The Pendulum.* Washington, D.C.: Smithsonian Institution, 1995.

Smithsonian Institution. *Brief Guide to the Smithsonian Institution.* National Publishing Co., 1956.

Smithsonian Institution. *Brief Guide to the Smithsonian Institution.* Publication 4507. National Publishing Co., 1963.

Smithsonian Institution, ed. *Official Guide to the Smithsonian.* Washington, D.C.: Smithsonian Institution Press, 1981.

Smithsonian Institution, ed. *Official Guide to the Smithsonian.* Rev. ed. Washington, D.C.: Smithsonian Institution Press, 1986.

Smithsonian Institution, ed. *Official Guide to the Smithsonian.* Washington, D.C.: Smithsonian Institution Press, 1996.

Smithsonian Institution, ed. *Official Guide to the Smithsonian.* Washington, D.C.: Smithsonian Institution Press, 2002.

Smithsonian Institution, ed. *Official Guide to the Smithsonian.* Rev. ed. Washington, D.C.: Smithsonian Books, 2007.

Smithsonian Institution, ed. *Official Guide to the Smithsonian.* 4th ed. Washington, D.C.: Smithsonian Books, 2016.

Smithsonian Institution, ed. *Seeing the Smithsonian: The Official Guidebook to the Smithsonian Institution, Its Museums and Galleries.* Washington, D.C.: Smithsonian Institution, 1973.

Smithsonian Institution, ed. *Smithsonian Institution Yesterday & Today.* Washington, D.C.: Smithsonian Institution, Office of Public Affairs, 1984.

Smithsonian Institution, ed. *The Smithsonian Experience: Science, History, the Arts… the Treasures of the Nation.* Washington, D.C.: Smithsonian Institution, 1977.

Smithsonian Institution, ed. *The Smithsonian Institution: A Description of Its Work*. Washington, D.C.: Smithsonian Institution, 1951.

Smithsonian Institution, ed. *The Smithsonian Journal of History*. Washington, D.C.: Smithsonian Institution, n.d.

Smithsonian Institution and CBS Publications, eds. *The Official Guide to the Smithsonian*. Rev. ed. Washington, D.C., 1976.

Smithsonian Institution and G. Brown Goode, eds. *The Smithsonian Institution, 1846–1896: The History of Its First Half Century*. Washington, D.C.: Smithsonian Institution, 1897.

Stephens, Carlene E. *On Time: How America Has Learned to Live by the Clock*. 1st ed. Boston: Bulfinch, 2002.

Stone, Roger D. *The Lives of Dillon Ripley: Natural Scientist, Wartime Spy, and Pioneering Leader of the Smithsonian Institution*. Lebanon, N.H.: Fore Edge, 2017.

Syz, Hans C., J. Jefferson Miller, and Rainer Rückert. *Catalogue of the Hans Syz Collection*. Washington, D.C.: Smithsonian Institution Press, 1979.

Taylor, Frank A. A National Museum of Science, Engineering and Industry. *Scientific Monthly*, 63(5) (1946):359–365.

Taylor, Frank A. *Catalogue of the Mechanical Collections of the Division of Engineering United States National Museum*. Washington, D.C.: Government Printing Office, 1939.

Taylor, Lonn, Jeffrey Brodie, and Kathleen Kendrick. *The Star-Spangled Banner: The Making of an American Icon*. 1st ed. New York: Smithsonian, 2008.

Vogel, Robert M. Assembling a New Hall of Civil Engineering. *Technology and Culture*, 6(1) (1965):59–73. https://doi.org/10.2307/3100952

Walker, William S. *A Living Exhibition: The Smithsonian and the Transformation of the Universal Museum*. 1st ed. Amherst: University of Massachusetts Press, 2013.

Warner, Deborah Jean. *Perfect in Her Place: Women at Work in Industrial America*. Washington, D.C.: Smithsonian Institution Press, 1981.

Weil, Stephen E. *Making Museums Matter*. Washington, D.C.: Smithsonian Institution Press, 2002.

Wright, Helena E. *The First Smithsonian Collection: The European Engravings of George Perkins Marsh and the Role of Prints in the U.S. National Museum*. Washington, D.C.: Smithsonian Institution Scholarly Press, 2015.

Yochelson, Ellis L., and Mary Jarrett. *The National Museum of Natural History: 75 Years in the Natural History Building*. Washington, D.C.: Smithsonian Institution Press, 1985.

Image Sources

This table lists source information for the images in this book. Most came from the Smithsonian Archives, and the relevant image numbers are shown. Although numbering conventions varied over time, the images are generally traceable using these numbers. The source listing "SIA Acc 03-040" refers to a single accession in the Archives of a large collection of exhibition slides. Images from this source were digitized by history project staff. Most are not numbered. Similarly, images attributed to sources other than the Archives were digitized by staff and are not numbered. These may not be traceable.

Abbreviations: SI – Smithsonian Institution; SIA – Smithsonian Archives; ACC – Accession Number in the Smithsonian Archives; MAH – Museum of American History; NPM – National Postal Museum

Image/Figure	Accession Number	Source
MAH exterior (front cover)	SI 72-5114	SIA
Bell's telephone (front cover)	SI EM.252599	SIA
1805 coin (front cover)	SI 2005-30130.tif	SIA
Jefferson Desk (front cover)	SI 2000-3201	SIA
Figure 1-1	SI 2008-15160	SIA
Figure 1-2	SIA 2011-1081	SIA
Figure 1-3	MAH-11115	SIA
Figure 2-1		Smithsonian Institution, *Brief Guide to the Smithsonian Institution: National Museum, National Collection of Fine Arts, National Air Museum, Freer Gallery, National Zoological Park* (National Publishing Co., 1962)
Figure 2-2	SIA2008-2452	SIA
Figure 2-3	MAH-66046	SIA
Figure 2-4	MAH-44173	SIA
Figure 2-5	SI 90-7265	SIA
Figure 2-6	MAH-9508	SIA
Figure 2-7	SI 2002-10640	SIA
Figure 2-8		Annual Report of the Board of Regents of the Smithsonian Institution, 1890, p. 22
Figure 2-9		NMAH History Office
Figure 2-10	MAH-4319	SIA
Figure 2-11	MAH-48727A	SIA

Image/Figure	Accession Number	Source
Figure 2-12	SIA 11-006	SIA
Figure 2-13	MAH-2964	SIA
Figure 2-14		Smithsonian Institution, *Brief Guide to the Smithsonian Institution: National Gallery, Freer Gallery, National Zoological Park,* (Smithsonian Institution, 1933)
Figure 2-15	SIA 2010-2719	SIA
Figure 2-16	AI-18942	SIA
Figure 2-17	SIA2012-6518	SIA
Figure 2-18	MAH-28515	SIA
Figure 2-19	SIA2010-2568	SIA
Figure 2-20	MAH-50700	SIA
Figure 2-21	SIA2010-2423	SIA
Figure 2-22	MAH-11064B	SIA
Figure 2-23		NMAH Division of Political History
Figure 2-24	MAH-19952	SIA
Figure 2-25	MAH-44931	SIA
Figure 2-26	SIA2007-0133	SIA
Figure 2-27	MAH-44518D	SIA
Figure 3-1		Museum of History and Technology, *Exhibits in the Museum of History and Technology,* Smithsonian Institution Publication 4720 (Washington, D.C.: Smithsonian Institution Press, 1968)
Figure 3-2		NMAH History Office, "Dedication of the Museum of History and Technology of the Smithsonian Institution, January 22, 1964"
Figure 3-3	MAH-P6411-29	SIA
Figure 3-4	MAH 11087-B	SIA
Figure 3-5		NMAH Public Affairs Office, "A New Museum of History and Technology" brochure
Figure 3-6	SIA2010-1796	SIA
Figure 3-7	SIA 2009-0003	SIA
Figure 3-8	SI 2002-10622	SIA
Figure 3-9	SI 73-2622	SIA
Figure 3-10		NMAH History Office
Figure 3-11		University of Pennsylvania Archives, Anthony Garvan Papers, UPT 50 G244, box 44
Figure 3-12	SIA-SIA2010-2878	SIA
Figure 3-13	SIA 63489-1967	SIA Acc 03-040

Image/Figure	Accession Number	Source
Figure 3-14	SIA-SIA2010-3467	SIA
Figure 3-15	SIA-SIA2010-2878	SIA
Figure 3-16	SI 74-410	SIA
Figure 3-17	SI 73-2386	SIA
Figure 3-18		SIA Acc 03-040
Figure 3-19	MAH-44321D	SIA
Figure 3-20		SIA Acc 03-040
Figure 3-21	SIA 2010-3408	SIA
Figure 3-22		SIA Acc 03-040
Figure 3-23	SIA 72-4770A	SIA
Figure 3-24	SIA 2010-3395	SIA
Figure 3-25		SIA, record unit 334, box 1, folder "Brochures"
Figure 3-26	SI #P-64135-cn	NMAH Division of Political History
Figure 3-27	SI 2003-43965	SIA
Figure 3-28	SI 3934	SIA
Figure 3-29	SIA2010-3475	SIA
Figure 3-30	SI x3936	SIA
Figure 3-31		SIA Acc 03-040
Figure 3-32		SIA Acc 03-040
Figure 3-33	SI 71-2067	SIA
Figure 3-34	SI 72-7786	SIA
Figure 3-35	SI 2003-43970	SIA
Figure 3-36		SIA Acc 03-040
Figure 3-37	SI 85-8372	SIA
Figure 3-38		SI Acc 03-040
Figure 3-39		NMAH History Office
Figure 3-40		SIA Acc 03-040
Figure 3-41		SIA Acc 03-040
Figure 3-42		NMAH Graphic Arts Division Photography Collection
Figure 3-43	ET2012-09708	SIA
Figure 3-44	ET2012-09732	SIA
Figure 3-45		NMAH Graphic Arts Division Photography Collection
Figure 3-46	SI 81-16338	SIA

Image/Figure	Accession Number	Source
Figure 3-47	NMAH 2001-10535	SIA
Figure 3-48	SI 2008-10468	SIA
Figure 3-49	OPA-1462	SIA
Figure 3-50	JN2015-5863	SIA
Figure 3-51	JN2015-5925	SIA
Figure 3-52	Object 0.217665.1	NPM
Figure 3-53	Object 0.052985.274.1	NPM
Figure 3-54		NPM, https://postalmuseum.si.edu/exhibition/collecting-history/photo-album
Figure 3-55		SIA Acc 03-040
Figure 3-56		SIA Acc 03-040
Figure 3-57		SIA Acc 03-040
Figure 3-58		SIA Acc 03-040
Figure 3-59	JN2015-7179 and JN2015-7177	SIA
Figure 3-60		SIA Acc 03-040
Figure 3-61		SIA Acc 03-040
Figure 3-62		SIA Acc 03-040
Figure 3-63		SIA Acc 04-030
Figure 3-64		SIA Acc 03-040
Figure 3-65		SIA Acc 03-040
Figure 3-66	SIA BotkinMural2	SIA
Figure 3-67		SIA Acc 03-040
Figure 3-68	SI 73-2842	SIA
Figure 3-69		SIA Acc 03-040
Figure 3-70	SIA 2010-2892	SIA
Figure 3-71		SIA Acc 03-040
Figure 3-72		Museum of History and Technology, *Exhibits in the Museum of History and Technology*, Smithsonian Institution Publication 4720 (Washington, D.C.: Smithsonian Institution Press, 1968), p. 84
Figure 3-73	SI 2009-2170	SIA
Figure 3-74	NMAH-2000-2211	SIA
Figure 3-75		SIA Acc 03-040
Figure 3-76	SI 2004-10283	SIA
Figure 3-77	NMAH2003-02637	SIA

Image/Figure	Accession Number	Source
Figure 3-78		SIA Acc 03-040
Figure 3-79		Museum of History and Technology, *Exhibits in the Museum of History and Technology*, Smithsonian Institution Publication 4720 (Washington, D.C.: Smithsonian Institution Press, 1968), p. 91
Figure 3-80	SIA-SIA2010-3276	SIA
Figure 3-81		SIA Acc 03-040
Figure 3-82		SIA Acc 03-040
Figure 3-83		SIA Acc 03-040
Figure 3-84	SI 75-7246	SIA
Figure 3-85		SIA Acc 03-040
Figure 3-86	Image 3634	NMAH Division of Electricity
Figure 3-87	SI EM.252599	SIA
Figure 3-88	NMAH-JN2014-3624	SIA
Figure 3-89	SIA-SIA2010-3373	SIA
Figure 3-90	SIA-SIA2010-3379	SIA
Figure 3-91		SIA Acc 03-040
Figure 3-92		SIA Acc 03-040
Figure 3-93		SIA Acc 03-040
Figure 3-94		SIA Acc 03-040
Figure 3-95		SIA Acc 03-040
Figure 3-96	NMAH-JN2013-1403	SIA
Figure 3-97		SIA Acc 03-040
Figure 3-98		SIA Acc 03-040
Figure 3-99		SIA Acc 03-040
Figure 3-100		SIA Acc 03-040
Figure 3-101		SIA Acc 03-040
Figure 3-102		SIA Acc 03-040
Figure 3-103		SIA Acc 03-040
Figure 3-104		SIA Acc 03-040
Figure 3-105	SIA 2010-3371	SIA
Figure 3-106	SI 72-8409-10	SIA
Figure 3-107		SIA Acc 03-040
Figure 3-108		SIA Acc 03-040

Image/Figure	Accession Number	Source
Figure 3-109	SIA 2010-2926	SIA
Figure 3-110	SIA 2010-2925	SIA
Figure 3-111		SIA Acc 03-040
Figure 4-1		NMAH History Office, museum brochure
Figure 4-2	SIA 76-6222-19A	SIA
Figure 4-3	SI 2012.201.B0097.0318	SIA
Figure 4-4		SIA Acc 06-163, box 3, *A Nation of Nations* brochure
Figure 4-5		SIA Acc 03-040
Figure 4-6		SIA Acc 06-163, box 3
Figure 4-7	SI 76-16880042	SIA
Figure 4-8		SIA Acc 03-040
Figure 4-9	SI 75-5421	SIA
Figure 4-10	*(right)* NMAH-ET2017-06801-000001	*(left)* SIA Acc 03-040, *(right)* SIA
Figure 4-11	SI 74-9747003	SIA
Figure 4-12	SI 75-7355005	SIA
Figure 4-13		SIA Acc 03-040
Figure 4-14		SIA Acc 03-040
Figure 4-15	SI 92-1783	SIA
Figure 4-16	SI 76-13650	SIA
Figure 4-17		NMAH History Office, *1876* brochure
Figure 4-18	SI 77-3205	SIA
Figure 4-19	SI 77-3182	SIA
Figure 4-20		NMAH Public Affairs Office Slide Collection 1876_005
Figure 4-21		NMAH Public Affairs Slide Collection 1876_2
Figure 4-22		"Preface" in Bicentennial Park, Smithsonian Institution brochure, files of Armed Forces Division, NMAH, 1971
Figure 4-23		"Preface" in Bicentennial Park, Smithsonian Institution brochure, files of Armed Forces Division, NMAH, 1971
Figure 4-24		NMAH Armed Forces Division, map of proposed National Armed Forces Museum
Figure 4-25		SIA Acc 03-040
Figure 4-26		SIA Acc 03-040
Figure 4-27		SIA Acc 03-040
Figure 4-28		SIA Acc 03-040

Image/Figure	Accession Number	Source
Figure 4-29	SI 73-10875	SIA
Figure 4-30		SIA Acc 03-040
Figure 4-31		SIA Acc 03-040
Figure 4-32	SI 72-7143	SIA
Figure 4-33		SIA Acc 03-040
Figure 4-34	SI 73-5906-05	SIA
Figure 4-35	SI 76763A	SIA
Figure 4-36	SIA RU000371 [73-5900] Productivity	SIA
Figure 5-1		NMAH History Office, brochure
Figure 5-2		*Smithsonian Torch*, March 1980, p. 1
Figure 5-3	SI 80-18141	SIA
Figure 5-4	JN2016-00256	SIA
Figure 5-5	SI 88-18759-06	SIA
Figure 5-6		NMAH Public Affairs Office Slide Collection
Figure 5-7		NMAH Public Affairs Office Slide Collection
Figure 5-8	NMAH 95-1154-7	SIA
Figure 5-9	SI 89-21361	SIA
Figure 5-10		NMAH Public Affairs Office Slide Collection
Figure 5-11	SI 85-7199	SIA
Figure 5-12	SI 87-3715	SIA
Figure 5-13	SI 86-4923	SIA
Figure 5-14	SI 86-49327	SIA
Figure 5-15	SI 87-3696	SIA
Figure 5-16		NMAH Public Affairs Office Slide Collection
Figure 5-17	SI 88-7304	SIA
Figure 5-18	SI 87-7856	SIA
Figure 5-19	SI 87-7867	SIA
Figure 5-20	SI 87-7860	SIA
Figure 5-21		NMAH Public Affairs Office Slide Collection
Figure 5-22	SI 89-3905	SIA
Figure 5-23	SI 89-3908	SIA
Figure 5-24	SI 87-1128	SIA
Figure 5-25	89-13614.14	SIA

Image/Figure	Accession Number	Source
Figure 5-26	SI 88-14336	SIA
Figure 5-27	SI 88-12519	SIA
Figure 5-28	JN2017-00247	SIA
Figure 5-29	SI 2005_4454693727_o	SIA
Figure 5-30	2005_4454707781_o	SIA
Figure 5-31	SI 90-15037	SIA
Figure 5-32	SI 90-14548	SIA
Figure 5-33	SI 90-7164	SIA
Figure 5-34	SI 90-14304	SIA
Figure 5-35	SI 90-15068	SIA
Figure 5-36	SI 92-15447	SIA
Figure 5-37	SI 92-15458	SIA
Figure 5-38	SI 92-15467	SIA
Figure 5-39	SI 92-15463	SIA
Figure 5-40	SI 92-15254-17	SIA
Figure 5-41	SI 92-15250	SIA
Figure 5-42		NMAH Public Affairs Office Slide Collection
Figure 5-43	SI 91-8325-5	SIA
Figure 5-44	SI 91-834	SIA
Figure 5-45	SI 94-9123	SIA
Figure 5-46	SI 94-1022_01	SIA
Figure 5-47	SI 94-0113	SIA
Figure 5-48	SI 94-9141	SIA
Figure 5-49	SI 94-8606	SIA
Figure 5-50		NMAH Public Affairs Office Slide Collection
Figure 5-51		NMAH Public Affairs Office Slide Collection
Figure 5-52		NMAH Public Affairs Office Slide Collection
Figure 5-53		NMAH History Office, *On Time* brochure
Figure 5-54	SI 2000-10974	SIA
Figure 5-55		SIA, record unit 551, box 31, folder "Frank A Taylor Dedication"
Figure 5-56		NMAH History Office
Figure 5-57		NMAH History Office

Image/Figure	Accession Number	Source
Figure 5-58		NMAH History Office
Figure 5-59		NMAH History Office
Figure 5-60		NMAH History Office
Figure 5-61	SI 83-7182	SIA
Figure 5-62	SI 83-15747	SIA
Figure 5-63	SIA2017-054255	SIA
Figure 5-64	https://www.flickr.com/photos/nationalmuseumofamericanhistory/	Smithsonian Flickr site
Figure 5-65	https://www.flickr.com/photos/nationalmuseumofamericanhistory/	Smithsonian Flickr site
Figure 5-66		NMAH History Office, screen capture
Figure 6-1		NMAH History Program Office, brochure
Figure 6-2	JN2012-0113, JN2012-0110 and RWS2012-04681	SIA
Figure 6-3	NMAH 2000-9252.08a	SIA
Figure 6-4	SIA 2003-22689	SIA
Figure 6-5	SI 2005-8250	SIA
Figure 6-6		Presentation by Skidmore, Owings, & Merrill, 2003
Figure 6-7		NMAH Director's Office
Figure 6-8		SIA, record unit 16-322, box 14, folder "SPWH Exhibition: Design Development, 2004"
Figure 6-9	2008-15487	SIA
Figure 6-10	NMAH 2000-1278	SIA
Figure 6-11	NMAH 2000-11249	SIA
Figure 6-12	NMAH 2000-2006	SIA
Figure 6-13	SIA 2009-12898	SIA
Figure 6-14	NMAH 2005-5785	SIA
Figure 6-15	NMAH 2005-5791	SIA
Figure 6-16	NMAH 2004-60891	SIA
Figure 6-17	NMAH 2004-56872	SIA
Figure 6-18	NMAH 2004-56874	SIA
Figure 6-19	NMAH 2009-9050	SIA
Figure 6-20	NMAH 2009-9067	SIA
Figure 6-21		NMAH Division of Political History
Figure 6-22	ET2011-09604	SIA

Image/Figure	Accession Number	Source
Figure 6-23	NMAH 6358311671	SIA
Figure 6-24	JN2019-00248	SIA
Figure 6-25	JN2012-1252	SIA
Figure 6-26	NMAH ET2012-11529	SIA
Figure 6-27	NMAH ET2012-11476-S	SIA
Figure 6-28	ET2018-01657	SIA
Figure 6-29	JN2012-0857	SIA
Figure 6-30	NMAH ET2015-04595-S	SIA
Figure 6-31	ET2015-04993	SIA
Figure 6-32	SI 2008-18666	SIA
Figure 6-33	JN2017-00851	SIA
Figure 6-34	JN2018-01910	SIA
Figure 6-35	MAH 2001-9771	SIA
Figure 6-36	SI 2001-9791	SIA
Figure 6-37	ET2019-00340	SIA
Figure 6-38	JN2015-6200	SIA
Figure 6-39	JN2015-6228	SIA
Figure 6-40	JN2015-6424	SIA
Figure 6-41	JN2015-6208	SIA
Figure 6-42		NMAH Public Affairs Office Slide Collection
Figure 6-43	ET2015-04421	SIA
Figure 6-44	ET2015-04446	SIA
Figure 6-45	NMAH 2009-10957	SIA
Figure 6-46	JN2015-6977	SIA
Figure 6-47	JN2015-6557	SIA
Figure 6-48		Report of the Blue Ribbon Commission on the National Museum of American History, March 2002
Figure 6-49	JN2017-00852	SIA
Figure 6-50	ET2017-06982	SIA
Figure 6-51	ET2017-07105	SIA
Figure 6-52	ET2017-06945	SIA
Figure 6-53	JN2017-00853	SIA
Figure 6-54	JN2017-00919	SIA
Figure 6-55	JN2017-00862	SIA

Image/Figure	Accession Number	Source
Figure 6-56	JN2015-8136_v1	SIA
Figure 6-57	JN2015-8136_v1	SIA
Figure 6-58	SI 2002-32306	SIA
Figure 6-59	SI 2002-32312	SIA
Figure 6-60	RWS2011-02833	SIA
Figure 6-61	SI 2005-6044	SIA
Figure 6-62	RWS2009-23697	SIA
Figure 6-63	SI 2009-3726	SIA
Figure 6-64	SI 2009-3739	SIA
Figure 6-65	ET2018-00636	SIA
Figure 6-66	EV_OCA_20120125_01_098	SIA
Figure 6-67	JN2017-00894	SIA
Figure 6-68	JN2018-01124	SIA
Figure 6-69	ET2015-04549	SIA
Figure 6-70	ET2015-12185	SIA
Figure 6-71	RWS2015-08225	SIA
Figure 6-72	RWS2017-02171	SIA
Figure 6-73	RWS2018-02442	SIA
Figure 6-74		NMAH Director's Office, presentation
Figure 6-75		NMAH Director's Office, presentation
Figure 6-76		NMAH Director's Office, presentation
Figure 6-77		NMAH Graphic Design Studio, presentation
Figure 6-78		NMAH Graphic Design Studio, presentation
Figure 7-1	SI 2005-30130	SIA

Index

About the Authors

David K. Allison is curator emeritus at the Smithsonian Institution's National Museum of American History. He earned his BA from St. John's College in 1973 and PhD in history from Princeton University in 1980. He was employed at the National Museum of American History from 1987 to 2019. During those years, he worked as curator, department chair, associate director for curatorial affairs, and senior historian. He was project director and curator for three large, multimillion-dollar exhibitions: *Information Age: People, Information and Technology* (1990), *The Price of Freedom: Americans at War* (2004), and *American Enterprise* (2015), and for several dozen smaller exhibitions and displays. Major publications that he has authored or coauthored include *New Eye for the Navy: The Origin of Radar at the Naval Research Laboratory* (NRL, 1981), *The Price of Freedom: Americans at War* (Marquand Books, 2004), *American Enterprise: A History of Business in America* (Smithsonian Books, 2015), and *The American Revolution: A World War* (Smithsonian Books, 2018).

Hannah Peterson earned her BA from St. John's College in 2018. She worked as an intern for both the Smithsonian Folklife Festival (2017) and the Smithsonian Institution's National Museum of American History (2018–2019). While earning her MA in history and literature from Columbia University in 2020, she authored her thesis, "Figures of the Author: Representations of Conversation and Community in 17th-Century French Literary Fairy Tales."